BENGAL

Communities, Development and States

Edited by

SEKHAR BANDYOPADHYAY
ABHIJIT DASGUPTA
WILLEM VAN SCHENDEL

MANOHAR
2026

First published 1994
Reprinted 2026

ISBN 978-81-7304-089-4

Published by
Ajay Kumar Jain *for*
Manohar Publishers & Distributors
4753/23 Ansari Road, Daryaganj
New Delhi 110 002

Printed and bound in India

BENGAL
Communities, Development and States

Contents

Acknowledgements

Most of the essays in this book were presented during a workshop on 'Development and Underdevelopment in Bengal: Castes, Communities and the State', held in Calcutta from 19 to 21 December, 1991. We owe a great deal to all those who contributed papers and took part in the discussions. The workshop was held under the auspices of the Eastern Regional Centre (ERC) of the Indian Council of Social Science Research (ICSSR). We wish to acknowledge our debt to the ERC for providing organizational support. We are grateful to the ICSSR for providing financial support under its Indo-Dutch Programme on Alternatives in Development (IDPAD). For permission to reproduce copyright materials we wish to thank the editors of the following journals: *Economic and Political Weekly*, *Modern Asian Studies* and *Journal of Social Studies*. Thanks also to Ritambhara Hebbar for preparing the index and the glossary.

Sekhar Bandyopadhyay
Abhijit Dasgupta
Willem van Schendel

1 Introduction

I

Since the Partition of Bengal in 1947 very little comparative research has been done on the economy and society of the 'two Bengals'. In this book an attempt has been made to explore some aspects of state formation, community problems, and development strategies since the colonial period.[1] The study of the two Bengals has assumed significance for a number of reasons. First, our knowledge about the socio-economic life of the vast majority of people living in this region is still far from adequate. Today, some two hundred million people make their home in the two parts of Bengal. The region is more populous than any country in the world, except China, India, Russia and the United States. Yet the study of Bengali society has not received the kind of attention it deserves. Second, development problems in Bengal have never been so acute as they are today. In terms of gross national product, per capita income, literacy and life expectancy at birth, Bengal is lagging far behind the developing countries of the world.[2] There can be little doubt that social scientists can play an important role in identifying factors affecting development processes in the region. Third, in addition to the size of the population and the acute development problems, the remarkable complexities in social life and the long common historical tradition make Bengal an extremely important and interesting field of study.

Administratively, Bengal is now split into two units: East Bengal is the sovereign state of Bangladesh and West Bengal

[1] The word 'community' has been used here in a broad sense to include castes, tribes and religious groups.

[2] In 1985-86 Bangladesh per capita income was only Tk.4,400, equivalent to US $147. Khan and Hossain [(1985),p.5] report that the poorest 40% of Bangladesh had a substantially lower per capita income, approximately Tk.2,450 or $82. In the mid eighties West Bengal's per capita income was around $150.

is a federal state within the Indian Union. This administrative division has resulted in profound political changes. East Bengal, always a Muslim majority area, became a part of Pakistan in 1947, and there is no reason to believe that the demand for a separate homeland did not have mass support among the Bengali Muslims. But domination and exploitation by the political elites from West Pakistan soon led to the rearticulation of the 'Bengali nationalism' among East Pakistanis, resulting in a revolt and the establishment of the new state of Bangladesh. West Bengal, on the other hand, visualised as the homeland of the Bengali Hindus by the Congress and the Hindu Mahasabha leaders in 1946-47, became a part of the Indian Union. As a result the West Bengalis, though occasionally complaining against domination and exploitation by the centre, have become increasingly more integrated into the new political system. Their distinctive identity is sometimes expressed in the new political vocabulary of 'centre-state relationship', but seldom articulated in terms of regional or linguistic exclusivism. Bengalis on the two sides of the international boundary have become part of two different political systems and no one would now consider a 'sovereign united Bengal', which was once a dream of Bengali politicians such as the Hindu Congressite Sarat Bose or the Muslim League leader Abul Hashem.[3]

Yet culturally, the region may still be considered as a clear-cut unit, the differences being not more than they were in 1905, when Lord Curzon decided to divide Bengal for politico-administrative reasons for the first time. First of all, despite differences in dialects, the region is bound by a common literary language, Bengali. Since the early twentieth century we can trace the emergence of what Sumit Sarkar has defined as 'the sense of unity among the Bengali- speaking people—a sentiment certainly by no means all-pervasive, but still extending far beyond the narrow coteries of zamindars,

[3] Shila Sen(1976), Gordon (1989).

lawyers, and Congress leaders...'[4] The sentiment perhaps persists even today, notwithstanding the political changes, and constitutes an emotional tie, not very clearly visible but perceptible nonetheless, between the two peoples on the two sides of the international boundary. A long common history and many shared cultural traits set this region off against the surrounding areas.

To put it in another way, Bangladesh and West Bengal are like Siamese twins who have been separated and have asserted their individuality. And although their recent life experiences have been quite different, they do remain identical twins, springing from the same historical roots. We can understand their social structures and dynamics only if we take account of their long and united experience before the surgeon's knife severed them. The study of the two Bengals is not only necessary to make sense of either of them, it may also provide important insights into processes of state formation. Like other separated 'Siamese twins' (e.g., the two Punjabs or the two Koreas), the two Bengals allow us to gauge the impact of different state policies on social development in what used to be one society. Just as human identical twins help us in understanding the complex interplay of biological and social factors in human development, so a careful study of 'severed societies' helps us in sorting out the role of states in social development.

However, the image of Siamese twins should not be taken too far, since they never became as completely separated as biological organisms. For example, continual migration of people occurred between East and West Bengal after Partition and many ideas continued to flow across the border.

Some 'severed societies' are even reunited after some time, recent examples being Vietnam, Germany and Yemen. Though that possibility is difficult to visualise for Bengal at present, the study of this 'severed society' nevertheless al-

[4] S. Sarkar(1973), p.22.

lows us to examine contrasts and similarities in social change in a more controlled situation than is usual in social science research. In this way we can advance our understanding of societies as on-going processes which are not predetermined, but which develop under the impact of ever-changing combinations of influences.

This book contains some of the contributions to a workshop held in Calcutta in December 1991. The workshop, organised under the auspices of the Indo-Dutch Programme on Alternatives in Development (IDPAD/ICSSR), came at the conclusion of two IDPAD research projects which involved a comparison of social change in rural East and West Bengal.[5] It brought together scholars with a research interest in the two Bengals. Its purpose was to take stock of ongoing research in the two parts of Bengal.[6] The workshop revolved around the study of development and underdevelopment in connection with the formation of communities and states in the colonial and post-colonial periods. Our main concern was to explore the many facets of development, the various conceptual frameworks that underlie development policies and, above all, how development affects various communities, their self-perception, and their own ideas of what development should mean for them.

The essays in this volume show that the state intervenes in the development process according to its own predilections, depending on the interests and views of those who dominate the state. Ruling elites may have different priorities, as is revealed in the quite different policies adopted in Bengal under the colonial state, the state of Pakistan, the state of Bangladesh and the Marxist government of West Bengal. But all policies have had a differential impact on various communities—Hindus and Muslims, higher castes and lower castes,

[5] The findings of these projects are reported in Willem van Schendel (1991) and Dasgupta (1991). One of the contributors to the present volume, Shyamali Ghosh, participated in the workshop,but did not present her paper. Ranajit Das Gupta, Smriti Kumar Sarkar, Anjan Kumar Datta and Samita Sen did not take part in the workshop, but contributed papers at a later stage.

[6] See Van Schendel and Dasgupta (1992) for a report on the workshop.

Bengalis and non-Bengalis etc.,—and often on different sections within each community.[7] This differential impact created new pressures which in turn had repercussions on development policies. Sometimes the state ignored these pressures for a time in order to satisfy the aspirations of the dominant community, but on other occasions new policy options were explored. In this book development is seen, not as a process initiated by either the state or the 'grass roots', but as a long-term process which is determined by the continual interplay of state policies and (often unforeseen) development at the level of communities. The study of development, it is felt, should therefore be conducted at both levels and in a much longer time perspective than is usually allowed for. The waxing and waning of communities determine the political expediency and actual implementation of development policies and vice versa. Both take time, and therefore, the study of historical examples of development policies may provide us with insights which we cannot yet derive from the study of the ongoing policies.

II

Several contributions to this volume explore how state policies impinged upon community formation in Bengal. The early colonial state and its convoluted concept of the 'rule of law', implemented by an alienated judiciary, created more confusion in indigenous agrarian society than it resolved. While its 'public law' was based on the principle of 'possessive individualism', the private law recognised older community identities and rights and thus put limits to individual freedom.[8] Despina Iliopoulou's study of colonial law in this volume emphasises the fact that agrarian relations in Bengal were not just shaped by the economic policies of the early colonial state, which, as Ranajit Guha has argued, were

[7] See Rahman (1986) and Schendel (1982) for discussions on the role of the state.

[8] For a detailed discussion of this aspect of the colonial legal system, see Washbrook (1981).

drawn from Whig ideas and Physiocratic economic theories.[9] The non-economic policies of the colonial rulers also had a profound impact on social relations which were now placed on an altogether different legal base. For example, Muslim and Hindu laws of inheritance had not been in force in the pre-colonial era, and their implementation in the early colonial period was instrumental in creating new claims on land which were contested in courts. Iliopoulou argues that court decisions disturbed family relations among the landed classes by creating property rights for women and by creating uncertainty about the new rules for the transmission of property. But on the whole, contrary to widely held notions, the courts undermined rather than protected private property rights in land. Equally important is the question which she asks with regard to the role of courts in deciding what constituted 'good' Hindu or Muslim practices: 'Did laws of inheritance, or similar laws constructed on the basis of religion, contribute to a colonial identity along religious lines?'

Indeed, the colonial concept of an Indian society divided along religious and caste lines had an important impact on the way communities were formed and dissolved in nineteenth and twentieth century Bengal. This colonial 'discourse of differentiation', as Bernard Cohn has called it,[10] began to replace other indigenous discourses on social structure and group relations and led to the articulation of community identities among various indigenous groups. Taking the Rajbansis of North Bengal as a reference group, Swaraj Basu examines how the colonial social policies made the lower caste people, in the context of their day-to-day humiliation at the hands of the caste Hindus, self-conscious and motivated to search for a more dignified place in society. But this place was defined in a cultural environment dominated by the official discourse on caste that was based on scriptural notions of hierarchy and rank. Therefore, instead of demanding a levelling of society, the Rajbansis, claimed to have origi-

[9] Guha(1963).
[10] Cohn (1987).

nated from a twice-born *varna* and invented traditions to support this mythico-historical claim. Colonial ethnography and social policies thus contributed to a reinforcement of traditional views of society, in which caste solidarities were considered to be legitimate and social segmentation natural.

But although cultural notions were important, economic development also played a crucial role in the formation of community identities and in determining the status of various castes in the ritual hierarchy. Smriti Kumar Sarkar's essay shows how unprecedented growth in the brass and bell metal utensil industry in the nineteenth century had resulted in social mobility for the Kansaris, a low ranking artisanal group traditionally associated with this craft. But their position was seriously threatened in the twentieth century, first by the intrusion of artisans from other castes into the utensil industry and then by competition from a new range of cheaper wares made of glass, porcelain, enamel, tin, iron and above all aluminium. It was against this background of a real threat to their traditional occupation that the relatively prosperous Kansaris felt the need for caste solidarity. They began defining and articulating a new caste identity for themselves. But as their movement was closely related to the fate of their occupation, it failed to strike roots because the majority of the members of the caste had already given up their unremunerative hereditary occupation and were no longer interested in the movement. The differential impact of development thus dismantled the community, despite attempts by a few to invoke the cultural symbols of solidarity.

Sekhar Bandyopadhyay, in his essay on the Namasudras of eastern Bengal, also argues that the differential impact of development created fissures within the communities and their movements therefore did not remain homogeneous in terms of goals and forms of action. In the Namasudra movement, for example, a conflict of interest soon emerged between the majority and the leaders. Most Namasudras remained concerned with perceived threats to their community honour, resentment against social disabilities and protest against economic exploitation. The leaders, on the other hand, were more concerned with cultural symbols of ritual rank and institutional concessions. Although these different concerns could be accommodated within a single movement, conflicts began to surface 'particularly in the thirties when the British government began to patronise such lower-caste movements in order to legitimise India's colonial connection'. The movement began to unravel as new identities came up which cut across or encompassed caste identity and different groups of Namasudras allied themselves with nationalist, Hindu communalist or class-based politics, from which they had long kept their distance as a result of being dominated by high-caste Hindus. This integration was made possible as the latter gradually acknowledged the political importance of the lower castes, now underscored by the constitutional arrangement of 1935 - once again an act of state intervention.

The Bhuimalis, another low-caste group of East Bengal, examined in this volume by Ratan Lal Chakraborty, had from the very beginning avoided a collision course. 'Unable to sustain their movement all on their own, they used their numbers to pursue the high-caste Hindus to support their claims. In this they were successful, and the demands of the Mymensingh Bhuimalis came to be projected under the leadership of the high-caste Hindu politicians.' This unlikely alliance between caste groups at opposite ends of the ritual hierarchy came about as a result of state action: proposed constitutional reforms made it necessary for high-caste politicians to harness the votes of other groups.

However, the possibilities of such a symbiotic relationship between caste Hindus and 'tribal' people have been questioned by many.[11] Like the lower castes, the hill people and 'tribal' groups of Bengal were also experiencing far-reaching changes in their economic and social life in the late nineteenth and twentieth centuries and were protesting

[11] See for example, Bose (1941).

against social and economic oppression by dominant groups, such as the colonial planters in the Duars or the Hindu-Muslim elites in the Chittagong Hill Tracts. The role of the state in marginalising such communities cannot be overlooked either. The essay by Van Schendel deals with changing identities, over a 200-year period, among a dozen non-Bengali groups inhabiting the Chittagong Hill Tracts in Bangladesh. It focuses on the link between the policies of successive states (British India, Pakistan, Bangladesh) and the creation of a new overarching identity in the seventies. The emergence of the *Jumma* identity 'was a bid for ethnic innovation, to cope with the political and economic consequences of loss of power, growing expendability to the state, and cultural marginalisation. This makes it an important case for students of ethnicity who have been much concerned with ethnic conflict but have given less attention to ethnic innovation (ethnogenesis) than to other forms of boundary crossing (especially ethnic assimilation, incorporation and secession).' Today one finds an attempt by the hill people to develop an indigenous model of state, society and culture. The term *Jumma* signifies the cultural separateness of the hill people from the Bengalis of the plains.

But the distinctiveness of 'tribal' cultural enclaves also broke down in certain specific situations. Ranajit Das Gupta examines one such situation created by the Oraon labour agitation in the Duars tea plantations of Jalpaiguri district in 1915-16. Although this movement was a continuation of the Tana Bhagat movement of the Oraons of Chotonagpur, it witnessed a convergence of vertical and horizontal solidarities. The Oraon labourers, in addition to being motivated by their 'tribal religious consciousness', also '*acted as workers*' and their movement therefore involved non-Oraon tribal, semi-tribal and even non-tribal workers. 'There was', Das Gupta writes, 'an *overlapping* of anti-British content..., class solidarity and tribal or ethnic loyalty.' But tribal separateness persisted at another level, as 'tribal anti-imperialism and [Bengali] bhadralok nationalism', he concludes, 'remained distanced from each other.'

If this bhadralok nationalism had suffered from anything during colonial period, it was the alienation of the Bengali Muslims. The theme of the emergence of a community consciousness among these, both at the grass roots level and among the elite, and its politicisation in the twentieth century has figured prominently in recent literature.[12] The role of the colonial state in this process is also well known. The Bengali Muslims, it is claimed, had developed an autonomous character, or indeed a 'subculture', based on the dual bond of religion and language which distinguished them from both the Bengali Hindus and the North Indian Muslims, and this sense of distinctiveness was reflected in their politics.[13] However, by the end of 1945 the Muslim electorate in Bengal was united solidly behind Jinnah and the Muslim League and their demand for Pakistan; all other forces in Muslim politics had lost their appeal.[14] Religion thus appears to have overshadowed the linguistic nationalism of the Bengali Muslims. But resurfaced linguistic consciousness in the fifties; it resulted in the language movement and eventually in the birth of Bangladesh in 1971.

The story does not end there, however. Shyamali Ghosh's essay demonstrates how in recent years the state has intervened to create a new national cultural identity for the Bangladeshis, based on their religious affinity. But is it posible for the state to effect culture change without clearly expressed popular approval? She takes as her example the controversy over the celebration of *Shahid Dibash* (Martyr's Day on 21 February) in Bangladesh in the eighties and shows how the state attempted to 'Islamise' this celebration in the face of popular resistance. She argues that this is just one example of a much older and broader tension between popular Bengali Muslim subculture and orthodox interpretations of Islam. She shows how by the eighties the Bangladesh

[12] See, R.Ahmed (1981), S.Ahmed (1974), Maitra (1984).
[13] For a recent exposition of this argument see Sarkar (1991).
[14] Sen (1976), Das (1991).

state, which had started out as a secular entity, had come to champion the cause of Islamisation. This brought it into open conflict with the heterodox, syncretistic heritage of the vast majority of the people of Bangladesh, leading to a stalemate. Yet the state itself is not solidly orthodox, as the allegiance of the various leaders to *pirs* (popular saints) shows. Ghosh concludes that 'the occasional invectives against un-Islamic practices and half-hearted measures towards "Islamisation" are meant only to make Bangladesh appear to be moving towards Islamisation. This provides Bangladesh with a better bargaining position in the Organisation of Islamic Countries, especially with regard to getting easy financial assistance, bilaterally or multilaterally, from the Islam heartland as well as making it possible for many Bangladeshi citizens to be gainfully employed in this region.' If the Bangladesh state would, however, attempt actually to impose the communal identity of orthodox Islam on its citizens, they would surely come to the defence of Bengali Muslim cultural symbols.

The complex relationship between community formation, gender and politics are highlighted in Samita Sen's contribution. Sen focuses on notions of gender, community and class among the working class in the jute industry of Calcutta between 1890 and 1940. Her essay explores 'the imagining of the woman as a victim of male sexual violence and its construction as the violation of community "honour" in communal discourse and in the discourses of racial and class resistance.' She argues that this image, which obscured the very real sexual oppression of women by men of their own class or community within the household, symbolised the anxieties attending the changes which the working class household underwent as a result of long-distance migration, industrial labour, urbanisation and industrial insecurity. These anxieties tied in with the political developments in Bengal in the first half of the twentieth century. Communal and nationalist politics used the image of Hindu women as victims of sexual violence by Muslim and European men. The harsh realities of living and working in the jute mill slums forced working class women to opt for 'temporary marriages', compromising their honour in the eyes of the elite. Working-class women were used as emblems of their community, but at the same time seen as sexually deviant; they 'alternated between the image of the victim, and the image of the morally flawed poor.'

These case studies, taken from the two Bengals, clearly show that none of the community identities prevalent in this region have been in any sense primordial. These have been constructed, articulated, dismantled and then again rejuvenated under certain specific historical circumstances and in response to various developmental processes or political changes initiated by the state. The differential impact of development ultimately determines peoples' perceptions of social identities and group affiliations. And such perceptions are expressed in cultural idioms which too are often enforced by the power of an interventionist state.

III

While the studies which we have discussed so far look at the social situation in Bengal from the viewpoint of communities, there are other essays in this volume which address it from a development perspective. They link the issues of development and underdevelopment with those of communities and states. Among these, Arjan de Haan's contribution is a report on West Bengal's jute industry and its workers. He argues that the decline of the jute industry, especially after 1968, was not inevitable but largely the result of faulty government policies. The negative image of the jute industry among policy makers resulted at least partly from the fact that it had been a colonial industry in which Bengalis were only marginally involved. He explores the reasons why the jute labourers were overwhelmingly non-Bengalis who had migrated over long distances. Rather than presenting them as victims of (colonial) capitalism, he asserts that their own view should be acknowledged: they benefited from industrial employment: 'they came to the industry to find some extra income ... to defend themselves against proletarianisation.'

Some of the problems of the agricultural sector are discussed by Abhijit Dasgupta and Anjan Kumar Datta. Returning to some of the issues raised in Iliopoulou's essay, they explain how state intervention is linked with changing agrarian relations in the post-colonial period. They explore factors accounting for the differential impact of technological growth on agrarian communities, especially on sharecroppers, and on sharecropping arrangements. Dasgupta's contribution reveals that the state policies in West Bengal and Bangladesh affected agricultural communities in two different ways. His closely researched comparison of two villages in adjacent border districts of West Bengal and Bangladesh deals with the social effects of state policies geared at technological innovation in agriculture. In both Bangladesh and West Bengal, the use of underground and surface water irrigation and the spread of HYV seeds, fertilisers and pesticides have led to an increase in agricultural production. But what about equity? Dasgupta takes two explanatory variables into account: state intervention in the interest of social justice and self-organisation by poor peasants to protect their rights. He shows how these two factors supported agricultural growth with equity in West Bengal. Unionisation helped poor peasants to become more aware of their rights which the state supported and expanded by means of legislation protecting the interests of the sharecroppers and agricultural labourers. By contrast, in Bangladesh a lack of organisation left poor peasants and labourers very much at the receiving end, while the state aimed at maintaining the status quo. As a result, agricultural growth has not brought any perceptible improvement in the condition of the rural poor in Bangladesh.

Datta discusses changes in sharecropping arrangements in Bangladesh in the context of the Land Reform Ordinance of 1984. According to him, even after the enactment of this ordinance, which aimed at offering tenurial security to sharecroppers, the terms and conditions of sharecropping arrangements are deteriorating. Besides extracting fifty percent of the produce, landowners impose a number of non-economic conditions while negotiating sharecropping contracts. Datta's detailed study of two villages points out that legislative measures alone cannot improve the condition of the peasantry in Bangladesh. 'What is needed is sufficient legal and institutional back-up. This calls for administrative support from the state machinery, and more importantly concerted actions from the tenants and poor labourers themselves.' In other words, while positive state intervention is necessary, what is also required is the initiative and self-organisation of tenants which in a not too distant past, united for collective action in support of their demand for *tebhaga* or the two-thirds share of the produce.[15]

This volume wishes to draw attention to the rich possibilities of comparative research into the development of the two Bengals. The essays in this book suggest questions which are rarely addressed in Bengal studies. For example, could the West Bengal model, identified by Dasgupta as a combination of state intervention and peasant initiative, be applied in Bangladesh? If so, would it yield more positive results for Bangladeshi peasants? Answering such questions would require a comparative analysis of the evolving relationship between peasants and the two states in Bengal. It is well beyond the scope of this book to do so. This book merely intends to suggest that it is worthwhile to do more, and more systematic, comparative research on Bangladesh and West Bengal. Such comparisons will bring out both similarities and contrasts and may suggest new angles to approach old issues. This will result in a sharper focus to Bengal studies. In this way, the study of two Bengals, which is concerned with a relatively small region of the world, can contribute more to an understanding of the interrelationship between communities, development and states, which is of worldwide interest.

---

[15] For details of this sharecroppers' movement in Bengal, see Sen (1972) and Cooper (1988).

References

Ahmed, R. (1981). *The Bengal Muslims, 1871-1906*, Oxford University Press, Delhi.

Ahmed, S. (1974). *Muslim Community in Bengal, 1884-1912*, Oxford University Press, Dacca.

Bandyopadhyay, D. (1979). West Bengal: Experience in Land Reform', *Mainstream*, Annual No., pp.29-31.

Bose, N.K. (1941). The Hindu Method of Tribal Absorption, *Science and Culture*, Vol.VII, pp.188-94.

Cooper, A. (1988). *Sharecropping and Sharecroppers' Struggles in Bengal 1930-1950*, K.P.Bagchi & Co., Calcutta.

Das, S. (1991). *Communal Riots in Bengal 1905-1947*, Oxford University Press, Delhi.

Dasgupta, A. (1991). *Rural Proletarianization in Eastern India and Bangladesh*, ICSSR/IDPAD Project Report.

Gordon, L. (1989). *Brothers Against the Raj: A Biography of Sarat and Subhas Chandra Bose*, Viking, New Delhi.

Guha, R. (1963). *A Rule of Property For Bengal*, Mouton & Co., Paris.

Khan, A.R. and M. Hossain (1989). *The Strategies of Development in Bangladesh*, The Macmillan, Houndmills.

Maitra, J. (1984). *Muslim Politics in Bengal 1855-1906: Collaboration and Confrontation*, K.P.Bagchi & Co., Calcutta.

Rahman, A. (1986). *Peasants and Classes: A Study in Differentiation in Bangladesh*, Oxford University Press, Delhi.

Sarkar, C. (1991). *The Bengali Muslims: A Study in Politicization 1912-1929*, K.P.Bagchi & Co., Calcutta.

Sarkar, S. (1973). *The Swadeshi Movement in Bengal 1903-1908*, Peoples Publishing House, New Delhi.

Sen, Shila. (1976). *Muslim Politics in Bengal, 1937-1947*, Impex India, New Delhi.

Sen, Sunil. (1972), *Agrarian Struggle in Bengal 1946-47*, Peoples Publishing House, New Delhi.

Van Schendel, W. (1982). *Peasant Mobility: The Odds of Life in Rural Bangladesh*, Manohar Publications, Delhi.

(1991). *Three Deltas: Accumulation and Poverty in Rural Burma, Bengal and South India*, Sage Publications, New Delhi.

Van Schendel, W. and A. Dasgupta. (1992). 'Development and

Underdevelopment in Bengal: Castes, Communities and the State', *Economic and Political Weekly*, April 4.

Washbrook, D.A. (1981). 'Law, State and Agrarian Society in Colonial India', in C.Baker, G.Johnson and A.Seal, (eds.), *Power, Profit and Politics*, Cambridge University Press, Cambridge.

2

Colonial Policy, Law and the Structuring of Social Relations in Bengal*

DESPINA ILIOPOULOU

The role of the colonial state in shaping processes of social transformation in Bengal has been discussed primarily in terms of economic policies. As a result, little attention has been paid to other types of state activity that may be equally relevant in discussing issues of development. In this paper, I will argue that a closer look at the processes which shaped the colonial milieu reveals the central role that non-economic colonial policies played in recreating rural society in a particular way. More specifically, I will examine the role of the state in organising and shaping agrarian relations during the administration of the East India Company by concentrating on colonial law and legal institutions. This approach provides, first, an alternative perspective for evaluating the historical roots of development and underdevelopment. Second, it enables us to look at relations between the state and agrarian classes, which are usually excluded from analyses which focus exclusively on class relations, and allows us to incorporate the colonial state as part of the social relations of rural society.

1.1 *Colonial Policy and the Zamindars*

From the point of view of colonial administration, the relationship between zamindars and the state during

* I would like to thank Zaheer Baber, Prof. Pradeep Bandopadhyay, Ena Dua, the editors and the seminar participants for valuable comments and suggestions in writing this paper.

the early period of colonial rule can be best described as a ruler-subject relationship. Zamindar, and large zamindars in particular, were hostile subjects — the only social group which had the potential to challenge the colonial administration.[1] Consequently, the handling of zamindari issues was reserved exclusively for consideration by the Governor-General. The perceived threat posed by the zamindars was two-fold: economic and political. At the latter level, the state had to compete with the zamindars for the political allegiance of the indigenous population; the colonial authorities felt that the zamindars had so much influence over the peasants and local functionaries that they could undermine colonial rule Such political influence could also intervene with the collection of agricultural revenues, a prime economic interest of the colonial administration. The colonial state therefore introduced substantive policies to guarantee revenue collection and undermine the position of the zamindars. But these policies had wider implications for agrarian relations in Bengal. Farming out revenue collection contributed to the parcellisation of zamindaris in addition to creating intermediate interests on land and disrupting the traditional relationship between zamindars and peasants (Mahmood [1970]). A similar objective dictated the separation of taluks from zamindari lands (Monckton Jones [1918], pp. 157,161).[2] By substituting the salaried *darogha* for the land-based magisterial authority of the zamindar, the state sought to divest the latter from his governing role while at the same time contributing to curbing rural unrest (McLane [1988]). Similarly, the

[1] The colonial administration was able to eliminate any political challenge from the indigenous governing class by undermining both its political and its economic basis. Removal from administrative positions and consequent distancing from land were successful policies in destroying the old regime.

[2] The separation of taluks is especially interesting in the light of earlier opinions held by the colonial administration. The letter to the Supervisors pointed out: 'The increase of Talooks is highly impolitic and detrimental to the general prosperity and to the diffusion of population in the country. The tenants of a Talook are possssed of so many indulgencies and taxed with such evident partiality and tenderness in proportion to the rest, that the talooks generally swarm with inhabitants while other parts are deserted....' (Colebrooke [n.d], p.182). See also Philips ([1876], p.399) for policies related to taluks.

abolition of *patwaris* and *kanungoes* aimed at curtailing the giving of false information on which to base revenue assessments (which had been common under the zamindars) and to improve record-keeping regarding agricultural rights and interests.[3]

1.1.2 *Organisation of Property: Indigenous Law and the State*

In addition to the above policies, there was one other policy which requires specific attention because it was designed explicitly with the purpose of minimising the political and economic role of the zamindars. This policy was the abolition of primogeniture in Bengal. In an attempt to curtail the control of the large zamindars over land and local population, the Hastings administration argued that primogeniture, the mode of transmission of large zamindaries, was inconsistent with indigenous laws of succession that could be observed in small zamindaries. Consequently, the authorities revised the policy so that zamindari lands could be divided among all legitimate heirs according to Hindu and Muslim laws of inheritance (Monckton Jones [1918], pp.159-60,161).[4]

The political expediency of this policy is thrown into clearer relief if we keep in mind that it coincided with resistance to changes in the law of inheritance in England Look-

[3] The colonial administration undertook to rectify the negative consequences of the abolition of the patwari and kanungo offices. However, its effort met with strong opposition from the zamindars and was never achieved in Bengal. Zamindari resistance to the re-introduction of these office indicates that the zamindars could use their monopoly of knowledge of agrarian Bengal to undermine the interests of the state as well as of the peasants. (See Government of India [n.d.]).

[4] The two modes of land transmission in large and smaller zamindaris suggest an interesting question regarding the origin of primogeniture in Bengal. The prevalence of Hindu and Muslim laws of succession in small zamindaris may signify that actual property rights over land were vested in small zamindars. Consequently, the land could be divided among heirs according to indigenous laws of inheritance. On the other hand, the presence of primogeniture in larger zamindaris indicates that the position of the zamindar did not signify a property status but the status of an administrative officer, the collector of revenue. Even an hereditary office like the one occupied by a zamindar could be divided among heirs. It is not surprising, then, that primogeniture was restricted to large zamindaris which were indeed administrative units established for the collection of revenue. In abolishing primogeniture in Bengal the colonial administration implicitly conferred property rights on the zamindars well before, and independently of, the implementation of Permanent Settlement. See Pal ([1925]) for a detailed exposition of this argument.

ing at the debates prevailing in England and the reasons for objections to the abolition of primogeniture there, it is clear that primogeniture was seen as a means of maintaining the *status quo* of a political order associated with control over land by a particular class (Brodrick [1872]; Kenny [1878]). The abolition of primogeniture in Bengal sought to achieve the exact opposite. It is no exaggeration to say that the zamindars were the ruling and governing class in Bengal, at least at the local level. The colonial policy was designed exactly to destroy this indigenous political structure by undermining its economic basis, control over land. Furthermore, provisions were made so that small properties would not be divided according to the Hindu or Muslim laws of inheritance because this could lead to unproductive landholdings (Monckton Jones [1918], p. 285). Obviously, the destruction of the large zamindars was behind the policy to eliminate primogeniture in Bengal.[5]

The initial legislation regarding transmission of zamindari estates allowed them to remain indivisible, if primogeniture was a family custom. This provision enabled interested parties to contest claims over customary practices in the courts, and between 1792 and 1813 the Sudder Diwani Adalat in Calcutta decided at least twelve cases in favour of indivisibil-

[5] I do not have any data directly indicating whether or not such provisions found their way into the actual legislation and, if they did, how they were actually implemented. However, some inconclusive evidence indicates that HIndu and Muslim laws of succession could be circumvented. A number of court cases relating to land disputes and instituted on the basis of Hindu and Muslim laws of inheritance were dismissed by the sudder Diwani Adalat in Calcutta on the rule of limitation (See Lal Rooder Pertab Sing v. Lal Dhokul Sing (1808); Mizra Husun ali v. Mizra Shureef and others (1811); Mt Zureenah Beebe v. Khajan Ali and others (1820); Ramdhun Sein and others v. Kishenkanth Sein and other (1821); Radha Mani Devya v. Suri Mani Devya and other (1831) (Morley [1850], pp.425-427).

The law of limitation, which fixed a limit of 12 years for the institution of suits relating to land, was incorporated in the 1772 and 1780 orders which established the Provincial Courts and the Suder Diwani Adalat. It also constituted part of Regulation III of 1793. At that time, the colonial administration believed that such a limit was prescribed by the Hindu and Muslim laws operating in Bengal. Regulation II of 1805 disputed the fact that such a limitation was embedded in indigenous laws. Nonetheless, it conceded that the law of limitation might have been a customary practice. Consequently, the law of limitation was constructed as customary law, whose origins were based not on indigenous custom but on the practices of the colonial administration.

ity (English Reports. Privy Council, Vol. 18, p. 374).[6] These cases indicate that customary practices were upheld during the early colonial period but the impact of litigation on the zamindars remains to be assessed.

The available evidence suggests that such litigation contributed considerably to the destruction of zamindaris, even in cases where heriditary practices could be established. Legal disputes took place over the property of the Nadia Raj and Bishnapur Raj.[7] An account of the legal battle between Choyton and Damundar Singh of the Bishnapur Raj provides useful insights into the consequences of litigation. The former, the elder son, claimed the whole zamindari on the basis of the customary law of primogeniture. The latter, his younger brother, demanded half of the zamindari according to the Hindu law of succession. In 1795, 22 years after the legal dispute was initiated and fought at various levels, the Sudder Diwani Adalat decided the case in favour of Choyton Singh. By this time Choyton Singh had already lost half of his zamindari lands as a result of revenue arrears. The financial loss involved in the long court battles between Choyton Singh and his brother and the effect of the dispute on the management of the estate were instrumental in the eventual downfall of the Bishnapur Raj. Moreover, the decision of 1795 formed the basis of a new war of succession among Choyton's eldest son and his ten younger sons, which further undermined the financial position of the zamindari (Islam [1971], pp. 136-139,140).[8]

[6] See cited cases Isshanchud Roy v. Isshurchud Roy (1792), Ramgunga Deo v. Doorgamunee Jobrau (1809), Baboo Ishurrepershand Sing v. Baboo Sahal Zada Singh (1803), Koonwur Bodh Singh and other v. Seonath Singh (1813), Gungagoing Sing v. Rajah Madho Singh (1804), Golam Husun Ali v. Zeinub Beebee (1801). Ali Buksh Khan v. Kaeem Beebee (1804), Mirza Moohummud and Hyaut-o-nisa v. Jareut-oz-Zohra Begum and others (1808), Wajih-on Nisa Khanum v. Mirza Husun Ali (1808), Omduton Nisa Begum v. Mirza Asud Ali (1809), Meer Nujib Ollah v. Mussummaut Doordana Khatoon (1805).

[7] See Kemm and Pringle, A Report on the Survey and Settlement Operations in the Nadia District, 1918-26. I would like to thank Dr Abhijit Dasgupta for bringing this case to my attention.

[8] In 1806 the government bought the remainder of the zamindari; after unsuccessful armed resistance by the family, all members were removed from Bishnapur by 1808.

We have no detailed documentation about the frequency of litigation like this or about the actual implementation of the new policy in the early colonial period.[9] But we do know that customary practices of zamindari inheritance were formally abolished by Regulation XI of 1793. Thereafter, land was to devolve exclusively according to Hindu and Muslim laws of inheritance. Other modes of land transmission were considered legitimate only if there was a will or another written and verbal declaration which specified these. The difficulty in producing such evidence and proving its legitimacy in court meant that the division of zamindari estates became the established norm.

Regulation XI of 1793 had also provided guidelines for the registration of zamindari shares in cases where a zamindari continued to be held jointly by several family members. However, subsequent organisational problems associated with the collection of revenue from numerous shareholders led to Regulation VI of 1807. Section 2 of this Regulation specified that zamindari holdings assessed under Rs 500 could not be registered as separate holdings. This meant an institutional restriction on the subdivision of zamindari shares (as far as the collection of revenue was concerned) but not on the actual division of rights to land. Eventually, even this limitation was abolished by Regulation 19, section 2, of 1814 (Appendix to the Select Committee 1832, Vol.III, Appendix No 6: 31).

Colonial administrators acknowledged that division of zamindaris posed a serious problem. They also recognised that policies requiring the registration of individual shares contributed to subdivisions of zamindaris. Nevertheless, they refrained from attributing any causal relationship between changes in the laws of succession introduced by the

[9] Some evidence suggests that the law was contested and circumvented. For example, the rebellion of heriditary chiefs in Midnapur led to the exemption of the area from the operation of the law. Transferring family property to religious trusts was another way of retaining control of property.

colonial state and land fragmentation. On the contrary: in 1856 the Lieutenant Governor of Bengal, Halliday, attributed land fragmentation to the Hindu law of inheritance. Commenting on the proposed amendments to the Sale Law (Act I, 1845), he objected to the recognition and registration of all zamindari shareholders on the ground that such a policy would encourage a 'rabbit warren' system of land ownership. He argued that the subdivision of zamindaries in Bengal districts had already created a 'pauper proprietary,' and that:

> 'the number of shares will go on increasing under the Hindoo Law up the limit of starvation, especially if encouraged and fostered by unlimited separate accounts at the Collectorate.' (Bengal Administrative Report 1856-57, pp. 103-105).

In 1831-32, A. D. Campbell held the courts responsible because they had administered the indigenous laws of succession in a rigorous way (Appendix to the Select Committee 1832, Vol III, Appendix 6, p.30; Campbell's Report to the 1831-32 Parliamentary Commitee on land revenue in the Bengal Presidency).

The above assessments ignored the fact that the responsibility for the division of zamindaris lay primarily with the policies of the colonial state which had imposed the implementation of indigenous laws of inheritance which had not been in force in the precolonial era. They also failed to take into account the fact that legislation was instrumental in creating new claims on land which were contested in the courts. Since these courts operated within the limitations set by the Regulations, Campbell's assessment is not altogether accurate. Nevertheless, the process of interpreting and implementing such legislation by the courts points to the arbitrary nature of legal decisions. In this regard, the courts were equally significant in institutionalising rights and interests over land.

1.1.3 *Religious Law and Land Fragmentation: the Case of Surjapur*[10]

The struggle over the division of the zamindari of Surjapur, situated in Purnea and Dinajpur, illustrates the extent of land fragmentation resulting from the new laws of inheritance. It also offers an insight into the working of the courts. The zamindari was established when Bibi Rowseen, the initial possessor, married Mahomed Saeed (See *Chart 1*). Primogeniture or monogeniture appears to have been the mode of transmission until 1793 when Fukurud-din Hossein died and the administration of the zamindari was entrusted to a manager. In 1801 Raja Akbar Hossein and Raja Deedar Hossein, Fukurud-din's sons, took direct possession of the property which was registered as a single unit at the collectorate.

Akbar Hossein died in 1813 without any male heirs; his first wife, Rani Zuhur-un Nissa, took possession of his share. Deedar Hossein, however, contested this and took the case to the Provincial Court of Murshidabad. He produced two documents to support his claim as the only legitimate heir. The first, a will left by his father, indicated that the zamindari should remain indivisible according to established family practice; the second, an *ikrarnamah* (agreement) between the two brothers, reiterated the family custom and at the same time was used as a disclaimer to female rights of inheritance. Rani Zuhur-un challenged the validity of the family practice on legal and factual grounds. First, she argued that any claims to customary practices contradicted Regulation XI of 1793. Second, she pointed out that between 1801 and 1813 the profits were divided equally between the two brothers; an act which in itself constituted admission of divisibility. Moreover, she argued that the zamindari could devolve to female members of the family since the zamindari had origi-

---

[10] The following account is based on the proceedings of two appeals to the Privy Council. See Rajah Deedar Hossein, Appellant; Ranee Zuhoor-oon Nissa, Respondent, and Rajah Enayet Hoosein, Appellant; Sayud Ahmed Reza and Mahammad Reza, Respondents (*English Reports, Privy Council,* Vol.18, pp. 368-383; Vol 19, pp. 298-307).

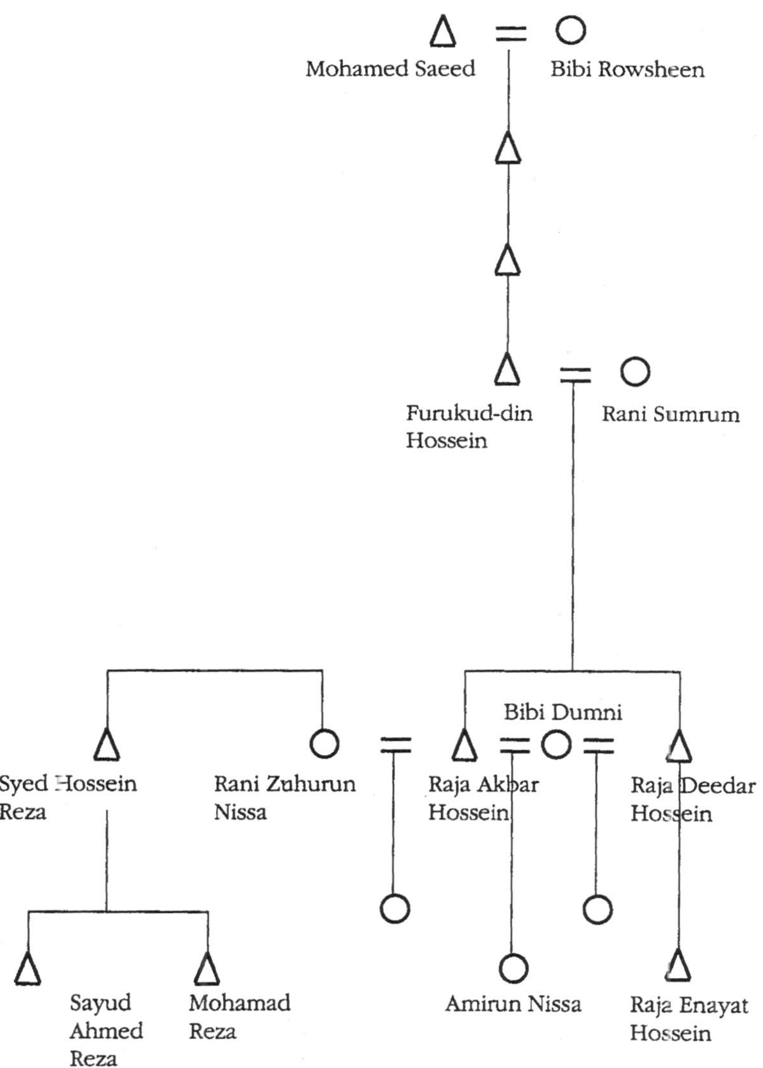

Chart 1: Family Chart of the zamindars of Surajpur

nally been the property of Bibi Rowsheen. She further substantiated her claims by producing two documents, executed by her husband during his life. The first, a bill of sale, transferred the property to her as a marriage-settlement; the second, a deed of gift, allocated some of his property to his daughters.

Four years later, in 1817, the Murshidabad Provincial Court decided the case in favour of Rani Zuhur-un. The decision was based on the authenticity of the documentary evidence produced in court. The documents produced by Rani Zuhur-un were treated as genuine, while those of Deedar Hossein were considered as fabrications. Moreover, the senior Judge of the Court argued that even if the latter's documents had been genuine, they were irrelevant to the case. The will could not be upheld as valid because it contradicted Muslim law; the *ikrarnamah*, an acceptable Muslim practice, was invalidated by the later execution of a bill of sale and a deed of gift.

An appeal was lodged before the Sudder Diwani Adalat. The case went through six hearings before different judges of the Court — a result of disagreements about the validity of the evidence and the interpretation of existing Regulations. The case was first heard by S.T.Goad, the fourth Judge of the Court. He dismissed Deedar's documents as fabricated, since there was no need for written evidence in establishing a customary practice. In doing so, he upheld the decision of the Murshidabad Provincial Court regarding Deedar Hossein's claims. However, he questioned the validity of the bill of sale and rejected the decree of the Murshidabad Provincial Court regarding the Rani's right to inheritance. He concluded that Raja Akbar's share of the zamindari should be divided among all his heirs according to Muslim law. The difference of opinion between the Mursidabad Provincial Court and the Sudder Diwani Adalat led to a second hearing before Courtney Smith, the Officiating Judge of the Adalat. He argued that none of the evidence brought before the court was valid. According to him, it was evident that the

Rajas of Surjapur did not have the power to pay for marriage settlements from the zamindari and that female members of the family were not allowed any power over the zamindari. He found that the family custom of indivisibility was applicable to the case and that the Regulation XI of 1793 did not bar a decision in favour of Raja Deedar. The last comment was based on established precedent by previous decisions of the Sudder Diwani Adalat.[11] Consequently, he reversed the previous decrees and appointed Raja Deedar as the only legitimate heir. It appears that Judge Goad objected to this decision, and the case was brought before Sir James Edward Colebrooke, the Chief Judge of the Adalat. Colebrooke concurred with Smith's opinion and affirmed his decision. Subsequently, Rani Zuhur-un filed a petition requesting a review of the judgement. This time the case was heard before the then Chief Judge of the Adalat, William Leycester, who altered Colebrooke's decision. He ruled that the family custom had not been established; if such a custom had existed in the past, it had been altered by the division of profits between Raja Akbar and Deedar when they held the zamindari jointly; even if such custom had been established, it would have been invalidated by Regulation XI of 1793. He argued against the establishment of any precedent by previously decided cases on the ground that the Regulation XI of 1793 became operational subsequent to its enactment. Similarly, he dismissed the issue of marriage settlements and divisions in the zamindari on grounds of irrelevance. He ordered that the half-share of the zamindari should be divided among the heirs of Raja Akbar according to Muslim Law, thereby reaffirming the initial decision of the Adalat. Two additional hearings were held before Judge Goad and Officiating Judge William Dorin. Both concurred with Leycester's decision. Judge Dorin provided an interesting new interpretation concerning the division of zamindaris and the operation of Regulation XI of 1793. Commenting on precedents, he argued that

[11] See note 6.

non-division of zamindaris could be accepted if a zamindari coincided with a Raj.[12] The Adalat had ruled in favour of family custom in such cases only when the disputing parties were Hindus. Since the Adalat had never decided an analogous case involving Muslims, the case under consideration had to be decided on the basis of the rules set by the Regulation XI of 1793. The final decision of the Sudder Diwani Adalat was given by Leycester, Goad and Dorin. It was ruled that the share of Raja Akbar was to be divided by his heirs. Raja Deedar was excluded from the list of legitimate heirs because it was discovered in the last two hearings that both litigants were Shia Muslims. The ruling was based on a 1808 decision of the Sudder Diwani Adalat which determined that according to a Shia *futwa* (law opinion), the rights of surviving daughters to their father's property override the rights of a brother.[13] In response, Raja Deedar filed a petition to the Court in 1823 arguing that Shia *futwas* were not in force in Bengal and consequently he appealed to the Privy Council in England. In 1842, the Privy Council affirmed the decision of the Sudder Diwani Adalat and gave a judgement on the operation of the Shia law of inheritance in Bengal. First, it justified the prevalence of Sunni law in the Indian Courts because Sunnis predominated in India's Muslim population. Second, it argued that this state of affairs did not contradict Regulation XI of 1793 which laid down the rule that the religious persuasions of the litigants would determine how property was divided.

In the meantime, both Rani Zuhur-un and Raja Deedar had died. The Rani died in 1835, leaving her brother Sayud Hossein Reza as her heir; his property was eventually inherited by his two sons, Sayud Ahmed Reza and Mahammad Reza. The latter, who had also inherited the property of his mother, Rani Sumrun, died in 1841, and left his only son Raja

[12] Raj rights to a zamindar were rare. They were confined to the old zamindaris and these were seen as exception to the rules of Regulation XI of 1793 (Appendix to the Select Committee 1832, Vol III, appendix 6, p.30).

[13] See *Wujib-on* Nisa Khanum and others v.Mirza Husun Ali (Morley [1850], p. 340).

Enayet Hossein as his heir. Following the decision of the Privy Council, a number of new law-suits concerning shares of Raja Akbar's property were instituted. One of these was started by Amir-un Nissa in 1844; she claimed her share of the property of her father, Raja Akbar, as well as that of her mother, Bibi Dumni, against Sayud Hossein Reza and later his sons. A controversy arose out of different interpretations by the Judges of the Zillah Court of Purnea, but it seems that in 1846 the court decided in favour of Amir-un on the basis of the Privy Council decision. Another case, involving Raja Enayet Hossein and Sayud Ahmed Reza and his brother, became more controversial and once again ended up in the Privy Council. This law-suit was started in April 1852 by Raja Enayet who claimed the legitimate share of his paternal grandmother from the property of Raja Akbar. He argued that according to the 1842 Privy Council decision his grandmother was a legitimate heir to a share of her eldest son's property. Rani Sumrun's share was inherited by his father Raja Deedar, who left him as his legal heir. Ahmed and Mahammad Reza argued that the descendent of Deedar Hossein did not have any legitimate claims to the property of Akbar Hossein. Moreover, the law of limitation barred him from any such claims since they had been in possession of the property for more than forty years. The judge of the Zillah court of Purnea ruled in May 1854 that the law of limitation was not applicable in this case since the case originated from the decision of the Privy Council in 1842, and it decided in favour of Raja Enayet. This decision was, however, dismissed by the Sudder Diwani Adalat in 1854 which ruled that the law of limitation was operable after all, since the present parties in the dispute were not the original litigants affected by the decision of the Privy Council. This decision was reversed once more by the Privy Council in 1858. The new judgement was based on the relevance of the 1842 decision on the present case as well as on the Shia law of inheritance. The Privy Council ruling gave possession of the zamindari lands to Raja Enayet because he was the heir to the property of his paternal grandmother, who in turn had rights to the disputed zamindari lands.

This detailed and perhaps confusing case indicates that a systematic analysis of court cases dealing with land disputes can be particularly useful in evaluating the impact of colonial institutions on rural society. The Surjapur case raises a number of important issues. First, it shows the role of legislation and courts in organising property and family relations, and in establishing women's property rights. It also indicates that, contrary to widely held notions about the role of colonial law as instrumental in implementing and reinforcing private property rights, the courts actually undermined rather than protected such rights. The uncertainty surrounding the outcome of a legal decision and the length of time involved in deciding legal disputes point to the ambiguous status of property rights.

Second, the adoption of indigenous religious laws of inheritance, as opposed to customary law, implies an institutionally imposed definition of what constituted a 'good' Hindu or Muslim. This poses an important historical question: did laws of inheritance, or similar laws constructed on the basis of religion, contribute to a colonial identity along religious lines? Whatever the case may be, religion did provide a legitimate means of creating and accommodating new interests in land. Disputes over transmission of property became a permanent feature of agrarian society. According to Halhed ([1832], p.22), wills proved to be 'never-failing sources of litigation' among Hindus. Our evidence on such litigation is considerable. For example, 1,705 original suits were instituted in the districts of Bengal on the basis of the Hindu and Muslim laws of inheritance in 1864 alone (Bengal Administrative Report, 1864-65, Appendix- Statement A1:ii-v). Simultaneously, however, religion provided a means of resisting colonial policy. The increase in the number of Muslim endowments, for example, can be seen as an attempt to keep family property intact (Kozlowski [1985]).

Third, the Surjapur case allows us to focus on a dimension of colonial rule that has been overlooked. It is well known that the enforcement and protection of indigenous law, customs and practices was assigned a privileged status by the colonial administration.[14] It could be argued that the cases of the Bishnapur Raj, Surjapur and others I have referred to support this argument. However, if we situate such cases in the general discourse on inheritance laws and the contradiction between customary and Hindu or Muslim law, we see that respect for indigenous law had very little to do with the construction and the implementation of colonial policy. The colonial state intervened by introducing and interpreting religious law regarding property. A good indicator of the degree to which religious law was respected by the colonial state is interference in the administration of religious endowments.[15] Regulation XIX of 1810 empowered the state to nominate and control the trustees and managers of endowments. Exclusion of legitimate heirs by institutionalising wills as legal and legitimate instruments for the transmission of property contradicted both Hindu and Muslim law.

Similarly, the abolition of primogeniture demonstrates the limited extent to which customary law was respected in Bengal. The colonial authorities were well aware that primogeniture was a customary practice. Nevertheless, they chose to implement a law against it in order to manipulate the manner in which property was transmitted. Whether one accepted or contested the new law, the outcome was gener-

---

[14] In the context of this paper, the political expediency of indigenous law is confined to internal factors. However, it is relevant to the discussion of external constraints operating on the colonial administration as well. Without going into a detailed exposition of this issue, it must be pointed out that this policy was a device to keep to a minimum British interference into the affairs of the EIC. The establishement of the Board of Control and the Supreme Court Calcutta gave ample opportunity to the British authorities to intervene in the administration of Bengal. One way of minimising such interference was to associate just administration with respect for indigenous customs and practices. The complexity of indigenous law, customary or otherwise, gave legitimacy to the claim that only EIC officials possessed the practical knowledge to comprehend and administer Indian society. For an analogous situation see C. Hill's discussion (1965) of the use of common law in limiting the power of the absolutist state by the emerging bourgeoisie in England.

[15] See Jawun Doss Sahoo, Appellant; Shah Kubeer-ood deen, Repondent (1840) (*English Reports. Privy Council,* Vol. 18, pp. 348-360); and Morley ([1850], pp. 549-556).

ally the same: a disintegration of large zamindari estates and a fragmentation of landed property.

1.2 *Permanent Settlement: Revenue and Non-revenue Payers*

The policies discussed above had important implications for the structure of landholding in Bengal and for agrarian society in general, but they failed to achieve their original goal of undermining the zamindars as a class. This failure was enshrined in the property rights which the Permanent Settlement explicitly vested in the zamindars. The implications of the Permanent Settlement for the legal status of zamindars and peasants were criticised from the start (Firminger [1812]). Nevertheless, it was not till the 1820s and 1830s, when the impact of the Permanent Settlement on agrarian society could be assessed and evaluated, that its validity came to be vigorously disputed (Appendix to the Select Committee 1831-32, Vol. III pp. 28, 256). Defenders of the policy maintained that the Permanent Settlement did not intend to give exclusive property rights to the zamindars, and this interpretation became more prevalent in the second half of the 19th century. It found its way into legislation, and informed court decisions, starting with the 1859 Rent Act and up to the Bengal Tenancy Act of 1885, which aimed to accommodate peasant rights which had eroded. The 1865 celebrated case of *Thakoranee Dassee v. Bishshur Mookerjee*, better known as the Great Rent Case, has been widely used to provide evidence that the rights of zamindars were limited by the rights of subordinate holders (Philips [1876], pp. 312-320).

The administrative and legal discourse of the 19th century centred around the intentions of the Permanent Settlement and absolved it of any malice. Some recent interpretations have, however, sought to re-evaluate the Permanent Settlement by focusing on its actual impact on rural society. For example, Frykenberg (1965) argued that the introduction of proprietary rights affected the upper echelons of agrarian society but had no impact on the cultivators of the soil. Similarly, Stokes maintained that legal rights to private property had no impact on the everyday life of rural society. He argued that 'rural society refused to be neatly segregated into the mutually exclusive roles of landlord, tenant, and labourer, and doubled or trebled these roles endlessly' (Stokes [1978], p. 3).

Such views cannot be squared with the reality of colonial Bengal. It is true that a multiplicity of statuses with various claims over land and the products of the soil was part of the agrarian reality, but such claims did not necessarily entail peasant proprietary rights. In many instances, as in the case of *patni* tenures, zamindars were instrumental in creating such claims but they resisted any institutionalisation of the property rights of other agricultural classes. Jaykrishna Mukherjee of Uttarpara, for example, actively sought to minimise existing property rights at his estates by resuming rent-free lands (Mukherjee [1975], p. 97). In other words, the ever-increasing multiplication of agrarian roles and statuses was not inconsistent with the destruction of existing peasant rights which took place simultaneously. Direct evidence of this is provided by the relatively few cases regarding eviction from land which came to the courts throughout the period of colonial rule. Not dispossession but rent increase, a major means of circumventing proprietary rights, formed the substance of the overwhelming majority of court cases.[16]

To understand the situation described above we need to take into account the meaning attached to the notion of property rights in the Permanent Settlement. Regulation III of 1794 defined as a proprietors of land those 'who pay the revenue assessed upon their estates immediately to Government' (Anonymous [1879], pp. 48-49). The association be-

[16] For example, in 1828-29 land-rent cases made up 20,239 of all summary suits disposed of and pending in the Calcutta division; only 624 were suits regarding dispossession. The same was true for the other divisions of the Bengal Presidency: Dacca - 6,320 rent cases, 97 dispossessions; Murshidabad — 7,689 and 616 respectively; Patna — 5,778 and 983 (Appendix to the Select Committee 1832, Vol III, Appendix No 5, Table XIV, pp. 556-558).

tween property rights and revenue payment embedded in the Permanent Settlement signifies the inability of the state to control zamindars — and the danger to revenue realisation that this failure implied. The policy sought to resolve this problem by redefining the relationship. The classification of proprietors as revenue payers meant the inclusion of the zamindars into the public domain and the institutionali-sation of their relationship with the state. Even though this relationship was still an unequal one, since it originated from the state, it was far from being a simple subject-ruler relationship. It established a direct contact between the two and incorporated certain rights and obligations on both sides. As long as the zamindars met their revenue obligations, they were guaranteed the protection and cooperation of the state.

The fact that only revenue payers and proprietors were in direct contact with the state meant that non-revenue payers and non-proprietors were excluded from the public domain. In other words, there was no direct institutional linkage between the state and non-revenue payers as far as property rights were concerned.[17] The only direct interaction between the state and non-revenue payers occurred in the criminal courts. For example, Morley's digest reported 187 criminal cases in which the government was directly involved. By contrast, it reported only nine cases relating to land tenure (three of them from Benares) in the Sudder Diwani Adalat in Calcutta, which involved direct litigation on the part of the government (Morley [1850], pp. 122-190, 402-407).

1.2.1 *Permanent Settlement: Rent Receivers, Rent Payers and the State*

The differentiation between revenue payers and non-revenue payers was analogous to another classification embed-

[17] Technically, a direct relationship between the state and non-revenue payers should have existed in *khas mahals*. I am not aware of any study indicating the position of non-revenue payers in such cases; it would be interesting to compare their circumstances with those of their counterparts under zamindars.

ded in the Permanent Settlement. According to its provisions, revenue payers were classified as rent receivers and non-revenue payers were classified as rent payers. The distinction between revenue and rent, first introduced in Bengal with the Permanent Settlement (Sen [1935], pp. 146-148), was consistent with the overall character of the Permanent Settlement. Rent signified a private contractual relationship between the two social categories, revenue payers and non-revenue payers, based on property relations. Furthermore, the exclusion of non-revenue payers from the public domain further reinforced the private status assigned to the relationship between rent receivers and rent payers. As J. E. Colebrooke noted in 1820, the zamindar was left to make his settlement with the peasants 'on such terms as he might choose to require' (Mookerjee [1919], p. 59). Thus, state non-interference became the official doctrine in Bengal (Beames [1961], p. 129).

It was this aspect of the relationship between the state and the agrarian classes that made it possible for the zamindars to extract concessions from the state at the expense of non-revenue payers. By using their status of revenue payers, the zamindars were able to dictate legislation dealing with processes of rent collection, such as the *Haptam* (Reg. VII of 1799) and *Pancham* (Reg. V of 1812) which undermined the position and rights of non-revenue payers.

1.2.2 *Civil Courts and the 'Private' Domain*

Under these circumstances, the only option available to peasants and other non-revenue payers was to take their grievances to the civil courts. As a matter of fact it was left to the courts to define and determine the rights of every description of landholders and tenants. The introduction of the Regulations of the Permanent Settlement was therefore followed by an enormous and non-manageable amount of law suits. By 1803 in some districtst the pending court cases far exceeded those decided or dismissed (Firminger [1812],

p. 116, Vol. I). In Burdwan 13,025 civil suits were decided in 1801, and from February 1815 to June 1818, 18,039 suits were decided. By contrast, few civil suits had been instituted prior to 1793. For example, in the district of Birbhum, which included Bishnupur and the Santal Parganas, only 112 cases were instituted in the civil courts between 1787 and 1793 (McLane [1988], pp. 32, 171, fn23).

The colonial administration tried to belittle the significance of the enormous litigation which followed the introduction of the Permanent Settlement. They attributed it first to the litigious nature of the indigenous population and second to the relatively low costs involved in instituting a law suit. However, in response to an inquiry on the functioning of the courts, which was initiated by the Wellesley administration in 1801, a number of local administrators rejected this interpetation. In one particular case, the judge of Midnapur, H. Strachey, pointed out that 'the complaints of these people are seldom or never litigious.' In addition, he observed that it was common to see 'a suitor, when stripped of his last rupee, and called upon for the fee on a document, produce in a court a silver ring or other trinket to beg that it might be received as a pledge; and after all, perhaps he was cast for want of money, to bring proof' (Firminger [1912], p. 592, Vol II). Thus while at one level the courts provided, at least in theory, the means of resisting the ever-increasing power of zamindars, in practice most people were unable to seek justice in the courts of law. Policies such as an increase of the fee for court stamps were implemented at various times in order to reduce the work load of courts, and the prolonged period in deciding cases acted against the interests of non-revenue payers and against the rights of the peasants in particular.

These institutional barriers did not affect the zamindars who could withstand and sustain prolonged litigation. As a matter of fact, the courts were extensively and effectively used by the zamindars in order to protect their interests and deprive non-revenue payers of their rights. The advantageous position enjoyed by the zamindars *vis-á-vis* other claimants can be demonstrated by considering court cases dealing with various claims over land. In one case a zamindar whose land had been sold for revenue arrears had held part of his zamindari under a *devottar* tenure. As a result of the sale, 1,452 *bighas* of *devottar* land had been bought by three different auction purchasers. The zamindar engaged in a legal battle with them which lasted thirty years; it involved the district (*zillah*) courts of Hughli and 24-Parganas, the Calcutta Provincial Court and the Sudder Diwani Adalat. In 1832, the latter ruled in favour of the zamindar and granted him to sue for *mesne* profits in one of the cases. At the same time, it suggested a review of previous decisions regarding the status of land bought by the second auction purchaser.[18]

The ruling of the court is significant because it indicates that the zamindars were in a position to win even in cases where land disputes originated from the operation of sale laws. In implementing the sale laws, the courts protected the revenue interests of the state and they normally decided in favour of auction buyers. Even actual proprietors were affected by public auctions, as the following case shows.[19] A portion of a zamindari estate was sold privately. The land was assessed and separated by the collector. However, divisions of estates had to be approved by the Board of Revenue and the Governor-General and in this case the collector had not obtained their sanction. As a result, the disputed land had been re-annexed and included in the public auction of the zamindari that took place later. The case was brought to the courts and the Sudder Diwani Adalat ruled that the private sale was invalid; the auction purchaser took possession of the land. The decision was based on a strict technical implementation of the Regulations. The reason why the sale had not been sanctioned by the Board of Rev-

[18] See *Kali Parshad Ray v. Heirs of Kheda Ram Mukhopadhya* (Morley [1850], p. 404).

[19] *Sham Rai and another v. Collector of Jessore and another* (Morley [1850], p. 572).

enue was considered immaterial and had not been addressed by the court. The court aso ignored the fact that records of the sale and the assessment were available at the collectorate. It is interesting to note that when the provisions requiring the the Board of Revenue and the Governor-General to sanction private partition were rescinded by Regulation XIX of 1814, the courts ruled that private partitions without any *butwarah* by the Collector constituted a legal severalty under Hindu law.[20]

In cases involving disputes between zamindars and peasants, the advantages which the legal structure provided the former are obvious. Loss of peasant property rights was the rule especially when land was sold in public auction for revenue arrears; sale laws gave power to auction purchasers to oust all but the resident ryots (Appendix to the Select Committee, 1832, Vol. III, p. 153). Even though extensive dispossession did not take place, as has been noted earlier, property rights eroded through the increase of rents. Enhancement of rent was accomplished in various ways. The sale laws facilitated this process by allowing public auction purchasers to increase rent directly or indirectly. The Regulations put a ceiling on the amount of rent which could be demanded, but the absence of detailed records on *pergunnah* rates undermined the ability of the courts to decide on such cases (Mookerjee [1919], p. 66). Moreover, the application of irrelevant precedents on rent disputes between zamindars and peasants by the courts[21] facilitated the formation of the doctrine that land rent was an annually recurring cause of action, thereby exempting rent enhancement from the operation of the law of limitation. Jaykrishna of Uttarpara had won one thousand summary suits relating to rent disputes and less than thirty had been reversed in appeals by the civil courts in the course of ten years

[20] *Raja Patni Mal and another v. Ray Manohur Lal and others; Baboo Kishenkomar Sahee v. Kunchun Konwar* (Morley [1850], pp. 485-486). For other cases relating to partition, see Morley [1850], pp. 478-487).

[21] See the cases involving disputes between zamindars, occupancy cultivators and dependent talukdars discussed in Anonymous ([1879], pp. 81-84).

(Mukherjee [1975], p. 71). According to the author of the *Zemindari Settlement of Bengal*, 'eminent judges have reasoned away the rights of the ryots' through a rigid and literal interpretation of the Regulations regarding proprietary status and rights for the enhancement of rent (Anonymous [1879], pp. 34,81).

The interpretation of law was part of the problems associated with the impact of courts on agrarian society. In many instances the courts had to decide cases which were not included in legislation. In such cases the courts exercised discretionary power based on individual judges' definition of justice. Consequently, judicial precedents were established by local courts which varied from district to district. According to Taniguchi ([1981], p. 46), such precedents or 'rule of practice' were important in regulating agrarian relations because they affected most agrarian classes. Disputes regarding *patni* tenures provide an illustration. In Hughli and Jungle Mahals the local courts had established a precedent of voiding inferior *patni* tenures when a superior *patni* tenure was sold. In Burdwan, however, the courts upheld the rights of inferior *patnidars*. As a result, the value of *patni* tenures varied in the three districts, and the Raja of Burdwan whose estate spread over the three districts had to adopt different policies towards the inferior *patnidars* (Taniguchi [1981], pp. 45-46). The litigation between the Raja of Burdwan and *talukdars* holding various grades of *patni* tenures led the government to commission an investigation which eventually led to the Patni Regulation (Reg. VIII of 1819). The legalisation of *patni* tenures did not mean, however, that the rights of inferior *patnidars* were protected. The Regulation specified that the sale of a *patni* taluk by a public auction, for rent arrears due to the zamindar, invalidated all inferior tenures. In enforcing the Regulation, the courts ruled against inferior *patnidars*, even though they themselves might not have been defaulters. At the most, the courts allowed inferior *patnidars* to sue for any damage that they might have sustained by the default of superior tenure holders.[22]

In this paper, I have focused on legislation and courts in order to provide additional insights into the processes which shaped agrarian society in Bengal during the first half of colonial rule. Particular emphasis has been placed on the objectives of colonial policies regarding indigenous law and the unintended consequences of such policies. In doing so, two issues were addressed: land fragmentation and the enabling effect of law in shaping new demands and claims over land. The role of colonial law and courts has been also assessed within the context of the Permanent Settlement and its implications for structuring the relations between the colonial state and agrarian classes. An examination of law suits involving claims over land by revenue and non-revenue payers has indicated, however tentatively, that the courts contributed to the uncertainty and erosion of property rights which involved tenures held by non-revenue payers, and in doing so, organised and regulated property relations. In this sense, the courts played an important role in the formation of the colonial agrarian milieu. A conclusive assessment of the courts, however, requires further research, especially in evaluating their contribution to regulating the relationship between the zamindars and various categories of non-revenue payers at the local level.

References

Anonyniys (1879), *The Zemindary Settlement of Bengal,* B.R. Corporation, Calcutta.

Appendix to the Select Committee of the House of Commons on the Affairs of the East India Company (1983). *Revenue,* Vol. III.

Beames, J. (1961). *Memoirs of a Bengal Civilian,* Chatto and Windus, London.

Brodrick, G. (1872). The law and custom and primogeniture, *Cobden Club Essays,* Second Series, Cassel, Petter and Galpin, London.

[22] *Mohun Geer Mohunt v. Radhamohun Ghutuk and others; Ramdoolal Misser v. Rammohun Sawunt and others* (Morley [1850], pp. 407-408).

Colebrooke, J. (n.d.) *Digest of Regulations - Supplement,* Calcutta.

English Reporters, (n.d.). *Moore Indian Appeals,* Vol 18 and 19, Privy Council, London.

Firminger, W.K. (1812). *The Fifth Report of the Selct Committee of the House of Commons on the Affairs of the East India Company:* 3 Vols. R. Cambray & Co. Calcutta.

Frykenberg, R.E. (1965). *Guntur District,* 1788-1848, Clarendon Press, Oxford.

Government of India (n.d.). *Papers Relating to the Bill to Amend and Consolidate the Law Relation to Canoongoes and Patwaries,* National Archives of India. New Delhi.

Halhed, D. (1832). *A Memoir on the Land Tenure and Principles of Land Taxation,* Samuel Smith and Co., Calcutta.

Hill, C. (1965). *Intellectual Origins of the English Revolution,* Clarendon Press, Oxford.

Islam S. (1971). *The Permanent Settlement in Bengal: A Study of its Operation,* Bangla Academy, Dacca.

Kenny, C.S. (1878). *The History of the Law of Primogeniture in England and its Effect upon Landed Property,* J. Hall & Son, Cambridge.

Kolowski, G.(1985). *Muslim Endowments and Society in British India,* Cambridge University Press, Cambridge.

Mahmood, A.B (1970). *The Revenue Administration of the Northern Bengal,* 1765-93, National Institute of Public Administration, Dacca.

McLane, J. (1988). Bengali bandits, police and landlords after the Permanent Settlement, in A. Young ed., *Crime and Criminality in British India,* University of Arizona Press, Tuscon.

Monckton Jones, M.E. (1918). *Warren Hasting in Bengal, 1772-74, with Appendixes of hitherto Unpublished Documents,* Clarendon Press, Oxford.

Mookerjee, R. (1919). *Occupancy Right: its History and Incidents,* Calcutta University Press, Calcutta.

Morley, W.H. (1850). *An Analytical Diggest of all Reported Cases Decided in the Supreme Courts of Juricature in India, in the Courts of the Hon. East India Company, and on Appeal from India,* Vol I, W.H. Allen and Co, London.

Mukherjee, N. (1975). *A Bengal* Zamindar*: Jaykrishna Mukherjee of Uttarpara and the Times, 1808-1888,* Firma K.L. Mukhopadhyay, Calcutta.

Pal. Radhabinod (1925). *The History of the Law of Primogeniture with Special Reference to India, ancient and Modern,* Calcutta University Press, Calcutta.

Philips, A. (1876). *The Law Relating to the Land Tenures of Lower Bengal,* Thacher, Spink and Co., Calcutta.

Sen, S. (1935). *Studies in the Land Economics of Bengal,* The Book Company, Calcutta.

Stokes, E. (1978). *The Peasant and the Raj,* Cambridge University Press, Cambridge.

Taniguchi, S. (1981). The patni system - a modern origin of the sub-infeudation of Bengal in the nineteenth century, *Hitotsubashi Journal of Economics,* Vol.22, No.1.

The Colonial State and the Indigenous Society: The Creation of the Rajbansi Identity in Bengal*

SWARAJ BASU

I

There exists a great deal of controversy among the scholars on the question of origin and identity of the Rajbansis of North Bengal. Let us take a look at some of these views. H.K.Adhikari (1907), a Rajbansi himself, noted:

> 'The Koch and Rajbansi did not belong to the same caste, they were different castes. The Rajbansis were superior to the Koches. Their origins were also different, and different were their occupations' (p.22).

A colonial observer, Montgomery Martin (1838), on the other hand, pointed out:

> 'I have no doubt, however, that all the Koch are sprung from the same stock, and that most of the Rajbangsis are Koch; but I am inclined to think, that many of the former are of different tribes, and having abandoned their impure practices, have been admitted to a communion' (p.538).

Suniti Kumar Chatterji (1974), the celebrated Bengali linguist, was however of the view that

> 'The masses of North Bengal areas are very largely of Bodo origin, or mixed Austric Dravidian-Mongoloid... They can now mainly be described as Koch, i.e., Hinduised or semi-Hinduised Bodo who have abandoned their original Tibeto-Burman speech and have adopted the northern dialect of Bengali... They are proud to call themselves as Rajbansis and to claim to be called Kshatriyas' (p.112).

* I am indebted to the editors of this volume for their comments on the earlier draft of this paper. However, the responsibility for any remaining error is entirely mine.

The three passages quoted above speak of three different identities of the Rajbansis, once a very low ranking peasant caste of north Bengal, and thus draw our attention to the most important problem of classification and categorization of local society in India during colonial period. It shows that the colonial administrators-cum-ethnographers and the contemporary Indian authors on caste have presented ambiguous and sometimes contradictory accounts of the social identities of different indigenous social groups. However, this confusion in the existing literature has a history of its own, which needs to be understood for comprehending properly the dynamics of caste among the Indians in the late 19th and the early 20th centuries.

The unique caste system that remained at the centre of Indian social order generated curiosity and interest among the Westerners - missionaries as well as colonial officials - who studied its origin, functioning and structure. As a result of this growing interest in the caste system, a number of surveys were made and several ethnological monographs were produced on racial and ethnic origins of various Indian social groups.[1] The reasons for this search were not merely academic and antiquarian interests of the colonial rulers; some recent works have tried to analyse what motivated such colonial ethnological enquiries. However, what seems equally important is the process through which this imperial perception of Indian society developed as a result of an interaction between the Western anthropological concepts and the indigenous knowledge of local society. And this new colonial ethnological discourse then motivated various indigenous social groups to create new histories of their own castes. Thus, partly in response to colonial attempt to redefine Indian society and partly as a result of their initiative to invent a more respectable identity for themselves within the existing

[1] Buchanan Hamilton surveyed some districts of Bihar and north Bengal in the first decade of the 19th century. The writings of Buchanan were edited and published later in 1838 by Robert Montgomery Martin as *The History, Antiquities, Topography and Statistics of Eastern India*; other works of the same genre on Bengal, are Dalton[1872], Hunter[1876], Wise[1883], Risley[1891], *Imperial Gazetteers of India*, Provincial series, 1909, *Census of India*, 1872 onwards, etc.

social hierarchy, the various social groups all over India, as also in Bengal, produced their own geneologies and mythical-historical accounts of their caste identities (for example, see Singha-Barman[1910], Biswas[1911], Ghosh[1924], Majumdar[1875]). The colonial period thus witnessed two trends in the study of caste — one initiated by the colonial rulers and the other by the indigenous elites. The two trends were complementary, as they influenced each other in a complex way.

The study of these two types of literature on caste does not clarify our knowledge about the exact status of the various social groups, as either they deal with imagined historical identities or with obsolete scriptural notions of status having no relevance to contemporary reality. But these ambiguities are indicative of a complex social phenomenon, i.e., the invention of new identities by the marginal groups in caste hierarchy. Taking the Rajbansis of north Bengal as a reference group, this paper would argue that the particular form in which the new identity was imagined by such lower and intermediary castes in the late 19th and the early 20th century Bengal, was basically the outcome of such competing discourses on castes and their historical origin.

II

The earliest reference to the Rajbansis is to be found in Buchanan Hamilton's report (Martin [1838]) and then they are mentioned in all subsequent ethnographic monographs, land revenue settlement reports, district gazetteers and census reports on Bengal. The districts in which they were to be mostly found were Rangpur, Cooch-Behar, Jalpaiguri, Dinajpur, Malda and Darjeeling in north Bengal, Purnea in Bihar and Goalpara in Assam. But about 89% of this caste population lived in just four north Bengal districts, i.e., Dinajpur, Rangpur, Jalpaiguri and Cooch-Behar.[2] They were

[2] According to the *Census of India*, 1921 (Vol.V, Part I, p.358), the total number of the Rajbansis was 1,727,111, of whom 1,530,712 lived in Cooch-Behar, Dinajpur, Rangpur and Jalpaiguri

the original inhabitants of north Bengal and the third largest Hindu caste in the whole province. But the Census Commissioners and the colonial ethnographers landed up in a major problem in determining the social status of these Rajbansis. Particularly problematic was the question whether the terms Rajbansi and Koch (the name of another dominant caste in north Bengal) were synonymous or not.

The area where the Rajbansis were to be found in large numbers formed parts of the old kingdom of Kamrup, of which modern Assam was also a part. We come to know from the history of Kamrup and medieval Assam that many tribal groups like the Kiratas, the Ahoms, the Khens, the Koches etc., ruled over different parts of Kamrup. Among these various groups, the Koches under the leadership of Viswa Singha established their control over the western part of Kamrup by the end of the 15th and the beginning of the 16th century (Acharyya [1984], Barua[1966], Chaudhury[1966], Basu[1983]). Nowhere at this stage do we find any reference to the Rajbansis in the history of this region. Nor is there any mention of the Rajbansis in the Parsian records, in the foreign accounts, in the *Assam-Buranjis* or in the *Darrang Raj Vamsavali* (the genealogical account of the Koch royal family) (Nath[1989], p.5). In the *Brahmavaivarta Puran* there is an exhaustive list of castes in Bengal. In this list also there is no mention of the Rajbansis, though there is a reference to the origin of the Koch.[3]

What then was the origin of the name Rajbansi? Opinions varied in different official and non-official works on the question. On the whole two general lines of argument developed — one by the colonial official-cum-ethnographers and the other by the Rajbansi caste publicists. In the colonial literature, the Rajbansis were generally regarded as a purified group of 'Koch' who had adopted Hindu culture and caste norms, abandoning their traditional tribal cultural practices and social customs. B.H.Hodgson wrote that when Viswa

[3] Report on Dinajpur district by Harimohon Sinha, in Risley Papers (in microfilm), Reel no.5, National Archives of India, New Delhi.

Singha, the grandson of Hajo and the founder of the Koch kingdom, embraced Hinduism, 'the country was renamed Bihar – the people, Rajbansi...' (Hodgson[1849], p.705).

W.W.Hunter also thought that the Rajbansis and the Paliyas were the offshoots of the Koch tribe. The Koch tribe first came to prominence by the close of the 15th and the beginning of the 16th century when they established the powerful Koch kingdom. During the reign of Viswa Singha, Brahmanism was introduced and the people including the king and his officers embraced the new religion. They abandoned the name 'Koch' on their conversion to Hinduism and took the name 'Rajbansi', which literally means 'Royal Race' (Hunter[1876], Vol.X, pp.255-56).

Herbert Risley in a similar way noted that the Koch, Koch-Mandi, Rajbansi, Palliya and Desi were the components of a large 'Dravidian tribe of North-Eastern and Eastern Bengal', as among them there were 'grounds for suspecting some admixture of Mongolian blood... Now the great majority of the Koch inhabitants of Northern Bengal invariably describe themselves as Rajbansis or Bhanga Kshatriyas - a designation which enables them to pose as an outlying branch of the Kshatriyas who fled to these remote districts in order to escape from the wrath of Parasuram... The original nucleus of the... Rajbansi was certainly Dravidian' (Risley[1891], Vol.I, p.491).

However, in the Census Report of 1901 E.A.Gait remarked that there was basis for the assertion of the Rajbansis of Rangpur that they did not resemble the Koches and had sprung from entirely different sources. Inspite of considerable racial intermixture in some places, the Rajbansis appeared to be a 'Dravidian tribe', and they probably owned the name long before the 'Mongoloid [Koch] kings' rose to power. But Gait also believed that: 'In Jalpaiguri and Kuch Bihar and in Goalpara in Assam, the persons now known as Rajbansi are either pure Koches who though dark have a distinctly Mongoloid physiognomy or else a mixed breed in which the Koch element usually pre-ponderates.'[4]

[4] E.A.Gait, *Census of India*, 1901, Vol.VI, Part I, pp.382-83.

The observations of other British ethnographers and officials like Dalton, Thompson, Vas, Strong and Gruning, on the origin of the Rajbansis more or less corroborate the same story.[5] To put it in brief, the colonial literature generally argued that the Rajbansis were a section of the Koch people who had abandoned their traditional cultural practices and had adopted the Brahmanical culture. There was also a belief among some colonial ethnographers that all the Rajbansis were not Koch and some of them were 'Dravidians' (whatever that term might mean), not 'Mongoloids' like the Koches. But due to subsequent racial intermixture the 'Mongoloid' element came to dominate over the 'Dravidian' among them.

In the indigenous literature on the other hand, the Rajbansis were referred to as different from and superior (in rank) to the Koch. But this assertion was made, it will be interesting to note, through the use of the same concepts, either Western anthropological ('Dravidian', 'Mongoloid' etc.) or ancient scriptural (i.e., varna status), borrowed from the official discourse. For example, Manomohan Roy wrote that: 'Irrespective of any question as to the identity or difference of origin, the Rajbansis and Koches form entirely distinct castes.' In social status the Koches were distinctly inferior to the Rajbansis, who had greater ceremonial purity. The physical feature of the great majority of the Rajbansis of Rangpur — except in the northern part bordering on Cooch Behar — were distinctly 'Dravidian', while the physiognomy of the Koches was decidedly 'Mongoloid'. 'I am inclined to think', Roy continues, 'that the distinction between the Rajbansis and the Koches in the Rangpur district is not a recent growth, but points to a real ethnological difference. The theory that the term Rajbansi is merely a recent title of the Koch who assumed it on the establishment of the kingdom of Kuch Bihar does not, on a close examination of the existing facts, appear to be a tenable one' (Roy[1902], pp.50-53).

[5] Dalton[1872], p.92; Vas[1911], pp.38-40; Strong[1912], pp.34-43; Gruning[1912], p.32; W.H.Thompson, *Census of India*, 1921, Vol.V, Part I, pp.356-58.

Hara Kishor Adhikari also argued that the Koches and the Rajbansis were not members of the same caste, but were different in many ways. The food habits, behaviour and customs of the Koches spoke of their lower social status, and the upper caste Hindus, including the Rajbansis, did not maintain social relations with them. The Rajbansis, on the other hand, should be regarded as an upper caste and it is borne out by their food habits, behaviour and customs. They performed all their ceremonies and rituals in the fashion of the Kshatriyas and other upper caste Hindus. Adhikari also objected to the contention that the Rajbansis adopted Hinduism during the reign of Maharaja Viswa Singha of Cooch Behar (in the early 16th century). According to him, the Rajbansis were Hindus before the reign of Viswa Singha and were recognized as Bhanga Kshatriyas. But as according to the shastras the term Bhanga Kshatriya had no meaning, so instead of this name they had come to be known as the 'Rajbansis' (Adhikari[1907], pp.21-25). Upendranath Barman also argued in a similar way that the Rajbansis were Kshatriyas and lived in the land called Paundra Desa, between the rivers Karatowa and Ganga. He refuted the arguments of the colonial ethnographers by citing examples from the Hindu shastras and puranas and wrote that the Rajbansis were claiming the Kshatriya status long before the 16th century (Barman,U.[1941], pp.1-55). Maniram Kabyabhushan, Manabhola Barman and many others of the Rajbansi literati also asserted the same mythico-historical claim of a Kshatriya origin (Barman,M. [1928], Kabyabhushan [1911]).

Thus the main argument of the Rajbansi caste publicists was that 'Koch' and 'Rajbansi' were not synonymous terms and the name Rajbansi was there long before the Hinduization of Viswa Singha, the Koch king, in the early 16th century. The name Rajbansi itself indicated that they were the descendants of the Kshatriyas. Yet they still wanted to be entered as Kshatriyas in the census reports, as they desired to differentiate themselves from the Koches, the Jalias etc. who 'also called themselves Rajbansis'.[6]

Some recent studies have also tried to focus on this question of origin of the Rajbansis; but as regards a conclusive answer, they are in the same confusion as their predecessors - the colonial ethnographers - were. While some of them think that the Rajbansis were the descendants of the Koches, others say that they were a 'mixed race' (Majumdar[1926], p.165; Dutt[1969], pp.142-43; Chatterji[1974], p.112; Das Gupta[1969]; Nath[1989], p.5). This debate, both old and recent, over the origin of the Rajbansis is to a great extent a legacy of the ethnological studies of the colonial period. It is therefore necessary to find out how this debate initially took shape, i.e., how the colonial ethnographers acquired their information and codified it into official knowledge and how the Indians responded to it and tried to confront it in its own terms.

III

Knowledge about local society was essential for the rulers to rule the local people effectively. So, starting from the early nineteenth century, with Buchanan's survey of some southern and eastern parts of India, there was a growing initiative on the part of the colonial rulers to have systematic information on various aspects of the local social order. Primarily to meet this requirement, and some times also due to the academic interests of some individuals, that a number of ethnological monographs were published, and district gazetteers or census reports prepared, giving details of castes and customs of local people.

The basic objective of these ethnological enquiries, as Risley observed, could have been '...to render available, for the use of scientific men in Europe, the large body of barbarous custom, both Aryan and non-Aryan, which still survives in India' (Risley[1891], Vol.I, p.vi). But even if we accept

[6] Prem Hari Barma to F.O.Bell, the Commissioner of Dinajpur, 31 October 1939, F.O.Bell Papers, (in microfilm), National Archives of India, New Delhi.

Risley's academic explanation, the doubts still persist as to why the colonial rulers attached so much importance to caste returns in the decennial census reports ever since 1872. Though caste was not always the central focus for all the colonial official enquiries on Indian society, it was from the 1840s that it increasingly occupied the prime position in such discourses on indigenous people. Laws could be enacted or imperial orders enforced, it was believed, 'only after a synthetic vision of the whole of Indian society had been officially constructed. The task of this construction was entrusted to a new apparatus of the government — the census' (Smith[1985], pp.171-72). Caste figured prominently in this census-based imperial vision of Indian social structure. Some recent works have discussed how this knowledge was used to strengthen and perpetuate colonial rule by exerting stricter social control (Cohn[1987], Carroll[1978], Bandyopadhyay[1990]. We shall discuss here how this colonial perception of caste had developed and how the indigenous traditions and beliefs on the one hand and the Western anthropological notions on the other mutually interacted to define the existing social categories and create new collective identities.

Caste was viewed by the colonial rulers as the essence of Indian society. James Mill wrote that caste was the key to understanding India (Inden[1990], p.57). The reason for this kind of notion was the existence of a corpus of Indian religious texts and their interpretation by the Indian pundits. The image of a society, permanently divided into four varnas (Brahman, Kshatriya, Vaishya and Sudra), with the Brahmans at the top of the hierarchy, was transmitted to the Westerners by the interpreters of Indian shastras. With this basic assumption, the Westerners then tried to construct an image of Indian society through their own subsequent reading of the Indian classical texts, particularly the laws of Manu.[7] But this did not make much difference in their already conceived notions on Indian society. Particularly in the period between

[7] Sir William Jones first translated into English the laws of Manu and the Indologists used it as the authoritative account on India.

the 1750's and the 1850's there were attempts by the missionaries and the Orientalists (though the motives were not necessarily the same) to construct an image of India on the basis of classical texts and their own experience of Indian social life. As a result of such endeavours the picture that emerged was that of a society which was very static, inflexible and compartmentalized into fixed caste categories. This depiction of Indian society to a large extent reflected the received wisdom.

The shift in colonial policies in India in the post-1850's led to a marked change in the process of formulating their notion about indigenous society. Besides depending on the classical literature, the colonial rulers also initiated systematic surveys of the Indian people, using the recently developed anthropological knowledge of the West. In other words, Western anthropological methods and European science now set the pattern for such ethnological enquiries. Instructions given to enumerators for collecting data on caste and the classification of the local population into such categories as Hinduized, semi-Hinduized, barbarians, aborigines etc., illustrate this point.[8] Risley's training in anthropometric scheme from contemporary European experts in the field, like Prof. Flower and Prof.Topinard, influenced his notions a great deal and he applied this methodology in the study of the tribes and castes of Bengal. (Risley [1891], Vol.I, Introduction) But this anthropometric method, based on race, colour, physical measurement, etc., failed to explain the inner complexities of the Indian caste system. Distinction between caste and sub-caste, caste and sect or the complex ethnic boundaries of various tribal groups remained a mystery to the colonial ethnographers (Conlon [1981], pp.105-12)

But there was no lack of initiative on their part to resolve this mystery, though the results were not always convincing. Actually the complex character of caste in a particular region or even all over India was one of the major reasons for this

[8] Risley Papers (in microfilm), Reel No.1, National Archives of India, New Delhi.

confusion and ambiguity in the classification of castes (Conlon [1981], p.107). For example, the 1872 census report noted: 'Many of those who in other provinces are classed among the lower castes of Hindus are, in the Bengal report, reckoned as semi-Hinduised aborigines.'[9] This complex character of indigenous society was further complicated by the process of enumeration in the census.

In the process of information collection the most important part was played by local informants. Shahid Amin has shown, in a different context, how the social prejudices and outlook of the informants to a large extent coloured the outlook of the colonial officials (Amin [1989], p.XXX). Writing on the caste history of the Rajbansis, Upendranath Barman has also observed that having no proper idea about local language and local society, the British authors depended for information on the non-Rajbansi immigrant caste Hindus working in the government offices. As the latter were not very favourably disposed to the local Rajbansis, their history was distorted in the official accounts (Barman,U. [1941], pp.28-29).

The official view on caste thus largely reflected the values and perspectives of the informants. In the completion of the census reports there were broadly three stages. Information was first collected at the local level; it was then scrutinized at the district level; and finally it reached the office of the Census Commissioner. So the information at the local level had significant contribution to the shaping of the final official version. And who were the informants at the local level? As the Census Reports noted, the enumerators were chosen mostly from among the *patwaries*, village headmen, *tehsildars*, *moktars* or *mohuris* and where literate men were not found, writers of the Deputy Commissioner's office worked as enumerators. [10] Generally, these people belonged to the upper castes, because there were very few among the

[9] *Memorandum on the Census of British India, 1871-72, General Reports*, Part I, p.20.

[10] H.Beverley, *Report on the Census of Bengal*, Vol.III, 1872, pp.18-43.

backward classes who were literate and could be eligible for the job (Risley [1891], Vol.II, Appendix IV, pp.189-90). So often these enumerators had a prejudiced view of society, coloured by a sense of contempt for the lower castes and the marginal groups. So the castes or any other social group which were traditionally backward had very little chance of being treated properly or their recent improvement in status being recognized duly in the census accounts of caste system.

The common people's own attitude to the census also might have denied them a proper place in it. Due to illiteracy and ignorance they had no idea about what the census meant and what was its basic purpose. Fear and prejudice generated many misconstrued notions about this official exercise,[11] and the people preferred to avoid it by all means. The enumerators, therefore, as Bernard Cohn suspects, took their liberty; '...they filled in the [census] forms on the basis of their own knowledge of their neighbours - particularly on questions of caste, language and religion' (Cohn [1987], p.248).

Cohn's suspicion seems justified when we go through the caste lists in different census reports. To illustrate this point we can take the example of the Rajbansis. Who the Rajbansis were — was a question which created a lot of confusion among the enumerators and this confusion was well reflected in the successive census reports. In the report of 1872, 1881 and 1891, the Koch, Rajbansi and Paliya were clapped together as Koch; in 1901 all subsections of Koch were recorded as Rajbansi; and in 1911 and 1921, the Paliyas were also recorded as Rajbansis. This was not a unique case, as Frank Conlon has cited a similar example of the Ambiga from the Madras census reports (Conlon [1981], p.112).

In cases of controversies the Census Commissioners usually took the Hindu shastras and their interpretations by local pundits as the final authority on caste. This kind of

[11] *Ibid.*, pp.54-55.

authentification by Brahmans lacked objectivity because the views of the pundits were coloured by traditional beliefs and their own prejudices. Emile Senart had expressed a similar reservation regarding the authenticity of the opinion of the Brahmans (Senart[1930], p.X). Yet the colonial officials could not overcome this limitation because the high caste indigenous elites were for them the major, if not the only, source of information on local social order.

The point which the above analysis has sought to emphasize is that the colonial literature on caste was the outcome of a close interaction between colonial ethnographers and the indigenous, usually high caste, informants. Particularly the placement of various castes in social hierarchy according to varna status and the scale of purity-pollution, was influenced largely by the social preconceptions and prejudices of these informants. And it was this distorted information which was then systematized through an application of Western anthropological concepts.

IV

But whatever might have been the process through which it took shape, the colonial ethnology by the early twentieth century had established a new discourse on caste ranking, in which issues like racial origin and varna status assumed supreme importance in determining the social status of groups. Since this discourse was essentially derived from Brahmanic scriptures, usually interpreted by upper caste commentators, it did not recognize social mobility among the ritually lower castes. Such lower castes, despite the improved social position of many of them, continued to be described as degraded. This was expressed either in scriptural terms, such as 'Sudra', 'Antyaja' etc., or in European anthropological vocabulary, such as 'Dravidian', 'Mongoloid' etc. This so called anthropological distinction of racial origins, often determined through a faulty application of anthropometric methods, was also based on an assumption of Aryan — non-Aryan dichotomy in Indian society, the lower castes being relegated to the latter category (Bandyopadhyay [1990], p.36). This classificatory scheme, based on varna and racial distinctions, was corroborated by empirical surveys and census enumerations, as the enumerators and the Census Superintendents had the same preconceived view of Indian society.

The official sanction behind this new discourse compelled the indigenous society to reconstruct its self-image accordingly. As a result, themes like varna status or racial origin assumed supreme importance in the indigenous discourse on caste. Particularly the lower caste elites, who had improved their secular status but remained degraded in official status ranking, now felt compelled to invent tradition to prove that they too belonged to the Aryan stock and to one of the three twice born varnas. The late 19th and the early 20th centuries witnessed such attempts by various caste groups to construct 'new' caste histories to prove their aspired social status. Such caste histories and chronicles written by the caste publicists on the basis of shastric interpretations and beliefs, like for example the Rajbansi accounts of their own origin (Singha-Barman[1910], Kabyabhushan[1911], Barman,U.[1941]), lacked historical authenticity. But that was because this literature had been the product of a particualr socio-cultural environment and was motivated by a set of politico-social aspirations, which require a closer examination.

The Rajbansis, as we have said, belonged to northern Bengal and were regarded as the autochthonous people of the region. Like many other intermediary and lower castes of Bengal they also formed their own caste associations, appealed to the government for recognition as Kshatriyas and published many pamphlets and books in support of their caste movement.[12] But before we get into their caste literature, let us see what motivated them to claim Kshatriyahood — a phenomenon which can only be understood if

[12] For details see, Basu [1993].

contextualized within the 19th century socio-cultural environment. Petitions and representations by the Rajbansi elites to the colonial authority to recognize them as Kshatriyas were not merely in emulation of the other mobile castes in different parts of India. There might have been similarities in the circumstances or in the methods followed; but the demand of the Rajbansis for a better status in Hindu society appears to have emanated from their own existential experience.

The changes that came in the wake of colonial rule had both direct and indirect influences on local society. Particularly from the early 20th century onwards colonial policy was given a new direction in order to safeguard the interests of certain disprivileged groups. In the sphere of education, public employment and in the local representative bodies, the government by official orders tried to protect the interests of such 'depressed classes' (Bandyopadhyay [1990], pp.52-84). The protective measures taken by the government had no doubt a rationale behind it. But by recognizing caste as an official category for providing social protection, the government policies legitimized caste identities.

If the colonial policies influenced the Rajbansi caste leaders to strive for collective caste mobilization, the local social situation itself provided sufficient ground for their assertion of a Kshatriya identity. They were the original inhabitants of north Bengal. But since the late 19th century, because of the abundance of land, possibilities of good business, job opportunities in government offices (as the local people were not in a position to compete) and the lure of the tea gardens, there was migration of a large number of outsiders, mostly upper caste Bengali Hindus, to different districts of north Bengal.[13] This immigrant upper caste group, by virtue of their closeness to the administrative power and their intelligence, gradually emerged as the dominant landholding class in the region.

---

[13] For details on the volume of migration to north Bengal districts, see A.Mitra, *West Bengal: District Handbooks*, (Calcutta, 1951): Cooch Behar, p.XXXVI, Jalpaiguri, p.LII, West Dinajpur, p.XII.

As the new dominant group was socially guided by the traditional Brahmanical cultural values, the Rajbansis who had a tradition and culture of their own, failed to get a respectable position in its status estimation. There were sharp dissimilarities between the cultural practices of these two groups and the upper caste gentry behaved in a rather haughty way with the local Rajbansis, stereotyping them as 'backward, uncultured and even *antyaj* [low born]'. [14] Disparagingly they were called *Babe*, which implied their cultural inferiority. The word was a distortion of *Baba he*, by which the Rajbansis generally used to address a person.[15] This attitude of cultural superiority of the immigrant upper caste Hindus and their general tendency to look down upon the local Rajbansis created a psychological barrier that prevented a closer relationship between the two groups. This alienation from the caste Hindus did indirectly promote caste solidarity among the Rajbansis.

This sense of alienation was further strengthened by the insults and humiliation that they experienced in their day to day life. In the Rajbansi caste literature there are numerous references to such humiliation by the upper caste Hindus. The latter regarded the Rajbansis as *antyaja*, who had no right to enter the places of worship on the occasion of any public celebration of pujas or to enter the kitchen in the upper caste households. Even water touched by them was not acceptable to the upper caste Hindus (Sarkar [1984], p.16). In his autobiography, Upendranath Barman (who became a minister in the Progresive Coalition ministry in 1941 and later was elected to the Constituent Assembly) has narrated his rather unpleasant memories of one such experience during his student days at the Cooch Behar Victoria College in 1916-20 (Barman,U [1985], pp.43-45). Accounts of similar experiences of caste hatred are not difficult to find in the

[14] A.K.Roy, 'Some Notes on the Kshatriya Movement in Northern Bengal', *Journal of Asiatic Society of Bangladesh*, Vol.XX, No.1, p.48.

[15] Interview with U.N.Barman taken by Ananda Gopal Ghose and Parimal Chandra Sen, *Madhuparni*, (in Bengali), Jalpaiguri Special Number, 1987, p.393.

writings of other Rajbansi public figures.[16]

The intensity of caste hatred and ill treatment that these people faced at the hands of the caste Hindus cannot perhaps be accurately measured from the above accounts taken exclusively from Rajbansi writings. But it is not difficult to deduce from those narratives that this community did not certainly occupy a very respectable social position in the status estimation of the upper caste Hindus. This resulted in the development of a sense of alienation among the Rajbansis, leading to the generation of a spirit of community solidarity among them. The search for Kshatriya identity was only a symbolic cultural expression of this emergent collective self-consciousness. And it was articulated through their caste literature.

Most of this Rajbansi caste literature was produced in the early 20th century, the period when the majority of the castes in Bengal were coming up with their own caste histories. The basic objective of the Rajbansi caste histories was also to create a convincing myth supporting their Kshatriya lineage. The common legend that we find in this literature is the story of annihilation of the Kshatriyas by the Brahman sage Parasurama. To escape from his wrath, it is claimed, the Rajbansis had left their original homeland, settled down in the Poundra Desha, i.e., northern Bengal, and had given up their sacred thread to hide their Kshatriya identity (Kabyabhushan [1911], pp.23-24; Singha-Barman [1910], pp.33-37; Barman,M. [1928], p.22; Barman,U.[1941], pp.1-15).

In his *Jag Sangeet* (a kind of *pala gan* or folk song), Rati Ram, a late 18th century Rajbansi poet, spoke about his royal lineage and said that because of Parasurama's threat to the Kshatriyas, they had come to northern Bengal and were living there as 'Bhanga Kshatriya Rajbansi'.[17] As we have al-

---

[16] Singha [1972], Preface; interview of Shrimati Hemlata Devi, daughter-in-law of Panchanan Barma, taken by Nripendranath Paul and Biman Chakraborty, *Madhuparni*, (in Bengali), Cooch Behar Special Number, 1396 BS, pp.502-03.

[17] *'Hai re rajar banse laviya janam'*
Parasuramer bhaye ebara saram,
Rane bhanga diya mora edeshe asiachhi
Bhanga Kshatri Rajbansi ei naame aachhi.'
Quoted in Singha-Barman [1910], p.49.

ready mentioned, before Buchanan's survey in the early 19th century we do not find any reference to the Rajbansis in the available historical records. In the absence of evidence, we cannot therefore expalin how in the 18th century Rati Ram became concerned with the Kshatriya identity of the Rajbansis. It is assumed however by some scholars that there was a general tendency among the tribal groups to move towards caste identity after they had established their political authority and had become economically dominant. The case of the Bhumij-Kshatriyas of south Manbhum, studied by Surajit Sinha, is well known (Sinha [1959]). But whatever might have been the situation in the case of the Rajbansis, i.e., whether they were a tribal group or not, Rati Ram's reference to Kshatriyahood was used by the subsequent Rajbansi caste publicists to construct elaborate legends on their historical origin. Hindu religious texts and pundits were quoted according to convenience to substantiate their argument.

Beside the Parasurama myth, there were also references to other legends in the Rajbansi caste literature. One of such stories is as follows:

> 'They [the Rajbansi Kshatriyas] were once the ruling race in this part of the country, sometimes with divided territories and different capitals, their last capital being Kamata Behar known also as Gosanimari now within the state of Cooch Behar. About 450 years ago sudden aggression made by Muhammadan invaders from Bengal brought about secretly by some non-Kshatriya traitors surprised and made away with the last Raja Kamteswar, leaving the people quite consternated and without a recognised head.'[18]

Hemanta Kumar Roy-Barma narrates yet another story about the Rajbansis' Kshatriya lineage. A branch of the Kamboj royal dynasty, belonging to north-western part of Kashmir, he writes, had established themselves in north Bengal in the 10th century AD and had ruled over this area. It can therefore be reasonably concluded, he argues, that the

[18] The Kshatriya Samiti Memorandum to the Indian Statutory Commission, *Indian Statutory Commission: Written Evidence, Bengal,* Vol.II, 1930, p. E/Beng.720.

Rajbansis of north Bengal originated from the Kamboj royal dynasty. After all, the word 'Rajbansi' also means the royal race. The kings in ancient India were Kshatriyas and hence the Rajbansis, having originated from a royal dynasty, should be considered as Kshatriyas as well (Roy-Barma [1988], pp.12-14).

Inspite of certain differences in all these accounts, the common thread that binds all of them together is the effort to create a convincing myth to prove the Kshatriya status of the Rajbansis. There is an important point to be mentioned in this context. Though popular belief in north Bengal holds them to be the descendants of the Cooch Behar royal family, which also claims Kshatriya status, the Rajbansi caste leaders would never agree to this association, as the tribal origin of the Cooch Behar Raj family was well documented in historical narratives. So, to be on safe side, the Rajbansi Kshatriya leaders preferred to trace their origin in the legends rather than in the recorded history of the Cooch Behar Raj Their caste literature therefore contained what may be called a constructed history, as this construction of a glorified and honourable past was their only natural response to the contemporary social reality which they were situated in and which they did not have the power to alter radically.

V

The colonial policy of redefining the local social order and providing patronage on the basis of caste identity on the one hand and the day to day oppression of the lower castes on the other had motivated the depressed groups like the Rajbansis to search for a dignified place in society. That this place was defined in terms of a varna category was because of a dominant official discourse on caste, that was based on the scriptural notions of an irrevocable hierarchy and immutable rank. Legitimated by the power of the colonial state, the official discourse compelled the indigenous groups to define their identities in terms of ancient categories. Myth, history and realities therefore intermingled in this process of redefinition of caste identities and this social process was amply reflected in the two sets of literature of the period, i.e., the colonial ethnography and the caste literature. The latter reflected the mental world of the different mobile aspiring social groups and their newly constructed self-images. But their terms of reference were determined by the colonial ethnography and the consequent colonial social policies, which reinforced the existing traditional view of society, in which caste solidarities were considered to be legitimate and social segmentation natural.

References

Acharyya,N.N. 1984. *The History of Medieval Assam*, Reprint, Gauhati.

Adhikari, H.K. 1907. *Rajbansi Kulopradeep* (in Bengali), Calcutta, 1314 BS.

Amin,S. 1989. 'Introduction', in William Crooke, *A Glossary of North Indian Peasant Life*, edited with an introduction by S.Amin, Delhi.

Bandyopadhyay,S. 1990. *Caste, Politics and the Raj: Bengal 1872-1937*, Calcutta.

Barman, U. 1941. *Rajbansi Kshatriya Jatir Itihas*, (in Bengali), Jalpaiguri.

Barman, U. 1985. *Uttar Banglar Sekal O Amar Jibansmriti*, (in Bengali), Jalpaiguri, 1392 BS.

Barman,M. 1928. *Kshatriya Tattva* (in Bengali), Santal Pargana, 1335 BS.

Barua,K.L. 1966. *Early History of Kamrup*, Gauhati.

Basu,N.N. 1983. *Social History of Kamrup*, Vol.II, Reprint, Delhi.

Basu,S. 1993. 'The Rajbansis of North Bengal: A Study of a Caste Movement 1910-47', Ph.D. thesis, Calcutta University (unpublished).

Biswas, S.B. 1911. *Namasudra Dwijatattva* (in Bengali), Barisal.

Carroll, L. 1978. 'Colonial Perceptions of Indian Society and the Emergence of Caste(s) Associations', *Journal of Asian Studies*, Vol.XXXVII, , No.2.

Chatterji,S.K. 1974. *Kirata Jana Kriti, The Indo-Mongoloids: Their*

Contribution to the History and Culture of India, Revised second edition, Calcutta.

Chaudhury,P.C. 1966. *The History and Civilization of the People of Assam to the Twelfth Century AD*, Gauhati.

Cohn,B.S. 1987. *An Anthropologist among the Historians and Other Essays*, Delhi.

Conlon, F.F. 1981. 'The Census of India as a Source for the Historical Study of Religion and Caste', in N.G.Barrier, (ed.), *The Census in British India: New Perspectives*, Delhi.

Dalton, E.T. 1872. *Descriptive Ethnology of Bengal*, Reprint, Calcutta, 1960.

Das Gupta,B. 1969. 'A Note on the Rajbansi', *Bulletin of Anthropological Survey*.

Dutt,N.K. 1969. *Origin and Growth of Caste in India*, Vol.II, Calcutta.

Ghosh,N.C. 1924. *Gopjatir Kshatriyatva*, (in Bengali), Mymensigh, 1331 BS.

Gruning,J.W. 1912. *Eastern Bengal and Assam District Gazetteers, Jalpaiguri*, Allahabad.

Hodgson,B.H. 1849. 'On the origin, Location, Numbers, Creed, Customs, Character and Condition of the Koch, Boco and Dhimal people, with a general description of the climate they dwell in', *Journal of Asiatic Society of Bengal*, Vol.XVIII, Part II.

Hunter, W.W. 1876. *A Statistical Account of Bengal*, Reprint, Delhi, 1974.

Inden, R.B. 1990. *Imagining India*, Cambridge, Massachussetts.

Kabyabhushan, M. 1911. *Rajbansi Kshatriya Deepak*, (in Bengali), Dinajpur, 1318 BS.

Majumdar,G.C. 1875. *Kayastha Kaustuv*, (in Bengali), Calcutta, 1282 BS.

Martin,M. 1838. *The History, Antiquities, Topography and Statistics of Eastern India*, Vol.V, London, Reprint, Delhi, 1976.

Mazumdar,D.N. 1926. 'Pseudo Rajputs', *Man in India*, Vol.VI.

Mitra,A. 1951. *West Bengal: District Hand Books*, Calcutta.

Nath,D. 1989. *History of the Koch Kingdom (c.1515-1615)*, Delhi.

Risley,H.H. 1891. *The Tribes and Castes of Bengal*, Reprint, Calcutta, 1981.

Roy,M. 1902. 'Some Notes on the Rajbansi', *Journal of Asiatic Society of Bengal*, Vol.LXXI, Part III, No.2.

Roy-Barma,H.K. 1988. *Koch Biharer Itihas*, (in Bengali), Second edition, Cooch Behar.

Sarkar,D.N. 1984. *Rai Saheb Panchanan*, (in Bengali), Rangpur, 1391 BS.

Senart,E. 1930. *Caste in India: The Facts and the System*, translated by E.Denison Ross, London.

Sinha,S. 1959. 'Bhumij Kshatriya Social Movement in South Manbhum', *Bulletin of the Department of Anthropology*, Vol.VIII, No.2.

Singha,P.R. 1972. *Kamte Rajye Paundra Kshatriya Itihas*, (in Bengali), Vol.I, Cooch Behar.

Singha-Barman,J.M.D. 1910. *Kshatriya Rajbansi Kula Kaumudi*, (in Bengali), Rangpur, 1317 BS.

Smith, R.S. 1985. 'Rule by Records and Rule by Reports: Complementary Aspects of the British Imperial Rule of Law', *Contribution to Indian Sociology*.

Strong,F.W. 1912. *Eastern Bengal and Assam District Gazetteers, Dinajpur*, Calcutta.

Vas,J.A. 1911. *Eastern Bengal and Assam District Gazetteers, Rangpur*, Calcutta.

Wise, J. 1883. *Notes on the Races, Castes and Trades of Eastern Bengal*, London.

4

Caste, Occupation and Social Mobility: A Study of the Kansaris in Colonial Bengal*

SMRITI KUMAR SARKAR

Caste in its traditional form was essentially an occupational system, as each caste or *jati* had a hereditary occupation assigned to it by religious sanctions. Since this occupation indicated the position of a caste in the ritual hierarchy and caste membership depended on birth, the occupational status of a caste was considered to be inviolable and immutable. No one had the right to encroach upon the occupation of other castes, nor could any one change his hereditary occupation without endangering his caste status. Yet in reality the situation was not so rigid. The traditional society always accepted new entrants, though branded them as lower jatis. Thus we find great discrepancies in the number of jatis listed in the *Dharmashastra* or in other medieval Sanskrit texts and those given in the relatively modern colonial census reports. The phenomenon suggests that limited occupational mobility was always permitted in society. An existing caste group or its dissident faction could scale the purity—pollution ladder by virtue of its material prosperity achieved through a change of occupation. Sometimes cultural attainments of a group also helped this process of mobility; but this happened only when the group was materially prosperous. Caste mobility, therefore, essentially arose out of 'an irresistible urge in the groups of low ritual status to relate their material achievements to a greater degree of

* This paper was originally presented at a seminar on "Communalism and Casteism in South Asia", held at the Department of History, University of Calcutta, on 11-12 April 1992.

purity for socially validating the position of eminence earned by them' (Sanyal [1981], p.26). The phenomenon became much more pervasive under the colonial regime, which destroyed both the political and the economic basis of the caste system, which now continued to exist only in the superstructural notions of purity and pollution (Sanyal [1981]; Bandyopadhyay [1990]).

In this essay I shall examine the question of caste mobility with reference to the Kansaris, a Bengali caste group of the traditional manufacturers of brass and bell-metal utensils. They have been chosen for the present study for two reasons. In Bengal in the nineteenth century, the Kansaris constituted the second largest artisan group, next only to the handloom weavers. Secondly, from a very low position in the traditional caste hierarchy of Bengal, the Kansaris had first climbed to the rank of *Nabasakh*[1] and then eventually came to occupy a position closer to that of the other higher castes. What is more important, unlike the Telis and the Sadgops, (Sanyal [1981]) the mobility process here did not involve any change of occupation or dissidence. In sharp contrast to similar other caste movements in colonial Bengal, the caste awareness in the case of the Kansaris came very late and the solidarity movement that started in the early twenties was linked more closely to the threats to their occupation than to any other social or cultural influence. And the movement ultimately failed to strike roots, as the majority of the caste population had by that time already changed their occupation and therefore found no attraction for it.

I

The brass and bell-metal manufacturing was the hereditary occupation of the Kansaris, originally forming a subgroup of the general metal-working caste of Karmakar or

[1] *Nabasakh* literally means 'nine branches'; the group included castes (originally nine) which were entitled to the services of Brahmin priests and water touched by their members was acceptable to the other higher castes.

Kamar. The Puranic mythology indicates the evolution of various sub-groups of the metal-working caste into distinct jatis through occupational differentiation. (Mukherjee [1894], p.4) In the earliest references, therefore, we have hyphenated caste names for the different occupational groups, like Lohar-Kamar, Tamar-Kamar, Swarna-Kamar, Chandi-Kamar, Pital-Kamar, Dhokra-Kamar and Ghatra-Kamar. All these groups later on hardened into separate endogamous castes.

In Bengal, the earliest specimen of brass vessels, from the Kalighat hoard, relates to the Gupta period. (Maity [1970], p.139) An inscription from Sylhet of the early medieval period refers to a *Kangsya*, i,e., *Kangsyakar* or Kansari, having the name of Govinda (Ray [1980], pp.192-93). The use of metal utensils in this region, however, does not seem to have become popular much before the medieval period. The Bengali literature of this period, the *Mangalkavyas* in particular, contain numerous references to copper, brass and bell-metal utensils, as also to the metal-working caste of Kansari or Kansabanik.[2]

Geographically, if the availability of copper, the basic metal for the Kansari's craft, is any indicator, then the utensil manufacturing in eastern India seems to have flourished first in the Dhalbhum-Singbhum region, where ancient remains of copper mining have been discovered (Forbes [1950], p.301; Naqvi [1968], p.223; Maity [1970], pp. 132-33). From this region it had entered Bengal as a migratory craft, possibly through Bankura-Purulia-Midnapore trail, which was indeed the exit route of the metal to the copper port of Tamralipta (Kosambi [1970], pp.140,163). The traditional Dhokra metal craft of Bengal also had its origin in the same region and had migrated to Bengal through this same route (Ghosh [1981], pp.58-61). And besides the use of the same kind of raw material (copper), the two crafts had also other things in common, particularly in so far as the nature of their demand and their technique of production were concerned.

[2] Dasgupta [1935], pp.220-21, 269; Sen [1920], pp.94-127; M. Chakraborty, *Chandi*, (in Bengali), (Basumati, Calcutta, nd), pp.70-71.

As a migratory craft, the metalware manufacturing in Bengal had its early growth in the western part of the province known as *Rarh*.[3] The region had a local supply of important metals like iron and copper.[4] The processing of these metals in the indigenous way was reported from these areas even in the early nineteenth century (Ball [1880], pp.224-225). It was through this region that copper used to travel from Singbhum to the copper port of Tamluk (or Tamralipta), as stated above. An early growth of the copper-based craft in this region was, therefore, quite likely both in view of the easy availability of the metal and its easier trade links with the agricultural plains of Bengal . The agriculturally fertile tract of the eastern Rarh (Burdwan) was the main centre of its growth in the *Rarhdesha*.

The concentration of the Bengali caste group called the Aguris in Burdwan also probably indicates a similar concentration of the traditional iron manufacturing in this area. The term Aguri is said to have been derived from the word *aag* (fire) and it literally means firemen (Watson [1907], p.27). Thus Burdwan had a tradition of excellence in all kinds of iron manufacturing (Collin [1892], p.7; Watson [1907], p.17). The stray settlements of Dhokra metal-smiths in Burdwan, some of which are still to be found (Ghosh [1981], p.58), also substantiates our contention of an early growth of the metal working craft in this region. We have also another conclusive evidence in the Sanskrit text *Brihatdharmapuranam*, written in the Rarhdesha in the thirteenth century AD; it also describes the Kansaris as one of the thirtysix castes of Bengal (Ray [1980], pp.33, 272, 316-317). Significantly, one of the Kansari sub-divisions, called Mahita, had its origin in Burdwan.[5]

However, the industry retained its migratory character for

---

[3] *Rarh Desha* includes the districts of Birbhum, Bankura, Purulia, the north-western part of Burdwan and the western half of Midnapore.

[4] H.Sanyal, 'Rarher Itihas Prasange Kayekti Katha', (in Bengali), Occasional Paper No.32, Centre for Studies in Social Sciences, Calcutta, pp.2-3.

[5] N.Pramanik, 'Gaude Kangsabanik', *Kangsabanik Patrika*, (Ranaghat), [hereafter *KBP*], Vol.I, No.3, 1330 B.S., pp.108-109.

a fairly long period and this can be explained in terms of the nature of the Kansari's work. Unlike the traditional weaver, the spinner, the carpenter, the oil-presser or the potter, the brazier could not hope to prosper in isolation in a remote village. The durability of the brazier's ware, in contrast to the fragility of the potter's pots, their nearest rival, made the demand for his utensils fairly inelastic. And since the latter could be safely carried to any distance, unlike the earthen pot, the brazier did not feel any compulsion to work on the spot. Then the availability of the brazier's metal also mattered.[6]

What I intend to emphasize here is the existence of the Kansaris for a very long period, but essentially as a peripheral group of metal workers, in a particular region, namely the south-western part of Bengal. This peripheral nature of their existence is clearly indicated by their social rank. The thirteenth century Sanskrit text *Brihatdharmapuranam*, though described them as an *Uttama Sankara jati*, ranked them below the Tantis (weavers), Gandhabaniks (spice-dealers), Napits (barbers), Gops (cowherds), Karmakars (metal-workers), Tamliks (betel nut traders) and even the Kumors (potters). Another contemporary text, *Brahmavaivartta-puranam*, also gives them a much lower rank within the *Sat Sudra* (pure Sudra) group of castes (Ray [1980], pp.316-319). In Mukundaram's *Chandimangal*, a late sixteenth century composition, we find reference to the Kansari's industry assuming a sedentary character. Even here the Kansaris are placed in the fifteenth position in a list of seventeen *Nabasayaka* (Nabasakh) castes.[7] What all this evidence conclusively suggests is the Kansaris' holding a position much lower than those of the other artisan groups, such as the Kamar, Kumor and Tanti.

But between the sixteenth and the eighteenth centuries, the Kansaris had considerably improved their social position. The source of this mobility was the eventual transformation

---

[6] For details, Sarkar [1991].

[7] M.Chakraborty, *Chandi*, *op.cit.*, pp.70-71.

of their occupation from a migratory craft to a flourishing industry, localised in larger centres like Saptagram, Nabadwip, Maldah, Bishnupur, Dacca, Mahmmudpur and Murshidabad. A prosperous group of Kansari merchants, trading both in their wares and raw materials, also emerged. Bharatchandra therefore describes them as one of the five leading merchant groups of Bengal.[8] After the degradation of the Swarnakars (Ray [1980], pp.316-317), the Kansaris came to occupy a definitely improved position among the metal working castes and also began to be served by the Brahmins (Mukherjee [1894], p.5).

The interrelationship between the Kansari mobility and the development of their trade will be clear if we look at their counterparts outside Bengal. In greater part of north India and Punjab, the Kaseras (local name for the Kansaris) enjoyed a higher social position than the other metal working castes like the Lohars and Sunars or the other agricultural castes like the Kunbis and the Ahirs (Dampier [1894], p.9; Johnstone [1888], pp.6-7; Shah [1912], pp.29-31). In Maharashtra, the Kaseras even used the sacred thread and were not much different from the Brahmins in their habits of food, drinks and rituals (Shah [1912], pp.29-31). But this did not happen in Assam, where the metal industry developed only in a later period. Here, utensil manufacturing not being a caste specific occupation, was usually undertaken by the members of such low ranking castes as Kalita, Koch and Kurat, the word *Kashar* being tagged on to their caste names as an indication of the occupation they followed.[9] Similarly in the hilly districts of the North Western Provinces and Awadh, where the industry had not flourished, the people making these wares were still called Dom-Tamota, indicating the low social rating of this occupation (Dampier [1894], p.9). In Maharashtra, Gujrat, the Central Provinces and northern India, the development of their occupation had helped the

---

[8] Bharatchandra, *Vidyasundar*, cited in Dasgupta [1935], p.220.

[9] Gait and Darrah, *Notes on Brass and Bell-metal Industries in Assam*, cited in Gupta [1908], pp.33-34.

Kaseras to enjoy a higher social position than that of the Tameras, Tambats or the Otaris (Shah [1912], pp.30-31) This happened much in the same way as the Kansaris of Bengal achieved a higher rank than that of their fellow Ghatra, Dhokra and Tamar Kamars.

II

At the beginning of the nineteenth century, therefore, we see that the Kansaris, by virtue of their wealth, had already succeeded in promoting themselves to a comparatively higher position than most of the other Nabasakh castes. But what was really striking about their social attitudes was the complete absence of any awareness of caste identity among them, the best evidence of which is a popular Kansari usage: '*Khai dai tama petai, jat pater dhar dharina*' (We eat and live merrily and work with copper, we don't bother about caste).[10] This absence of 'caste identity' was however due to a system of internal division based on territoriality. The caste was divided into a number of *gain* or *sampraday* - the most important of them being Mahita, Saptagrami, Mahutpuri and Mahmudpuri - each of which was associated with a particular place name and maintained an insulated social existence [11]

A brief discussion on these sub-divisions of the Kansaris, it seems, would be useful here. The word *gain* originates from *gan* or place of residence. The sub-divisions were, therefore, associated with the important centres of localization of the utensil industry in pre-colonial Bengal.[12] Thus the sub-group called Mahita had its name from a small place called Mahata in Burdwan. Saptagram, the famous port city of medieval Bengal, lent its name to another group. The Mahmudpuri Kansaris, the largest of these sub-divisions got

---

[10] *KBP*, Vol.II, No.4, 1331 BS, pp.168-170; P.B.Datta, 'Amader Safar', in *KBP*, Vol.I, No.1, 1330 BS, p.72.

[11] S.C.Nandan, *Bange Kangsabanik*, (in Bengali), (Calcutta, nd); N.Pramanik, 'Gaude Kangsabanik', *op.cit*, ,pp.108-109; A.K.Nandy, 'Mahmudpuri Samajer Kramabistar', *KBP*, Vol.I, No.4, 1330 BS, pp.144-145.

[12] S.C.Nandan, *Bange Kangsabanik*, cited by A.Datta in *KBP*, Vol.I, No.1, 1330 BS, Appendix.

their name from Mahmudpur or Muhammadpur in Khulna.[13] A slightly different version of their origin suggests that the Mahmudpuri Kansaris were originally the residents of the pargana Mamudabad. A revenue division, comprising parts of the districts of Nadia, Jessore and Faridpur, Mahmudabad was formed during the early years of the Sultani administration in Bengal.[14] There is also reference to a fourth group called the Mahutpuri, which is believed to have derived its name from that of a place called Mahutpur in the district of Maldah.[15]

These *gains* were thus associated with the larger centres of localization of the utensil industry in late medieval Bengal. Significantly, the process of the *gain* formation was also linked with that of the rise and decline of the urban centres. And since the process of urbanization was interlinked with the political situation and the economic system of the country, a sudden change in these conditions in the early eighteenth century Bengal led to a discontinuation in the process of *gain* formation among the Kansaris. The absence of proper communication, the fear of religious persecution and above all business competition led to the eventual cessation of inter-group social exchanges. Thus these Kansari sub-divisions or the *gains* eventually became endogamous groups, each using different sets of surnames, performing different patterns of rituals and enjoying different ranks. The Mahmudpuris, for instance, stood at the lowest rung of the Kansari hierarchy and with them the members of the other *gains* even refused to dine. The reason for this social ostracization of the largest sub-group was their alleged defilement during the invasion of their city, Muhammadpur, by Murshid Quli's army.[16] Thus even after centuries of separation from their places of residence , which their *gain* names were associated with, the various Kansari groups were keen

[13] A.K.Nandy, *op.cit.*, pp.144-145; N.Pramanik, *op.cit.*
[14] N.Pramanik, *op.cit.*, Vol.II, p.7.
[15] S.C.Nandan, *op.cit.*; A.K.Nandy, *op.cit.*
[16] Samaddar [1910], pp.236-243; Sarkar [1976], p.416; A.K.Datta, *op.cit.*

about maintaining their *gain* identity and distinctiveness. To the non-Kansari, the Kansaris would always introduce themselves as Saptagrami-Kansari or Mahita-Kansari, thus giving their *gain* identity a preference over that of their caste, which indeed could be called, *a la* Irawati Karve, a 'caste cluster' rather than a caste (Karve [1977], p.19).

Besides these *gains*, there was also a broad division between a small minority of rich Kansari *mahajans* (merchants) and the rest of the working Kansari population. Although this division in Bengal was not as sharp as the one existing between the Kaseras and the Thateras or Thatiars in northern India (Shah [1912], pp. 29-31), the two groups, the Kangsabaniks and the Kansaris as they were known in Bengal, held widely different social positions. Equally important were the regional divisions. For instance, the Kansaris of western Bengal generally claimed a higher social status than those who had earlier migrated to eastern or northern Bengal, irrespective of their *gains*.[17] As a counter measure, the latter group, in an attempt to artificially raise their status, dropped their individual surnames like Das, Datta, Nath, Nandy or Pramanik and replaced these by the more prestigious common title of Kangsabanik,[18] originally used by the affluent Kansari mahajans or merchants.

At the beginning of the nineteenth century, therefore, feelings of 'caste' solidarity were remarkably low among the different groups of Kansaris. The nineteenth century, however, brought in unusual prosperity to many of them. From a highly centralised urban craft of the pre-colonial period, the utensil industry now spread to all parts of Bengal. In 1872, Hunter had observed with regard to Nadia that among the district artisans, the Kansaris stood next in importance to the weavers (Hunter [1973], p.101). In fact, Hunter's observation was largely applicable to the whole of Bengal excluding only Bakarganj, Jalpaiguri and Khulna, where traditional

[17] For the pattern of Kansari migration in the late pre-colonial period, see Sarkar [1991].

[18] Rabilochan Roy Kangsabanik, Letter to the Editor, *KBP*, Vol.I, No.1, 1330 BS.

metalware industry was not very important.[19] The *Report on the Survey of Cottage Industries in Bengal* thus stated: 'Next to handloom weaving, the most striking and widespread home industry is that of brass and bell-metal manufacture'.[20] The Indian Industrial Commission also held the same view.[21] T.N.Mukherjee in his monograph on the utensil industry of Bengal had described the industry as a 'thriving one' (Mukherjee [1894], p.27). Writing nearly two decades after him, J.G.Cumming also held a similar view (Cumming [1908], p.22). The workforce engaged in this industry also tended to grow even in the early twentieth century. Between 1901 and 1911, the census occupational tables recorded a 36% growth in the number of braziers, not withstanding the considerable reduction in the geographical area of the province of Bengal.[22] In 1901 as many as fifty workers per ten thousand population in Bengal were engaged in this industry, thus constituting the largest segment of the braziers working in the whole of British India. (Shah [1912], pp.31-32)

Throughout the nineteenth and the early twentieth centuries, therefore, the metalware industry of Bengal had a significant growth. But how to explain it when the handloom weaving industry had been declining during the same period? Since a detailed discussion of this phenomenon is not necessary here, I shall briefly refer to the main contributory factors.

Unlike the handloom weaving industry, the traditional weaving industry of Bengal did not suffer from foreign competition. The industry had in its favour a very high degree of persistence of traditional consumption habits. For the traditional Hindu society these wares had a sacred utility sanctioned by religion.[23] As the purer gold and silver vessels were

[19] *Report on the Survey of the Cottage Industries in Bengal*, (Calcutta, 1924, 2nd Edition, 1929), (hereafter *RSCI*), pp.89-93, 124-126.

[20] *Ibid*, p.6.

[21] *Report of the Indian Industrial Commission*, 1919, p.163.

[22] *Census of India*, 1901, Vol.IA, Pt.II, p.376; *Census of India*, 1911, Vol.V, Pt.I, p.542.

[23] In the Code of Manu the vessels of gold and copper were considered to be of first class purity, followed by those of silver and brass and then came bell-metal. The iron vessels were considered to be impure for eating purposes. See, Shah [1912], p.25.

costly, brazier's wares formed the most important articles for regular domestic use. Only the potter's wares could compete with these utensils in point of cheapness, but there was a prejudice against their regular use (Shah [1912], pp.17,21). 'A Hindu', writes Buchanan in his account of Dinajpur, 'considers it as impure to use any vessel of potter's ware more than once' (Buchanan [1833], p.75). Therefore, 'the poor Hindu will generally use a platter of leaves, when he is unable to afford more noble ware' (Dampier [1894], p.3). And then the traditional utensil industry had an intrinsic strength of its own. For, it was also a form of indigenous art - a feature that protected the industry against foreign competition. Furthermore, the traditional brazier could to his advantage use old or scrap wares as his raw materials and keep the prices of his wares relatively low.

The industry had also been encouraged by the rapid growth of jute cultivation in the eastern districts of Bengal. This is indicated by the emergence of a number of new centres of brass and bell-metal manufacturing in these areas in the nineteenth century, as well as by the movement of the Kansaris in large groups from the western to the eastern districts of Bengal during the same period.[24] For instance, a large group of Kansaris had migrated from Khagra in Murshidabad to Budhpara in Rajshahi (Gupta [1908], p.39). Another group of Khagra Kansaris had moved to the larger village of Kalam, which later emerged as the foremost centre of the traditional metalware industry in Rajshahi.[25] A third group had left Khagra for Dacca.[26] Similar waves of migration from other centres could also be clearly related to the new prosperity brought about in that region by the cultivation of jute. 'Forty crore of rupees were paid for jute crop in one year (1906) and of this sum 15.5 crore were clear profit.'[27] This increased

[24] B.K.Das, 'Adam Sumari' (Results of the Kansari Census), *KBP*, Vol.II, 1331 BS, No.3, , pp.116-117, No.4, pp.165-167; C.Datta, 'Dinajpur O Rangpurer Kangsabanik Samaj', *KBP*, Vol.I, No.4, 1330 BS, pp.187-189.

[25] *KBP*, Vol.II, No.1, 1331 BS, p.33.

[26] *Report on the Survey of Brass and Bell-Metal Industry in Bengal*, (Calcutta, 1939), (hereafter *BBMI*), p.10.

[27] *Census of India*, 1911, *op.cit.*, p.65.

cash flow to the jute-growing areas seems to have increased the demand for utensils, given the rural society's love for these wares as marginal luxury items, which could also be exchanged for cash at times of distress.[28]

The increasing urbanization and the steady growth of middle class demand also helped the industry to grow. The case of Calcutta is an excellent example of such development. The growth of this metropolitan city had attracted braziers from different parts of Bengal, particularly from the neighbouring districts of Nadia, Burdwan, Murshidabad, Jessore and the 24-Parganas.[29] Calcutta also had a Kansari population of its own, settled in and around Kalighat since long before the place had come under British occupation. A section of the Kansaris of Nabadwip were called Kalighati - the name suggests their early migration from Kalighat to Nabadwip in the late medieval period.[30] Subsequent Kansari migration to Calcutta led to the emergence of new centres of the industry in the city. The largest of such centres was Kansaripara in Banarasi Ghosh Street, having one thousand Kansari workers in 1924.[31] The absence of the Saptagrami Kansaris in Kansaripara of Calcutta[32] suggests that the centre had emerged subsequent to the early migration of the Saptagrami braziers to Bhowanipore.[33] The old centre of the industry at Bhowanipore had a tremendous expansion dur-

[28] 'Whenever the Hindus have a small saving they generally buy a little jewellery and metal utensils. But usually these articles serve them no good. Because, whenever they are in need of some cash they get these wares mortgaged with the rural mahajan at half of their values and within a few days those articles are invariably lost to pay for their credit and interest charges.' - English translation of the report published in *Samachar Darpan*, 24 March 1827, cited by B.Bandyopadhyay, *Sangbadpatre Sekaler Katha*, Vol.I, 1818-1830, (Calcutta, 1356 BS), p.187.

'Copper being the chief metal used for domestic utensils and easily saleable when necessity arises, is in large demand in times of plenty and is instantly thrown on market in bad years...' *Imperial Gazetteer of India*, Vol.III, cited in Shah[1912], p.21.

Also see *Report of the Contai Relief Committee*, 9 September 1943, cited by Greenough [1982], p.197.

[29] The origin of the Kansaris of Calcutta is clearly indicated in the Kansari census conducted by the Bangiya Kangsabanik Sammilani. See, B.K.Das, 'Adam Sumari' (Results of the Kansari Census), *KBP*, Vol.I, No.1, 1330 BS, Appendix E; Vol.II, 1331 BS, No.3, pp.116-117; No.4, pp.165-167.

[30] J.Roy, 'Nabadwipe Kangsabanik' *KBP*, Vol.I, No.1, 1330 BS, pp.14-15.

[31] *RSCI*, p.42.

[32] B.K.Das, *op.cit.*, Vol.II, No.4, 1331 BS, pp.165-167

[33] *RSCI*, p.115; Mazumder [1927], p.36.

ing the early British period. In the mid-nineteenth century, however, the Bhowanipore Kansaris gave up *en masse* their hereditary occupation and took to jewellery work,[34] a phenomenon which we will discuss later. But what needs to be mentioned here is that the growth of Calcutta had also encouraged some of the outlying centres of the industry, like Kharar, Matiari, Ranaghat or Shantipore, to expand.[35]

The railways also played an important role. The earlier system of transport, slow and uncertain as it was, always discouraged the movement of metal wares, which had a low value relative to its weight and bulk. Both the collection of raw materials and the marketing of his products thus created for the traditional brazier a difficult problem of transport, which in its turn limited the size of his actual market. The difficulties of transport led to localization of the industry in towns or villages on the important waterways or crossroads of trade.[36] The railways by making transport easier and cheaper had thus encouraged the industry to expand.

Finally, the introduction of the imported metal sheet, brass sheets in particular, gave the utensil industry an unprecedented stimulus. Prior to the coming of these sheets from England, various types of brass were locally manufactured for the making of utensils. The introduction of metal sheet, therefore, led to a significant improvement in the organizational and the functional efficiency of the brazier's workshop. Both in colonial India and Africa the use of mill yarn had caused the traditional handloom to expand. Similarly the introduction of metal sheet encouraged the production of brass wares in Bengal.

III

The growth in their industry in the nineteenth century, by encouraging both vertical and horizontal mobility, had

[34] *BBMI*, p.15; Raychaudhuri [1964], p.212.

[35] For details see Sarkar [1991], Chapter V.

[36] All the old large centres of this industry, namely Saptagram, Maldah, Nabadwip, Dacca, Mahmudpur and Khagra stood on important rivers.

brought in significant changes in the structure of the Kansari *samaj* ('community'). The vertical mobility was evident in the Kansaris' attaining a greater social respectability, largely by virtue of their wealth which they had now accumulated through their expanded business and other means. The horizontal mobility, on the other hand, broke open the cocoons of their *gains*, although the *gain* divisions did not immediately disappear. It will be appropriate here to explain these developments in brief.

With the growth of their hereditatry trade, a section of the Kansaris, larger than the earlier group called Kangsabanik in pre-colonial Bengal, became immensely rich. Benimadhav Nandan and Taraknath Pramanik of Simla-Kansaripara (Calcutta), Kalicharan Datta of Ranaghat, Lalbehari and Gurudas Das of Nabadwip were a few prominent members of this group. Although many of them invested in landed properties, they did not, unlike the Tilis, Sahas, Subarnabaniks and Gandhabaniks, leave their hereditary occupation. Manufacturing utensil in large factories and trading in both utensils and raw materials remained the basic source of their wealth. Gurudas Das of Nabadwip, for instance, had 360 *arats* (godowns) of utensil, each giving him an annual profit of Rs. 5000 on a moderate estimate. Local tradition has it that even his *gomasthas* (agents) used to travel on elephants.[37] And even more important than him was perhaps Taraknath Pramanik. Known as the *Kangsabanik-kula-tilak* (Glory of the Kangsabanik caste), he was often described as the richest man in his community.[38]

Significantly, most of them diverted a part of their profits to the cause of social services. Thus they had built temples, constructed bathing *ghats* and other buildings of public utility, besides spending huge sums every year in charity to the poor and in performance of religious ceremonies.[39] Clearly

---

[37] *KBP*, Vol.II, No.4, 1331 BS, pp.168-170; P.B.Datta, 'Amader Safar', *op.cit.* p.72.
[38] P.B.Datta, 'Amader Safar', *op.cit.* p.19;.Mukherjee [1894], p.23.
[39] J.N.Bhattacharya, *Hindu Castes and Sects*, (Calcutta, 1896), cited in P.B.Datta, 'Amader Safar', *op.cit.*, p.69.

these activities were aimed at attaining greater social respectability. It also indicates the growth of an awareness about their ritual status not conforming to their material position. Evidently this went against the traditional Kansari attitude of indifference to their 'caste' status, as stated earlier.

Besides this section of immensely rich Kansari mahajans, the general material condition of the Kansaris had also significantly improved during this period. One evidence of this general prosperity was the increasing disassociation of the Kansaris from the labourious part of their work, which they now left to the people of lower castes, such as Handi, Dom, Bauri etc. Since they could not afford to promote temple-building and other public utility services, like their more affluent caste fellows, they began to adopt other accessible symbols of higher ritual status, like the use of sacred thread (of three knots), elaborate rituals of marriage like those of the higher castes and a shorter period (15 days) of defilement after a death in the family.[40] All these indicated a Kansari desire to be ranked among the higher castes.

This desire to climb up the ritual hierarchy was accompanied by some other developments that weakened their internal divisions and helped the growth of a movement for 'caste' solidarity. In the nineteenth century the pre-colonial localized pattern of the industry had broken down. A number of new centres had emerged, while the existing ones had further expanded. Eitherway, it disorganised the earlier system of production, with the result that the trade and manufacturing activity of a particular centre could no longer remain the exclusive preserve of a single *gain*. In larger new centres like Calcutta, the Kansaris of different *gains* and regions came to settle, leading to greater social interaction between them.[41] Similar interaction also resulted from the free flow of wares facilitated by the new transport system.

However, it was the introduction of the factory-made

---

[40] J.N.Kangsabanik, 'Noakhalir Patra' (in Bengali), Letter to the Editor, *KBP*, Vol.1, No.1, 1330 B.S.

[41] For details see Sarkar [1991], Chapter V, Section 3.

metal sheet that ultimately served as a catalyst in the process of 'community' formation. In the traditional structure of the industry, as stated above, the making of the necessary ingots of brass was as labourious and time consuming a process as was the manufacturing of wares from it. Further, the process of preparing these alloys, which actually determined the quality of the product, was a closely guarded secret jealously maintained by the Kansaris. One such formula, popular among the Saptagrami Kansaris, for instance, describes the manufacturing of bell-metal in the following way: '*Satay doay karo jaro tate ano tate garo*' (Make an alloy of seven parts of copper and two parts of tin. Get it to the furnace and strike it into shape while it is hot) (Mukherjee [1894], p.7). But the coming of metal sheet made metal casting altogether redundant and thus was gone the secretive aspect of the Kansari's occupation, opening it to the multitude of low castes, desirous of changing their occupation in favour of the purer or more profitable ones.

In fact the intrusion of artisans of other castes into the utensil industry had started even before the coming of the metal sheet. Buchanan stated in his account of Sahabad that the Sonars of Sahabad had joined the occupation of the Kaseras and had become pedlars of utensils (Buchanan [1934], p.404). Similarly, in north-western India and Punjab also, the Lohars and Sunars were found to be working with the brazier's metal (Dampier [1894], p.9; Johnstone [1888], pp.6-7). Significantly, most of the early entrants to the Kansari's occupation came from the other metal-working castes. Subsequently, however, mostly the low caste people took up this occupation. In 1908, Cumming thus found the Bagdis and Kaivarttas handling bell-metal in Berhampore (Cumming [1908], p.116). In Bankura a large number of Telis had joined this industry (Mukherji [1978], p.88). Similarly, in Birbhum men of all castes participated in this manufacture,[42] while in Calcutta nearly every low or middle ranking caste

[42] *RSCI*, p.17.

(like Rajak, Bhuimali, Jugi, Bagdi, Duley, Mahishya) had representation in the utensil industry (Mukherji [1978], p.88). We have similar evidence for most other centres of this industry as well (Mazumder [1927], p.28). And the same thing happened also in other parts of India. G.R.Dampier observed with regard to the North Western Provinces and Awadh in the late 1890's: 'That a Lohar or a Sunar should leave his particular metal and engage in the manufacture of brass and copper goods is not astonishing, but the Kunbis, a purely agricultural caste or that Kalwars, whose ordinary business is to distil and retail liquor, should adopt this trade is very surprising.' (Dampier [1894], p.9) In Punjab also the Lohars, Ahirs and Kumhars were found to be engaged in this work (Johnstone [1888], pp.6-7).

This intrusion of various castes completely changed the traditional caste character of the utensil industry. An unofficial estimate of the early 1890's thus found the Kansaris constituting only 30.32 percent of the total number of people engaged in this industry (Mukherji [1894], p.5). By 1924 the percentage had fallen to an alarming low of 23.66 percent. This was revealed in an occupational survey of the Kansaris conducted by their own organisation, the Bangiya Kangsabanik Sammilani.[43] Admittedly, the Kansaris, being in their herediatry occupation and therefore in a familiar field, were in a dominant position within the industry. And it was the Kansari mahajans who had earlier encouraged the admission of low caste people as cheaper replacements for the hereditary Kansari workers. But in the long run, this process came to threaten their position. Thus in eastern and northern Bengal, the traditional Kansari families in the manufacturing business failed in competition with their one time workers, who had later turned into shop owners producing cheaper utensils.[44] In Maldah, for instance, 84 per cent of the intermediary trade in utensil had slipped out of the hands of the

[43] B.K.Das, 'Adam Sumari', *KBP*, Vol.II, 1331 BS, No.3, pp.116-117, No.4, pp.165-167, Vol.III,1332 BS, No.1, p.12.
[44] Gupta [1908], p.39; J.N.Kangsabanik, *op.cit.*

Kansaris.[45] In Calcutta they were facing a similar competition from the more powerful Marwari merchants of Burra Bazar.[46]

The late nineteenth and the early twentieth centuries also witnessed the coming of an entire new range of cheaper wares of glass, porcelain, enamel, tin, iron, and above all aluminium — all came in quick succession and inevitably impinged on the traditional utensil industry. The post-war price rise further encouraged the diffusion of these cheaper wares throughout the province. This resulted in a complete reversal of the earlier situation where the Kansari's utensil had to compete only with the potter's ware and that too from a point of advantage.

It was really in this background of a positive threat to their traditional occupation that the necessity of caste solidarity was more desperately felt by a larger number of Kansaris outside the ranks of the few rich mahajans. The Bangiya Kangsabanik Sammilani, on the model of the Bangiya Tili Jati Sammilani (1901), was formed in 1921 with the primary intention of integrating various Kansari sub-divisions or *gains*.[47] For the sake of homogeneity, the Sammilani encouraged inter-*gain* marriages, but restricted marriages outside the geographical area of its jurisdiction. It also tried to make all Kansari marriages subject to its prior approval.[48] Within a few years its branches spread out to nearly all the leading centres of this industry.[49] Annual conferances were held with much fanfare; publication of a quarterly journal, *Kangsabanik Patrika*, was started from 1923; and a Kansari bank was established in Calcutta with the intention of facilitating their trade and manufacture. The membership of this association was restricted only to the Kansaris and was not open to the non-Kansari practitioners of their trade. This was, therefore, a clear attempt to mobilize the 'community' and to draw its social boundaries.

---

[45] *RSCI*, p.137.
[46] *KBP*, Vol.I, No.1, 1330 BS, p.31.
[47] *KBP*, Vol.I, No.1, 1330 BS, Appendix B.
[48] *Ibid.*
[49] See *KBP* volumes for details.

If we analyse the essays and letters published in the *Kangsabanik Patrika*, we will find that this solidarity movement emphasized two points. Firstly, they demanded a higher ritual status for their 'caste' and for that purpose sent petitions to the census authority for being classed as Vaishyas. They also passed repeated resolutions denouncing the texts which included their caste in the Nabasakh group. The texts thus denounced were *Jasohar Khulnar Itihas* by Satish Chandra Mitra, *Sambandha Nirnay* by Lalmohan Vidyanidhi and *Siddhanta Samudra* by Dharmananda Mahabharati. Along with this, to establish the Vaishya origin of the caste, pedantic papers were read at the first annual conference of the Sammilani by such eminent persons as Bipin Behari Das, Sarat Chandra Nandan and Ray Bahadur Kali Charan Datta.[50]

Secondly, the Sammilani tried to apprise the Kansaris in particular and the people in general of the danger that had of late befallen their hereditary trade. And it was this threat perception that also largely determined their attitudes to nationalism and the colonial state. They were critical of the nationalists as they had failed to denounce, far less to stop, the increasing import of the cheaper wares. A passage from the pages of the *Kangsabanik Patrika* would more clearly reveal this mentality:

> 'Now-a-days, in our country swadeshi feelings are running high. For this reason most of our countrymen are using, instead of foreign cloth, either coarse handloom products or cloth produced by the Indian mills. People generally prefer handloom to mill-made cloth. But can the self-respect of our country be maintained by using only [indigenous] cloth? True swadeshi calls for the use of all kinds of indigenous goods. Boycott of aluminium and enamel wares and the use in their place of hand-made indigenous wares of brass and bell-metal also form important components of the swadeshi spirit'.[51]

But this did not certainly mean that the Kansari leaders were keen about an all out extension of the spirit of swadeshi as an offensive against the colonial state. In the

[50] *KBP*, Vol.I, No.1, 1330 BS, Appendix B.
[51] *KBP*, Vol.I, No.3, 1330 BS, p.116.Translation author's

annual meetings of their Sammilani, *Rajbhakti* (loyalty) resolutions were regularly passed and the editorial notes in their journal often lamented that 'even living under the protective umbrella of British rule, the Kansaris are not being able to improve their lot.'[52] The Kansari movement thus reflected a political attitude of ambivalence, which was clearly related to its origin, i.e., the state of their industry. And this very origin also explains why the attempt to forge a 'community' failed so soon.

IV

At the forefront of the solidarity movement there were four main groups of Kansaris, each group wanting to use the movement for different purposes. First of all there was the small group of extremely rich Kansari mahajans, whose position had been threatened by the factors already explained. There was next a still smaller group of Western educated Kansaris, like Sarat Chandra Nandan, who had a successful legal career in Alipore court and was willing to mobilize a support base to carve out a position for himself within the new institutional politics of colonial India. The third group consisted of the Mahmudpuri Kansaris, who had been somehow eking out, irrespective of their occupation, an extremely isolated social existence within the Kansari samaj since the early eighteenth century. And they now looked for integration and social rehabilitation. The last group, and certainly the most important and the largest group interested in the solidarity movement, consisted of those who had given up their hereditary occupation in favour of that of the Swarnakars or goldsmiths. For obvious reasons they deserve some special attention.

The Kansaris switching over to the occupation of goldsmiths formed a sizeable group and their occupational movement did not fit into either the prosperity-mobility or the

[52] Editorial, *KBP*, Vol.I, No.2, 1330 BS.

impurer-purer occupational movement models. Although Bhowanipore in Calcutta offers the most interesting case of such movement, with 89 out of 142 families of original Kansari settlers switching over to goldsmith's craft, (Raychaudhuri [1964], p.212) it was not certainly an exceptional development. Traditionally, the Kansaris of Bengal made cheaper ornaments from brass, bell-metal, copper or tin for the poorer sections of the society,[53] like their counterparts in other corners of India. (Buchanan [1934]; Johnstone [1888]; Dampier [1894]) Significantly, they did not make gold or silver ornaments because of the social stigma attached to such occupation. In Bhowanipore, the Kansaris had taken to the latter occupation in the early nineteenth century, while their fellow-men in the Sovabazar-Pataldanga areas (also in Calcutta) followed them a little later.[54] What is really surprising, however, is the similar movement of the Kansaris in the mofussil centres as well, as we have positive evidence of such movement in Dinajpur, Rangpur, Bagura and Midnapore in the late nineteenth century.[55]

A relative rise in profitability, compared to their hereditary occupation, has been widely held to be the most plausible cause of such movement. An increasingly indifferent social attitude to various artisanal trade, in the context of an increasing inter-craft mobility, also made an important contribution towards this development. But the most important factor was the increasing competition of cheap labour coming from other castes. Thus the small group of Saptagrami Kansaris at Bhowanipore started manufacturing gold and silver ornaments in the early nineteenth century, when they began to lose their traditional utensil market to the new Kansari factories coming up in the Banarashi Ghosh Street of Calcutta. In 1924, the locality had as many as 110 such factories, which served as feeder to the Burra Bazar shops.[56] It

[53] A.K.Nandy, 'Jatiya Shilpa O Byabasay', *KBP*, Vol.VII, Nos.4-6, 1336 BS, p.42.
[54] *Arthik Unnati*, (Calcutta, Monthly), Vol.II, No.9, 1334 BS, p.645.
[55] *Ibid; RSCI*, p.25; C.L.Datta, 'Dinajpur O Rangpurer Kangsabanik Samaj', *KBP*, Vol.I, No.4, 1330 BS. p.188.
[56] *RSCI*, p.42.

may be recalled here that the Saptagrami Kansaris had been living in Bhowanipore long before the coming of the British. In the districts also, we have the similar evidence of the competition coming from the low caste and particularly the Muslim artisans joining the hereditary occupation of the Kansaris.[57]

Whatever might have been the reasons behind some of the Kansaris joining the goldsmith's profession, this created a serious identity crisis for them and consequently they were very keen about maintaining their 'caste' identity. Some of these families thus adopted the title of Kangsabanik in addition to their individual surnames.[58] They also avoided all sorts of social relations with the Swarnakars, who were traditionally assigned a very low position in the ritual hierarchy of Bengal, although the two groups had regular contacts at the business level. The caste solidarity movement for these people thus offered a solution to their identity problem arising out of an inverse relationship between their material position and the purity of their new occupation.

But the caste solidarity movement failed to strike roots among the majority of the Kansari population and, therefore, it soon petered out after some initial years of hectic activities. As the movement was closely related to the fortunes of their hereditary trade, it had absolutely no meaning for the large number of Kansaris who had already given up their caste occupation by volition. The occupational survey of the Kansaris conducted by their Sammilani in 1923-24 found the proportion of such dropouts to be as high as 71 per cent.[59] To this vast segment of the caste population, except those who had changed to goldsmith's profession, the solidarity movement had no significance at all. It was only to the small section of the Kansaris, still owning old type domestic units of manufacture, that the movement held out a hope of some relief, i.e., relief from the competition of the cheaper wares

[57] *BBMI*; also see the district reports regularly published in the *KBP* volumes.
[58] See advertisements of a number of these jewellery firms in the *KBP* volumes.
[59] B.K.Das, 'Adam Sumari', *op.cit.*

and that of the products of the larger factories of bigger mahajans. But they too were disillusioned soon about the utility of such a movement. And then the movement had to encounter constantly the opposition of the new trade associations, like the Calcutta Brass Dealers' Association, controlled by the Burra Bazar merchants and similar other suburban associations of Dacca, Nabadwip, Khagra etc.,[60] whose interests the propaganda activities of the Kansari Sammilani had evidently threatened. The movement, therefore, soon lost its momentum and was reduced to an inconsequencial existence.

The history of the Kansari movement in Bengal, however, shows how the ups and downs in the condition of an industry determined the social rank of a caste traditionally associated with it. The organization of this industry determined the internal structure of that 'community', shaped divergent aspirations among its various segments, created social compulsions for solidarity among them and finally created conditions for the disintegration of the 'community' that existed in the imagination of some people but did not appeal to others.

References

Ball, V. (1880). *Tribal and Peasant Life in 19th Century India*, Calcutta, Reprint, New Delhi, 1985.

Bandyopadhyay, B. (1949). *Sangbadpatre Sekaler Katha*, (in Bengali), Calcutta, 1356 BS.

Bandyopadhyay,S. (1990). *Caste, Politics and the Raj: Bengal 1872-1937*, Calcutta.

Buchanan, F. (1833). *A Geographical, Statistical and Historical Description of the District or Zilla of Dinajpur in the Province or Subah of Bengal*, Calcutta.

Buchanan, F. (1934). *An Account of the District of Sahabad in 1812-1813*, Patna.

[60] *Report of the Bengal Industrial Survey Committee*, 1945, (Calcutta, 1948), p.25; S.K.Basak, 'Dhaka O Dhakar Bahirer Tama Pital O Kansa Shilpa', (in Bengali), *Arthik Jagat*, 15 September 1941.

Collin,E.W. (1892). *Report on the Existing Arts and Industries in Bengal, 1890*, Calcutta.

Cumming, J.G. (1908). *Review of the Industrial Position and Prospects in Bengal*, Calcutta.

Dampier, G.R. (1894), *A Monograph on the Brass and Copper Wares of the North Western provinces and Oudh*, Allahabad.

Dasgupta, T.C. (1935). *Aspects of Bengali Society from Old Bengali Literature*, Calcutta.

Forbes, R.J. (1950). *Metallurgy in Antiquity*, Leiden.

Ghosh,B. (1981). *Traditional Arts and Crafts of West Bengal*, Calcutta.

Greenough, P.R. (1982). *Prosperity and Misery in Mòdern Bengal: The Famine of 1943-44*, New York/Oxford.

Gupta, G.N. (1908). *A Survey of Industries and Resources of Eastern Bengal and Assam for the 1907-1908*, Shillong.

Hunter, W.W. (1877) *A Statistical Account of Bengal*, Vol.II, London, Reprint, Delhi, 1973.

Johnstone, D.C. (1888). *Monograph on Brass and Copper Ware in the Punjab in 1886-87*, Lahore.

Karve, I. (1977). *Hindu Society - An Interpretation*, Third Edition, Poona.

Kosambi, D.D. (1970). *Culture and Civilization in Ancient India*, Delhi.

Maity, S.K. (1970). *Economic Life in Northern India*, Delhi.

Mazumder, J.K. (1927). *Cottage Industries of Bengal*, Calcutta.

Mukherjee, T.N. (1894). *Monograph on the Brass and Copper Manufactures of Bengal*, Calcutta.

Mukherji, Meera. (1978). *Metalcraftsmen of India*, Calcutta.

Naqvi, H.K. (1968). *Urban Centres and Industries in Upper India, 1556-1803*, Bombay.

Ray, N.R. (1980), *Bangalir Itihas:Adi Parba* ,Vol.I, (in Bengali), Calcutta.

Raychaudhuri, A. (1964). 'Caste and Occupation in Bhowanipore in Calcutta', *Man In India*, Vol.44, No.3, September.

Samaddar, J.N. (1910). 'Raja Sitaram Roy', *Bengal Past and Present*, Vol.V.

Sanyal, H.R. (1981). *Social Mobility in Bengal*, Calcutta.

Sarkar, J.N. (1976). *A History of Bengal*, Dacca.

Sarkar, S.K. (1991). 'Small-Scale "Unorganized" Industries of Bengal and their role in the Industrial Economy of the Province, 1900-1947', Unpublished Ph.D. thesis, Calcutta University.

Sen, P.C. (1920). 'Prachin Bangla Sahitya Haite Bangalir Dainandin Jiban O Samajik Achar Byabaharer Parichay', (in Bengali), *Bangiya Sahitya Parishat Patrika*, Vol.27, No.3, 1327 BS, pp.94-127.

Shah, P.G. (1912). 'The Copper and Brass Industries of India' in *Report of the Indian Industrial Conference*, Bunckipore, 1912, Calcutta.

Watson, E.R. (1907). *A Monograph on Iron and Steel Work in the Province of Bengal*, Calcutta.

5

Development, Differentiation and Caste: The Namasudra Movement in Bengal, 1872-1947

SEKHAR BANDYOPADHYAY

I

The equilibrium between caste, class and power that was usually maintained in traditional Hindu society in pre-colonial Bengal (Ray [1980], pp.324-25; Sanyal [1981], pp.19-26), tended to break down as the new colonial state introduced certain changes in the opportunity structure. The customary production relationship, it is believed, was replaced by contract, as land was made into a marketable commodity. New professions were created and were thrown open to talent, while trade in collaboration with the European companies offered new possibilities of self-improvement for the trading communities, which were otherwise confined to limited markets. The result of these developments is believed to have been greater diffusion of wealth across caste lines, which led to upward social mobility, threatening to disrupt the relations of power in society. But if census occupation data are to be trusted as indicators of certain broad general trends, if not as faithful reflections of actual social reality (Conlon[1981]), then even in the early twentieth century (1901-1931) we would find that this mobility was fairly restricted and only rarely was there any movement from the bottom up. Sizeable sections of the population could still be found in their hereditary caste occupations, indicating only a differential impact of development which the colonial state had initiated in India in a very limited way.

Economic mobility, in other words, was not certainly corporate and as a result, class lines could be found to be cutting across the caste boundaries (Bandyopadhyay [1990a], pp.104-108). This phenomenon in a significant way conditioned the consciousness of the various caste groups and consequently had a profound impact on the various lower caste movements that were being organised in colonial Bengal during the late nineteenth and the early twentieth centuries.

Indeed during this period all over India members of almost every caste, despite their common ritual rank, had become differentiated in terms of economic and social status. But this fact of differentiation, though recognised in a number of empirical studies, has not so far been properly related to the dynamics of their social awakening and political movements. Such movements are usually interpreted either as expressions of social ambitions motivated by relative economic prosperity (Bailey [1958], p.VII; Hardgrave [1969], p.263; Zelliot [1973], p.39; Washbrook [1975], pp.176-77), or as manifestations of social protest against degradation and disabilities (Gough [1963], pp.174-75; Jha,H. [1977], p.556; Pandey [1983], pp.71-74). The first analytical framework ignores the element of protest involved in all such movements. But on the other hand, those who romanticise the element of protest tend to overlook the fact that the ideological hegemony of the constituted order had set limits to the imagination of these protestant lower castes and had ultimately led to the cooption of the more advanced section among them, if not of all of them, thus neutralising their social protest to a large extent.

Both these explanations are, in other words, based on the same underlying assumption that a caste, at least in terms of consciousness, represented an undifferentiated group of people. It is this conceptualisation of 'community' as a monolith which is questionable, as these movements were motivated neither only by an ambition for social climbing, nor by a protestant spirit alone. On the contrary, in a single caste movement we may find the convergence of both the trends, represented by different sections within the same caste. It was perhaps only when such a convergence occurred that a 'community' could be constructed, in the sense that its boundaries could be more sharply defined. This usually took place through a complex process which brought into sharper focus the commonality among that particular group of people, i.e., their low ritual status, and thus articulated, despite differentiation, their 'collective self'. The 'community' then invented its own tradition, created its myths and heroes and used various symbols, both verbal and non-verbal, to give a concrete shape to this collective identity. Attempts at self-affirmation by such submerged groups required the breaking of the barriers of deference which involved them in conflict, both violent and non-violent, with those who enjoyed social authority and so were used to being revered. Such conflicts further marked out the lines of demarcation separating the 'community' from the rest of the society.

But over-emphasis on such incidents of conflict often deflects our attention from the less dramatic moments of accommodation and/or disintegration of a 'community' and of its social movement. In other words, a convergence of the various streams of consciousness, of multiple ambitions and grievances of the various sections within a caste at a particular historical juncture, did not necessarily eliminate the possibility of divergence or fracturing of the 'community' at a subsequent stage. This could take place due to increasing differentiation resulting from a differential impact of development on a caste, rendering the ideological hegemony of its leadership ineffective. This could also have been due to the unfolding of a qualitatively different socio-political process that might result in the redrawing of the social boundaries and articulation of other forms of identities within the same group. If we look just at a particular historical conjuncture, then a caste or community might appear as a static monolith. But if we observe it in its involvement in a movement over a longer historical period - experiencing variously the impact of the politico-economic developments of the colonial period then the mutations in the community formation process actually would come into sharper focus. The point which this essay seeks to drive home is that none of these movements, and in particular the one under review, the Namasudra movement in Bengal between 1872 and 1947, were homogeneous movements, as in them we may detect various levels of consciousness and different forms of action, yet all encapsulated into one.

II

Numerically, the Namasudras constituted the largest Hindu caste group in eastern Bengal and the second largest in the whole province (9.8 percent). They lived mainly in the six eastern districts of Bakarganj, Faridpur, Dacca, Mymensingh, Jessore and Khulna; these districts in 1901 contained 75 percent of the total population (1,852,371) of this caste. Within this geographical region, again, their major concentration was in the marshy tracts of north-west Bakarganj, South Faridpur, the adjoining Narail and Magura subdivisions of Jessore and the Sadar and Bagerhat subdivisions of Khulna. In this contiguous area lived almost half of the Namasudra population of Bengal[1] and therefore it may legitimately be called their principal inhabitation zone. This geographical anchorage, which may perhaps be explained in terms of the tribal origin of these people (Basak[1911], p.67; Wise[1883],p.257; Risley[1891], pp.183-85), was certainly one of the sources of strength for this community, and its allocation to Pakistan after the Partition in 1947 contributed to the decline of their movement.

The Namasudras had a very low social status among the Hindus of Bengal. According to ancient Indian texts, the Chandals, as they were earlier known, were untouchables

[1] *Census of India*, 1901, Vol.VI, Part I, pp.395-96; Vol.VIA, Part II, Table XIII, p.246; *Bengal District Gazetteers*, B Volume, (Calcutta, 1933) for the districts of Bakarganj, Faridpur, Jessore and Khulna; Risley[1891], p.189; Das[1961], p.1.

(Jha,V.[1986-87],pp.1-36). But untouchability in its strict sense was never a problem in Bengal. The thirteenth-fourteenth century *puranas* refer to the Chandals of Bengal as an *antyaja* or a 'low-born' mixed caste or *sankarajati*, but do not indicate that they were looked down upon as untouchables.[2] Even Raghunandan, who is regarded as the most conservative *smritikara* of sixteenth-century Bengal, speaks of restrictions on marriage and commensality with the Chandals, but does not categorically insist that their touch should be avoided by all means (Chakraborti[1970], pp.33,256-61). The literary evidence of the *Mangalakavya* of the sixteenth-eighteenth century also suggests that the Chandals lived within the precincts of the village or town and were not regarded as *antebasi* (dwellers on the periphery), as had been enjoined by Manu.[3] Several enquiries in the early twentieth century also revealed that the so-called untouchables suffered less in Bengal, as compared with their counterparts in other regions.[4] And this was perhaps one of the reasons why the lower caste movements were also less powerful in Bengal than in other parts of India.

However, the Chandals were subjected to various forms of social disabilities which had created a considerable social distance between them and the privileged high caste Hindu bhadralok. Though the latter did not actually practice untouchability, they often verbally invoked the notion in order to affirm their social authority (Palit [1915], pp.2-3). This social distance was further accentuated by the specific class situation of the region. In 1911, about 78 percent of the actual earners among the Namasudras lived on agriculture.

[2] *Brihaddharmapuranam*, edited by H.P.Shastri, Bibliotheca Indica, Asiatic Society of Bengal, (Calcutta, 1888), p.578; *Brahmavaivarttapuranam*, edited by Panchanan Tarkaratna, (Calcutta, 1391 BS), pp.22,25,27.

[3] Mukundaram, *Chandimangala*, edited by Sukumar Sen, Sahitya Academy, (New Delhi, 1975),p.81; also see, Bharatchandra, *Annadamangala*, in *Bharatchandra Granthabali*, edited by Brojendranath Bandyopadhyay and Sajani Kanta Das, Bangiya Sahitya Parishat, (Third edition, Calcutta, 1369 BS), p.171.

[4] Report (of the enquiry) by H.E.Stapleton, DPI, Bengal to Secretary, Government of Bengal, [hereafter GB], Education Dept., 22 March 1929, GB, Appointment (Appointment) Dept., File No.5M-114 of 1928, February 1930, Proc. Nos. 7-20, West Bengal State Archives (hereafter WBSA).

Among this agricultural population, only 1.15 percent were 'rent receivers', while the rest have been referred to in census reports by various terms as 'farm servants', 'cultivators' or 'field labourers'. Other evidence suggests that many of them were tenant farmers, with or without occupancy right, and others were sharecroppers (*bargadars*) whose number was increasing towards the 1920's. But the more important fact was that landholding in this region was monopolised by the high-caste Hindus and the Saiyad Muslims. In the Dacca, Rajshahi and Chittagong divisions, where the Namasudras mainly lived, 80.82 percent of the 'rent receivers' belonged to these social categories, while only 3.78 percent of them were Namasudras. Thus the most fundamental dichotomy in Bengal agrarian relations, i.e., between rent-payers and rent-receivers, coincided in this situation with the caste hierarchy. And this contradiction was further accentuated by various forms of oppression, such as subinfeudation, exaction of illegal cesses, non-fixity of rent and replacement of easy cash rents with heavy produce rents. However, the situation also suggests that there was differentiation within the community, as a small group had moved up the social ladder, by taking advantage of the process of reclamation that had started in the area since the mid-nineteenth century. Some of them had also taken to moneylending and petty trading and later to education and various professions. But the census occupation data indicate, if these are to be trusted at all, that this upwardly mobile group constituted even less than 2 percent of the caste population in 1911.[5]

We may surmise therefore that the vertical divisions within the community were not as yet sharp enough to destroy its internal unity or prevent the emergence of a shared sense of group identity. The peasantry had already been alienated from the oppressive high-caste gentry of the region, and the upwardly mobile section was numerically so small and economically so weak, with such a low ritual rank, that

[5] *Census of India*, 1901, Vol.VIA, Part II, pp.480-81; *Census of India*, 1911, Vol.V, Part II, pp.370-73; for further details see Bandyopadhyay [1989], pp.175-81.

they could not identify themselves with the high-caste bhadralok. And their newly acquired secular status made them more conscious of their paradoxical social position. A sense of self-respect had also developed among the masses as they emerged as a settled peasant community through constant encounter with a hostile nature in the vast marshy lands and came into contact with such liberal religious sects as Gaudiya Vaishnavism or Kartabhaja Sampraday and other local religious preceptors as Sahlal Pir in the eighteenth century, all repudiating the caste system and preaching equality among human beings (Beveridge [1876], pp.260-65; Jasimuddin [1977], pp. 36-42,259,262). Thus the two segments within the community, despite their different interests and aspirations, also shared a common desire to defy or overthrow the social authority of the higher castes who had dominated them socially and economically for such a long time. And this also gradually pushed them away from the mainstream of nationalist politics, which in Bengal had become identified with the high-caste Hindu bhadralok. This alienation was rooted in an ideology that emanated from their own reconstruction of the past and perception of the present, which varied in significant ways from those of the nationalists.

III

The social movement of the Namasudras had started in 1872-73 in the Faridpur-Bakarganj region and had taken the form of a social and economic boycott of the higher castes who had refused to attend the funeral ceremony of the mother of a prominent Namasudra village headman. The movement then continued for about six months during which fields remained untilled, roofs unthatched and no Namasudra could be found to be serving the higher castes in any manner (Bandyopadhyay[1989], pp.183-84). They could not however sustain the movement for a long time and the failure of this initial move was followed by the development of an organised religious sect called Matua. It derived its social attitudes, rituals and notions of cosmology from the established traditions of Vaishnavism, but adapted them to suit their particular social need of interrogating the existing relations of power. Its preceptor, Sri Guruchand Thakur, who came from a big peasant family, preached like many other Vaishnava *gurus* the gospel of personal devotion, elimination of caste, and equality among all men and women. But apart from that he also preached a work ethic attuned to the requiremnts of an upwardly mobile community. While the Bengali bhadralok society remained immersed in Vedantism as preached by Ramakrishna, insisting on renouncing material wealth to seek spiritual salvation, Guruchand was asking his disciples to become educated and earn money in order to become respectable. '*Hate kam mukhe nam*', or salvation through performance of worldly duties, was his teaching for the disciples, who were almost exclusively Namasudras. As the higher caste Vaishnavas refused to have any social relations with them, the followers of Matua developed a greater sense of group solidarity. The need for solidarity was also given importance to by the guru himself, as one of his teachings, '*jar dal nei tar bal nei*', i.e., those who do not form a group do not have power, essentially conveyed the message of community formation for collective action. Regular *Kirtan* (collective singing of devotional songs), which was perhaps the only ritual of the sect, gave it a congregational character and continually reinforced its group solidarity through a shared experience of devotion. Other periodic gatherings of the devotees, for example on the occasion of the Baruni mela, provided for further social mobilisation (Sarkar[1916]; Haldar,M.[1943]; Haldar,N.[1985,1986]; Haldar,P.[1986])

It was around the Matua sect that the Namasudra social movement began to develop in the late nineteenth century, and Orakandi, the ancestral village of Guruchand in the district of Faridpur, virtually became its headquarters. Apart from this sect, a *samiti* (association) was also started in 1902 and regular 'uplift meetings' were organised to disseminate the message of the caste movement. Other media, such as the performance of *jatra* (a form of folk theatre) and the weekly collection of *mushti* (a handful of rice) from every household, were used for the purpose of mobilisation. And from 1912, the Bengal Namasudra Association, with its district units, provided the movement with a regular organisational network (Mead[1911], pp.12-14; Haldar,M.[1943], pp.110-114, 119-120; Das[1961], p.38; Ray,R.[1914], p.37; Biswas[1931], pp.157-160; Bose[1975], p.158; O'Malley[1912],p.50).

However, as the movement made progress, two levels of consciousness and two forms of action gradually became clearly discernible, one represented by the elite leaders and the other by their peasant followers. The first and foremost demand of the Namasudra leaders was for the public recognition of their new name 'Namasudra' instead of the old despised 'Chandal', which was ultimately dropped in the census of 1911. Along with this, they also went in for other forms of cultural adaptation and sought to appropriate symbols that would indicate their higher ritual status. For example, they referred to their Brahman origin, manipulated scriptural evidence to prove it, forbade their women from visiting market places, performed eleven days' mourning and above all began to don the sacred thread.[6] The existing discourse of 'Sanskritisation' cannot perhaps explain this behaviour, as it ignores the element of protest involved in it. What such lower caste people were actually trying was to appropriate certain symbols of authority and divest them of their symbolic significance. For example, as the lower castes began to don the sacred thread, which was the most authentic symbol of social authority, the early twentieth century Bengali bhadralok began to call it '*siki paisar suto*' or a thread worth a quarter of a penny (Ray[1926],p.493). However, the protest of the Namasudra elites ultimately ended in

[6] *Census of India,* 1901, Vol.VI, Part II, pp.480-81; *Census of India*, 1911, Vol.V, Part I, Subsidiary Table V, pp.351-55; Risley[1891], pp.184,186; Haldar,M.[1943], pp.255-58; Das[1961], pp.37,68; Badoi Biswas[1911], pp.90-99.

an endorsement, perhaps a subconscious endorsement, of the existing ritual order. The myths that they used to evince their higher ritual status were derived directly from the corpus of traditional Hindu religious scriptures. And the way in which these were constructed makes it clear that they did not visualise a levelling of the social hierarchy, nor the ritual order turned upside down. They were only seeking legitimation for a higher ritual status for themselves within the existing structure (Badoi Biswas [1911], pp.45-53; Sarma[1913],pp.6-9).

At a secular level, the leaders of the Namasudras had realised that education and employment were essential for the economic development of the commuity and, more significantly, that these were now the new sources of higher social status. Unfair competition with the higher castes, as well as various forms of overt or concealed discrimination, were, according to them, the reasons for their lack of access to educational institutions or exclusion from public employment. Hence, the colonial policy of protective discrimination initiated since 1906 in favour of the Muslims also inspired the Namasudras to ask for the same privileges. Some concessions in matters of education and employment were also granted to them in the 1920's and the early 1930's. But in spite of that, their position did not improve noticeably, mainly due to the local officials' non-compliance with such orders.[7]

The other grievance of the Namasudra leadership concerned their exclusion from the new representative institutions. Although their position in the local bodies had gradually improved, their representation in the provincial legislature was still minimal. This fact of under-representation in the context of the possibilities of greater devolution of power made the Namasudra leadership apprehensive of a high-

[7] *Namasudra Suhrid,* May 1911, 'Selections from Vernacular Newspapers in Eastern Bengal and Assam' for the week ending 24 June 1911, GB, Appointment (Appointment) Dept., File No.1D-1, November 1922, Proc. Nos. 114-117, Appendix E, p.XV, Appendix F, p.XVII; File No.1D-1, October 1923, Proc. Nos. 3-19; File No.4-D-10 of 1930, June 1931, Proc. Nos.36-41, Appendix A & B and KW, p.3; Appointment Dept., File No.8L-35 of 1932, B April 1933, Proc. Nos. 429-430; WBSA.

caste oligarchy. Therefore, after the announcement of the Montagu-Chelmsford Reform proposals, in two conferences in 1917 and 1918 they demanded 'communal representation' to ensure the future progress of the backward classes.[8] Consequently the Reform Act of 1919 provided for the nomination of one representative of the Depressed Classes to the Bengal legislature. But apart from this solitary member, such classes still remained unrepresented, and the Namasudra majority constituencies continued to return only caste-Hindu candidates.

This continuing frustration of their political ambitions had led to the development among the Namasudra leaders of a certain sense of attachment to the Raj and suspicion about nationalist politics which had come to be identified with the high-caste Hindu bhadralok. But this position was also rooted in an ideological construction of the nature of colonial rule and this construction was based on a particular perception of history which differed from that of the nationalists. As the latter portrayed the establishment of colonial rule as a break with a glorious past, the Namasudras considered the new regime to be an improvement over that past. Therefore all political movements against British rule appeared to be steps in historical retrogression or attempts to put the clock back and hence against what they considered to be their legitimate community centric interests (Ray,R.[1909], pp.155,158; Biswas,R.[1921], pp.17, 124; Biswas, B.[1921], pp.19,31). This explains why they opposed the Swadeshi movement quite actively, condemned the Home Rule agitation, and even in the age of Gandhian mass politics stayed away from the Non-Co-operation, Civil Disobedience and the Quit India movements, despite the endeavours of the nationalist leaders and Gandhi himself to win their sympathy (Biswas,R.[1921], pp.72-78,85-90; Haldar,M.[1943],pp.168-76, 262,403,413-15,442-43).

---

[8] *Bengalee*, 6,10,11 November 1917; *The Statesman*, 6 November 1918.

IV

This rejection of the nationalist politics was not just an affair of the elites. It was common at the lower level too, as the leaders were successful in convincing the peasantry that nationalism was an ideology of the high-caste gentry. Such an identification of the Swadeshi movement was quite easy as most of the leaders and volunteers in eastern Bengal came from these social groups and were frequently using their coercive power to compel the peasants to participate in their movement (Sarkar,S.[1973], pp.355-60). The latter detested it and the antipathy that was generated persisted through the days of the Non-Cooperation, Civil Disobedience and Quit India movements.[9] But this non-participation in, and sometimes active opposition to the nationalist movement need not be taken as a manifestation of loyalty to the British. On the contrary, it was more an expression of protest against social and economic injustices perpetrated on them by their high-caste landlords, many of whom were in the leadership of the movement against the Raj. Indeed, the attitude of the Namasudra peasantry towards the government was rather ambivalent. Usually they preferred the distant ruler to the oppressors nearby and frequently resorted to bazar-looting and house-breaking to harass their overbearing landlords, who usually belonged to the higher castes. But whenever the authorities, in the name of maintaining law and order, intervened and sided with the landed classes, as they did on a number of occasions in Faridpur in 1909, the Namasudra peasantry did not hesitate to take up arms against the police, who represented in that local situation, and also in the consciousness of the peasants, the colonial state.[10]

What the behaviour of the Namasudra peasants always

[9] GB, Home(Confidential) File Nos. 599 of 1930, 597(1-3) of 1930, 345(1-3) of 1931, WBSA; Bengal Legislative Council Proceedings, (hereafter BLCP), Vol. 7, No.2, 20 February 1922, p.9.

[10] Government of India, [hereafter GI], Home(Political), March 1909, Proc. No.105: April 1909, Proc. No.52; May 1909, Proc. No.131; B November 1909, Proc. No.34; December 1909, Proc. No.16; National Archives of India (hereafter NAI).

reflected was a yearning for social honour and an urge to escape economic exploitation. For these purposes, they sometime sided with the government against the nationalists. Sometimes, they allied themselves with the Muslims against the high-caste Hindus, as in parts of Jessore, Khulna, Faridpur and Mymensingh in 1908-09.[11] But on other occasions they fought pitched battles with the Muslims, primarily to uphold their community honour, as in various pockets of Jessore, Khulna, Bakarganj and Faridpur in 1911, 1923-25 and 1938.[12]

The Namasudra peasantry had so long remained with their caste leadership because the latter quite effectively had evolved a caste ideology by articulating what were essentially certain peasant grievances. They constantly harped on such issues as the exploitation and harassment of the 'low-caste peasantry' by the 'high-caste landlords' or the 'domination of the bhadralok politicians', and raised various peasant demands in public meetings and in the legislative council.[13] As some of these leaders, at least in their use of popular rhetoric, proposed to alter the established structure of social authority, they did succeed in mobilising the masses in support of their politics.

But from the 1930's the Namasudra leaders gradually began to forget their peasant followers. The shift appears to have started from the 1930 Khulna district conference, which was described as a meeting not of the Namasudra peasants, but of their educated and professional descendants. It was at this gathering that their leader Guruchand emphasised that political power was absolutely necessary for the uplifting of the social and material condition of the community and for

[11] *Mussalman*, 29 May 1908; O,Malley [1912], p.50; GB, Politicai (Police) Dept., File No. P5R-1, B July 1911, Proc. Nos. 326-328, WBSA; GI, Home(Political), B October 1907, Proc. No.47; June 1909, Proc. No.125; B September 1909, Proc. No. 47, NAI.

[12] GB, Police Dept., File No. P5R-11/23, B May 1924, Proc. Nos. 110-149; File No. P5R-2(4-12)/25, B March 1926, Proc. Nos. 95-103, WBSA.

[13] Haldar,M.[1943], pp.168-76, 413-15; Rajani Kanta Das, *Bangiya Namasudra Conference* , (Pirojpur, 1922), pp.9-11, 20-23; BLCP, Vol.I, No.6, 1 April 1921, p.79;Vol.3, 4 July 1921, p.72; 7 July 1921, pp.306-8; 12 July 1921, pp.495-96; Vol.7, No.3, 27 February 1922, p.3.

getting access to this power, participation in institutional politics was essential.[14] Since then, barring a few occasional public meetings, one or two appeals to the government or a few council questions,[15] there was nothing for the rural poor on the agenda of this upwardly mobile professional leadership. There was also a marked decline in mass mobilisation and organisational efforts at the village level, as the leaders became more and more Calcutta-based. Since the institutional concessions which they had been looking for had already been provided in the new constitutional arrangement of 1935, there was no longer a necessity for numbers and hence a palpable neglect of the masses, especially after 1937.

It was from the beginning of the 1930's that the Namasudra leaders became preoccupied with constitutional politics. They welcomed the Communal Award, condemned the Poona Pact as 'Dr.Ambedkar's political blunder', but then rallied behind it when there was a non-Congress caste-Hindu backlash against it. But it was only 'by necessity' and 'not by choice' that they had accepted the pact which had taken away the advantage of a separate electorate.[16] In this way, as the leaders became more and more institution-oriented, their movement also became faction-ridden, and from 1932 onwards we find two rival organisations trying to represent the Namasudra community. The institutional concessions they were now asking for would hardly benefit the rural poor, who were ill-equipped to take advantage of these, and as a result the movement began to lose its popular appeal.

The Praja movement by offering a more class based political programme for the peasants further corroded the support base of the Namasudra leadership. In fact from the early twentieth century the Namasudra peasantry had been showing independence of action in mobilising themselves on ex-

---

[14] *Matua Mahasangher Lakshya O Karmasuchi*, (The Aims and programmes of the Matua Mahasangha), (in Bengali), (Second edition, Thakurnagar, 1394 BS), pp.9-10.

[15] BLCP, Vol.34, No.3, 31 March 1930, p.632; Vol.41, No.1, 20 February 1933, p.44.

[16] GI, Reforms Office, File No.199/R-1932, NAI; BLCP, Vol.41, No.2, 14 March 1933, p.99.

clusively peasant issues, such as for the commutation of high produce rents into easy cash rents in the first decade of the twentieth century,[17] or for the three-fourths share for the bargadars or sharecroppers in the late 1920's (Sarkar,T.[1987], pp.38-41). But in a more organised way, the Krishak Praja Party under the leadership of Fazlul Huq had successfully mobilised a large section of the Muslim and Namasudra peasantry of eastern Bengal. Younger Namasudra leaders like Jogendranath Mandal and Birat Chandra Mandal were behind the mobilisation of the Namasudras under the banner of this new tenants' party. But before the election of 1937 the Krishak Praja Party abandoned the Scheduled Caste constituency in order to compete with the Muslim League for Muslim votes (Khan[1982], Chapter II; Das[1961], p.55). As a result, the Namasudra peasantry was left with no other choice and had to support their caste leaders. But the fact that many of their established leaders lost the election in 1937 proved that around this time the Namasudra peasantry did not fully approve of the politics of their caste leaders. On the other hand, nor could the Congress take advantage of the situation, as only one of the elected Namasudras in that year was a Congress nominee. In an unreserved constituency in Bakarganj, inhabited predominantly by the Namasudras, Jogendranath Mandal as an Independent candidate defeated a Kayastha Congressite, Saral Datta, who was a nephew and indeed the political successor of Ashwini Kumar Datta.[18] This shows the attitude of the Namasudra peasantry and their determination to stand by somebody of their own caste who had shown sympathy for their cause.

V

The Namasudra movement till about 1937 looked more

[17] *Final Report on the survey and Settlement Operations in Bakarganj District, 1900 to 1908*, by J.C.Jack, (Calcutta, 1915), pp.167-68 and Appendix G-I, G-II, G-V, G-VII, G-IX.

[18] GB, Home (Constitution and Elections) Dept., File No.R3E-27, May 1937, Proc. Nos.1-13, WBSA.

like a parallel stream of consciousness, and was not certainly a distributary of any of the mainstreams of nationalist politics in Bengal. But the dominant streams of politics began to capture the parallel streams during the last decade of colonial rule when the transfer of power became a distinct possibility. By the time Bengal was partitioned and India achieved independence, the Namasudras had moved away from their political alienation and had integrated into the existing political mainstreams in the province. But as their movement encapsulated various forms of consciousness, its integration into the mainstreams also took place at different levels and was expressed in a variety of forms.

At an institutional level, the Namasudra leaders till 1937 had maintained a distance from the Congress, as indicated by the result of the election, returning only one Congress nominee out of 13 successful candidates from that caste and the subsequent support of these 'independent' legislators for the Muslim League - Praja Party coalition ministry under Fazlul Huq (Bandyopadhyay [1990a], pp.181-182). But soon they were disillusioned, as the new ministry did precious little for the benefit of the Scheduled Castes[19] and Mukunda Behary Mullick, their representative in the cabinet, was publicly criticised in early 1938 in a meeting at Kanchrapara.[20] The Congress now tried to capitalise on this disaffection to appropriate the Scheduled Caste movement, as the importance of the Scheduled Caste lobby in the legislature could no longer be ignored. With the death of Guruchand in March 1937 also disappeared the major influence that had kept the Namasudra movement away from Congress politics and the Calcutta Scheduled Caste League, formed in early 1937, became the new connecting link between the two groups. Among the prominent Namasudra leaders associated with this new organisation was Pramatha Ranjan Thakur,

[19] *Amrita Bazar Patrika*, 23 February 1938.

[20] *Amrita Bazar Patrika*, 29 March 1938; *Hindustan Standard*, 3 February, 22 March 1938.

Guruchand's grandson.[21] On the Congress side, the persons who were instrumental to this emerging new alignment were the two Bose brothers, Subhas and Sarat. At a meeting in Albert Hall on 13 March 1938, Subhas Bose, now the Congress President, described Guruchand as 'a superman' who had 'regenerated the Hindus of Bengal by infusing new life into them'.[22] Three days after this meeting, about twenty Scheduled Caste legislators, including a number of prominent Namasudras like P.R.Thakur and Jogendranath Mandal, assembled at the residence of Sarat Bose and decided to cooperate with the Congress and withdraw their support for the Coalition ministry. [23] They formed a new legislative party, known as the Independent Scheduled Caste Party, with Mandal as the Secretary, and decided 'to work in cooperation with the Congress...'.[24]

Gandhi also personally met a number of prominent Namasudra legislators in Calcutta on 18 March 1938. On his personal invitation, P.R.Thakur set out on a tour of the Congress ruled provinces in July and on his return made a press statement that he was very impressed with the achievements of the Congress governments in ameliorating the conditions of the Scheduled Castes.[25] In August there were ten Congress sponsored resolutions against individual ministers of the Huq cabinet. The resolution against the Namasudra minister M.B.Mullick was moved by his fellow caste leader P.R.Thakur, who was supported by another Namasudra legislator Jogendranath Mandal. The voting pattern on the no-confidence motions showed that at least 16 out of the 31 MLAs from among the Scheduled Castes had now switched over to the side of the Congress.[26] As for the Namasudras, this position was formally endorsed on 29 May 1939 at the All

[21] *Amrita Bazar Patrika*, 21 November 1937.

[22] *Amrita Bazar Patrika*, 15 March 1938; *Hindustan Standard*, 13 March, 15 March 1938.

[23] *Hindustan Standard*, 18 March, 19 March 1938.

[24] *Amrita Bazar Patrika*, 3 April 1938.

[25] *Amrita Bazar Patrika*, 29 July 1938; Barman [1985], pp.73-75.

[26] *Bengal Legislative Assembly Proceedings*, [hereafter *BLAP*], Vol.53, No.2, 8 August 1938, pp.14-16; 10 August 1938, pp.118-124.

Bengal Namasudra Conference at Tamluk, where P.R.Thakur, in his presidential address, advised his community to 'join the National Congress and fight for India's freedom'.[27] The political alienation of the grandfather now was decisively replaced by the integrationist ideology of his grandson's generation. And it was with their support that in October 1941 the Muslim League backed Huq ministry was toppled and a new Congress supported Progressive Coalition ministry (popularly known as the Shyama-Huq ministry) was installed, with the Rajbansi leader Upendranath Barman as the new minister representing the Scheduled Castes (Barman [1985], pp.81-84).

However, not all of the Namasudra leaders liked the idea of integration with the Congress and by now there was a clear division within the movement. During all these years the other section of the Namasudra leadership which had gathered around M.B.Mullick, had stuck to the earlier stand of advocating moral and material support for His Majesty's government. As usual, they were demanding more jobs and educational opportunities and were trying to expose the hollowness of such Congress-led movements as those for temple-entry or the removal of untouchability.[28] The proposed Cripps Mission and the new possibilities of getting constitutional concessions had temporarily brought the Mullick group for the first time closer to the pro-Congress Thakur group. On 26 March 1942 they announced the decision to send a joint delegation to Delhi to represent their case before Stafford Cripps.[29] But the chances of a permanent rapprochement disappeared with the failure of the Cripps Mission.

The signs of a fresh realignment could again be seen when a large number of Scheduled Caste people assembled at Calcutta on 26 April 1942 and formed a new organisation called the Bengal Scheduled Caste League, with Jogendranath Mandal as its president. Initially the new

[27] *Hindustan Standard*, 2 June 1939.
[28] *Amrita Bazar Patrika*, 8 September, 16 November 1939, 24 January 1940.
[29] *Hindustan Standard*, 24,26 March 1942.

organisation had retained a pro-Congress stand and condemned the arrest of Gandhi during the Quit India movement.[30] But Mandal was already sore about the Congress due to the Subhas Bose controversy; and further disenchantment followed when in 1943 he joined the Muslim League-led Nazimuddin ministry, which the other Scheduled Caste leaders boycotted for being 'entirely communal' (Barman [1985], p.84; Mandal [1975], p.51). However, the new cabinet had included another Namasudra minister Pulin Behary Mullick (Mukunda Behary's brother) and a Rajbansi leader Premhari Barma, while Mukunda Behary himself became the Deputy Leader of the new Coalition Party. The situation indicates the existence of a great schism within the Namasudra leadership. Two months later was formed the Bengal branch of the All India Scheduled Caste Federation, which Ambedkar had started in 1942. Jogendranath, now more committed to Ambedkarite politics, became its first president. In April 1945, in its first provincial conference at Gopalganj (Faridpur), he announced in his presidential address that 'the first and foremost aim' of the Federation would be to establish the 'separate political identity' of the Scheduled Castes.[31] But at this juncture he was not certainly speaking for the entire community. Many of its important leaders had decided to boycott this conference, which, according to one account, only three out of thirtyone Scheduled Caste MLAs of the province had attended. Ambedkar was probably aware of the situation and therefore cancelled his scheduled visit to the conference at the very last moment.[32]

At this point the 'integrationists' certainly appeared to be representing the majority position within the Namasudra and for that matter within the entire Scheduled Caste movement

[30] *Amrita Bazar Patrika*, 28 April, 1 September 1942.

[31] Jogendranath Mandal, *Sabhapatir Abhibhashan, Pradeshik Tapsili Jati Federation, Pratham Pradeshik Mahasammelan,* [Presidential Address, Scheduled Castes Federation, First Provincial Conference], Gopalganj, 24th & 25th April 1945, pp.9-10.

[32] 'Good Sense Has Dawned on Dr. Ambedkar', by B.C.Mandal, 12.5.45, Shyama Prasad Mukherjee Papers, Speeches and Writings by Others, II-IV Instalment, Serial No.8, Nehru Memorial Museum and Library [hereafter NMML].

of Bengal. This was amply reflected in the results of the election of 1946, in which only one official candidate of the Scheduled Caste Federation won and that was its president Jogendranath Mandal. Mukunda Behary won as an Independent candidate from his home constituency Khulna. But by contrast, Congress Scheduled Caste candidates won in 24 reserved seats out of a total of 30. The Rajbansi leader Prasannadeb Raikat and the Namasudra leader P.R.Thakur had won the election as Independent candidates;[33] but both of them formally joined the Congress later. The 1946 election results thus clearly showed that there was a complete reversal of the 1937 situation, when among the 32 elected Scheduled Caste candidates only 7 had Congress affiliation. By now the Congress appears to have appropriated the Scheduled Caste movement and had marginalised the 'separatists' among the Namasudras and the other Scheduled Castes, and in view of the extended franchise, election results may also be taken to reflect the popular mind to some extent.

The electoral debacle of the Scheduled Caste Federation continued in the election for the Constituent Assembly as well. Of the six Scheduled Caste candidates elected to this body by the Bengal Legislative Assembly, there was only one representative of the Federation and that was B.R.Ambedkar himself, who had to depend on his Bengal friends because of difficulties at his home province Maharashtra. Other successful candidates from Bengal, given the composition of the Assembly, were all Congress nominees, while those defeated included Jogendranath Mandal and M.B.Mullick. Indeed, Ambedkar was the sole representative of the Federation from the whole of India in the Constituent Assembly and therefore even the British government now refused to recognise this organisation as the true representative of the Scheduled Castes. The Secretary of State announced in the House of Lords that it was the Congress which would represent the

---

[33] Press Information Bureau, Govt. of India, 'The General Elections (1945-46), The Legislative Assembly - Bengal', May 23, 1946, GI, Reforms Office, File No. 106/3/45-R, NAI.

Scheduled Castes in the constitution making body.[34]

In Bengal the marginalisation of the Ambedkarites was completed when Jogendranath Mandal joined the Muslim League ministry led by Suhrawardy and after the great Calcutta killing in August 1946 opposed, along with M.B.Mullick, the no-confidence motion against the ministry. An 'Open Letter' of the riot victims appealed to him to '...cut off all connection with the League Ministry ... and thus regain the sympathy and support of all...'[35] But he was not very keen about it, as his alliance with the League bore fruit in October 1946 when Jinnah nominated him as the League's representative from Bengal in the Interim Ministry. Soon, however, the politics which Mandal stood for lost its significance as in a by-election in July 1947 the Bombay Congress legislature party nominated Ambedkar to the Constituent Assembly, leading subsequently to his selection as the Chairman of the Drafting Committee of India's constitution and eventually to his inclusion as the Law Minister in independent India's first government (Zelliot [1988], pp.193-194). The appropriation of the Scheduled Caste politics by the Congress was now complete, even though it appeared to be more effective at the apex than at the bottom.

VI

Since 1938 the leaders of the Namasudra community were mostly involved in what may legitimately be called faction-ridden elite politics. And as they more and more integrated with and came under the protective umbrella of the Congress, their interest in the mass movement diminished even further. Most of the leaders as well as their organisations became almost wholly Calcutta based and only occasionally did they visit the countryside 'to enquire into the

---

[34] 'Lords Debate on India: Text of Secretary of State's Speech', GI, Home (Political), File No. 51/2/46-Poll(I), NAI.

[35] *Amrita Bazar Patrika*, 4 September 1946.

conditions of the peasants'.[36] And even more rarely did they speak of any peasant demand, as the agenda of their various meetings clearly indicate.[37] What we can perhaps read in this situation is a continually increasing mental and physical gap between the Namasudra leaders and their predominantly peasant followers.

What the Namasudra peasants were doing since 1937 is a matter of conjecture in view of the absence of any direct evidence. There is no reason to believe that they had exhausted their spirit of protest against the inequities of Hindu society. For example, in 1937-38 they had organised in village Simulghar in Habiganj sub-division of Sylhet district a prolonged movement to win their right to put on shoes in the presence of caste Hindus and occasionally this movement also lapsed into violence.[38] But on the other hand, there is also strong evidence to suggest that the Namasudra masses at this stage were developing a greater identification with the Hindu community and this Hinduisation at times tended to overshadow their caste identity.

The articulation of the Hindu identity of the Namasudra masses was the direct result of the endeavours of a number of Hindu organisations. The Hindu Mission, for example, had been active among these people since the early 1930's and by 1938 it had intensified its activities.[39] It was around this time again that Swami Pranabananda of the Bharat Sevashram Sangha had started working among the Namasudras of Jessore, Khulna, Faridpur and Bakarganj in order to mobilise them to enhance the power of the Hindu

[36] *Hindustan Standard*, 8 June 1939, 18 January 1942; that all the Scheduled Caste organisations and their leaders had become Calcutta based is indicated by the numerous notices of meetings of these organisations published in the two Calcutta dailies, the *Amrita Bazar Patrika* and the *Hindustan Standard* between 1937 and 1945.

[37] See for example, *Hindustan Standard*, 28 June, 29 June, 30 July, 17 September, 22 November 1938, 14 January, 15 February, 9 July 1939, 2 May 1940, 11 March, 26 April 1942; *Amrita Bazar Patrika*, 20 April, 17 September 1938, 29 August 1939, 13 March, 26 March 1940, 19 March, 6 May, 14 December 1941, 26 April, 28 September 1942.

[38] *Hindustan Standard*, 24 July 1938.

[39] *Amrita Bazar Patrika*, 29 April 1938; *Hindustan Standard*, 21 June 1938.

community.[40] But most crucial in this respect were the endeavours of the All India Hindu Mahasabha which particularly devoted its energy towards the mobilisation of the Scheduled Caste peasantry since 1939-40. By 1944 in eastern Bengal it had started 65 rural branches in the district of Bakarganj, 50 in Dacca, 43 in Faridpur, 29 in Jessore and 31 in Khulna. All these districts were thickly populated by the Namasudras and some of these branches were located in areas known for Namasudra activism in the past.[41] And furthermore, there is evidence to suggest that in these districts some of the local Scheduled Caste leaders were receiving money from the Mahasabha in order 'to organise the Scheduled Caste people',[42] and organisations like the Dacca Namasudra Samiti had become much too keen to maintain cordial relationship with its leader Shyama Prasad Mukherjee.[43]

The impact of such organised efforts to articulate the Hindu identity among the Namasudras could be seen very easily in the communal riots that subsequently broke out between them and the Muslims. There had been a series of riots between the two communities in the past as well; but these were of a more secular character. There were communal frenzy centring around land disputes, protection of women or for the honour of the community - only rarely there was any overt use of religious idioms. And simultaneously with confrontation there was co-operation as well (Bandyopadhyay [1990b]). But the situation began to change since the 1940's, as due to the Hindu Mahasabha influence the Namasudras now began to confront the Muslims not simply as Namasudras (as they did previously) but as Hindus as well.

This new mood became palpably clear after the Dacca

[40] Swami Vedananda, *Sree Sree Jugacharya Jiban Charit*, Bharat Sebashram Sangha, (Calcutta, 1398 B.S.), pp.355, 379-386.

[41] Hindu Mahasabha Papers, File No. P-32, 1944, NMML.

[42] Shyama Prasad Mukherjee to U. N. Edbar, 13 October 1944, Shyama Prosad Mukherjee Papers, II-IV Instalment, Subject File No. 90, NMML.

[43] Mohan Lal Mandal, President, Dacca Namasudra Samity, to Shyama Prosad Mukherjee, 29 June 1946, Shyama Prosad Mukherjee Papers, II-IV Instalment, Correspondence, Serial No. 849, NMML

riot of 18-21 March 1941, as the new high pitch temper of politicised communalism affected the Namasudras as well. Simultaneously with the Dacca riot, another riot broke out in Khulna on 20 March 1941 in which 'one Namasudra Hindu village and one Moslem village [were] burnt to the ground'.[44] Nothing more is known about this riot; but its timing perhaps suggests that it was not caused by any land dispute or quarrel over cattle. It was from this time that the Hindu Mahasabha volunteers started working in this area and the result was that in June 1944 the Namasudra and Muslim mobs in Bagerhat in the district of Khulna were openly confronting each other with such highly politicised communal slogans as '*Hindu sakti ki joy*' [Victory to Hindu power], '*Shyama Prasad jindabad*' [Long live Shyama Prasad] and, on the other hand, '*Muslim sakti ki joy*' [Victory to Muslim power] and '*Shyama Prasad dhansa houk*' [Let Shyama Prasad be destroyed]. The local officers in Khulna had good reasons to believe that these ill feelings in the area had been 'instigated by the organisers of the Hindu Mahasabha'.[45]

By 1946-47 the Namasudra peasants in eastern Bengal were definitely more conscious of their Hindu identity and were sufficiently vocal in their support for the Hindu Mahasabha demand for a separate homeland for the Bengali Hindus. At different villages in the interior of the districts of Bakarganj, Faridpur and Khulna, the Namasudra peasants in overwhelming numbers participated in meetings held to demand the incorporation of the Hindu majority areas of these districts into the new province of West Bengal which would be a part of the Indian Union.[46] And this was the sentiment shared also by their leaders, except Jogendranath Mandal, who supported the 'sovereign united Bengal' proposal of

[44] Telegram from Governor of Bengal to Viceroy, 20 March 1941, GI, Home (Political), File No.5/25/41-Poll(I), NAI.

[45] 'Report of the Commissionar, Presidency Division on allegations against the conduct of the Police and local officers in connection with the communal riots in Mollahat P.S. on 26 May 1944 and subsequently', GB, Home (Political) Confidential File No. 272/44, WBSA.

[46] For details of these meetings, see AICC Papers, File No. CL-14(B), 1946, NMML; GI, Reforms Office, File No. 41/3/47-R, Part III, NAI.

Sarat Bose and the Abul Hashim- Suhrawardy group of the Bengal Muslim League . When the partition issue was put to vote in the Bengal Assembly, all but four Scheduled Caste MLAs voted for the Congress-Mahasabha scheme to keep West Bengal as a Hindu majority province within the larger political unit of India (Gordon [1989], pp.581-582, 586). But the partition ultimately did not help the Namasudras, as they lost their territorial anchorage. Contrary to their hopes and in spite of their pleas, the entire area which we earlier identified as their principal inhabitation zone went to East Pakistan and not to West Bengal. And the post-partition violence, as F.C.Bourne, the last British Governor of East Bengal reported in 1950, left many of them with 'nothing beyond their lives and the clothes they stand up in.'[47]

But there was also another level of integration for the Namasudra peasantry of eastern Bengal. The same people who responded positively to Hinduisation, also participated in the more class-oriented movements. We have already mentioned how the Krishak Praja Party had mobilised them in the 1930's and why it subsequently abandoned them in 1937. At this juncture, the Bengal Provincial Kisan Sabha, founded in March 1937, tried to harness the protesting spirit of the lower caste peasantry in Bengal. Even though in 1938-39 it had only 50,000 members all over the province (Sen[1982], pp.75-78), it was from mid-1937 that 'Krishak Samitis on Communistic lines' began to be formed in districts like Khulna, Faridpur and Bakarganj, where the Namasudras constituted the majority among the Hindu peasants.[48] Such Communist efforts at 'cultivating the Kisans'[49] increased after the Bengal Provincial Krishak conference was held at Rangpur on 28-29 June 1942 and the ban on the Communist Party was lifted in July.[50]

---

[47] Note by Governor of East Bengal to Nurul Amin, Prime Minister of East Bengal, 24 February 1950, Bourne Papers, MSS.Eur.E.364, India Office Library.

[48] 'Fortnightly Report on the political situation in Bengal for the first half and second half of March 1937, GI, Home (Political), File No. 18/5/1937-Poll, NAI.

[49] GI, Home(Political), File No.7/5/42-Poll(I), NAI.

[50] GI, Home (Political), File No. 7/15/42-Poll(I), File No. 177/42-Poll(I), NAI.

The outcome of such mobilising efforts could be seen at the time of the Tebhaga movement in 1947, as the main participants in this movement in eastern Bengal came from among the Namasudra sharecroppers of Faridpur, Khulna and Jessore. In some of these areas, however, the attention of the agitators were from time to time deflected, sometimes because of outside machinations, towards their traditional rivalry with the Muslim neighbours and this no doubt weakened the movement (Cooper [1988], pp.225-26, 253, 256-57, 260). But this phenomenon also indicates that their loyalties to 'class' 'religion' and 'caste' had remained juxtaposed; none could displace the others, nor did these identities ever converge. On the other hand, the traditional caste leaders of the Namasudras did never even bother about this sharecroppers' struggle and remained aloof, if not directly hostile like their Rajbansi counterparts in north Bengal. This shows that the process of divergence in the Namasudra movement had already set in and that their 'community' identity, constructed so carefully in the nineteenth and the early twentieth centuries, was being dissolved, reshaped and redefined.

For the Namasudras of Bengal, to put it in general terms, their caste identity coexisted with the broader national, class and religious identities. At times one might precede over the others; but this did not mean that the other competing identities were completely displaced. Their notions of community were neither wholly autonomous nor absolutely static and its boundaries were continually redrawn as they were exposed to various ideological influences and organisational mediation.

VII

This particular case study of the Namasudra movement in Bengal between 1872 and 1947 shows that such movements did not remain homogeneous all along, as in them at different points in time we may detect various levels of consciousness, different sets of goals and also varied forms of action, but all compressed into one. Thus while the masses remained concerned with their perceived threats to community honour, resentment against social disabilities and protest against economic exploitation, the relatively more advanced section within the same group cared more for ritual symbols and looked for institutional concessions. Both the sections in their own ways thought of reworking the power relations in indigenous society. The relation between them was therefore symbiotic, as both perhaps felt the same need, consciously or otherwise, to subvert the hegemonic ritual order. But this symbiosis did not mean that all possibilities of conflict or disjunction were permanently eliminated.

On the contrary, at a later stage, particularly in the 1930's, when the colonial government began to patronise such lower caste movements in order to legitimise India's colonial connection, all sorts of realignments began to take shape. Some of their leaders found it more convenient to be integrated into the more dominant political structure, i.e., the Congress. This was also to some extent inevitable, as the political goal of these leaders was not ultimately to separate themselves from the larger community, but rather to ensure for themselves a position of power within the political nation, which for all practical purposes Congress had come to represent by the beginning of the 1940's. The Congress also recognised their power within the institutionalised political arena, as defined by the constitutional arrangement of 1935, and this further facilitated the integration. The masses, on the other hand, also carried on their unfinished battles for social and economic rights, sometimes through the traditional forums of their caste based community; but it was no longer considered to be the only source of power. So sometimes they were in alliance with the nationalists, sometimes with the Hindu communalists and in some cases were also organised around more directly class based programmes and organisations. In other words, the movement which had once started as a 'lower caste movement' began subsequently to move in different directions as various other identities that cut across or encompassed the caste identity were in the process of formation or articulation. It is these complexities, rather than the assumed homogeneity and unilinear progress of such movements which are required to be probed into. And such probings alone can answer the all important question why these lower caste protests failed to alter the dominant power structure in India, except only in some areas or to a very limited extent

References

Badoi Biswas,S. 1911 *Namasudra Dwijatattva*, (in Bengali), Barisal.

Bailey,F.G. 1958. *Caste and Economic Frontier*, Delhi.

Bandyopadhyay,S. 1989. 'Social Protest or Politics of Backwardness? The Namasudra Movement in Bengal, 1872-1911', in Basudeb Chattopadhyay, H.S.Vasudevan and Rajat K.Ray (eds), *Dissent and Consensus: Social Protest in Pre-Industrial Societies*, Calcutta.

Bandyopadhyay,S. 1990a. *Caste, Politics and the Raj: Bengal 1872-1937*, Calcutta.

Bandyopadhyay,S. 1990b. 'Community Formation and Communal Conflict: Namasudra-Muslim Riot in Jessore-Khulna', *Economic and Political Weekly*, 17 November.

Barman,U. 1985. *Uttar Banglar Sekal O Amar Jibansmriti*, (in Bengali), Jalpaiguri, 1392 BS.

Basak,G.C. 1911. *Bangiya Jatimala*, (in Bengali), Second edition, Dacca, 1318 BS.

Beveridge,H. 1876. *The District of Bakarganj: Its History and Statistics*, London.

Biswas,B. 1921. *Kuloddeepan Namahchandrika*, (in Bengali), Barisal, 1328 BS.

Biswas,R. 1921. *Jatiya Jagaran*, (in Bengali), Calcutta.

Biswas,S. 1931. *Jatitattva O Namasyakulodarpan*, (in Bengali), Dacca.

Bose,N.K. 1975. *The Structure of Hindu Society*, translated from Bengali by Andre Beteille, New Delhi.

Chakraborti,B. 1970. *Samaj Sanskarak Raghunandan*, (in Bengali), Second edition, Calcutta.

Conlon, F. 1981. 'The Census of India as a Source for the Historical Study of Religion and Caste', in N.G.Barrier, (ed.), *The Census in British India: New Perspectives,* New Delhi.

Cooper,A. 1988. *Sharecropping and Sharecroppers' Struggles in Bengal 1930-1950,* Calcutta.

Das,N.C. 1961. *Namasudra Sampraday O Bangladesh,* (in Bengali), Calcutta, 1368 BS.

Gordon,L. 1989. *Brothers Against the Raj: A Biography of Subhas and Sarat Chandra Bose,* New Delhi.

Gough,K. 1963. 'Indian Nationalism and Ethnic Freedom', in David Bidney, (ed.), *The Concept of Freedom in Anthropology,* The Hague.

Haldar,M. 1943. *Sri Sri Guruchand Charit,* (in Bengali), Calcutta.

Haldar,N. 1985. *Srihari Darshan,* (in Bengali), Thakurnagar, 1392 BS.

Haldar,N. 1986. *Matua Dharma-Tattva-Sar,* (in Bengali), Thakurnagar, 1393 BS.

Haldar,P. 1986. *Matua Dharma Darshan,* (in Bengali), Thakurnagar, 1393 BS.

Hardgrave Jr., R.L. 1969. *The Nadars of Tamilnad,* Bombay.

Jasimuddin. 1977. *Murshida Gaan,* (in Bengali), Dacca.

Jha,H. 1977. 'Lower Caste Peasants and Upper Caste Zamindars in Bihar (1921-1925): An Analysis of Sanskritisation and Contradiction between the two Groups', *The Indian Economic and Social History Review,* Vol.XIV, No.4.

Jha,V. 1986-87. 'Candala and the Origin of Untouchability', *The Indian Historical Review,* Vol.XIII, Nos.1-2, July-January.

Khan,M.E.H. 1982. 'A.K.Fazlul Huq and Muslim League in Bengal 1906-1947', Unpublished Ph.D. thesis, Punjab University, Chandigarh.

Mandal,J. 1975. *Mahapran Jogendranath,* (in Bengali), Vol.I, Calcutta, 1382 BS.

Mead,C.S. 1911. *The Namasudras and Other Addresses,* Adelaide.

O'Malley,L.S.S. 1912. *Bengal District Gazetteers, Jessore,* Calcutta.

Palit,H. 1915. *Bangiya Patit Jatir Karmee,* (in Bengali), Calcutta, 1322 BS.

Pandey,G. 1983. 'Rallying Round the Cow: Sectarian Strife in the Bhojpuri Region, c.1888-1917', in R.Guha, (ed.), *Subaltern Studies II,* Delhi.

Ray,K. 1926. 'Jatyabhiman', (in Bengali), *Bangabani,* Vol.V (1st half), No.5, Ashadh 1333 BS.

Ray, N. 1980. *Bangalir Itihas: Adi Parba,* (in Bengali), Third edition, Calcutta.

Ray, R. 1909. *Namasudra Darpan,* (in Bengali), Vol.I, Khulna, 1316 BS.

Ray, R. 1914. *Saral Namasudra Dwijadarpan,* (in Bengali), Khulna, 1321 BS.

Risley,H.H. 1891. *The Tribes and Castes of Bengal,* Vol.I, London, reprint, Calcutta, 1981.

Sanyal, H. 1981. *Social Mobility in Bengal,* Calcutta.

Sarkar,S. 1973. *Swadeshi Movement in Bengal, 1903-8,* New Delhi.

Sarkar,T. 1987. *Bengal 1928-1934: The Politics of Protest,* Delhi.

Sarkar,T.C. 1916. *Sri Sri Harileelamrita,* , (in Bengali), Faridpur 1323 BS.

Sarma,P.1913. *Namasudrachar Chandrika,* (in Bengali), Jessore.

Sen,S. 1982. *Peasant Movements in India: Mid-Nineteenth and Twentieth Century,* Calcutta.

Washbrook,D. 1975. 'The Development of Caste Organisation in South India, 1880 to 1925' in C.J.Baker and D.A.Washbrook, *South India: Political Institutions and Political Change, 1880-1940,* Delhi.

Wise,J. 1883. *Notes on the Races, Castes and Trades of Eastern Bengal,* London.

Zelliot,E. 1973. 'Learning the Use of Political Means: The Mahars of Maharashtra', in R.Kothari, (ed.), *Caste in Indian Politics,* New Delhi.

Zelliot,E. 1988. 'Congress and the Untouchables, 1917-1950', in R.Sisson and S.Wolpert, (eds.), *Congress and Indian Nationalism,* Delhi.

6

A Caste Movement in Mymensingh

RATAN LAL CHAKRABORTY

Caste has become a popular subject of research for modern historians and sociologists who study the problem from many angles. Too often, however, they view caste as a social phenomenon unaffected by political movements. Caste politics have often been narrowed down to the relationship between so-called 'dominant castes' and lower castes, although there is a body of literature dealing with caste mobility in the nineteenth and twentieth centuries against the backdrop of broader socio-religious, political and nationalist movements.[1] This paper examines a caste movement in the district of Mymensingh, now in Bangladesh. The movement is placed in the context of the anti-Partition *Swadeshi* movement of Bengal, which was launched by the high-caste Hindu landlords and *bhodrolok* (gentry) of Bengal who were organised in the Congress Party. What was remarkable about the Mymensingh caste movement was a conciliatory move which resulted in a compromise which was agreeable to both the high-caste Hindu landlords and bhodrolok, and the aspiring low-caste people.

Mymensingh was the largest district of Bengal; it was

[1] For details, see, Sekhar Bandyopadhyay, (1990) *Caste, Politics and the Raj: Bengal, 1872- 1937,* Calcutta K.P. Bagchi & Company; Hitesranjan Sanyal, 'Continuities opf Social Mobility in Traditional and Modern Society of India: Two Case Studies of Caste Mobility in Bengal,' *Journal of Asian Studies,* Vol. XXX, 1971, pp. 315-39; Rajat K. Ray, (1984) *Social Conflict and Political Unrest in Bengal, 1875-1927,* Delhi; Hetukar Jha, 'Lower Caste Peasant and Upper Caste Zamindars in Bihar, 1921-1925: An Analysis of Sanskritization and Contradiction between the Two Groups,' *The Indian Economic and Social History Review,* Vol. XIV, No.4; C.J. Baker and D.A. Washbrook, *South India: Political Institutions and Political Change, 1880-1940,* Delhi, 1975, pp. 176-77; D.L. Sheth, 'Caste and Politics: A Survey of Literature,' in Gopal Krishna (ed.) *Contributions to South Asian Studies,* Delhi: Oxford University Press, 1979, pp.161-97; A.K. Roy, 'Some Notes on the Ksatriya Movement in North Bengal,' *Journal of the Asiatic Society of Bangladesh,* Vol.XX, No.I, April, 1975, pp. 47-71; Sumit Sarkar, 'The Conditions and Nature of Subaltern Militancy: Bengal from Swadeshi to Non-Co-operation, c.1905-1922,' in Ranajit Guha (ed.), *Subaltern Studies,* Vol. III, Delhi: Oxford University Press, 1984, 271-320.

subdivided in big zamindaris (estates) mostly owned by high-caste Hindus. It occupied the highest position in Bengal with regard to the cultivation of jute, which fetched a high price at the time. All the well known Hindu castes of Bengal were represented in Mymensingh. Most zamindars were Brahmans or Kayasthas. There were also many bhadrolok families, especially in Netrokona and Kishoregonj.[2] The district was also well known for its large and turbulent Muslim tenantry and a long history of agrarian unrest.[3]

The lower castes were very numerous in Bengal. Judging by their names, these were originally formed out of local tribes which had been reduced (or compelled) to taking up occupations which the community to which they were subject looked down upon. Sweeping was one such occupation; in Bengal, sweepers belonged chiefly to the castes of Bhuinmalis and Haris. It has been suggested that 'both are of the same stock, a *Kol* or Deltaic tribe of early settlement. The Bhuinmali is found in the north and east of the province, the Hari in the west and centre.'[4]

But we need to investigate this idea about origins put forward by a European writer. This paper examines the claims put forward by the Bhuinmalis themselves concerning their caste status and their struggle to get these recognised during the Swadeshi movement.

The Bhuinmali (or Bhuimali or Bhumali[5]) occupied a low position in the caste hierarchy. Both economically and socially the Bhuinmalis were inferior to other Hindu castes. The

[2] 'The families of so-called *kulin* Kayasthas who accompanied the originals from Kanauj are strongly represented in the Ghoses, Boses, Guhas, Mitras and Dattas of the Tangail sub-division.' F.A. Sachse, *Bengal District Gazetteers: Mymensingh*, Calcutta: Bengal Secretariat Book Depot, 1917, p.39.

[3] John R. McLane, 'The 1905 Partition of Bengal and the New Communalism,' in Alexander Lipski (ed.), *Bengal East and West*, Asian Studies Center, Michigan State University, South Asia Series, Occasional paper No. 13, 1970, pp. 58-60.

[4] Athelstane Bains, *Ethnography: Castes and Tribes*, Strassburg: Verlag Von Karl J. Trubner, 1912, pp. 85-86.

[5] For details of the Bhuinmalis, see Digindra Narayan Bhattacharjee, *Mali Jatir Udbhodhon*, Rangpur, 1320 B.S. and *Mali Jatir Itihas*, Rangpur, 1321 B.S.; U.N. Mukherji, *The Malis of East Bengal*, Calcutta, 1911 (**I.O.L. Tract No. 1080**); Govinda chandra Byseck, *Caste System in Bengal: Its Baneful Effects and Their Remedy*, Mymensingh, 1900. (**I.O.L. Tract no. 902**).

Bhuinmalis of East Bengal were regarded as *chhotolok* (low-caste people) by the upper-caste bhodrolok: they were not allowed the services of *shrotriya* barbers. The origin of this prohibition is obscure. Mymensingh appears to have been the stronghold of the Bhuinmali caste in Bengal. It has been suggested that Bhuinmalis were numerous in those places where the demand for labour in servile positions was high.[6]

In many districts of Bengal, Haris and Bhuinmalis were synonymous. According to H.H. Risley, 'it seems probable that the Bhuinmali of the east are really the Haris of other parts of Bengal disguised under a more big-sounding name.'[7] Local proverbs current in East Bengal support this view.[8] In the Population Censuses (1872-1911), the Bhuinmali and Hari castes were entered under separate headings as 'semi-Hinduised aborigines.' But the Bhuinmalis vehemently protested against this because they considered it ignominious to be classed with the Haris.

The Social Position of the Bhuinmalis

Traditionally Bhuinmalis were village servants who provided menial services to both the Hindu and the Muslim communities. They were employed in cutting brushwood, repairing footpaths, sweeping the outer part of the houses of zamindars, and preparing the *marocha* (area of the marriage ceremony). They performed the duties of *mashalchi* by carrying the torch at Hindu wedding ceremonies. The Brahmans

[6] H.H. Risley, *The Tribes and Castes in Bengal*, Calcutta: Bengal Secretariat Press, 1891, pp. 105-107.

[7] Ibid.

[8] I have interviewed one barber of Barisal district (Mr. Sarat Chandra Shil) about their reasons for boycotting the Bhuimalis. He told me about the connection between Bhuimalis and Haris, citing stories from the *Sastras*. He recited the following *sloka* strophes from his memory, saying that these were well known to Hindus:

'Dom, Chandal, Hari
Tak, Prokiti, Mirigibai
Ei Tin Roger Oisad Nai.'

He had heard from his father that the Mymensingh Zamindars allowed the Bhuimalis to be shaved by the 'Shrotriya napit,' and the repercussions of this decision were felt in his village. The Bhuimalis pleaded for the same status in the local market, and they were then accepted as 'Jalchal.'

and zamindars forced them to live in a servile position, to accept small, less remunerative and sub-human jobs, and to lead a highly restricted social life. Bhuinmali sweepers were never allowed to enter a Hindu house; another maid called *dasi* or *chhokri* was employed to sweep the floors of rooms and passages. Apart from these jobs around the house, Bhuinmalis also provided labour for levelling the *sraddha* ground and for constructing the shed in which the votive offerings were placed. Other important social services included playing music at Hindu weddings and working for many low castes such as the *Chandals*, and even for Muslim peasants, without a sense of dishonour.[9] In fact, they performed all the tasks repudiated by other so-called 'depressed castes' of Bengal.

Bhuinmalis were subject to various forms of discrimination. Traditionally they, like other low castes in rural Hindu society, were obliged to live in separate hamlets outside the area where the other villagers lived.[10] This spatial expression of their low position can still be observed: in some parts of East Bengal the huts of Bhuinmalis are located in the extremity of a village, preferably at the end of a Hindu *para* (neighbourhood) or within a Muslim para. Another example of discrimination was provided by the washermen who would go so far as to wash the clothes of Bhuinmalis but would refuse to bring them to their huts; the Bhuinmalis had to collect their clothes from the washermen's house. Ferrymen (*patni*), on the other hand, could not refuse to take them across. In Tangail, the ferrymen were even obliged to ferry them across rivers free of charge.[11]

---

[9] *The Bangalee* 18 April, 1911.

[10] Athelstane Bains, *Ethnography: Castes and Tribes*, Strassburg: Verlag Von Karl I, Trubner, 1912, pp. 85-86; Ramkrishna Mukherjee, *The Dynamics of a Rural Society: A Study of Economic Structure in Bengal Villages*, Akademie-Verlag: Berlin, 1957, p.111.

[11] 'About fifty years ago there was a difference between the two communities. The zamindar in those days was the supreme court of arbitration. He judged the merits of the case. The fault was found to be on the side of the Patnis and the order was that the Patnis should pay a fine of two thousand rupees to their opponents. The Patnis could not pay such a large sum and it was settled by mutual agreement that the Patnis would not in future charge the Malis anything to ferry them across the rivers.' U.N. Mukherji, *The Malis of East Bengal*. p.2

Although the Bhuinmalis had a low social status, they had Brahmans of their own who were regarded as degraded by the rest of the Hindu community (*potit Brahman*). The Bhuinmalis generally worshipped Krishna and they celebrated all the popular Hindu festivals. They had their own *gurus* who played an important role in their spiritual life. They were greatly attracted by Chaitanya liberalism and could be classed as Boishnobs (Vaisnabs).

In the course of the nineteenth century some Bhuinmalis were able to change their occupation; many became cultivators and some carpenters, smiths, shopkeepers, and watchmen (*chowkidars*).[12] They made strenuous efforts to send some of their children to school; by the beginning of the twentieth century many of them were found to have received English education and some were even employed in Government offices.

The Bhuinmali Movement

Aspirations to have one's communal dignity (*samajik morjada*) acknowledged were by no means uncommon in Bengal. These had nothing to do with claiming a higher ritual rank. In the first decade of the twentieth century, however, a new type of caste consciousness developed among the Bhuinmalis of Mymensingh which did involve a claim to higher ritual rank. This new consciousness developed out of an 'upward economic movement and consequent social differentiation.'[13] Moreover, the decennial censuses inspired the Bhuinmalis, like many other low castes, to claim a higher status in the ritual hierarchy. To them, Sanskritisation provided an opportunity for the entire caste (*jati*) to achieve upward mobility within the existing ritual structure. The high price of jute, which had become widely cultivated in East Bengal, had improved the economic condition of many cultivating Bhuinmalis and this helped them in their struggle to

---

12 U.N. Mukherji, *The Malis of East Bengal*, p.3.

13 L.S.S. O'Malley, *Census of India, 1911, Vol.V: Bengal, Bihar and Orissa and Sikkim Part- I Report*, Calcutta: Bengal Secretariat Book Depot, 1913, p.497.

achieve higher ritual and social rank as well.

The caste movement developed in Mymensingh after 1871 when the first scientific Census was initiated.[14] In the Census of 1901 the Bhuinmali community was entered as 'unclean feeder.' The Bhuinmalis of East Bengal protested against this designation and claimed that it lacked any foundation whatsoever. In their application to the Census Superintendent they argued that most of their community belonged to the Vaisnab sect. They demanded entry in the Census as 'Bhumi-mali' under the surnames of Dass, Bhuia, Hazra, Biswas, Sarkar and Poddar.[15] Similarly, during the Census operations of 1911 the Bhuinmalis of East Bengal claimed the title of 'Bhumi Das.'[16] The nationalist movement and consequent political polarisation by now gave a strong impetus to their demands.[17]

---

[14] The Hoddis obtained the services of 'potit Brahmans' for the performance of the rituals in 1900, but were debarred from the service of barbers and washermen. In 1908 they applied for such social privileges to the Zamindars of Sherpur, paying them the usual 'nazarana' (payment for interview with a superior). During the Census of 1901 the Haliadas of Mymensingh pleaded for the social status of Mahisyas. This was not a movement of only low castes. The Brahmans of the Jugis, Sutradhars and Shahas claimed to be Shrotriya Brahmans and they were accepted as Svarna Brahmans. Similarly, among the Muslims the Kulus and Jolas also applied for the social titles of Bepari and Karikar. Kedernath Majumder, *Mymensingher Bibaran* (Mymensingh, 1904), pp. 24-25. Khagesh Kiran Majumder, "The People of Mymensingh: An Ethnological Review,' *Mymensingher Jiban & Jibika*, Bicentennial Memorial Souvenir, Mymensingh District Board, Mymensingh, 1987, p.26.

[15] The application was signed by the Bhuinmalis of Barabashalia, Sakrail, Parakhi, Shinragi, Bhadra and Kaijuri, Bajitpur, Haridrapur and Ramagopalpur of Mymensingh; Bibandi, Bhagyakul, Lohaganj, Srinagar of Dhaka; Adamdighi of Bogra; Keshabkati of Barisal; Sadarpur of Faridpur; Sialkhol of Pabna; Natore of Rajshahi. *The Bengalee* 8 March, 1911, p.7, c.2.

[16] L.S.S. O'Malley, *Census of India*, 1911, p.443. The Census data give the following information regarding the decline of the Bhuinmalis as a caste.

Bhuinmalis of Mymensingh District, 1901-1921

1901	18,632
1911	15,377
1921	8,068

During the Census operation of 1911 the Bhuinmalis of East Bengal claimed to have the title of Bhumi Das. They took the Census as an opportunity to obliterate caste distinctions. The reliability of the figures is highly questionable because the Bhuinmali caste is often spoken of as 'Mali' in Eastern Bengal. From the large increase in the numbers returned for the true Mali caste, otherwise known as Malakar, it seems probable that, in view of the steep decline suggested by the statistics given above, many Bhuinmalis were entered as Malis in the later censuses. *Census Reports*, 1910-1921; N. Sen Gupta, 'The Census and Caste,' *The Dacca Review*, Vol.I, No.6, September, 1911, p.200.

[17] Jnanbrata Bhattacharyya, 'Examination of Leadership Entry: Bengal Peasant Revolt, 1937-1947,' *Journal of Asian Studies*, Vol.XXXVII, No. 4, August, 1978, p.621.

The Bhuinmali caste movement focussed specifically upon one grievance: the denial by the 'shrotriya napits' (caste barbers) to serve them.[18] The issue throws considerable light on caste relations in East Bengal in general. Barbers had to have a large number of customers in order to earn a good living. Why then did they refuse to shave the Bhuinmalis? Were they under pressure from local high-caste Hindus? Did they fear being excommunicated by their fellow caste members? And why should the Bhuinmalis be so anxious to be served by the barbers? In some similar communities, some members acted as barbers for the rest of their community; why did the Bhuinmalis not adopt the same procedure? And if they longed for a caste barber to work for them, why did they not invite barbers from Bihar or the United Provinces, as was a practice among other low-caste Hindus of Bengal?

Barbers refused to serve Bhuinmalis because they occupied a higher rank in the ritual order (*Navashak*) than the Bhuinmalis. Even if some of them would be tempted to work among the Bhuinmalis, the other Hindus (*beradari*) would threaten to boycott them. Such a boycott meant enormous financial and social loss for the barber because the upper-caste Hindus not only had great control over local society but barbers were also their tenants.[19]

It was for this reason that the Bhuinmalis focussed upon the refusal by the barbers to attack their inferior position: it was a badge of their degradation within the caste system.[20] This was why they were not interested in hiring a barber from elsewhere. They also felt it was a disgrace because they needed the permission of the zamindars to settle an outside barber in their village. In the days of the Swadeshi movement the Bhuinmali demand for the service of caste barbers became prominent. Bhuinmalis tried to obtain favourable religious rulings from complaisant Brahman pundits, the tradi-

[18] Shrotriya means caste status acquired through birth or original caste. *The Bengalee,* 5 December, 1910, p.5.

[19] L.S.S. O'Malley, *Census of India,* 1911, p.440-41.

[20] *The Hitabadi*, 25 Kartick, 1317 B.S.

tional law-givers in Hindu society. Liberal Hindus in Mymensingh did not object to this as long as their own social and economic status remained unaffected, but orthodox Hindus deplored it.[21]

The Bhuinmalis of Mymensingh approached local Brahmans who, against payment of money, were willing to give their consent in writing.[22] Barbers serving Bhuinmalis would not run any risk regarding their position in society, nor would the work degrade them. Armed with these permissions (*vyavashthas*), the Bhuinmalis approached the zamindars who still held considerable authority in the community.[23]

The Bhuinmalis found that the time was right for them. A social reform movement, initiated by different social and religious organisations in Bengal and elsewhere in India, sought to incorporate low castes by giving them a better ritual status in order to stop them abandoning the Hindu faith. The general decline of Hinduism was attributed mostly to the rigidity of caste; Christian missionaries, who had considerable influence among the lower castes in East Bengal, actively exploited this.[24] At this time some social conferences were held in Mymensingh at which local political leaders and social reformers passionately denounced the servile condition of low-caste people.[25] The idea of social reform was seen to receive support from these high-caste Hindus, both local and from other parts of the country, who defended it on both

---

[21] *The Monthly Shourav* (published from Mymensingh), Vol.8 No.9, Jaistha, 1327 B.S., pp. 184-85.

[22] 'So to the Brahmans they went, not emply-handed by any means. The Brahmans gave their *panti* 'permits',-their opinion in writing, that the Napits could serve the Malis without any risk to their position in society or any degradation attending the work. Most of the Brahmans took money for the "opinion".' *The Bengalee*, 4 April, 1911.

[23] *The Bengalee*, 21 October, 1910.

[24] 'The greater impetus for the uplift of the Pariah however, had come from the Hindu's desire to put into operation a policy calculated to counteract the propaganda of the Christian missionary that has been winning the low castes out of the Hindu into the native Christian fold,' *The Bengalee*, 21 October, 1910.

[25] 'It indicates a widespread movement towards freedom on the part of the outcastes all over India as a result of the forces that have been at work during the last fifty years to rouse them out ot their apathy and despair.' *The Bengalee*, 23 October, 1910.

political and religious grounds.

As we have seen, the Bhuinmalis succeeded in obtaining the consent of Brahmans by payment of money. However, Brahmans often lacked practical power to enforce their commands, so their consent had little immediate value. The Bhuinmalis therefore turned to the zamindars who considered it in their interest to support the Bhuinmalis. Pramathanath and Raja Manmatha Nath of Santosh gave their consent and support to the Bhuinmali movement and even Rani Dinamoni, an influential zamindar and a conservative lady, was persuaded, probably by other landlords who anticipated the danger of caste agitation. It was thought that the Bhuinmalis might join in the agrarian unrest then current in Mymensingh.[26]

But the landlords, local politicians and even social reformers (such as Sashibhusan Tarafdar, Monomohan Mitra, Surendranath Roy, Upendranarayan Neogi and Nath Bandhu Guha) did not give their support unconditionally. The zamindars of Tangail demanded four hundred rupees from the Bhuinmalis for making the barbers *kholasa* (open, accessible) to them. It was a long-practised custom to give landlords '*nazarana*' for any interview or benefaction, and they exploited that custom even when granting social recognition.

To support their demand the Bhuinmalis organised a large public meeting in Tangail on 29 March, 1910. But the meeting was cancelled by the police who considered it a Swadeshi activity. The Bhuinmalis then appealed to the Lieutenant-Governor of Eastern Bengal and Assam to prove that their activities were non-political. On 25 October, 1910, the meeting was finally held. At this large gathering in Tangail two barbers came forward to shave Bhuinmalis.[27] Many photographs of the shaving ceremony were taken, telegrammes were sent to the newspapers, and important speeches were delivered by the local high-caste Congress leaders. Every care

[26] *The Bangalee,* 4 April, 1911.
[27] *Amrita Bazar Patrika,* 27 October, 1910.

was taken to show that the landlords and local leaders had command over the entire thing and that it was an expression of their magnanimity to the lower castes of Mymensingh. Caste fellows of the barbers who had attended the meeting, however, threatened within a month to boycott those who had joined hands with the Bhuinmalis. The two barbers who had shaved Bhuinmalis were summoned by members of their caste to renounce their new clientele. Their refusal to do so ultimately led to their excommunication from the caste. At this juncture landlords-cum-local political leaders interfered for political reasons and brought the matter to an end.[28]

The Swadeshi Movement

The Partition of Bengal and the Swadeshi movement which followed it put a strain on relations between Hindus and Muslims in Bengal. James Campbell Ker, a contemporary official, remarked,

> 'When the Partition took place the state of Hindu-Mahomedan feeling in Eastern Bengal, never very cordial, became very bad. The Hindu rightly or wrongly considered that the Mahomedans were taking things with a high hand, while the Mahomedans possibly thought that their improved status enabled them to retaliate for some of the oppression they had suffered at the hands of Hindu landlords and petty officials in the past.'[29]

The caste reform movement was aimed at achieving political gain for the Hindus as a community by increasing its numerical strength and using Hindu votes as a counter-

---

[28] Similar inter-caste rivalry took place in many areas. Looking at the frenzy the Hindoo Patriot commented: "The movement is intended to foster the growth of a feeling of union among the numerous castes which compose Hindu society. But in effect, it is calculated to rouse the sleeping lion of orthodoxy, to set one caste against another and divide, not merely the members of the same caste or sub-section of caste, but even those of the same family. We are afraid that, in this sense, the movement will not hasten, but rather retard, real reform and progress.' *The Hindoo Patriot,* 7 October, 1912, p.5.

'The unmerited severity inflicted by the high caste Hindus upon the low castes besides keeping the latter in a socially, intellectually, morally, and materially depressed state, is responsible for inherently weaking the body politic of the whole land.' *The Bengalee,* 21 October, 1910.

[29] James Campbell Ker, *Political Trouble in India, 1907-1917,* Calcutta: Superintendent Government Printing, 1917, pp. 8-9.

weight to the Muslim vote.[30] The Hindu zamindars and high-caste local political leaders suddenly needed the low castes; they assumed the role of social reformers out of political interest. They tried to accommodate the demands of the lower castes in return for their political support.

Growing Antagonism between Hindus and Muslims

Although the Bhuinmali movement focussed on religious issues, it was more than a religious movement. It should be realised that the Bhuinmali movement took place in a largely Muslim society. About two-thirds of the total population of Mymensingh were Muslims; no less than 90 percent of these were illiterate and made a living as tenants and servants. Most Hindus were educated people who drew their income from landed property or were engaged in other non-agricultural pursuits. The Muslim *ryots* (tenants) held land under Hindu zamindars. The Tenancy Act had improved the position of the ryots and this had strained relations between between them and their landlords who now found it more difficult to enhance and realise rents.[31] The attitude of the high-caste Hindu landlords of Mymensingh towards their tenants is well demonstrated by the writings of a contemporary observer, Nirad C. Chaudhuri who remarked,

> 'our fourth feeling was mixed concern and contempt for the Muslim peasant, whom we saw in the same light as we saw our low-caste Hindu tenants, or, in other words, as our live-stock.'[32]

The Swadeshi movement accentuated the differences between Hindus and Muslims. The Muslim leaders of rural East Bengal, who were *jotedars* (holders of intermediate landed

---

[30] L.S.S. O'Malley, *India's Social Heritage,* Oxford: Clarendon Press, 1934, p.51.

[31] But in official circles it was thought that zamindar interest was best served by the Bengal Tenancy Amendment Bill, 1906. It has been remarked officially: 'Under this Bill substantial benefits are to be conferred on landlords, and they may be apprehensive that these benefits will be withdrawn by Government in case they associate themselves with public movements which may have for their object criticism of Government measure or of Government action.' Government of Bengal, *Legislative Department* , A Proceedings November, 1906, No.1.

[32] Nirad C. Chaudhuri, *The Autobiography of an Unknown Indian*. Bombay, Jaico Publishing House, 1988, (First publlished 1951), p. 235.

interests), opposed the anti-Partition Swadeshi movement which was launched by the Hindu zamindars and bhodrolok. The *ulema* (religious teachers) took a leading part in alienating the Muslim tenantry from the Swadeshi movement.[33] Tensions increased, Muslim tenants refused to cultivate lands of high-caste Hindu landlords, and riots occurred.[34] In this situation of increasing agrarian unrest, the Mymensingh zamindars probably considered it wise to improve their relationship with the low-caste Bhuinmalis who were also tenants.

At the same time, however, the local Muslim landlords and leaders were courting the Bhuinmalis. They expressed their sympathy with the movement. Muslim landlords encouraged their low-caste Hindu tenants against the Swadeshi movement. Large numbers of Muslims attended every Bhuinmali meeting and Muslim leaders would speak in glowing terms against their degraded condition. They would contrast the humiliating position of the Bhuinmalis with their own dignified position in society, and they would promise that 'if they, the Malis, would join them, then their demand would be fulfilled.'[35] The Muslims also encouraged the Bhuinmalis by promising to bring about changes if they would embrace Islam.[36]

---

[33] Taj ul-Islam Hashmi, *Peasant and Politics in Eastern Bengal*, 1920-1947, Unpublished Ph.D. Thesis, University of Western Australia, 1986.

[34] The Hindu zamindars of Iswarganj intimidated their Muslim tenants into cooperation in the Swadeshi movement. From early 1906 onwards the mentality of paying lower rates of rent became dominant among the small agriculturists of Mymensingh, while the Muslim tenants declined to cultivate the lands of the high-caste Hindu landlords. The outbreak of rioting connected with the Swadeshi movement was related to the agrarian conditions and the Cadastral Survey arranged by the authorities, under the charge of Abdul Momen in 1907-08. *Charu Mihir*, 23 January, 26 & 27 February, 1906; F.A. Sachse, *Final Report on the Survey and Settlement Operations in the District of Mymensingh*, 1908-1919, Calcutta: The Bengal Secretariat Book Depot, 1920, Appendix, p.1.

[35] A well-known zamindar of East Bengal sent word to a leader of the Malis that, if they would give up the 'Babus' and the 'Swadeshis,' he would see to it that they got their Napits (barbers). U.N. Mukherji, *The Malis of East Bengal*,p. 13.

[36] 'The Mahomedans have dangled many tempting baits before them, and have promised to do much for the Malis, if only the Malis would embrace Islam, But the Malis have refused to quit their ancient fold. The have everything to gain from the Mahommedans and nothing to lose. Hinduism, so far as can be judged, has nothing to give them, and only delights in heaping additional burdens upon them; and yet the Malis are staunch. There is something noble, something heroic, something infinitely touching in this resolution of theirs.' *Ibid.*, p.18.

The Partition of Bengal (1905) therefore brought about a new polarisation in agrarian relations in Mymensingh. The district became a stronghold of the Swadeshi movement and the question of boycotting foreign goods assumed a different character here with the growing antagonism between Hindus and Muslims.[37] There occurred serious riots in many places in Mymensingh. The leaders of the Swadeshi movement (mostly high-caste Hindus of the petty zamindar class) tried to exert pressure on their tenants to participate in the Swadeshi movement. The bulk of these tenants were, however, Muslims. Between these two groups stood a powerful body of Muslim jotedars who had a remarkable influence on the Muslim tenantry, as Rajat and Ratna Ray have remarked correctly:

> 'The social peculiarity of East Bengal which fed the growing political conflict in the province was that the zamindars and *taluqdars* in the area were mostly high caste Hindus, while the large *jotedars* under them were almost invariably Muslims of peasant stock.'[38]

From 1907 onwards large-scale communal disturbances broke out in many areas of Mymensingh. These effectively destroyed the basis of the Swadeshi movement there, as Muslim jotedars tried to win over low-caste Hindus in their fight to capture power in the Union and Local Boards which had so long been monopolised by high-caste Hindus.[39] Sekhar Bandyopadhyay has shown that aggrieved backward castes sometimes did join with the Muslims against high-caste Hindus.[40]

---

[37] *Fortnightly Report on Native Papers in Bengal,* 27 April, 1907 *Dhaka Prokash,* Weekly, 15 *Baishakh-7 Asvin,* 1314; *Unofficial Commission of Enquiry into the Mymensingh Disturbances, Report and Evidence,* Calcutta, 1908, India Office Library and Records, Tracts No. 1098(a); Sumit Sarkar, *The Swadeshi Movement in Bengal,* New Delhi: People's Publishing House, 1973, pp. 393-98.

[38] Rajat and Ratna Ray, 'Zamindars and Jotedars: A Study of Rural Politics in Bengal.' *Modern Asian Studies* Vol .9, No.1, 1975, p.101.

[39] *Bengal Legislative Council Proceedings,* 24 November, 1921, Speech of Ekramul Haq.

[40] Sekhar Bandyopadhyay, 'Protest and Accommodation: Two Caste Movements in Eastern and Northern Bengal, c. 1872-1937', *The Indian Historical Review,* Vol.XIV, Nos. 1-2, p.228: L.S.S. O'Malley, *India's Social Heritage,* Oxford: Clarendon Press, 1934, p.46.

But there was a third party courting the Bhuinmalis. Christian missionaries had been fairly successful in converting low-caste Hindus to Christianity. In *A Dying Race*, U.N.Mukherjee argued that conversion to Christianity and Islam was partly responsible for smaller numbers of Hindus. The Hindu drive to accommodate the Bhuinmalis had much to do with this perceived danger.[41]

Conclusion

On the crest of the economic improvement brought about by jute cultivation, and in response to the new thinking about caste resulting from the population censuses, the Bhuinmalis of Mymensingh first pursued the strategy of sanskritization as a means of getting a higher caste rank. They used the traditional power and legitimacy of Brahmans to achieve their end, but it soon became clear that the authority of the Brahmans among the Mymensingh Hindus had declined and continued to do so during the Swadeshi movement.[42] The Bhuinmalis then considered other options. They did not form a caste association of their own, probably because their numbers were too small and they lacked a strong charismatic leader. Unable to sustain a movement all on their own, they used their numbers to persuade the high-caste Hindus to support their claims. In this they were successful, and the demands of the Mymensingh Bhuinmalis came to be projected under the leadership of high-caste Hindu politi-

41 U.N. Mukherji was elected vice-Chairman of the Bengal Provincial Congress, while Surendra Nath Roy and Anath Bandhu Guha - who was a very influential members of the Mymensingh Bar Council, were elected members of the Executive Council of the Bengal Provincial Congress. It is worthy of note that all of them were associated with the drive to accommodate the Bhuinmalis in the existing Hindu Society. Later U.N. Mukherji, Surendra Nath Roy, Anath Bandhu Guha, Surya Kanta Some, Akhilbandhu Guha became members of the Reception Committee of the Conference of the Bengal Provincial Congress in 1911. Upendra Narayan Neogi went a step further by emphasising the need of the entry of depressed classes as Hindus in the Census in order to strengthen the voting power in the local bodies. *The Bengalee*, 3 March, 1911, p.5 and 7 March, 1911, p.5.

42 For details, see Surendra Munshi, 'Tribal Absorption and Sanskritisation in Hindu Society,' *Contributions to Indian Sociology*, Vol. 13 No. 2, 1979, pp 293-315; U.N. Mukherji, *The Malis of East Bengal*, p.9.

cians. These politicians in turn used the Bhuinmalis to prop up their own entrenched position at the apex of local society. This was particularly urgent because the proposed constitutional reforms threatened this position unless sufficient numbers of votes could be harnessed to their cause. This was the background of the unlikely alliance between these castes at opposite ends of the ritual hierarchy in Mymensingh during the Swadeshi period.

7

The Invention of the 'Jummas': State Formation and Ethnicity in Southeastern Bangladesh*

WILLEM VAN SCHENDEL

This paper deals with socio-cultural innovation in the hills of southeastern Bangladesh. Outsiders have always been struck by the ethnic diversity of this area. The literature —written mainly by British civil servants, Bengali men of letters, and European anthropologists — presents a picture of twelve distinct 'tribes', all practising swidden or shifting agriculture, locally known as *jhum* cultivation.[1] In addition, there are Bengali immigrants who do not engage in swidden cultivation.

In the following pages I shall review the evidence on the persistence of these groups and I shall argue that the prevalent view is too static and fragmented; it should be replaced by a more integrated approach to social structure and process in the hills. The need for such a new approach is especially clear if we look at long-term process; I shall reconstruct ethnic persistence

* This article first appeared in *Modern Asian Studies*, 26:1(1992), pp.95-128. It is reprinted by permission.

[1] These groups, with rough estimates of their numbers in 1981, are Chakma (260,000), Marma (120,000), Tippera (40,000), Tongchengya (25,000), Mru (22,000), Mrung/Riang (10,000), Bawm (7,000), Khumi (3,000), Sak (2,000), Pangkhua (2,000), Khyang (1,500) and Lushai (500). In 1951 there were 26,000 Bengalis in the Chittagong Hill Tracts (or 10% of the total population, up from 2,5% in August 1947), by 1981 about 260,000 (35% of the total population). Recent reports assert that Bengalis now make up about 45% of the population. For an older but most detailed count by mother tongue and religion, see Census of India, 1931.

Bedrohte Zukunft: Bergvölker in Bangladesh (Zurich: Völkerkundemuseum der Universität Zürich IWGIA-Lokalgruppe Zürich, 1988), 13; Pierre Bessaignet, *Tribesmen of the Chittagong Hill Tracts* (Dacca: Asiatic Society of Pakistan, 1958), 4; P.B. Chakma, 'Chittagong Hill Tracts and its Development', *Bangladesh Journal of Buddhist Studies*, 3:1 (May 1986), 45-46; 'Fresh Influx in Tripura', *Times of India* (June 23,1989); 15. *Census of India, 1931-Volume V; Bengal & Sikkim, Part II, Tables* (by A.E. Porter) (Calcutta: Central Publication Branch, 1933), 194, 197.

and innovation on the basis of documentation covering the last 200 years. This brings together travellers' accounts, colonial records, anthropological monographs, government publications, statements by a political party, writings by human rights activists, and press reports. Although this is important in its own right (information is scattered and needs to be synthesized), it can also be seen as a small contribution to the integration of anthropological and historical insights. What interests me particularly is the relation between local and regional patterns of change, a theme much broader than the present inquiry.

In this paper I use ethnic identity more as a socio-cultural than as a psycho-cultural concept.[2] My interest is in exploring how the self-perception of groups is related to their social position. What is the relationship between changing social circumstances and the emergence of a new group identity? To what extent does a new identity emerge as a spontaneous response to changing external circumstances and to what extent is it created by a conscious effort? What is the system of symbols and interpretations on which an emerging group identity rests? These are the principal questions which I address.

The hill area of southeastern Bangladesh is today known as the Chittagong Hill Tracts, subdivided in three districts.[3] It forms part of a mountain range which stretches north for some 1800 km from western Burma to the point where it meets the eastern Himalayas in China. Apart from the narrow strip (roughly 280 by 60 km) now administered from Dhaka, and the Chinese-administered northern tip, this mountain range is divided almost equally between India and Burma. It is inhabited by a bewildering variety of people speaking a wide range of languages, adhering to various creeds, and organized socially in different ways. Anthropological researchers have established that the Chittagong Hills are the home of people belonging to twelve groups, although there

[2] Cf. Anya Peterson Royce, *Ethnic Identity: Strategies of Diversity* (Bloomington: Indiana University Press, 1982), 17-33.

[3] For over 120 years it was administered as the Chittagong Hill Tracts District; in 1983 this district was split into the Khagrachari Hill District, the Rangamati Hill District, and the Bandarban Hill District.

are fewer languages and fewer religions. These groups had never developed a particular sense of unity; Lewin reported that 'none of them appear to have any general term for all hill dwellers'.[4] It was only after colonial annexation in 1860 that this section of the mountain range began to take on a separate identity; neighbouring parts of the range were colonized at different points in time and were administered separately. In 1947 British rule came to an end; during the Partition that split British India, the Chittagong hills were awarded to Pakistan. When Bangladesh seceded from Pakistan in 1971, the Chittagong hills became part of the new country. The hills now have a little over half a million inhabitants, less than one percent of the total population of Bangladesh. In addition, tens of thousands of people from this area are said to be living in refugee camps in the neighbouring Indian state of Tripura. Among the population of the Chittagong hills, in-migration has made the Bengali population the fastest-growing in recent years.

1. *Ethnic Identities before British Rule*

Documentation on the Chittagong hills is fairly rich from the late eighteenth century onwards. Before that time, there are scattered references to life in the hills, mostly in relation to events on the coastal plain. For centuries this plain was a battleground between three centres of power that sought to expand their spheres of influence. Arakan to the south, Tripura to the north, and Bengal to the northwest held the plain in turn. From the sixteenth century onwards they had to contend with newcomers, notably Portuguese traders and pirates, Burmese state agents and Mughal emissaries; the expansionism of these newcomers led to an increasingly confused interplay of alliances and counter-alliances. When the Mughals were defeated by the British in the mid-eighteenth century the Chittagong plain passed into the British

[4] T.H. Lewin, *Wild Races of the Eastern Frontier of India* (Delhi: Mittal Publications, 1984 [originally published in 1870]), 73.

sphere of influence, but British hegemony continued to be contested by the Burmese till the early nineteenth century.

References to the adjacent hills, which were beyond any formal state administration till 1860, usually crop up in connection with political refugees from Burmese or British territory seeking shelter there, or in connection with the cotton trade which increasingly had taken on the shape of state tribute during the Mughal period.[5] The earliest detailed travel account dates from the 1790s. Surprisingly, this extensive and important manuscript by Francis Buchanan has been ignored by historians of the region; it provides unique insights into ethnic identities in the hills.[6]

During his trip Buchanan interviewed people and asked them about their own 'nation' or 'tribe' as well as about others in the hills. The groups which he came across were the Marma (Marama[7]), the Chakma (Saksa[8]), the Mru (Moroo-sa[9]), the

---

[5] In the precolonial period both raw cotton and hill textiles were exported from the port of Chittagong. Suniti Bhushan Qanungo, *A History of Chittagong, Volume One (From Ancient Times Down to 1761)* (Chittagong: Signet Library, 1988), 615. Cf. A.M. Serajuddin, 'The Origin of the Rajas of the Chittagong Hill Tracts and their Relations with the Mughuls and the East India Company in the Eighteenth Century', *Journal of the Pakistan Historical Society*, 19:1 (January 1971), 51-60.

[6] 'An account of a Journey undertaken by Order of the Board of Trade through the Provinces of Chittagong and Tiperah, in order to look out for the places most proper for the cultivation of Spices, by Francis Buchanan, M.D.' (Manuscript (1798), British Library ADD 19286) (hereafter: Buchanan). I am grateful to Richard Eaton for drawing my attention to this manuscript and to Francis Rolt for providing me with a copy.

[7] This group was commonly known as 'Joomea (Mogs)' to the Bengalis of the plain, but their leader Kaung-la Pru [Kong Hla Phru] explained that 'the proper name of the Joomeas is Ma-ra-ma, and that they have resided in this Country from time immemorial'. (Buchanan, 91)

[8] 'I found that the men, except a few words, understood no other language [than Bengali]. They say that they are the same with the Sak of Roang or Arakan: that originally they came from that country; and that on account of their having lost their native language, and not having properly acquired the Bengalese, they are commonly called in ridicule Doobadse. They call themselves Saksa, which word corrupted has, I suppose, given rise to their Bengalese name Sagma or Chakma. From the few words of their native language, which they retain, it is evidently a dialect of the Burma, nearly the same with that of Arakan. Their religion is that of Godama, corrupted by their having adopted many Braminical superstitions, and especially bloody sacrifices to the Devtas.' (*ibid.*, 114)

'A priest, who assumed the name of Poun-do-gye or Great royal virtue, informed me, that the Chakmas have in general forgot the Roang language: but that it is the dialect spoken by the Sak-mee, who still live in Arakan. The books, which this priest has, are written both in the Roang character and dialect.' (*ibid.*, 121)

[9] 'They call themselves Mo-roo-sa..They said they knew no god (Takoor), and that they never prayed to Maha-moony, Ram, nor Khooda...their native tongue has some affinity to that of the Burmas.' (*ibid.*, 67-68. Cf.97).

Bawm (Bon-zu[10]), the Zo (Zou[11]), the Sak (Thaek[12]), the Mrung (Doingnak?[13]), and the Tippera[14], in addition to some Bengalis, Baruas and Arakanese who were neither swidden cultivators nor permanent residents. He described how complex the ethnic situation in the hills was, and how variable ethnic boundaries. There was no question at all of isolated 'tribes' living in distinct territories; on the contrary, there were several 'multi-ethnic' arrangements, e.g villages inhab-

[10] Buchanan was unable to interview Bawm and had only second-hand information on them: 'the Bonjoogies are by the Rakain [=Arakanese] and the Joomeas [=Marma] called Bon-zu..They have a number of slaves, originally prisoners of war: and many Lan-ga have settled among them, and are subject to their Prince.' (*ibid.*, 91, 92).

'The chief of the Bonjoogies, as I am told here, is by the Chakmas called Tai-koup. His subjects are said to be numerous, and to consist of two tribes, the Bon-zu, and Loo-sai. From the head of every family in his dominions Tai-koup receives an annual tribute of one basket of rice, and one piece of cotton cloth'. (*ibid.*, 123).

[11] 'Their language has some affinity to the Burma: but they did not seem to understand the Ma-ra-ma dialect, a proof perhaps of their not having been long dependent on Kaung-la-pru. They name their own tribe Zou. By the Ma-ra-mas they are named Lang-ga, which by the Bengalese is corrupted into Lingta. By the Bengalese they are commonly called Koongky, which we have corrupted into Kooky, or as it is written in the Asiatic Researches Cuci.' (*ibid.*, 98-99). Other 'rude tribes' that Buchanan heard about include Khumi (Hkwe-myi), Shein-du, Hkyaw and Kaung-me. (*ibid.*, 41, 68; cf. 123, 139a).

[12] Again, Buchanan did not meet any Sak personally. He writes about 'a people, whom they [=the Chakma] name Sak, and the Bengalese name Chak. These people are evidently the Thaek of the Burmas.' 'In order to distinguish the Sak settled here, from those called Sak-mee, who still live in Arakan, the [Chakma] priest calls them Moishang Sak.' (*ibid.*, 56, 121).

[13] Buchnan's references to this group, which he could not meet personally, are confusing in the light of later reports. He is evidently talking about the Mrung, a group closely related to the Tippera, but also refers to 'Deinea', apparently a form of the word 'Doingnak', which was later used for a group in Arakan as well as for the Tongchengya of the Chittagong hills who, according to later reports, split off from the Chakmas in 1782 (Lewin, *Wild Races*, 164-165, cf. 182-183). There is not mention of 'Tongchengya' in Buchanan's manuscript. Were 'Doingnak' and 'Mroung' a single group? Or did Buchanan lump two groups together? He was told:

'The Tiperah and the Mroung...dress alike, and speak the same language. From some circumstances in collecting the revenue these Mroungs are frequently called Wa-the Mroo. From some similar circumstance the Mroo proper [Mru] are called Lay Mroo..It is to be observed that both Mroo and Mroung are by the Bengalese called Moroong. To distinguish the last mentioned tribe from the Mroo they are often called Deinea Moroong'. (Buchanan, 78, 79; cf. 81).

[The Marma leader Kaung-la Pru said that] 'the Mroung and Tiperah dress in the same manner, and speak Dialects of the same language, having to each other as great an affinity as the Burmas and the Rakain [=Arakanese] have.' (*ibid.*, 91) 'The Mroung wear their hair tied in a knot on the nape of the neck, by which they may easily be distinguished from the Mo-roo [Mru], who wear their knot of hair on the forehead.' (*ibid.*, 70; cf. 68, 75).

[14] 'The tribe named Tiperah, Tipperah, or Teura.' The Dewan, or Minister, of the Tippera Raja told him, 'that the Tiperah, Reang, and Alynagur, are of the same nation, and speak dialects of the same language. The different names arise from the places they inhabit.' (*ibid.*, 35, 164).

ited by swidden cultivators belonging to different language groups;[15] villages that were 'ethnically stratified', being inhabited by an ethnic group together with its debt peons from different groups;[16] and villages where the leaders had servants from several other groups.[17] Moreover, 'chiefs' often collected tribute from households belonging to an amalgam of ethnic groups.[18] And all groups were continually on the move, not only because of their style of agriculture but also because of raids and warfare.

What is remarkable about Buchanan's account is that he makes an effort to understand ethnic identities from 'within', from the viewpoint of the people concerned. This concern for an 'emic' perspective contrasts with his contemporaries and many later writers who content themselves with describing the people of the Chittagong hills in terms of the ethnic categories used by their Bengali neighbours. Thus Macrae makes a distinction between 'Choomeas', 'Mugs' and 'Kookies or Lunctas'.[19] Lewin, writing seventy years later, explains that Bengalis distinguish two classes: friendly tribes near the Chittagong plain, referred to as 'Joomas', and all others, referred to as 'Kookies', especially if they are unable

---

[15] E.g. Marma and Sak, Marma and Bawm, Mru and Arkanese. *Ibid.*, 62, 67, 90, 104.

[16] E.g. Chakma keeping Tippera debt peons, and Bawm keeping Lang-ga debt peons/prisoners of war. *Ibid.*, 98, 115.

[17] The Marma leader Kaung-la Pru had: 'about twenty Hindoo Servants, and still more Mohammedans, his Dewan or Minister being of that Religion. the domestic who takes care of his table is a Rajbunjee [=Barua, a Buddhist Bengali].' Even a minor Marma chief entitled Umpry Palong had two Bengali servants. Taubboka [Tabar Khan], the Chakma leader, also had Bengali servants, and a Tippera boy was reported to serve a Chakma monk. (*Ibid.*, 63, 93, 120, 122).

[18] Kaung-la Pru, the Po-mang-gre ('Great Captain') of the Marma, ruled over Marma, Mru, Mroung, Tipera and Lang-ga subjects who paid him tribute. (*Ibid.*, 34-35, 39, 67-68, 70, 75 (insert), 81, 98, 101) The minor Marma chief 'Umpry Palong' received tribute from Marma and Bawm. (90)

Taubboka [Tabar Khan], the Chakma *Mang* (which Buchanan translates in English with 'Prince' and in Bengali with 'Raja' - and renders in Burmese script as *min* (= '*min*, ruler), had Chakma, Koongky and Bengali subjects in the Chittagong hills; he was also a zamindar in parts of the Rangunia region in the plains, where he had his main residence and received tribute from Bengali and Barua subjects (108-109, 120-121, 142-143, 144-145). The *Ta-kang* ('Prince': also Mang or Raja) of the Bawm received tribute from Bawm, Lushai and Langga, (69, 90-92, 123, 136-137)

[19] John Macrae, 'Account of the Kookies or Lunctas', *Asiatick Researches*, 8:5 (1801), 184. Cf. John Rawlins, 'On the Manners, Religion, and Laws of the Cùcì's, or Mountaineers of Tipra', *Asiatick Researches*, 2:12 (1790), 187-193.

to speak Bengali.[20] The term 'Mug' (also frequently spelled 'Magh' or 'Mugh') is another blanket term often used by Bengalis to refer to their eastern neighbours.[21]

2. *Two Views of Ethnic Identities since 1860*

The ethnographic map of the Chittagong hills remains confused well into the twentieth century. Officials such as Lewin (1869, 1870), Hutchinson (1906) and Mills (1927, 1931) produced more or less detailed accounts of the different groups living in the area,[22] and the colonial population cen-

[20] Lewin, *Wild Races*, 73. Forty years later Hutchinson, who described the inhabitants of the Chittagong hills as 'more or less savages', concurred: 'The Bengali of the plain divides the inhabitants into two classes. Those able to understand the vernacular of Bengal are designated as Jumiyas, while the others are distinguished as Kukies.' The 'Kookies', whose ethnic identities long remained a puzzle to British and Bengalis alike, were sometimes subdivided on practical grounds. According to a report of 1862 they, 'are locally known and divided by two general names, as "Mela" (friendly) and "Ghyr Mela" (unfriendly). The former may be roughly said to live to the West of a line drawn North and South from Burkal: the latter live to the East of that line.' R.H. Sneyd Hutchinson, *Eastern Bengal and Assam District Gazetters: Chittagong Hill Tracts* (Allahabad: Pioneer Press, 1909), 14. Government of Bengal, Judicial Department, Political Branch, Proceedings 226-227 (April 1862).

[21] Cf. Francis Buchanan's remark: 'I find, that the appellation of Mug is given by the people of this province [=Bengal] to all the Tribes, and nations, east from Bengal, who as differing from the Hindoos, and Mussulmans, are considered as having no cast, and as therefore being highly contemptible.' (28; cf. 56).

The term also was, and continues to be, used more specifically but confusingly to refer to the following distinct groups: Arakanese (or Rahkain or Rakhine), Marma, and Barua. Sometimes these were distinguished by labels such as 'Jhumia Mughs', 'Roang Mughs', 'Inland Mughs', 'Hill Mughs', and 'Barua Mughs', but these labels were not used consistently. Cf. Lewin and *East Pakistan District Gazetteers*. The derivation of the word is unknown, and various explanations have been put forward — the most fanciful no doubt being Pogson's suggestion that Maghs are Magi, hence Jews. For other conjectures, see Risley, Ghosh, and Bernot.

Lewin, *Wild Races*, 95-96, 302; *East Pakistan District Gazetteers: Chittagong* (Dacca: East Pakistan Government Press, 1970), 114-117. *Captain Pogson's Narrative during a tour to Chateegaon, 1831* (Serampur: Serampore Press, 1831) 70; H.H. Risley, *The Tribes and Castes of Bengal; Ethnographic Glossary* (Calcutta: Firma Mukhopadhyay, 1981 [orig, 1891]), Volume I, 28-29; Jamini Mohan Ghosh, *Magh Raiders in Bengal* (Calcutta, etc.: Bookland, 1960), 17-25, Lucien Bernot, *Les paysans arakanais du Pakistan Oriental: l'histoire, le monde végétal et l'organisation sociale des réfugiés Marma (Mog)* (Paris/The Hague: Mouton, 1967), Volume I, 49-54.

[22] T.H. Lewin, *The Hill Tracts of Chittagong and the Dwellers Therein, with Comparative Vocabularies of the Hill Dialects* (Calcutta: Bengal Printing Company, Ltd., 1869); *Wild Races*; R.H. Sneyd Hutchinson, *An Account of the Chittagong Hill Tracts* (Calcutta: Bengal Secretariat Book Depot, 1906); J.P. Mills, 'Report on the Chiefs of the Chittagong Hill Tracts' and 'Proposals Regarding the Chiefs' (typescripts, 1927); J.P. Mills, 'Notes on a Tour in the Chittagong Hill Tracts in 1926', in *Census of India 1931, Volume V: Bengal & Sikkim*, Appendix II, 514-521.

See also the travel account by Emil Riebeck, *Die Hügelstämme von Chittagong: Ergebnisse einer Reise im Jahre 1882* (Berlin, 1885).

suses attempted to clarify the statistical picture, but it is only with the arrival of professional anthropologists in the 1950s that the 'emic' perspective first hinted at by Buchanan reasserts itself strongly. Important insights resulted from studies by a group of German anthropologists (Löffler, Spielmann, A. Mey, and W. Mey[23]); these studies, begun in the mid-1950s, came to an abrupt end in 1971 when the hills were sealed off.[24] Other studies from this period were done by Lévi-Strauss, Bessaignet, D. and L. Bernot, and Sopher.[25] The latest addition is Rosén-Hockersmith's study of the Barua community, living on the border of the hill region.[26] It is unfortunate that many of these studies have been published only in European languages that are little understood in the region — German, French, and Swedish. On the other hand, Bangladeshi scholars have done relatively little work on the Chittagong hills.[27] It should be realized that the Bangladesh universities lacked departments of anthropology, and that professional anthropologists were

---

[23] E.g Lorenz G. Löffler, 'Chakma and Sak: Ethnolinguistische Beiträge zur Geschichte eines Kulturvolkes', *Internationales Archiv der Ethnographie*, 50, (1964), 72-115; Lorenz G. Löffler, 'L' alliance asymétrique chez les Mru (Pakistan oriental)', *L'Homme* 6.3 (1966), 68-80; Claus-Dieter Brauns and Lorenz G. Löffler, *Mru: Bergbewohner im Grenzgebiet von Bangladesh* (Basel/Stuttgart: Birkhauser, 1986); Hans-Jurgen Spielmann, *Die Bawm-Zo; eine Chin Gruppe in den Chittagong Hill Tracts (Ostpakistan)* (Heidelberg: Südasien-Institut, 1968); Almut Mey, *Untersuchungen zur Wirtschaft in den Chittagong Hill Tracts (Bangladesh)* (Bremen: Uebersee-Museum, 1979); Wolfgang Mey, *Politische Systeme in den Chittagong Hill Tracts, Bangla Desh* (Bremen: Uebersee-Museum, 1980).

[24] The special status of the Chittagong hills was abolished in 1964 and the hills were officially closed to outsiders in that year but some anthropological research could be carried on till 1971. See Brauns and Löffler, Introduction.

[25] Claude Lévi-Strauss, 'Le syncrétisme religieux dans un village mog du territoire de Chittagong', *Revue de C'Histoire des Religions*, 141:2 (1952), 202-237; Pierre Bessaignet, *Tribesmen of the Chittagong Hill Tracts* (Dacca: Asiatic Society of Pakistan, 1958); Denise Bernot and Lucien Bernot, *Les Khyang des collines de Chittagong (Pakistan oriental): Matériaux pour l'étude linguistique des Chin* (Paris: Mouton, 1958); Lucien Bernot, *Les paysans arakanais*, 2 Volumes; Lucien Bernot, *Les Cak: contribution a l'étude ethnographique d'une population de langue loi* (Paris/The Hague: Mouton, 1967); David E. Sopher, 'Population Dislocation in the Chittagong Hills', *Geographical Review*, 53 (1963), 337-362; David E. Sopher, 'The Swidden/Wet-Rice Transition Zone in the Chittagong Hills', *Annals of the Association of American Geographers*, 54:1 (1964). 107-126.

[26] Eva Rosén-Hockersmit, Buddhismen i Bangladesh: En studie av en minoritetsreligion (Uppsala: Religionshistoriska institutionen vid Uppsala universitet, 1985).

[27] For an overview of anthropological studies, see Mahmud Shah Qureshi (ed.), *Tribal Cultures in Bangladesh* (Rajshahi: Institute of Bangladesh Studies, Rajshahi University, 1984).

rare indeed.[28] Historians too have practically ignored the Chittagong hills, and most of the unpublished records cited in this paper have not been used before.[29]

As a result of these factors, little up-to-date information on the people of the Chittagong hills has been available to the Bengalis living in the plains that form the rest of Bangladesh, and a remarkably stagnant view of the hill people has prevailed among them throughout the twentieth century. This view is composed of various elements. First, there are strong echoes of nineteenth-century European views of non-western peoples, particularly those formalized in classic anthropological assumptions of unilinear social evolutionism from a state of 'savagery' or 'barbarism' to that of 'civilization'.[30] Nineteenth-century British writers on the hill people described them as 'primitives', 'savages', and 'wild hill tribes', and these terms continue to be encountered frequently in contemporary writings in Bangladesh. Second, these ideas are superimposed on ancient South Asian conceptions of a crucial distinction between civilized society and nature. This distinction, expressed by the terms '*grāma*' (village) and '*araṇya*' (forest), implied a complementary but unequal relationship between the inhabitants of these two realms.[31] The combination of these two traditions has led to a dominant Bengali view that assumes the Chittagong hill people to be 'isolated remnants' of some hoary past that have

[28] The first Department of Anthropology was established at Jahangirnagar University in the early 1980s.

[29] Bangladeshi historians who have done work on the 18th century are Serajuddin, Chakraborty and Islam. The most extensive work on the 19th and 20th centuries was done by Wolfgang Mey; he based himself on annual administration reports and published selections of records. See Serajuddin, 'The Origin of the Rajas'; A.M. Serajuddin, 'The Chakma Tribe of Chittagong Hill Tracts in the 18th Century', *Journal of the Royal Asiatic Society of Great Britain and Ireland*, No.1 (1984), 90-98; Ratan Lal Chakraborty, 'Chakma Resistance to Early British Rule', *Bangladesh Historical Studies*, 2 (1977), 133-156; Sirajul Islam, 'Tribal Resistance in Chittagong Hill Tracts (1776-1787)', in: Nishit Ranjan Ray (ed.), *Saga of Freedom* (Delhi: People's Publishing, 1983), 122-129; Wolfgang Mey, *Politische Systeme*, 5.

[30] For example, in 1879 the area beyond the eastern boundary of British India was described as: ' a large area of mountainous and forest land inhabited by tribes who, paying no tribute to, and independent of, the British Government, revel in a state of almost unrestrained barbarism.' (*Administration Report on the Hill Tracts, Northern Arakan for the Year 1877-78*) (Rangoon: Government Press, 1879), 6)

[31] Cf. J.C. Heesterman, *The Inner Conflict of Tradition: Essays in Indian Ritual, Kingship, and Society* (Chicago and London: University of Chicago Press, 1985), 118, 170-171.

preserved their culture unchanged from time immemorial. They are backward and childlike, and therefore need to be protected, educated, and disciplined by those who are more advanced socially. The relationship between Bengalis and hill people is seen as one of guardianship, and Bengalis assume the responsibility to 'uplift' their charges, to bring them into contact with the modern world. This 'mission civilisatrice', akin to the colonialist's 'white man's burden', is nowadays translated in terms of development policies carried out or at least nurtured by the state. This whole attitude of guardianship over 'primitive' people is summed up in the expression 'our tribes' which is commonly used when talking about the hill people. The use of the term 'tribe', an exceedingly vague and confusing term in South Asia (quite apart from the anthropological debate concerning this term[32]), also reflects the idea that all hill people belong to a single category, and that differences between them are of minor consequence. What is underlined is the wide gulf separating 'primitive' tribals from 'civilized' Bengalis, and their presumably unchanged symbiosis.[33] These ideas, which might be termed 'tribalist',[34] are voiced most clearly by Abdus Sattar, a prolific and influential writer on tribal affairs in Bangladesh in the 1970s:

> 'The Shendus, Pankhos, Mrus, Murangs, and Bonjugis of the Chittagong Hill Tracts are yet to receive even a peripheral contact

[32] Cf. M. Sahlins, *Tribesmen* (Englewood Cliffs, N.J.: Prentice-Hall, 1968); M.H. Fried, *The Notion of Tribe* (Menlo Park, Cal.: Cummings Publishing Company, 1975); Andre Béteille, 'The Definition of Tribe', in Romesh Thapar (ed.), *Tribe, Caste and Religion in India* (Delhi: Macmillan, 1977), 7-14.

[33] Cf. Begum Ismat Ara Mazumdar, 'Kaptai — Coexistence of Civilized and Tribal 'People', in: 'Chittagong Hill Tracts: An Observer Supplement', *The Bangladesh Observer* (12 November 1985), 7-8; and the quotations in Wolfgang Mey, "Es ist verboten, die Chittagong Hill Tracts zu betreten: Siedlungsgebiete der CHT-Völker', in: Wolfgang Mey (Hrsg.), '*Wir wollen nicht euch — Wir wollen euer Land'; Macht und Menschenrechte in den Chittagong Hill Tracts/ Bangladesch* (Göttingen and Vienna: Pogrom Taschenbücher, 1988), 32-36.

[34] Such representations of the 'tribe' are based on the presumption that all tribes share characteristics that are fundamentally different from, even opposite to, those of civilized people. Principal among these are 'childish' qualities that betray a lack of socialization: immoderately emotional behaviour (revelry, sensuality, extravagance, cruelty, fear of the supernatural) and naivety (credulity, incapacity to plan for the future). This discourse may be referred to as 'tribalist' because of its similarities to the Orientalist representation of 'the Orient.' Cf. Edward Said, *Orientalism* (New York: Vintage Books, 1979).

with the civilized world. Their way of life is timeless. Their cultural configuration is still intact, the outlines still hard and sharply drawn against the contrasting background of civilization with no sign of dimming. Their religious beliefs and practices completely insulates [sic] them against the demands of modernism. Even their economy is antidiluvian [sic]...'[35]

'If there is no education it will further widen the gap between the civilized and the pre-civilized. Isolated and left behind, the tribes will become more inward-looking and aggressive.'[36]

'The tribals are usually simple, credulous and jovial folks As long as they have enough to eat they are not much bothered by worries. The elders give themselves up to singing and dancing while children play or frolic.'[37]

'They are of deep interest to any one who wants to discover man in his raw form.'[38]

Juxtaposed to this rather stagnant external image of the people of the Chittagong hills as tribes lost in time, or 'people without history',[39] is an historic experience and internal images of ethnic relations which are strikingly different. A reconstruction of the historical development of ethnic identities is far from easy and cannot be more than preliminary: historical records did not concentrate on questions of changing identities to any great extent, the anthropological work done on the area is rather old, and writings by hill people themselves derive mostly from one group, the Chakmas. Nevertheless, the following corrections can be made.

First, the idea of unchangeable tribes frozen in time cannot stand the test of historical scrutiny. There is ample evidence of historical change affecting each group, and for

[35] Abdus Sattar, *Tribal Culture in Bangladesh* (Dacca: Muktadhara, 1975), 6-7.
[36] *Ibid.*, 4.
[37] *Ibid.*, 7.
[38] Abdus Sattar, *In the Sylvan Shadows* (Dacca: Saquib Brothers, 1971), 4.
[39] The term is taken from Wolf. It goes without saying that other views are also expressed among Bengalis in Bangladesh; but these are rarely heard, have little or no influence on national policy, and appear to be restricted largely to the academic community. Even in the most vocal collection of these counter-views to date (Qureshi (ed.), *Tribal Cultures*) the 'dominant view' manages to reassert itself occasionally. Cf. Mazumder's article, and Mey's experience in 1968: 'Again and again I was told, even by educated Bengalis: "They are savages; they are still leaving in the stone age. They do not know plough cultivation and are underdeveloped."'

Eric R. Wolf, *Europe and the People without History* (Berkeley: University of California Press, 1982); Mazumder, 'Kaptai'; Wolfgang Mey, 'Es ist verboten', 35 (my translation)

several of them, e.g. the Chakma, Tongchengya and Mrung, there is information allowing us to suggest how and when they came into being. For example, the Mrung are thought to have developed out of a group of Tippera who were taken to Arakan as prisoners of war and who began to move back north when the Burmese invaded Arakan, ending up in the southern Chittagong hills.

Second, the present distribution of different groups in the hills is far from 'traditional'; complex patterns of migration into and out of the area have been occurring for centuries. Almost all people have been highly mobile, not just in the short term and over short distances as a result of their shifting style of cultivation, but also over long distances over a long time span. The main movement into the Chittagong hills has been from the south, with minor migrations occurring from the east and north. Some of the people who arrived from the south are thought to represent fragments of larger state societies that have become separated and through a process of devolution turned into 'tribal' groups. Others never belonged to state societies; they represented the small-scale, mostly acephalous groups that abounded in the mountain range. These different groups certainly did not conceive of themselves as a single social category.

Third, they also did not form rigidly-bounded units. Even a highly exclusive group like the Mru, which tended to frown on exogamy and usually lived in separate villages, did allow marriage with one other group, the Pankhua. Moreover, we have seen that many villages were multi-ethnic, either because two or more 'tribes' lived together, or because a village dominated by one ethnic group also contained a number of war captives or debt-peons from other groups. Finally, 'chiefs' and other intermediaries with the state often presided over multi-ethnic groups of dependents. Therefore, although boundaries did exist, they were often far more blurred than the dominant view presumes.

Finally, the hill people had been involved in extensive networks of tribute and trade at least as long as states had been rising and falling in southeastern Bengal, Tripura and Arakan. For example, they were linked with Bengal's major industry, cotton textiles, as both producers of finished products and providers of raw cotton to the factories around Chittagong town and in Noakhali district. When cotton textiles became precolonial Bengal's foremost export product, the Chittagong hill people became tied into an ever denser network of overseas trade, not only as growers of cotton but also as providers of timber to Chittagong's ship-builders. Far from being isolated from the wider world or survivals from some primeval period, their continual contacts with outsiders, mostly Bengalis, shaped their economic, political and cultural development. The cultural distinctiveness of the different groups in the Chittagong hills should be regarded as an outcome of these interactions.

3. *Competing Cultural Models*

A crucially important aspect of relations between Bengalis and the inhabitants of the Chittagong hills was that the hill people had access to two competing models of state society and culture: the South Asian (represented by its Bengali variant) and the Southeast Asian (in the form of its Burmese/Arakanese variant). In this respect they differed fundamentally from many small peoples on either side of this great cultural divide who had access to one model only. Historically, there are clear fluctuations in the use that the people of the Chittagong hills made of the two models. Some groups leaned more towards one than the other, but all of them changed over time. The Tippera perhaps went farthest in their attempt to emulate the South Asian model. Their leader styled himself a '*raja*' (king, ruler) in the Hindu tradition, and Hindu elements clearly played an important part in Tippera religion. In other matters (e.g. dress style) they also followed Bengali examples. But despite a degree of Hinduization and Bengalization, they remained clearly separate. Not only was their language quite distinct, but they also stood out for their syncretic religion, their kinship system, and their economic activities. At the other end of the spectrum are the Marma, whose very name actually signifies that they perceive themselves as Burmese.[40] The Marma called their leaders '*mang*' ('ruler', 'governor', with the Burmese connotations of that word) or '*po-mang*' ('great captain'; Bohmong[41]), and village-level leaders were referred to as '*rua-sa*' (often Bengalized to 'roaja' in the literature), once again a reference to the Burmese system of 'village eaters' or local representatives of the state.[42] In between these two extremes stand the Chakma in whose history both models are seen to vie for dominance. Burmese elements are strong in their religion, in which Burmese Buddhist elements abound. But their language is so strongly influenced by the Chittagonian dialect of Bengali that it has been described as a Bengali dialect rather than a separate language. Chakma political culture also reflected influences from both South and Southeast Asian models. Chakma leaders adopted Islamic names during the Mughal period (even though this did not imply any religious change) but they used titles ('*mang*', '*khan*') derived from both Buddhist and Muslim traditions.[43] Only during the early-colonial period did the Bengali cultural model become dominant among the Chakmas: the chiefly family adopted Bengali titles ('raja', '*rani*', '*dewan*') and introduced some Hindu rituals in its religious observances. At the same time a myth of 'western' origin developed which linked the Chakmas firmly to South

---

[40] But see Bernot's critical remarks about this popular notion. Bernot, *Les paysans arakanais*, 41-42.

[41] Buchanan, who translates Mang as 'Prince', states that the titles Ta-kang and Po-mang, too, 'are titles analogous to our term Prince: and are the Rakain [Arakanese] pronounciation of သခင် [tha-hkyin] and မင် [min], the Burma titles for the Sons of their King, and bestowed also upon Officers of high rank.' (91).

[42] Bernot, *Les paysans arakanais*, 84, 86-87.

[43] Cf. Buchanan, 119-121. The suffix 'khan' is usually interpreted as an attempt on the part of the local chiefs to adapt to Mughal practices. It is more likely that the term derived from immigrant Muslims from Arakan. See Serajuddin, 'The Origin of the Rajas', 51-60.

Asia rather than Southeast Asia.[44]

Many more examples could be given of the competing influence of the Burmese and Bengali models among the hill people and the ways in which they were combined with the various local cultural traditions. Historically the changing influence of these models appears to be linked with changing trade routes, which were in turn influenced by the vagaries of state formation in the plains. Trade between hills and plains consisted largely of the exchange of cotton yarn, textiles and forest products for salt, dried fish, and manufactures. Some Chittagong hill people traded with Bengalis in the Chittagong plain, others with the Arakanese in the south. Some trade must also have been carried on with the Burmese in the Irrawaddy valley to the east, but that area remained beyond the reach of European travellers till the late nineteenth century, and very little is known about eastward trade routes.

4. *Enter the State*

The Chittagong hills had never been incorporated in a state till the British annexed them in 1860. This does not mean that the hill economy had not been thoroughly influenced by its contacts with the outside world long before that. The Mughal state extracted a tribute in cotton, and a demand for certain products had led to some economic specialization in the hills. But it is important to realize that before annex-

---

[44] Many Bengalis claim roots in more western parts of South Asia or even in West Asia because such 'western' connections are considered prestigious. Nineteenth century Chakmas' claim to be descendants of Ksattriya migrants from 'Champa(k)nagar', thought to be in north India, can be interpreted as an effort to invent a tradition that might lead to both Sanskritization and Bengalization. As we have seen, Buchanan (114) recorded the story of an Arakanese origin, which was also suggested by the Chittagong Qanungo's report in Government of Bengal, Proceedings of the Committee of Revenue, 6 May 1784, cited in Serajuddin. 'The Origin of the Rajas', 52ff; and quoted partly in Serajuddin, 'The Chakma tribe', 95-97 The Champanagar story was first recorded in Lewin, *The Hill Tracts*, 62-63; cf. Lewin, *Wild Races*, 170; J.P. Mills, 'Notes on a Tour'; Bessaignet, 88ff; Syed Murtaza Ali. 'Hill Tribes of Chittagong', in: *East Pakistan: A Profile* (Dacca: Orient Longmans, 1962) 227-228. For critiques, see Wolfgang Mey, *Politische Systeme*, 38-43; and Serajuddin, 'The Chakma Tribe', 90-98.

ation the hill people were free agents who were feared by the plains people for their independence and military prowess. An uneasy symbiosis between the settled cultivators of the plain and the swidden cultivators in the hills was punctuated by raids that hill people would carry out on villages in the plain whenever they felt their rights were being encroached upon. Retaliation was extremely difficult because the hill people were invincible on their own turf.

The British Indian state was the first that was both strong enough to conquer the hills and had a reason to do so. The direct cause of annexation was a military one: it was a retaliation for raids on British territory that were carried out, not by the people of the Chittagong hills, but by hill people living further to the east, in the section of the mountain range now known as Mizoram. The point of formal annexation was that the British could now station troops on the eastern borders of the new hill district to fend off attacks from the east. These attacks had become more frequent as a result of increasing internecine warfare leading to territorial expansion in which 'Kookies' (Koongkies, Kukies, Cucis), now better known as Chin, Lushai, or Mizo, were involved.[45]

Colonial annexation had far-reaching consequences. A small section of the mountain range was now parcelled off as a new district called the Chittagong Hill Tracts. It was administered from Calcutta as part of the province of Bengal. This administrative set-up was unique; the bulk of the mountain range, which the British conquered gradually in the late nineteenth century, was ruled from Assam and Burma.[46] After 1860 the Bengali cultural model suddenly assumed a more prominent position in the Chittagong hills

---

[45] This development on the borders of British-controlled areas in Bengal and Lower Burma is likely to have been related to dislocations of old trade routes. Standard explanations refer mostly to possible population expansion in the Chin-Lushai hills, but the connection with colonial state formation and trade should not be overlooked. For a capsule history of the Chins, see Bernot and Bernot, *Les Khyangs*, 7-14. Cf. footnote 101.

[46] Only 'Hill Tippera', present-day Tripura, was an exception. It was given a special status as a Princely State in communication with the Government of Bengal.

than it had done in the past, and its emergence was linked directly to colonial domination.

5. *From Kin-ordered to Territorial Authority*

Perhaps the most radical change which colonial domination brought about was the abolition of kin-ordered modes of authority. In the Chittagong hills surplus extraction had been based largely on personal ties between chiefs and followers. Kinship and fictive kinship had been the underlying ideology legitimizing the chiefs' power. This system, which was also important in the precolonial Burmese state,[47] was anathema to the territorial system of surplus extraction that had long been in force in the Bengal plains. A territorial system was now introduced in the Chittagong hills, and existing chiefs were treated as subordinate territorial lords. The Chakma chief, for example, held some lands in the plains. Here he had the status of a *zamindar* (superior landholder and tax collector) under British-Indian law. The British tended to treat his position in the hills as subsidiary to his status as a zamindar.[48] After 1860 he and two other chiefs (the Bohmong chief in the southern hills, and the Mong chief in the north) were made responsible for tax collection in well defined areas of the Chittagong hills. Other chiefs were made answerable to them, and taxes were demanded on a territorial basis rather than on the basis of a personal following, as before. The chiefs became agents of the state with centralized power based on a principle of authority that was new in the hills.[49] Introduction of indirect rule in

[47] The precolonial Burmese state relied heavily on surplus extraction by means of non-territorial 'crown service groups' (ahmudan). Cf. John S. Furnivall, *An Introduction to the Political Economy of Burma* (Rangoon: People's Literature Committee & House, 1957), 28-41.

[48] Government of Bengal, Judicial Department, Political Branch, Proceedings 22-23 (September 1876), 'Report on the Administration of the Chittagong Hill Tracts for 1875-76', 30.

[49] Mey, *Politische Systeme*, analyzes this change at length. In addition to the three chiefs, there were at first, 'several petty Chiefs holding settlements in the Hills of new settlers, chiefly consisting of deserters from Independent Tipperah, under the local name of Noabad Kapass Mehals..' Government of Bengal, Judicial Department, Political Branch, Proceeding 226 (April 1862).

the Chittagong hills was advocated but never introduced;[50] although the chiefs were allowed some of the trappings of 'native rulers',[51] they were 'always treated as tahsildars and rent-collectors'.[52]

6. *A Policy of Exclusion*

A second crucial change was at first less apparent. Not only did the people of the Chittagong hills become incorporated in a state for the first time in their history, they also became minorities overnight. The state to which they now belonged was dominated by British and Bengali interests, and the political and social relations between the hills and the plains were reversed. Bengali mores gradually came to be the standard against which the cultural and social life of the people of the Chittagong hills was judged. A process of legal and commercial 'Bengalization' of the hills set in with such force that British officials began to worry about

---

A most eloquent advocate was Lewin (1869):

'They [=the chiefs] are on the spot, and have enormous local influence, and in my humble opinion they are the legitimate instruments of rule placed ready to our hand. I would subordinate them in every way to our authority. *Let them be guided or checked as need be, but within their own limits I would have their authority paramount.*' (emphasis in original) (Government of Bengal, Political Department, Political branch, Proceedings 100-101 (May 1917), Appendix A: 'References regarding the position of the Hill Tracts Chiefs.') Cf. the instructions of the Government of Bengal in 1860, quoted in Lewin, *Wild Races*, 63.

[51] In 1874 the government decided to confer on the new Chakma chief, Harish Chandra (ruled 1873-1885), the title of 'Raja' in order to underline his dependence on 'the pleasure of the paramount authority.' But it was not deemed 'desirable that any representative of Government should take part in the ceremonies incident on installation to the guddi [throne]; that would, I think, be assigning undue importance to the matter.' In the event, the Deputy Commissioner at Rangamati presented the Chakma chief with a *sanad* (deed of grant) and *Khilat* (dress of investiture) in return for a *nazar* (ceremonial present), but did not take part in further ceremonies. The *sanad* read:

'For William 24-3-1874 — In recognition of your position as the head of the Chukma tribe in the Chittagong Hill Tracts, I hereby confer upon you the title of "Raja" for your life, — Northbrook,' Government of Bengal, Judicial Department, Political Branch, Proceedings 15-17 (February 1874) and Proceeding 3 (April 1874).

On the history of the Chakma chief's family, see Lewin, *Wild Races*, 162-163; Ali, 'Hill Tribes', 229; Wolfgang Mey, *Politische Systeme*.

[52] Government of Bengal, Political Department, Political Branch, Proceedings 1-2 (June 1918), 'Issue of a warning to the Mong Chief, Chittagong Hill Tracts, for dereliction of duty'.

it.[53] Bengali pleaders and moneylenders were particularly successful, and the authorities soon sought to stop their activities on the ground that they fleeced the 'innocent' and 'ignorant' hill men. The state decided not to tolerate private accumulation by Bengali entrepreneurs; this could undermine its new territorial system of surplus extraction and might also lead to trouble in the hills, as the recent Santal rebellion had revealed forcefully.[54] Consequently, the colonial authorities constituted themselves the protectors of 'tribal' rights in the Chittagong hills.[55]

The Chittagong hills were made an excluded area, a policy which was formalized in the Chittagong Hill Tracts Regulation of 1900.[56] This regulation stemmed the tide of Bengalization but also isolated the hill people from the rest of Bengal. Far from being a charter for regional autonomy or a protection of 'tribal' rights (as some would have it[57]), it

---

[53] As early as 1866 this was voiced strongly:

'I think it is unadvisable that Bengallees of all descriptions should be allowed ingress at will into the hills. Several cases of extortion have come to my own notice where Bengallees have forced hill men to give them money by the threat of a false complaint, and on the other hand murders of Bengallees for reasons unknown are by no means uncommon, and the authors of the crime have to the best of my knowledge in no one instance been ascertained.' (Government of Bengal, Judicial Proceedings 83-84 (July 1866). Cf. Lewin, *Wild Races*, 62-68; Hutchinson, *An Account*, 42; Mills, 'Notes on a Tour', 514.

[54] In 1855 the Santal rebellion had erupted in hill country some 400 km to the west, across the deltaic plains of Bengal; the area had still not been 'pacified' by the time the Chittagong hills were annexed. See e.g. Tarapada Ray (comp.), *Santal Rebellion: Documents* (Calcutta: Subarnarekha, 1983); Dhirendronath Baske, *Shaontal Gonoshongramer Itihash* [History of the Mass Struggle of the Santals] (Calcutta: Pearl Publisers, 1976); Ranajit Guha, *Elementary Aspects of Peasant Insurgency in Colonial Bengal* (Delhi: Oxford University Press, 1983).

[55] The appointment of a 'Superintendent of Hill Tribes' was ostensibly: 'to administer justice to the Hill people in our jurisdiction, and to prevent that oppression and plunder of poor and ignorant savages by the crafty Bengallee moneylender which may lead, as in the case of the Sonthals, to violence and bloodshed.' (Government of Bengal, Judicial Proceedings 142-143 (December 1862)).

This policy was also followed in the adjacent portion of the mountain range which the British annexed as the Hill Tracts of Arakan. Here a Superintendent was appointed in 1866; his job was described in equally high-minded terms: 'The Superintendent — a specially selected officer — has brought justice, administered in the simplest and most paternal form, to their doors.' (Report on the Progress made in the Arakan Division from 1826 to 1869; in: *Report on the Progress of Arakan under British Rule from 1826 to 1875* (Rangoon: Government Press, 1873).

[56] For the text of this Regulation, see Hutchinson and Chakma. The excluded status of the Chittagong hills was confirmed during administrative changes in 1935. Hutchinson, *An Account*, Appendix A; and Siddhartha Chakma, *Froshongo: Parbotyo Chottogram* [Topic: Chittagong Hill Tracts] (Calcutta: Nath Brothers, 1392 B.E. [1985-86]). 149-162.

[57] E.g. Hutchinson (*An Account*, 32): "The policy of the Government is to interfere as little as possible with tribal customs'.

marked the onset of a process of 'enclavement' in which the hill people were denied access to power and were subordinated and exploited directly by their British overlords.[58] This was exemplified by various manipulations. First, the colonial state claimed ownership of all land in the hills:

> 'It appears advisable, as opportunities occur, to make the semi-civilized tribes inhabiting these hills understand more and more that the lands they occupy form an integral portion of Her Majesty's dominion in India, and that the Government alone is the fountain of all honor.'[59]

It was entirely in line with this position that the government declared large tracts of hill country to be 'reserved forests' and denied hill cultivators access to what they had always considered as commons.[60] Similarly, high-quality land was given out to European entrepreneurs, especially to tea planters, but these enterprises proved relatively unsuccessful.[61] Second, repeated efforts were made to supplant swidden cultivation in the hills by settled plough cultivation

---

[58] For applications of the concept of 'enclavement', developed by Edward H. Spicer, see George P. Castille and Gilbert Kushner (eds.), *Persistent Peoples: Cultural Enclaves in Perspective* (Tucson: University of Arizona Press, 1981).

[59] Government of Bengal, Judicial Department, Political Branch, Proceedings 22-23 (September 1876), 'Report on the Administration of the Chittagong Hill Tracts for 1875-76', 30. This principle determined not only the position of common cultivators, but equally that of the Chiefs, in the eyes of the colonial state: 'The Chiefs of the Chittagong Hill Tracts have no title to the ownership of the land which is vested exclusively in the Crown: they exercise only the delegated right of collecting taxes and rents on behalf of Government.' (Government of Bengal, Political Department, Political Branch, Proceedings 1-2 (June 1918), 'Issue of a warning to the Mong chief, Chittagong Hill Tracts, for dereliction of duty').

[60] In 1871 almost all forest area was designated 'Government Forest'. A few years later five reserved forests were created in which no cultivation was allowed; together they covered an area of 3,500 km2 (or 26% of the total area, which covers 13,000 km2). The District Gazetteer of 1971 states that the total area of reserved forests was 2,600 km2 and that of unclassed state forests 8,800 km2 (20% and 67% of total area, respectively) before the Kaptai lake was created; afterwards the figures were 2,400 km2 (18%) and 8,200 km2 (62%), with the lake taking up 663 km2 (5%).
See Hutchinson, *An Account*, 1,29-31, 51; Mey, *Politische Systeme*, 120-122; *Bangladesh District Gazetteers: Chittagong Hill Tracts* (Dacca: Bangladesh Government Press, 1971), 99; cf. Anti-Slavery Society, *The Chittagong Hill Tracts: Militarization, Oppression and the Hill Tribes* (London, Anti-Slavery Society, 1984), Appendix 4.

[61] Tea, coffee and orange plantations were establlished in the 1860s , as were teak plantations in the 1870s, but only tea was successful for some time. The main problem was the labour supply. See Administration Reports for various years, and Mey, *Politische Systeme*, 121-124.

because this was expected to yield a higher state revenue and to be less 'wasteful' of timber resources and land:

> 'Our object should be to put a stop to *jum* culture and induce the people to settle and cultivate by the plough, making land revenue the basis of our district settlement.' [62]

Swidden cultivation was also prohibited on government estates in the plains district of Chittagong; this led to a trek of swidden cultivators into the hill district and to a further physical isolation from Bengalis.[63] Third, the authorities began to move groups of hill people to new locations. Although the reason sometimes offered was that these cultivators had 'exhausted' the soil, these forced moves were all to the east and served mainly to strengthen the border against

---

[62] T.H. Lewin, in a letter to the Government of Bengal (1872), quoted in Hutchinson, 49-50. The idea had already been voiced a century earlier (1784), and again in 1798 and 1829. After 1860 a considerable correspondence developed on the topic of plough cultivation in the Chittagong hills. The general feeling was that it should be encouraged:

'The advantages of this scheme would be —

1st, that we would spur the hillmen into getting civilized and settling down; there would be no danger of being [sic] any scarcity of land, or the hill people being ejected by outsiders, or of the immigrants oppressing or disagreeing with them;

2nd, we would get the country cleared and opened out to the rest of India;

3rd, we would have a population which would serve as a barrier against the wild tribes to the east;

4th, in ten or fifteen years the state would begin to draw a large.revenue from this district;

5th, the district from the clearing of the jungle would become healthy.'

(Government of Bengal, Revenue Department, Land Revenue Branch, Proceeding 54 (May 1872), letter by a.W. Cochrane) Cf. letter of 6 May 1784 from Govt to Mr. Irwin, Chief of Chittagong and letter 21 April 1829 from Mr. Halhed, Commissioner, both quoted in Lewin, *Wild Races*, 58-60; see also Buchanan, 103. For a dissenting view, see Hutchinson, *An Account*, 47-54, and for a modern contribution, Nafis Ahmad, *A New Economic Geography of Bangladesh* (Delhi: Vikas, 1976), 111-113.

[63] In 1798 Buchanan had observed large communities of swidden cultivators in the hilly parts of the Chittagong plain. Chakma, Marma, Bawm, and Tippera were found in such places as the low hills between Mirsarai and Sitakund, Chattarua in the north, the Songu valley as far west as Dohazari, around Rangunia, Harbang and Chakaria, on Maheshkhali island in the Bay of Bengal, and down the coast south of Cox's Bazar. See Buchanan, 13, 14, 19-20, 32, 46-50, 54, 69, 86, 89-90, 147, 152.

On the prohibition of swidden cultivation on government lands in the plains district, see Government of Bengal, Judicial Department, Political Branch, Proceedings 22-23 (September 1876), 'Report on the Administration of the Chittagong Hill Tracts for 1875-76', 21; and J.B. Kindersley, *Final Report on the Survey and Settlement Operations in the District of Chittagong 1923-1933* (Alipore: Bengal Government Press, 1939), 6.

invaders.[64] And finally, the colonial authorities encouraged outsiders to settle in the Chittagong hills. Their policy was distinctly anti-Bengali:[65] while they continued to forbid Bengalis to migrate to the hills, they made considerable efforts to establish settlements of plough-cultivating Gurkhas and Santals on erstwhile 'tribal' land.[66]

The British were not so much interested in preserving the rights of the hill people as in making the Chittagong hills yield a good revenue for the colonial exchequer. Their interest focused on taxes gathered from the cultivators via the territorial chiefs but also on revenue from trade. The chief items of hill produce were timber, boats, grass, cane, cotton, umbrella leaves, and bamboo.[67]

This colonial policy of excluding Bengalis and isolating the hill people was not entirely successful because the hill

---

[64] 'As the lands in the vicinity of Bunderban have become exhausted by repeated jhooming, it was found necessary that the Mugh [Marma] population of the Sungoo valley should be moved eastward, where virgin soil was available along the right bank of the river. The movement, however, was checked by the fear of raiders.'

Similarly, Khumis and Bawm [Bunjoogies] were to be moved to the frontier to protect the 'weaker tribes behind', and Tipperas entering the Chittagong hills from Hill Tipperah (now Tripura) were induced to settle in the far east, north of Barkal. Government of Bengal, Judicial Department, Political Branch, Proceedings 22-23 (September 1876), 'Report on the Adminstration of the Chittagong Hill Tracts for 1875-76', 2; Government of Bengal, Revenue Department, Land Revenue Branch, Proceeding 15 (September 1873).

[65] It is interesting to see how selective this policy was, and how changeable official views on Bengalis. In the Hill Tracts of neighbouring Arakan Bengalis were welcome immigrants. Here the authorities did not perceive them as rapacious fleecers of ignorant tribals but as 'timid'. According to the Administration Report of 1877-78, plough cultivation should be stimulated at the foot of the hills around Myouktoung, and it should be carried out by 'the timid Chittagonian immigrants who are commencing to arrive here' (*Administration Report on the Hill Tracts, Northern Arakan for the Year 1877-78* (Rangoon: Government Press, 1879), 14).

[66] The Gurkhas were allowed to *jhum* for the first few years, and then had to switch over to plough cultivation. Lewin argued that 'The introduction of Goorkha colonists into our scantily peopled Hill Tracts would, I think, be productive of unmixed good'. (Government of Bengal, Revenue Department, Land Revenue Branch, Proceeding 53 (May 1872). Other groups were also welcomed (e.g. Banthallees, Dangurs, Assamese), but: 'Bengallees are the only race which I would exclude; they have an unhappy bias at least. The classes of them that would be likely to come in here have to [*sic*] usury litigation and fraud; they would be of no use in frontier protection, and they would worry the hillmen as they do so far as they are allowed at present'. (*ibid.*, Proceeding 54).

[67] These and other products and the rates levied on them were itemized in a highly detailed manner (e.g. thirteen different kinds of timber) in Revenue Department, Land Revenue Branch, Proceedings, 120-122 (March 1862). See also the Annual Reports of the Chittagong Hill Tracts, e.g. the one for 1878-79, in Judicial Department, Political Branch, Proceeding 11 (September 1879), 2-3.

people did not always co-operate. In precolonial days trade had been carried on by hill people coming down to markets near the foothills[68] and by Bengali tradesmen entering the hills by boat.[69] The British tried to stop the latter entering the hills and encouraged the establishment of permanent hill markets (*bazars*). But this proved unpractical: most hill people preferred bartering with traders at home to walking long distances to one of the thirteen new markets, and the British had to withdraw the prohibition in 1877. Once again,

> 'the trade of the country is in the hands of a class of men called *Bhasania beparis*, or "floating traders", who go up the rivers in boats well stocked with articles of all kinds, stopping at the villages to trade.'[70]

The colonial policy of exclusion meant that only certain economic and ecological niches were open to the hill people. They had no say in administrative affairs and decisions were made for, not with, them. They were not allowed to cultivate outside the Chittagong hills (unless they changed to plough cultivation, which was impossible because it would require them to relinquish their lifestyle completely[71]). And as the local economy became more commercialized and external trade grew, hill people played an ever smaller role in it. They had become minorities who had restricted rights in the territory that they had been assigned and were powerless outside it.

---

[68] E.g. Bajalia on the Songu river, described by Buchanan (88-89) as a 'market place made by [Marma chief] Kaung-la-pru for the convenience of his people, who here exchange their Commodities for those of the Bengalese. A Mussulman attends here, and procures all the luxuries of Bengal, that are wanted by the Chief.'

[69] During his trip in 1798 Buchanan reported extensively on Bengali trade in the Chittagong hills. See his observations on pp. 34, 117, 118-119, and 134-135.

[70] Judicial Department, Political Branch, Proceeding 11 (September 1879): 'Annual Report of the Chittagong Hill Tracts for 1878-79', 3. Cf. Lewin, *Wild Races*, 23-24, Hutchinson, *An Account*, 44-46.

[71] In the words of the Report on the Administration of the Chittagong Hill Tracts for 1875-76:

"Hillmen dislike cultivation by the plough alone, because they cannot under that system grow cotton and the vegetables and fruits produced in jhooms...It is no light thing to change the method of life of an intensely conservative people ' (Government of Bengal, Judicial Department, Political Branch, Proceedings 22-23 (September 1876), 29).

7. *Erosion and the End of Exclusion*

A relatively high level of self-sufficiency allowed the hill people to continue enjoying reasonable living conditions. The main articles that they required from outside were salt and dried fish; they produced their own staple foods and clothes long after the people in the plains had become dependent on the market. After 1892, when Mizoram had finally been annexed and all raids had stopped, life in the Chittagong hills became remarkably peaceful. Isolated and fairly self-sufficient, its population began to grow.[72] Migration to other parts of the mountain range was still possible in the colonial period but the territorial system of tax collection hampered it. The result was that migration continued to take place mainly within the jurisdictions of territorial chiefs, and population pressure began to rise. Although population densities were far lower than on the plains, the hills began to be over-cultivated, leading to lower yields from swidden cultivation, the cultivation of larger fields, shorter periods of fallow, and noticeable erosion from about 1940.[73] In an attempt to mobilize new resources some cultivators added plough cultivation in the river valleys to *jhum* cultivation on nearby hill slopes, a move they had resisted earlier when the authorities advocated it but no economic necessity had been felt.[74] The agrarian system of the Chittagong hills had become over-

[72] Lorenz G. Löffler, 'Carrying capacity, Schwendbauproblem in Südostasien', in: *VIe Congrès International des Sciences Anthropologiques et Ethnologiques, Paris 1960* (Paris, 1963), Volume 2, 1, 179-182.

[73] *Ibid.*, 179-180, 182.

[74] In 1869 Lewin remarked:

'Throughout the whole of the Hill Tracts, I know no single instance of a hill man cultivating with the plough; indeed, it is rare to find a man earning his livelihood in any other way save by joom [swidden] cultivation.'

Three years later A.W. Cochrane, the officiating Deputy Commissioner of the Chittagong Hill Tracts, wrote: 'I do not believe that the hill men will ever devote themselves to it [=plough cultivation] unless urged by emulation, and having the advantages brought clearly before them'. He attributed this reluctance to the 'dislike to change characteristic of them and other half or quarter civilized people'.

For the later shift to plough cultivation, see Löffler and Sopher.

Lewin, *The Hill Tracts*, 13; Government of Bengal, Revenue Department, Land Revenue Branch, Proceeding 54 (May 1872). Lorenz G. Löffler , 'Der Uebergang vom Schwendbau zum Ackerbau im Chittagong-Gebiet' (unpublished ms, n.d.); Sopher, 'The Swidden/Wet Rice Transition Zone.'

extended. The excluded nature of the area had kept all non-agricultural employment away, with the result that the hill people were faced with an economic crisis.[75]

In addition to this largely internal development there were external changes which would deepen the crisis. In 1947 British India disintegrated into India and Pakistan and the Chittagong hills, though practically devoid of Muslims, were awarded to (East) Pakistan.[76] The area continued to have a special status but soon attempts were afoot to change it. This was understandable as both land tax and revenues from cotton and forest produce had become much less important. The new power-holders were looking for new ways to make the Chittagong hills productive and these made the colonial policy of isolation redundant. The state was no longer interested mainly in the products of hill people's labour, e.g. in the form of taxes and cotton; increasingly it was the land on which they lived that interested the state.

The decision to exploit the hills as a source of hydro-electric power turned out to be momentous. East Pakistan had very few other sources of energy, and only the Chittagong hills offered an opportunity to harness water resources. To this end a huge lake was created to the north and east of a barrage at Kaptai village between 1959 and 1963. Large tracts of land were flooded, depriving tens of thousands of cultivators of their best lands, and many more of their homesteads. In all over 100,000 people, or 'more than one quarter of the total population of the district', were displaced.[77] Although some compensation was given to those affected, it proved insufficient to start them over

[75] The one sizeable factory in the Chittagong Hill Tracts was at Chandraghona, on the border with the plains. Employment at the Karnafuli Paper Mills, which used bamboo cut in the hills, was a predominantly Bengali affair. According to the District Gazetteer, hill people constituted less than 0.5% of the labour force of 3,920 'at one stage of its normal operation.' *Bangladesh District Gazetteers: Chittagong Hill Tracts*, 139; cf. Wolfgang Mey, *Politische Systeme*, Appendix, iv.

[76] The anomalous nature of this decision and the confusion around the 'Radcliffe Award' in the Chittagong hills in August 1947 are discussed in Siddhartha Chakma, *Proshongo*. Cf. S.P. Talukdar, *The Chakmas: Life and Struggle* (Delhi: Gian Publishing House, 1988), 47-58.

[77] *Bangladesh District Gazetteers; Chittagong Hill Tracts*, 42.

again.[78] Prospecting for oil and natural gas, which had been undertaken as early as 1908 in the Chittagong region, was resumed after the birth of Bangladesh.[79]

The Bengali nation-state was a relative late-comer in the region. Its establishment marked an important change in the hills; from 1971 the dominant Bengali view of ethnic relations in the hills came to inform state policy as never before.[80] It could hardly come as a surprise that the final blow to the colonial policy of exclusion and isolation was dealt in the 1970s, when the hills were opened to Bengali settlers. The lowlands of Bangladesh had fallen victim to disastrous poverty which, despite a large inflow of foreign development aid, showed every sign of increasing. Erroneous conceptions of the 'emptiness' and underutilized agrarian wealth of the hills combined with ideas about the superiority of (Bengali) plough cultivation in the presentation of settler migration to the Chittagong hills as a partial solution to both overpopulation in the plains and underdevelopment in the hills. Considering dominant Bengali conceptions of the hill people's cultural backwardness, settling Bengali peasants in the hills was also assumed to contribute to their cultural development.

---

[78] According to various sources 650 km2 (5% of the total area of the Chittagong Hill Tracts) were flooded, destroying 40% of the arable land. The Gazetteer states that compensation was adequate but Almut Mey and Wolfgang Mey disagree.

Cf. *Bangladesh District Gazetteers: Chittagong Hill Tracts*, 42-44, 99; *Population Census of Bangladesh 1974; District Census Report Chittagong Hill Tracts* (Dacca: Bangladesh Bureau of Statistics, 1979), 12; Almut Mey, *Untersuchungen*, 280-287; Mey, *Politische Systeme*, 210-218; Ahmad, *A New Economic Geography*, 123.

[79] The national oil company, Petrobangla, reached a 25-year agreement with Shell Petroleum Development for oil exploration in the Chittagong hills and plain in 1981. Wolfgang Mey (ed), *They Are Now Burning Village After Village: Genocide in the Chittagong Hill Tracts, Bangladesh* (Copenhagen: International Work Group for Indigenous Affairs, 1984), 120-122.

[80] In 1972 a delegation from the Chittagong hills met Bangladesh's new leader, Sheikh Mujibur Rahman, demanding regional autonomy, retention of the Regulation of 1900, continuation of tribal chiefs' offices, and a ban on in-migration. Mujibur Rahman replied that fulfilling such demands would encourage ethnic feelings and, according to Montu, he advised the delegation to go home and 'do away with their ethnic identities.' In 1975, during a visit to Rangamati, the district headquarters, he 'addressed the tribals as brethren and told them to become Bengalis, to forget the colonial past and join the mainstream of Bengali culture. At this, the tribal people left the meeting.' Successive governments in Bangladesh have not departed from this basic position, despite occasional gestures towards preserving 'tribal culture'.

Kazi Montu, 'Tribal Insurgency in Chittagong Hill Tracts', *Economic and Political Weekly* (6 September 1980), 1551; A.B. Chakma, 'Look Back from Exile: A Chakma Experience', in: Wolfgang Mey (ed.), *They Are Now Burning*, 58.

8. *Resistance and Abandonment of the Bengali Model*

It soon became clear that this was hardly the way in which the people of the Chittagong hills perceived the invasion of their land. A long history of passive resistance against the state now came to an end as open rebellion broke out.[81] Bangladesh armed forces moved in and full-scale guerrilla warfare ensued.[82] New migrants could only be brought in under army protection and they could only persevere because they were given arms. By 1990 continuous war had produced thousands of casualties, led to an exodus of perhaps 70,000 hill people now languishing in refugee camps in Tripura state (India),[83] and elicited international protests against the policy of the Bangladesh government, which was

[81] There had been one sizeable rebellion against British expansion between 1776 and 1787 (see Buchanan, Serajuddin, Chakraborty and Islam); in 1864 a short-lived revolt by the minor chief 'Ougyphroo' took place against the Marma chief. Ougyphroo thought that he was to be the Marma chief 'and that his dominion was to extend all over the Hill Tracts and from Cox's Bazaar to the Mugh Bazaar at Dacca.' (Government of Bengal, Judicial Department, Political Proceedings 187 (June 1865)), Serajuddin, 'The Origin of the Rajas', 54-55; Chakravorty, 'Chakma Resistance'; Sirajul Islam, 'Tribal Resistance'. Cf. Lewin, *Wild Races*, 57.

[82] See e.g. Amnesty International, *Unlawful Killings in the Chittagong Hill Tracts* (London: Amnesty International, 1986); Survival International, *Bangladesh — Chittagong Hill Tracts Report for 1988: No End to Human Rights Abuses* (London: Survival International, 1988); Kazi Mahmudar Rashid, 'A Study on Administration of Indigenous People of the Chittagong Hill Tracts' (typescript, 1980); Devasish Roy (Chakma Raja) et al., *04/05/89 Ing roj brihospatibar Rangamati Parbotyo Zelar Longodu Upozelar upojatiyoder biruddhe shongotito shohingsho ghotonar protibade smaroklipi* [A Memorandum in Protest Against the Genocidal Attacks on Tribals in Langadu Upazilla, Rangamati Hill District, on Thursday 4 May, 1989] (typescript petition, Rangamati, 1989); Siddhartha Chakma, *Proshongo*; Wolfgang Mey, *Politische Systeme*; Wolfgang Mey, 'Es ist verboten'; Wolfgang Mey (ed.), *They Are Now Burning*.

[83] The Bangladesh government estimates the number of refugees to be much lower. In 1987, at a time when Indian officials talked of 50,000 refugees, the Foreign Secretary of Bangladesh said that there were 29,920. Since then there have been various estimates, from 24,000 according to Bangladesh officials (June 1989) and 45,380 according to an Indian observer (June 1988) to 70,000 according to the JSS (May 1989). Cf. Bangladesh Groep Nederland, 'Bangladesh: Refugees from an Unknown War — Bangladeshi Tribals in India', *IWGIA Newsletter*, 53/54 (May/August 1988), 35; S. Kamaluddin, 'Bangladesh — Tribal Insurgents Try to Disrupt Hill Council Polls: Intimidatory Tactics', *Far Eastern Economic Review* (29 June 1989), 24; Survival International, *Bangladesh-Chittagong Hill Tracts Report for 1988*, 3; R.S. Dewan, 'The Jumma Representative's Statement on the Systematic Genocide of the Helpless Jumma People of the Chittagong Hill Tracts being carried out by the Bangladesh Armed Forces' (Working Group on Indigenous Populations, United Nations Economic and Social Council, Geneva, 31 July - 4 August 1989), 5; cf. 'Fresh Influx'.

branded as genocidal and ethnocidal.[84]

It is not my intention to deal with the ongoing conflict in the Chittagong hills itself; this has been done in detail elsewhere. Here I wish to concentrate on one aspect that has received little attention: the cultural repercussions of the conflict. I have indicated that the Bengali cultural model became dominant from the 1860s onwards and that it was linked with state power. The people of the Chittagong hills had to come to terms with administrative institutions that had been developed in Bengal, they had to learn the Bengali language to communicate with agents of the state, and local cultures developed a relationship with Bengali culture which was distinctly ambiguous. Efforts to adapt to and participate in Bengali culture were counterbalanced by assertions of the worth of each local culture.[85]

Up to 1947 direct interaction between hill people and Bengalis had been somewhat restricted but the end of British rule brought the hill people into closer contact with the Bengali population of the plains. In this period the first organizations emerged to bring together all people living in the Chittagong hills. Earlier organizations had concentrated on single language groups;[86] but now three new organizations, established between 1946 and 1950, opposed the merger of the Chittagong hills with Pakistan to various degrees, aimed at 'taking care of local needs and complaints', and were concerned with minority rights.[87] These organizations failed to attain their

[84] E.g. Wolfgang Mey (ed.), *They Are Now Burning*; Amnesty International, *Unlawful Killings*; Survival International, *Bangladesh — Chittagong Hill Tracts Report for 1988*.

[85] Bengali disdain for the people of the Chittagong hills has been amply documented, beginning with Buchanan in 1798. By contrast, hill people's feelings of superiority towards each other and towards Bengalis have been rarely recorded. See, however, Bernot's analysis of the ambivalent sentiments of Marmas towards their Bengali and Mru neighbours. Bernot, *Les paysans arakanais*, 748-750; cf. discussion in Wolfgang Mey, *Politische Systeme*, 232-233.

[86] In 1915 Rajmohan Dewan had started the 'Chakma Jubok Shomiti' (Chakma Youth Association), and in 1928 this was followed by Ghonoshyam Dewan's 'Chakma Jubok Shongho' (Chakma Youth Society). See Siddhartha Chakma, *Proshongo*, 5-6.

[87] These were the 'Hill Men Association' (1946?), the 'Parbotyo Chottograme Jono Shomiti' (People's Association of the Chittagong Hill Tracts; 1947), and the 'Hill Tracts People's Organization (1950). Kazi Mahmudar Rashid, 'A Study on Administration', 28; Siddhartha Chakma, *Proshongo*, 6-22.

aims and in 1957 student protests against political repression in the hills led to the formation of an underground *Pahari Chhatro Shomiti*' (Hill Students' Association). This association formed the organizational core of agitations against the Kaptai hydro-electric project and the abolition of the district's special status. With the establishment of an underground party known as the 'Chittagong Hill Tracts Welfare Association' in 1966 the political organization of the hill people entered a new phase. For the first time proponents of armed struggle against the government came to the fore. After the war between Bangladesh and Pakistan in 1971 the Welfare Association was dissolved; it was supplanted by the '*Parbotyo Chottogram Jono Shonghoti Shomiti*' ('*Jana Samhati Samiti*'; Chittagong Hill Tracts People's Solidarity Association).[88] This party, usually referred to as the JSS, has been the main political organization in the Chittagong hills since then.[89] It has become best known under the name of its armed wing, the '*Shanti Bahini*' (Peace Troops), which confronted the Bangladesh army and groups of armed in-migrants ('Village Defence Parties') from 1975 onwards.[90]

Increasing political organization in the Chittagong hills signalled the progressive abandonment of the Bengali cultural model. The ultimate break came with the mass in-migration of Bengali peasants in the late 1970s. A remarkable cultural innovation occurred which was reflected in the emergence of a new term to designate the people of the

---

[88] Kazi Mahmudar Rashid, 'A Study on Administration', 29; cf. A.B. Chakma, 'Look Back from Exile', 35-62.

[89] Other organizations exist but appear to be much weaker or inactive. These organizations, most of which the JSS considers creatures of the Bangladesh government, include the Pahari Jono Kolyan Shomiti [Hill People's Welfare Association], Tribal Convention, Marma Unnoyon Shongshod [Marma Development Council], Tripura Unnoyon Shongshod [Tripura Development Council], Hill District Co-ordination Committees, and Headmen's Association. It is significant, however, that a recent protest against killings in Longodu, signed by representatives of several of these organizations 'on behalf of the tribal people', also spoke of 'genocidal attacks' and demanded the removal of all Bengali settlers from the Chittagong hills.

Cf. *An Urgent Statement of the Jana Samhati on the Parbatya Zilla Parishad Zilla Parishad Bills Placed in the Jatiya Sangsad (Parliament) by Bangladesh Government* (n.p.: Department of Information and Publicity, Parbatya Chattagram Jana Samhati Samiti, 18th February 1989), 3; Devasish Roy et al., *04/05/89 Ing roj brihospotibar Rangamati.*

[90] C.M.T., 'Beleaguered Tribals,' *Far Eastern Economic Review* (6 October 1988), 8.

Chittagong hills. They were now called '*Jumma*'. An old pejorative term for 'swidden cultivator' in the Chittagonian dialect of Bengali, it had been appropriated by the JSS in its attempt to unify all hill people under one social umbrella. It is remarkable that this term came up at a time when many hill people had been forced to give up swidden cultivation.

9 *The Creation of a People*

What are the characteristics of the 'Jummas'? It is difficult to see them as an ethnic group in the traditional, cultural sense: they share neither a single language nor a single religion. The type of collective identity the term Jumma seeks to create is based more on social than on cultural characteristics, and the fact that the inhabitants of the Chittagong hills now frequently use the terms 'Jumma people' and 'Jumma nation' to refer to themselves indicates that a process of 'nation-building' is under way.[91] The mental construction of a 'Jumma nation' shows various aspects, and the ultimate success or failure of this attempt hinges on the future importance of these aspects in the minds of the hill people.

First, the demarcation of cultural boundaries is pre-eminent in the development of the Jumma identity. Although internally diversified, Jummas highlight their *cultural separateness* from Bengalis. In religious terms they stress their non-Islamic religious outlook[92] and in linguistic terms the fact that Bengali is not their mother tongue. Old negative stereo-

[91] E.g. *Urgent Statement* (1) speaks of the 'national entity of the Jumma people' and claims: 'The Jumma national unity and solidarity has been jeopardised dividing ten linguistically different Jumma national minorities into three Zilla Parishads.' The third use of 'national' apparently refers to Bangladesh. In 1985 the JSS had spoken of Jumma peoples ('the Jumma Peoples were compelled to organize a Movement for ensuring their National Identity and the integrity of their Motherland'), but significantly the plural was later dropped. Central Executive, Jana Samhati Samity, 'An Open Letter to Lt. General Ershad, Chief Martial-Law Administrator of Bangladesh, on his October 3 Proclamation' (printed leaflet dated 25 November 1985),2.

[92] In the 1970s Jummas were often equated with Buddhists because the majority of the hill people consider themselves Buddhists. More recently, this has been played down in deference to non-Buddhist influences among the hill people: e.g. Hinduism among the Tippera, Christianity among the Lushai and Bawm-Zo, and the local religions such as that of the Mru.

types of Bengalis play an important role. Around 1960 Bernot reported about Marma perceptions:

> 'The Bengali is the administration, the police, the greedy merchant, the sometimes unscrupulous money-lender, and so on; the Marmas' list is endless. But the Bengalis are also men who have left behind their wives in the plains.. and among them are beggars, coolies, boatmen, and famine.'[93]

New negative roles in which the Jummas have cast Bengalis since then include those of rapist, torturer, killer, extortioner, and arsonist. Older positive roles (teacher, friend, partner, patron, protector, broker) are conspicuously absent from the recent literature.

The Jumma identity does not signify a return to the old Burmese cultural model; rather it is the first serious attempt to develop an indigenous model of state society and culture. English is now often preferred to Bengali, which has served as a lingua franca in the hills since it supplanted Arakanese at the beginning of the colonial period. Attempts to revive the local linguistic heritage can also be observed, e.g. in a trend towards giving newborn babies Jumma names instead of the Bengali names that were fashionable a generation ago. Some efforts are also being made to resuscitate the old Chakma alphabet, which had been almost forgotten.[94] Cultural purification, i.e. the removal of Bengali influences that are now felt to be 'alien', is so far less pronounced than the demarcation of the cultural boundaries between Jummas and

---

[93] Bernot, *Les paysans arakanais*, 749-750 (my translation)

[94] The Chakmas now speak a language closely akin to Chittagonian Bengali but used to speak an Arakanese dialect which was already largely lost when Buchanan visited them (see footnote 8). Lewin (*Wild Races*, 307) reported, however that Arakanese was the lingua franca in the Chittagong hills, 'spoken and understood by everyone', as late as the 1860s.

The Chakma language was written in a script closely related to the Burmese script; during the 20th century it was gradually replaced by the Bengali script. The best introduction to the history of the Chakma language is Lorenz G. Löffler, 'Chakma und Sak'. See also C.R. Chakma, *Changma Kodha Bhandal/Chakma Bhashar Obhidhan* [Dictionary of the Chakma Language] (Calcutta: Pustok Biponi, 1391 B.E. [1984-85]); C.R. Chakma, *Jug-Bibortone Chakma-Jati (Prachin Jug)* [The Chakmas Through the Ages (Ancient Period)] (Calcutta: Pustom Biponi, 1394 B.E. [1987], 13; Dulal Choudhuri, Chakma Probad [Chakma Proverbs] (Calcutta: Pustok Biponi, 1980); and Maniruzzaman, 'Notes on Chakma Phonology', in: Qureshi (ed.), *Tribal Cultures*, 73-89.

Bengalis. Racial overtones have also been weak; the physical differences between 'Indic' Bengalis and 'Mongoloid' hill people that so preoccupied the British do not appear to figure prominently in the self-image of the Jummas in the 1970s and 1980s.

A second aspect that is being stressed is the possession of a Jumma *homeland* that needs to be protected against non-Jumma outsiders. The connection between nation and land is not traditional among swidden cultivators who used to consider land as a free gift of nature, not the possession of mortals. But territorial thinking has developed strongly in reaction to proprietary claims by the British crown and its successor governments, the introduction of private property rights in land, and exploitation of the region's resources.[95] Among the inhabitants of the Chittagong hills, whose precolonial forebears did not feel any particular closeness to each other because they happened to occupy the same tract of hill land, the possession of a homeland has now become a core element in the construction of a shared identity. Jummas now identify strongly with, and only with, the hills that the British carved out as the Chittagong Hill Tracts and that Bangladesh received as a colonial inheritance.

Third, the creation of the Jumma identity depends crucially upon the awareness that the hill people share a unique *historical experience*. This sets them apart from Bengalis but also from inhabitants of other parts of the mountain range. The emergence of the Jumma identity is accompanied with re-interpretations of that experience. The present war has enormously intensified feelings among the hill people that they have *always* been beleaguered by outsiders. The inven-

---

[95] JSS resistance led to the discontinuation or suspension of various development projects in which the Dhaka government was involved, e.g. a Swedish-funded forestry project, Australian-funded road-building project, and oil prospecting by Shell. An overview of the government development programme can be found in 'Chittagong Hill Tracts'. Anti-Slavery Society, *The Chittagong Hill Tracts*, 37-41; 'Shantibahini activities hinder road works in Ctg Hill Tracts', *New Nation* (13 February 1986); Syed Murtaza Ali, 'Hill Tracts solution in sight?" *Holiday* (12 September 1986), 5,7; 'Chittagong Hill Tracts: an Observer Supplement', *The Bangladesh Observer* (12 November 1985).

tion of a 'national' tradition can be observed in attempts to highlight Jumma prosperity and unity in the past and to focus on harmonious historical relations between different hill peoples rather than on conflicts between them. In this way a collective identity that has blossomed as a result of shared experiences in recent times is projected onto the more distant past.[96]

And finally, the hill people are striving to develop the 'indigenous cultural model' they have begun to adopt. In the 1980s they established contact with various international organizations of, or concerned with, '*indigenous peoples*', and they came to see their struggle increasingly in terms of human and minority rights. This was also the period in which they began to participate in new nation-wide organizations of minority groups in Bangladesh.[97] The cultural model which is spreading among the inhabitants of the Chittagong hills emanates from the experiences of minorities as far apart as Australia and Scandinavia. It is couched increasingly in 'Fourth World' terms and stresses their inalienable right to self-determination.[98]

10. *A Successful Identity?*

Is it possible to 'will' a collective identity into existence? To what extent has the JSS being successful in propagating the new Jumma identity? Is it an ethnic identity in the making, emerging nationalism, or a political pipe-dream? JSS documents have embraced the concept wholeheartedly and

[96] For a general analysis of 'invented traditions' and attendant re-interpretations of the past, see Eric Hobsbawm and Terence Ranger (eds.), *The Invention of Tradition* (Cambridge: Cambridge University Press, 1983), 1-14.

[97] Several other ethnic minorities live elsewhere in Bangladesh; their numbers are smaller and they live more dispersed than the Chittagong hill people. National organizations called Bangladesh Adibashi Upojati Kolyan Federation (Bangladesh Aboriginal-Tribal Welfare Federation) and Aboriginal Development Services of Bangladesh were established around 1980. Information can be found in their journals, *Matir Manush* (People of the Soil) and *Aronyok* (Forest People).

[98] 'But circumstances so led them [the Jumma peoples] that at last, a full decade ago, they had to take to Arms in demand of SELF-DETERMINATION...The War of Self-determination shall run unabated.' Central Executive, 'Open Letter', 2.

there are indications that the JSS enjoys broad support in the Chittagong hills. But it would seem that there are various obstacles to the acceptance of Jumma ethnicity or Jumma (sub)nationalism. First, the Jumma identity will have to compete with distinct local-group identities that are well established and do not show signs of fading. But of course no collectivity is homogeneous; it always overlaps with others, e.g. gender, class, kin group, and region. People are capable of having multiple identities, and the different local groups may well adopt the Jumma identity in addition to their local identity. Second, acceptation of the Jumma identity depends on the degree to which old inter-group perceptions can be neutralized. For example, some groups consider themselves more 'advanced' than others; this is especially clear in the traditional division between 'river-valley' groups (e.g. Marma and Chakma) and 'hill-top' groups (e.g. Bawm, Mru and Khumi).[99] Third, group size varies from a few hundred to several hundred thousand; if the smaller groups fear their cultural heritage will be swamped in a Jumma identity that is dominated by the largest groups, they may well be tempted to repudiate the Jumma label. Fourth, different ethnic groups have been affected differently by Bengali in-migration and repression, and it is conceivable that allegiance to the Jumma identity will vary accordingly.

At present it is impossible to know to what extent these obstacles operate. Bangladesh government sources either ignore the Jumma identity or denounce it as a figment of the imagination of some misguided Chakma 'miscreants[100]' who try to disturb peaceful relations between Bengalis and hill

[99] E.g. Mey, *Politische Systeme*, 226-246; Bernot, *Les paysans arakanais*,748-750.

[100] Amnesty International reports that the term miscreant is 'offically used for Shanti Bahini forces'. They are also frequently called 'terrorists' but the authorities no longer dismiss them as simple criminals. In the words of Major-General Abdus Salam, Area Commander of the Chittagong Hill Tracts, as reported in the Bangladesh press: 'We are not fighting just a bandit group. the insurgents are really quite deep into their mission and they are organized and motivated.'

Amnesty International, *Bangladesh: Report of a Mission Concerning Reported Human Rights Violations in the Chittagong Hill Tracts*, 24-30 January 1988 (London: Amnesty International, 1988), 5; Moinuddin Naser, 'Shantibahini now uses remote control explosives', *Holiday*, 25:24 (12 January 1990), 8.

people by means of an illegal organization. It is true that Chakmas are very visible in the JSS. It would be highly surprising if they were not: they are the largest group in the Chittagong hills, they have an educated elite, and they have been among those who have been most severely affected, first by the Kaptai lake and later by in-migration and militarization. But the other groups in the Chittagong hills are not absent from either the JSS or the casualty list. It is certainly too simplistic to dismiss the JSS as a Chakma organization and 'Jummaization' as a Chakma ploy. On the other hand, too little is at present known about inter-ethnic relations in or outside the JSS, or the use of symbols of Jumma adherence, to allow us to judge the degree to which the Jumma identity has struck roots in the Chittagong hills.[101]

So far the resistance movement against the Bangladesh army and Bengali in-migration has been supported by an ideology which leans heavily on ethnic pride and the right to self-determination. Its demands parallel those of the two great nationalist movements in which the hill people have participated to some extent: the Independence movement against British rule, and the Bangladesh movement against Pakistan.[102] Both these movements were successful and resulted in national states. Like them the Jumma movement is a solidarity movement: it endeavours to achieve self-determination by projecting a clear socio-cultural identity and by constructing a sharp image of the external enemy. But unlike them it cannot fall back on an already well-established 'internal' identity. At present its unity within appears to rest squarely upon the awesome opposition without; ultimately, however, its success will depend largely on the extent to which the people of the Chittagong hills come to perceive themselves primarily as Jummas.

[101] The cultural and political problems surrounding the search for an acceptable generic name for all the 'Chin-Kuki-Mizo-Zoumi' groups inhabiting the area to the east of the Chittagong hills should alert us to the potential limitations of the use of 'Jumma' in the Chittagong hills. Cf. H. Kamkhenthang, *The Paite: A Transborder Tribe of India and Burma* (Delhi: Mittal Publications, 1988), esp. 1-11.

[102] See e.g. Siddhartha Chakma, *Proshongo*; and A.B. Chakma, 'Look Back from Exile', 35-62.

Even so, what an autonomous Jumma region would look like remains vague. There are at least two factors that might undermine the attempt to establish the Jumma identity as a dominant ethnic category in the future. First, there is the old controversy between those who consider the indigenous political tradition of the Chittagong hills to be one of democratic equality, as exemplified by the 'acephalous' political systems of some groups, and those who consider it to be one of hierarchical centralism, as exemplified by chiefly rule. It remains to be seen if the Jumma identity can survive the competition between these views, and the social programmes they entail. Second, Jumma self-determination may easily come into conflict with other regional movements in the mountain range. There is, for example, a movement for 'Greater Mizoram' which claims parts of the Chittagong hills.[103]

The emergence of the Jumma identity can be understood as a warning signal, a symbolic response to the calamitous meeting of two incompatible views of ethnic relations in the Chittagong hills. These met under conditions of very unequal power, and the creation of the 'Jummas' was an act of defiance. It signalled that after the mid-1970s ethnic fusion, in which hill people would assimilate to Bengali culture, and ethnic persistence, in which hill people would hang on to indigenous identity systems, were both increasingly unrealistic. Instead, it was a bid for ethnic innovation, to cope with the political and economic consequences of loss of power,

[103] 'A part of Zoram lies in the eastern part of the Chittagong Hill Tracts of Bangladesh..The Zo clans in Bangladesh are Bawmzo, Asho (Khyang), Khami, Lusei, Masho (Mru), and Pankhu.' Vumson, *Zo History, with an introduction to Zo culture, religion and their status as an ethnic minority in India, Burma, and Bangladesh* (Aizawl, Mizoram: the Author, 1986), 316. Cf. Subir Bhaumik and H.C. Vanlalruata, 'Sailo's grand strategy: The former CM has picked up the Greater Mizoram cause to come out of the political wilderness', *Sunday* (19-25 June 1988), 64; Ramesh Menon, 'Mizoram — Wild Dreams: Plans to carve a new state', *India Today* (30 June 1988), 63-67.

growing expendability to the state, and cultural marginalization. This makes it an important case for students of ethnicity who have been much concerned with ethnic conflict but have given less attention to ethnic innovation (ethnogenesis) than to other forms of boundary crossing (especially ethnic assimilation, incorporation and secession).[104]

The Jumma identity turns enclavement upside down. It signifies the choice for an 'ethnic strategy' in politics: the Jummas themselves now seek isolation from the dominant culture and from the state that represents it, and they resist what they consider an infringement of their cultural boundaries. Worldwide, ethnic strategies can be seen as thoroughly modern responses to economic and political change.[105] Such strategies can also be observed in several parts of the mountain range. But nowhere else have hill people been given so little local autonomy, become so marginalized vis-à-vis the state, and been confronted with such in-migration. These factors, as well as the cultural diversity of the Chittagong hill people and the peculiarities of the Bangladesh state, defy easy comparisons with other groups employing ethnic strategies in the region. The Jummas are neither 'Bangladeshi Nagas' nor 'Bangladeshi Jharkhandis'.[106] Their movement is

---

[104] Similarly the ethnic consequences of migration are usually studied among in-migrants; the Chittagong hills case reveals that this is insufficient: it may result in critical ethinic change among the 'receiving' population. J.A. Fishman, 'Language and Ethnicity', in: Howard Giles (ed.), *Language, Ethnicity and Intergroup Relations* (London etc.: Academic Press, 1977), 15-57; Royce, *Ethnic Identity, 108-141.*

[105] Smith mentions six main strategies; in the Jumma movement the dominant one is 'autonomism' but 'separatism' is a second option. Anthony D. Smith, *The Ethnic Revival in the Modern World* (Cambridge: Cambridge University Press, 1981), 15-17. Cf. Fishman, 'Language and Ethnicity', 35-38.

[106] The cultural diversity of the Chittagong hill groups (with their separate links with Arakan, Chin country, Tripura, and Bengal) is greater than elsewhere in the mountain range, where overarching collective identities were usually available for diverse cultural groups from an early age. The 'Naga' identity is a case in point; it helped overcome local antagonisms and organize resistance in the far north from a much earlier date, first against the British, and then against the independent Indian and Burmese states.

Similarly, the 'Jharkhand' identity was first used in Chhota Nagpur and Santal Parganas in 1938, and followed the much older concept of 'diku' (alien oppressor) which had fired earlier rebellions; however, the Jharkhandi identity is even now 'an extremely amorphous concept'. Threre are many historical, political and economic differences between the Jharkhand and Jumma movements, e.g. the role of the Jharkhand urban middle class, the activities of Christian missionaries, extensive 'non-tribal' support, and close links with all-India political parties from the 1930s.

not simply an 'inter-ethnic alliance'; it seeks the creation of a new 'national' collectivity, based on a homeland created by colonialism and decolonization, in the face of extreme adversity.[107] I have indicated that this development can be explained by the unusual combination of factors affecting the Chittagong hills. The inhabitants of this area did not share a 'traditional' sense of unity but were nevertheless ecologically and socio-culturally isolated from the plains peasantry. The Bengali majority attained national statehood relatively late and a largely stagnant view of ethnic relations prevailed among those who held state power. In the new state the hills were a small border region with a minute population. An active policy of economic exploitation elicited local protests which went unheeded until armed resistance to in-migration, which hill people regard as an attempt to unload the effects of mass poverty in the plains at least partly on themselves, led to militarization, warfare, and international attention.

Discussion is clearly possible concerning the extent to which hill people have accepted the Jumma identity in addition to their older ethnic identities. The intensity of the conflict and the clear cultural boundaries between hill people and Bengalis make it likely that the Jumma identity is now more salient than ever.[108] But the point here is not whether it has been universally accepted or whether the old ambivalence towards the Bengali model has turned into complete rejection; this seems unlikely but cannot be verified at present. This paper has sought to explain why in recent years a new identity has been 'invented' at all, and found a mea-

---

Singh S.M. Dubey, 'Inter-Ethnic Alliance, Tribal Movements and Integration in Northeast India', in: K.S. Singh (ed.), *Tribal Movements in India* (Delhi: Manohar Publications, 1982), Volume I, 1-25; *The Naga Nation and its Struggle against Genocide* (Copenhagen: International Work Group for Indigenous Affairs, 1986); K.S. Singh, 'Tribal Autonomy Movements in Chotanagpur', in: K.S. Singh (ed.) *Tribal Movements,* Volume II, 1-29; Nirmal Sengupta, 'Background to the Jharkhand Question', in: Normal Sengupta (ed.). *Fourth World Dynamics: Jharkhand* (Delhi: Authors Guild Publications, 1982), 3-39.

[107] The distinction between 'ethnic group' and 'nation' becomes rather arbitrary in acute conflicts: 'when nations stand in a conflictive relationship with one another, the confrontation bears many of the earmarks of ethnic conflict.' Royce, *Ethnic Identity*. 84.

[108] On the 'saliency' of ethnicity', see Fishman, 'Language and Ethnicity', 32-34.

sure of acceptance. This in itself is a reflection of important and irreversible change: 'once [ethnic] boundaries have been invested with interpretations and enactments, these acquire a logic and dynamic of their own, and can become... exceedingly difficult to alter.'[109] As the most outspoken socio-cultural response to the political crisis in the Chittagong hills, the concept of 'Jumma' is here to stay, and will have to be taken into account by anyone planning to resolve that crisis.

[109] Fishman, 'Language and Ethnicity', 26.

Oraon Labour Agitation: Duars in Jalpaiguri District, 1915-16*

RANAJIT DAS GUPTA

This paper deals with a widespread agitation that took place among the tea plantation labourer of Duars in Jalpaiguri district in north Bengal. Starting in several gardens in November 1915, it spread rapidly to a large number of tea gardens stretching over the extensive Duars plantation tract and continued till mid-1916. Although the agitation was a short-lived one, it had several distinctive features. But till now it has not received any attention from scholars. It is hoped that a discussion of various aspects of the agitation will be of help in enriching our understanding of tribal as well as of plantation labour protest movements in our country.

I

The agitation was, in fact, an extension of the Tana Bhagat movement that had originated among the tribal peasant — specifically speaking, the Oraon peasants — engaged in settled agriculture in the Ranchi district of Chhotanagpur in April 1914.[1] Initially, the Ranchi movement had the character of a religious and social reform movement, but eventually came to have important economic and political dimensions.

---

* This is a revised version of part of a longer paper entitled 'Ambiguities of Class Formation: Plantation Capitalism, Workers and Collective Action in Duars, 1890s-1947' brought out in January 1987 in the working paper series of the Indian Institute of Management, Calcutta. In writing this paper I have benefitted much from discussion with Asok Sen, Barun De and Surendra Musnshi. I alone am responsible for all the shortcomings. For a Bengali version see 'Duarse Sramik Pratibad', *Madhuparni*, December, 1987, pp. 191-281. It is to be added that the research for this paper has been supported by the Centre for Management Development Studies of the Institute.

[1] For account and analysis of the Tana Bhgat movement see Sarat Chandra Roy, *Oraon Religion and Customs*, Calcutta, 1928 (1985 reprint). pp. 339-403; Nirmal Kumar Bose, *Some Indian Tribes*, National Book Trust, New Delhi, 1972, pp. 140-41; and Stephen Fuchs, *Rebellious Prophets: a Study of Messianic Movements in Indian Religions*, Asia Publishing House, Bombay, 1965, pp. 38-42.

The movement was basically based on the aspirations of Oraon peasants for deliverence from the exploitation and oppression of the *zamindars*, *mahajans* and *sarkar*.[2]

In its origin the Tana Bhagat movement had features which have come to be known as messianic.[3] In early 1914 the movement was launched by one Jatra Oraon who had mysterious dreams. The Oraons were called upon to 'pull out' (*tana*) ghosts and evil spirits which they had till then tried to appease but which were now held responsible for their misery. They were asked to abstain from meat and liquor and thus to purify and reform their lives. Participation in certain community dances and festivals too were forbidden.[4] They were also told to give up ploughing their fields, which entailed cruelty to cow and oxen but failed to protect them from poverty and famine. In this, in the form of a yearning to go back to pre-settled forms of agriculture, a protest against exploitation by the landlords and the government was discernible. Some of the *tana bhagats* even stopped payment of rents to their landlords and ploughing. They were, moreover, called upon to do no work as coolies and labourers under men of other castes and tribes. The latter aspect referred to labour in the tea gardens as well as in the fields of the large landholders in many districts of Bengal and Bihar.[5]

As stated already, it was a messianic movement and it was believed that god (whom they called *dharmes*, the 'just', the supreme being or Bhagwan, the bountiful) would send a messiah down to earth to redeem the Oraons from their

---

[2] See Roy, op cit, pp. 344-46. Roy himself was a loyalist and denied that the movement had any anti-government thrust (p 346).

[3] Cf Fuchs, op cit; and David Hardiman, 'Adivasi Assertion in South Gujarat: The Devi Movement of 1922-3' in Ranajit Guha (ed), *Subaltern Studies III*, Oxford University Press, New Delhi, 1984, p 210 and n 36.

[4] It is tempting to view this socio-religious effort in terms of Srinivas' sanskritization thesis (See M N Srinivas, *Social Change in Modern India*, University of California, 1966). But there are serious difficulties in the sanskritization interpretation. See Hardiman, *loc cit*; pp 212-14; and Surendra Munshi, Tribal Absorption and Sanskritization in Hindu society', *Contribution to Indian Sociology* (New Series), Vol.13, No. 2, 1979, pp 293-319.

[5] Roy, op cit., p 342; and Bose, op cit, p 141.

miserable plight. Sometimes, the messiah was identified with Birsa, the Munda rebel of late 1890s, and sometimes with German *baba* or benign god (Kaiser Wilhelm II?) who was at war with the British.[6] The movement also looked forward to a millennium or a 'golden age'. It, however, soon assumed forms that were considered dangerous by the colonial government. It threatened to break out into open revolt against the *dikus* (outsiders) and all exploiters and oppressers. Along with this, various symbols of 'modern civilization', such as railways, steamboat and bicycle had to be 'pulled out' or expelled, as the suffering of the Oraons came in the wake of their introduction.[7] Thus, these reactions signified a rejection of colonial capitalist penetration and associate instruments.

II

The reverberations of the movement in Chhotanagpur soon came to be felt in distant Duars.[8] In the wake of the launching of tea plantations in the Duars in the mid-1870s, with the active assistance of the colonial state, large scale migration of tribal, particularly Oraon peasants had been organized by the planters — overwhelmingly Europeans — to the Duars tea gardens.[9] The Oraon migrants in the Duars numbered about double the number of the number of the Munda and Santhal migrants taken together.[10] But the migrant tribal-peasants-turned-into-wage labourers on the tea gardens had a deep attachment for their homes and lands in Chhotanagpur and Santhal Parganas. In his report on 'survey and settlement' work in the Ranchi district during 1902-1910 Reid, the settlement officer, observed:

[6] Fuchs, op cit.

[7] See Bose, op cit, p 142.

[8] Duars was a 2,053 miles tract in Jalpaiguri district, the northern-most plain district in undivded Bengal.

[9] For labour migration to the Duars plantations see Ranajit Das Gupta, Economy, *Society and Politics in Bengal: Jalpaiguri 1870-1947*, Oxford University Press, Delhi, 1992.

[10] According to the 1921 census report, in Jalpaiguri district the Oraons numbered 1, 15, 350, (*Census of India*, while the Mundas and Santhals were respectively 34, 601 and 23, 488 Vol V, *Bengal*, Pt II, Table XIII).

> Large number of those who emigrate to Assam and the Duars return, if they are able to save a little money, and buy back the farms they had lost, or some land in the vicinity.[11]

Continuing he reported:

> A considerable percentage of emigration is periodic and non-permanent. The Oraons especially emigrate in large number... during the cold weather, when there is little or no work to do in their field and return home before the monsoon breaks to being the cultivation of their fields.[12]

In view of this persistence of connections with Ranchi, it was quite natural that the Tana Bhagat movement had its echoes among the Oraons in Duars. But this movement was not just a replication of the movement in Ranchi. The *specificity* of its locale, particularly the British dominated plantation economy and the horrible exploitation and oppression of plantation labour in duars, had its *distinctive imprints* on the movement.

The year 1916 was a war year and the stir came to be viewed by the planters and the colonial government as well with considerable alarm. In his address to the annual general meeting of the Duars Planters Association (DPA) held in January 1917, W L Travers, DPA chairman, spoke of the 'great anxiety' caused to the Europeans planters by the outbreak of what was considered by them as 'a new and dangerous movement amongst the Oraons' in the early months of 1916.[13] In the Bengal government's *Report on the Administration of Bengal* for 1916-17 it was stated that labourers of several gardens were 'said to be eschewing meat and strong drink and singing songs containing references to a Germany victory'.[14]

From available evidence it is found that the agitation consisted of two phases, though, as we shall see these were

[11] J. Reid, *Final Report on the Survey and Settlement Operations in the District of Ranchi 1902-1910*, Government Printing, Bihar, Orissa and Patna, p. 10, para 20.

[12] Ibid, p 11, para 20.,

[13] *Detailed Report of the General Committee of the Duars Planters Association* (here after DPA Report) for 1916, p vii.

[14] Government of Bengal, *Report on the Administration of Bengal during 1916-17*, p 17.

never clearly demarcated. In this first phase, it was primarily a socio-religious reform movement. There was an initiation ceremony, and those who passed this ceremony called themselved *bhagats* or devouts. Their utensils were destroyed, and drinking of *hari* (rice beer the drinking of which was an important part of the tribal social life) and *daru* (the country liquor) were prohibited. All meat except white goats and white fowls became a taboo. Those Oraons who did not go through the ceremony were excommunicated and the fear of excommunication perhaps persuaded many Oraons to join the movement.[15]

At the initial stage, the stir was viewed by the planters as an expression of aspiration of social and spiritual movement and, hence, the planters and district administration were not much perturbed. In the address referred to above Traverse observed:

> Many of the ideas connected with the first stage were excellent, and had the movement stopped there, it would have been encouraged by planters.[16]

But there was a swift transition to the second phase characterized by an anti-British and anti-planter content and direction, and these were infused with Oraon religiosity. It was this latter aspect which was one of the factors that gave the agitation a wide appeal.[17] According to the official version, the movement in the Duars had a political orientation from the very beginning and with the unfolding of the movement this became increasingly pronounced. In the trial of Bania Oraon, Laudha Oraon and Mangra Oraon, all tea garden workers, for their allegedly leading role in the movement, the prosecution case was that since November 1915 Oraon tea garden workers had been

> holding meetings at night and singing hymns to the 'German Father', whom they invoke[d] as if he was a god, calling on him to

[15] *DPA Report* for 1916, p xi.

[16] Ibid, p vii.

[17] See in this connection Partha Chatterjee, 'Agrarian Relations and Communalism in Bengal, 1926-1935', in Guha (ed), *Subaltern Studies I*, Oxford University Press, Delhi, 1982, p 31.

come and drive out the English, whom they compare[d] to devils, and give an independent raj to the Oraons.[18]

It is possible that the prosecution exaggerated the political tone of the movement. But undoubtedly one major distinguishing feature of the Duars movement was its much stronger political orientation than the one in Ranchi. In connection with the second phase, another important feature deserves to be mentioned. Though throughout its course the movement by and large remained peaceful, it was in this phase that it came to exibit a relatively militant tone. In their exchanges with the garden authority or in their defiance of the latter which are mentioned below this tone is discernible. Inter-tribal solidarity was another distinctive feature that came to be manifested. Though the movement was a movement of the Oraon workers, it did not remain confine among them alone. It came to involve, as shown later, several non-Oraon tribals and semi-tribal groups too.

The incident that first brought the movement to the notice of the district administration indicated the political dimension unmistakable. The official account of the movement is given below:

A man named Charua Oraon cut his wife's throat and then cut his own. He told the police that the villagers had asked him to 'sing the name of the Germans' and had threatened that, if he did not, a devil named Logo would kill him. He had his wife resolved to kill themselves rather than be killed by a devil...He said that an unknown man was always telling him to recite something, and that as he refused, everyone abused him and his wife, so they resolved to commit suicide.....[19]

Charua was too badly wounded to explain what he refused to recite and died in the jail hospital.

The event was reported to the police on January 25, 1916. Subsequently the superintendent of police made enqui-

[18] National Archives of India (NAI). Home Political. A Nos 280-81 of June 1916 'Oraon Unrest in Bengal, Bihar and Orissa. Judgement of the Special Tribunal appointed under the Defence of India Act in the Oraon Case (hereafter NAI 'Oraon Unrest'), p 5.

[19] Ibid, p 5.

ries to find out what the 'mysterious recitations' were. On February 25 he receivcd a letter from the manager of the Tasati tea estate, containing

> a list of eight Oraon men and six Oraon women who were holding seditious meetings and calling to the 'German Father' to come and save them. The manager said that they were upsetting the coolies on his garden and that it was rumoured that there would be a row at the Fagua Puja (March 18 to 21).[20]

On March 1 the DPA chairman informed the police that a meeting of garden managers was held to discuss the Oraon unrest, but they could only discover that 'mysterious meetings' were being held at night and that trouble at the *Fagua Puja* was apprehended. On March 2 the manager of Sarugaon tea estate intimated the police that Hasru, a *sardar* in the garden, was involved in the movement and 'was adopting a threatening attitude towards the garden staff...,'[21]. P T Monckton, the superintendent of police (SP), went to the Tasati tea estate on March 1 and interrogated some Oraon labourers. Dublai and Letho, two Oraon *sardars*, repeated to him the words of two of the songs sung at the meetings. The next day Monckton arrested ten Oraons in that garden, including Letho, who allegedly had helped the holding of the meetings.[22]

On March 4 an informal meeting of the DPA Committee was held and this was attended by the Deputy Commissioner of Jalpaiguri and also the SP. From the proceedings of the meeting the following is learnt:

> On one garden he (the SP) considered the movement had gone very far, and there was a distinct *seditious* element in connection with the German Raj. Again, on another garden he had been called in for, the coolies had *refused* to work, saying that they had *no allegience to the British Raj.* The coolies were almost in mutiny saying that the German Raj was comming in to govern the country...[23] (emphasis added).

---

[20] Ibid, p 5.
[21] *DPA Report* for 1916, p. ix.
[22] NAI 'Oraon Unrest', p 5.

The meeting was told by one member of the committee:

> ...the idea was held that the Germans would take possession of the Raj, and that those who helped the Germans would be rewarded by gifts of land in (Chhota) Nagpur, their ancient country.[24]

Another member told the meeting:

> ...there was a secret movement with a view to exterminate the Sahibs. The vow was sworn by god, Germany and blood.[25]

The managers reported acts of open defiance of authority. In Sarugaon tea estate Hasru and Kandru refused to work. When asked by the manager if they were taking part in the movement, Hasru shouted in a loud voice, 'who said so?', and when the manager ordered him to put down his hoe and report to the office, he and Kandru and another man threw down their hoes and ran away....[26] In the trial of three Oraon workers of the Gurjangjhora tea estate (western Duars) the prosecution referred to another instance of collective defiance. The estate manager was informed by the *chowkidars* that the Oraon workers of the garden were having meetings and songs in lonely places and intended to abstain from flesh food and liquor and lead a religious life. But this information alarmed the manager and he sent for two Oraon leaders. They came accompanied by forty Oraon workers. The leaders were asked to leave the garden and go elsewhere. But they refused to be separated from others on the ground that it would interfere with their prayers. They then left the manager and while they were leaving they were "heard to mutter something in Oraon language which the garden officers did not understand". But the manager's servant interpreted it to mean, "if we beat him, what will happen?"[27]

---

[23] *DPA Report* for 1916, pp 285-86.
[24] Ibid, p 286.
[25] Ibid, p 286.
[26] NAI 'Oraon Unrest', p 6.
[27] An account of this incident was given in the *Amrita Bazar Patrika* May 10, 1916, editorial entitled' The Oraon Unrest: the Second Case'. The editorial sharply criticized the government attitude. *Amrita Bazar Patrika* wrote another editorial in its issue of May 2, 1916. Both the editorials were considered 'objectionable' by the Criminal Intelligence Office and there was a move for prosecuting the Patrika under the Defence of India Act. See NAI Home Political Deposit, No 12 of June 1916.

These instances of course need to be considered with caution. With reference to the Gurjangjhora incident *Amrita Bazar Patrika* (a nationalist English daily published from Calcutta) of May 10,1916 editorially observed, "there is no evidence to show if the servant interpreted the coolies correctly or not". As pointed out in the same editorial, "among so large a population not a single act of violence or rowdyism...was reported."[28] Yet it is evident that the movement had a distinct anti-British political overtone. The political response of Oraon labour to both British rule and planters' domination and the Oraon political aspirations found expression in the Oraon labour agitation which, it may be reiterated, had a tribal religious diemension too. All this came to be articulated *inter alia* in the collective singing, often continuing till midnight. Despite the ambiguity, the following song composed by Letho, a *sardar* in the Tasati T E, and cited during the trial of Oraon workers as evidence of sedition, shows the Oraon political attitude:

German Baba is coming,
Is slowly slowly coming;
Drive away the devils Manaldanal:
Cast them adrift in the sea.
Suruj Baba (the sun) is coming;
The Devils of the Oven, will be driven away
And cast adrift in the sea.
Tarijan (the stars) is coming
Is slowly slowly coming,
Is coming to our very courtyard
The chigri devils will be driven away
And cast adrift in the sea.[29]

One prosecution witness told the special tribunal appointed to try the tribal workers, mainly Oraons and a few non-Oraons, who were alleged to have had taken leading

[28] Ibid.
[29] Cited in NAI 'Oraon Unrest', p 7.

role in the movement:

> ....there is a hidden meaning in the song...the new school of Oraons call the English devils (deos) and...the devils of the Oraons referred to in the song are the Englilsh.[30]

Asked by one of the commissioners if he had ever heard the song and knew its meaning, Birsai, another witness, said:

> ...Yes, he had heard it, and it meant that the Germans were coming to make war, and the government people would be thrown into the sea. He said that new school always speaks of the Germans as Suruj Baba (the sun)...and that Tarijan Baba also meant the Germans, while of the devils Manaldanal meant the English, and the devils of the Oraons (*sic*) [oven] or hearth meant those Oraons who did not join the new movement.[31]

The special tribunal in its "Judgement in the Oraon Case" accepted this interpretation:

> Now it is certain that the Oraons are not under any mistaken notion as to who and what the Germans are. Two or three witnesses have told us that export of tea from the garden was stopped for a time in December [1915], and they heard from the managers that it was because there was war between the English and the Germans. And when the price of salt and foodgrains rose in the market the *modis* [grocers] and *mahajans* also told them that it was due to the war with the Germans. So it appears that the new Oraons are deliberately invoking the head of the king's enemies as if he were a god and calling on him to come and cast certain devils into the sea.[32]

The special tribunal further stated:

> The devils cannot be spiritual devils, and it is highly probable that they represent the English, Manaldanal is a particularly exacting devil to whom, if an ancester once sacrificed a bullock, all his descendants must for ever sacrifice a bullock. Such a devil might well be chosen to represent the government. And unless it was chosen for this purpose Manaldanal would not be likely to be mentioned at all.

While the details of his interpretation may not be correct, that the song had an anti-imperialist content is unmistakable.

---

[30] Ibid, p 7.
[31] Ibid, p 7.
[32] This citation and the next one is from ibid, p 7.

And further, this was informed with tribal religious *consciousness*.

At this stage it is appropriate to raise several questions: how did the movement start in Duars? How was it organized? How did its message spread? That the Chhotanagpur connections of the Oraons who had migrated to the Duars were never totally snapped but were, infact, retained and quite intimate has been noted earlier. Available evidence suggests that some Oraons coming from Chhotanagpur brought the message of the movement to the Duars. Travers reported:

> Now this belief came to the Duars from Chhotanagpur. The disseminators were often young intelligent boys who appear who have learnt the part of a preacher of the new faith....[33]

In early 1916 the manager of the Sarugaon tea estate reported to the police that an Oraon named "Landroo had come from Chhotanagpur and was preaching the new movement".[34] From the special tribunal judgement it is learnt that Landroo's brother Hasru was a *sardar* in the Tasati garden and several meetings were held in his courtyard as far back as November 1915. Dublai and Letho, two other *sardars* in Tasati, too were prominently involved in the movement.[35] All this suggests that while the movement came from Chhotanagpur through young Oraons moving to the Duars, some of the *sardars*, though certainly not all, played a crucial role in organizing the network.

What were the mechanisms of transmission of the message of the movement? There must have been, to borrow the language from a major work on peasant insurgency, "a variety of means which were all specific to a preliterate culture..."[36] As Child, one DPA committee member reported:

> ...six week ago a message — a letter with a few rupees and some rice — had come from Manabari (TE) and had been passed from hand to hand among his *sirdar* and then sent on to Hope (TE) and

---

[33] *DPA Report* for 1916, pp viii-ix.
[34] NAI 'Oraon Unrest', p 5.
[35] Ibid, pp 5-6.
[36] See Ranajit Guha, *Elementary Aspects of Peasant Insurgency in Colonial India*, Oxford University Press, Delhi, 1983, p 226.

other gardens.[37]

It is not surprising that the British planter found all this incomprehensible: The meaning of the message was unknown to him.[38] The managers and the British administrators repeatedly referred to 'mysterious meetings', 'mysterious recitations', 'unknown message', and so on. In fact, such meetings and songs were among the important 'instruments of transmission' and mobilization of the Oraon workers. Travers in his address referred to above stated:

> ...mysterious meetings were held at night, in lonely places where interference by others was improbable. The Oraons attented armed with bows and arrows, axes and spears, and sentries were posted who threatened to kill any stranger who approached. He knows that at this meeting songs were sung in which the aid of the German *baba* was invoked. They were taught and believed that the British Raj was coming to an end, and that if they aided the Germans the latter would give them loan in their ancient country where a subsidiary Oraon Raj would be established. Not only were the British sahibs to be driven out, but also the Mundas and Mohammedans.[39]

Continuing he said:

> All this was mixed and confounded with superstitions in the most extraordinary way — in fact, many of the Oraons regarded the German *baba* as a god...not as the Kaiser... one sirdar afterwards confessed that a picture of the German maharaja, seated between two gods, had been passed from hand to hand among those in the movement in his garden. Many other facts came to light, but undoutedly the idea underlay them all, that the British Raj was coming to an end, and at a given signal the Oraons were to help exterminate the British sahibs.[40]

The spread of the movement with its pronounced anti-British and pro-German tone and aspirations for Oraon raj caused great alarms in the minds of the planters as well as the government officials. Though there was no report of any overt acts of violence such as assaults, riot or murder, the collective mobilization of the discontended and agitated

---

[37] *DPA Report* for 1916, p. 286.
[38] Ibid, p 286.
[39] Ibid, p viii.
[40] Ibid, pp viii-ix.

tribal workers and several incidence of open defiance of the garden management amounted to a frontal confrontation with the authority. In the prevailing atmosphere these came to be regarded as a threat to the existing order. The March meeting of the DPA committee attended, among others, by the deputy commissioner and SP who discussed in details the measures for supressing the agitation and also for mobilizing loyal *sardars* from among the Oraons.[41]

Following the meeting garden *sardars* were made special constables and held responsible for maintenance of peace in the gardens, and armed police pickets and police camps were set up in different parts of Duars to keep watch on the restive Oraons.[42] Many arrests were made and a special tribunal was appointed under the Defence of India Act to try the 'ringleaders'. Some of the arrested Oraons were sentenced to rigorous imprisonment for varying periods.[43] The *Fagua Puja* passed off without any disturbance and by late 1916 the agitation subsided.

But the planters remained in a state of apprehension about the recrudescence of the movement. Thus, when Ghura, *alias* Somra, who was considered as 'one of the instigators in the Oraon unrest' and was sentenced to six months' imprisonment, returned to the Duars in March 1917 after his release from jail there was a consternation among the planters, and they pressed the district police authority for taking action against him.[44] In response to this the superintendent of police wrote to the DPA chairman:

> In forwarding a list of the [29] Oraons [sic] convicted in this district, I write to request you to arrange with the managers of tea gardens concerned that they may not be re-employed in gardens if they come back again, from their native homes after their release from jail.[45]

---

[41] Ibid, pp 287-88.

[42] Ibid, p ix.

[43] We have come across a lis — of names of twenty nine tribals — both Oraons and non-Oraons — convicted in Jalpaiguri district between June and December, 1916. *DPA Report* for 1917, pp.426-27.

[44] Ibid, pp 422-27. See the correspondence between the DPA chairman and several garden managers on the one hand and the superintendent of police on the other.

[45] This citation and the next one is from ibid, p 425.

He further wrote:

> ...such Oraons who have been given lands or *jotes* or who have relations settled in Jalpaiguri district should not be allowed to call themselved permanent settlers of this district and to this end it is most desirable that grants of land to them or to their near relations should be withdrawn.

In May 1917 in the neighbouring Terai plantation area in the Darjeeling district there was a limited outbreak of a similar agitation.[46] In Jalpaiguri district, however, there was no fresh outbreak of the movement.

III

Any analysis of the nature of this short-lived ferment is full of complexities. The movement had three distinct strands: religious, social and political. However, three strands which were present through its course interacted and interpenetrated with each other giving a considerably complex character to the movement. It is this aspect which led R H Craddock, a government of India official, to speak of the movement in the following language:

> It is a curious and interesting case how modern events become garbled up with superstition and demonology among unsophisticated folk of this kind.[47]

But to Craddock the movement represented largely 'superstition and demonology'. He and many of the colonial officials were not in a position to understand the language, idiom and 'code' of the struggle of the tribal workers. J W Nelson of the criminal intelligence office, however, showed somewhat greater perception. He mentioned three aspect of the movement:

1. Economic unrest due to the rise in prices, which was attributed to evil spirits and witches — hence attempts to drive evil spirits out of the villages and the murder of supposed witches.

[46] NAI Home Political, Deposit 68 of June 1917. Fortnightly Political Report for first half of May 1917.

[47] NAI 'Oraon Unrest', p 2.

2. A religious revival of a highly emotional type with secret all night meetings and the singing of *mantras*.
3. A social movement, closely connected with the religious movement, directed towards elevation of the caste. Hence the prohibition of animal food and intoxicating drink, resolution not to work as palki bearers, etc. As in all such movements the influence of Hindu ideas obvious.[48]

In this observation one finds an indication of an awareness of a complex inter-relationship between religious fervour, social reform efforts and concern about economic issues. Nelson, however, did not mention the issue of political power underlying the agitation among the tribal workers. But on the basis of analysis of an Oraon song sung in the Duars another official hinted at the political dimension:

> Some portions of the song suggest that the movement is an attempt to purify the tribal religion and to cast off superstitions and get rid of corruption of ancient faith...It appears probable that the restriction of flesh food to white goats and white fowls is based on their being the proper offerings to Dharmesh and is connected with a scheme for driving out foreign [*sahib* or white] devils.[49]

The socio-religious aspect mentioned above was a common feature of many of the tribal protest movements in India under British rule. But, in addition to that, the Duars movement had a distinct political orientation. The Oraon songs sung in the Duars repeatedly and emphatically spoke of driving out the British and the establishment of an independent Oraon Raj.

In their vision of an independent Oraon Raj the Oraon workers came to look upon the Germans as their 'liberators'. This led the British planters and some colonial officials to suspect German hands behind the Oraon agitation.[50] The Oraon workers, described by Craddock as the 'unsophisticated folk', were thought to be incapable of acting on their own. Hence, they must have been 'manipulated'. It should be added that the British rulers and their associates had always tried to explain anti-imperialism and any popular mobilization in terms of manipulation by an external agency such as

---

[48] Ibid, p 3.
[49] NAI 'Oraon Unrest', p 2.
[50] Ibid, p 2.

German and Russian powers, disgruntled Indians etc. But despite efforts made by the prosecution, no foreign, that is, German manipulation could be established. As a matter of fact, available accounts show that the German missionaries stayed away from the movement. The participation of the Christian Oraons too was negligible.[51]

But how one is to explain the Oraon view of the Germans and even of the Kaiser? The explanation lies basically in the specific historical context. The immediate international background was one of victories won by the Germans in the early years of the war. The dislocating impact of the war on the tea export, tea industry and the employment in the industry was experienced by the Oraon workers. They were told by the *Mudis* (grocers), *kayas* (Marwari traders in the Duars) and moneylenders that the sharp rise in the prices of salt and food grains were due to the war. The reverses suffered by the British gave rise to the rumours that the British Raj was not only in crisis but also coming to an end. Here was a rumour about weakening of the authority structure eventually leading to the breakdown of authority. All this came to be associated with the might of Germany. It was against such a background that the enemy's enemy came to be viewed by the Oraons as a friend and, indeed, even as their emancipator. It will not be inappropriate to mention here that during the war years large section of revolutionary nationalists too were looking upon Germany as an ally to the nationalist cause.

Taking all relevant aspects into consideration it can be stated that in its origin, direction and content the ferment was basically indigenous and autonomous — autonomous in relation to non-tribal or any outside leadership and organization. It was an instance of self-mobilization based on tribal solidarities and its roots lay in the miserable social existence

[51] The judgement read: One characteristic of the movement is that all Christian Oraons were excluded from the meetings. So it cannot have been deliberately organized by any German missionary. Yet the special tribunal gave the verdict:..."it seems clear that it must have been started either by some German agent or by some agitator or by some imposter" (NAI 'Oraon Unrest',p 8, para 5).

condition of the tribal workers in the Duars plantation area and also the tribals in general in Chhotanagpur. The call in the song to drive away the devil Manaldanala, a particularly exacting devil, perhaps representing the British government indicated an urge to abolish the British rule. Moreover, the worship of the German emperor reflected a deification of the British king's enemies, and the English were relegated to the position of one among a host of tribal devils.

In all this the anti-imperialist dimension of the movement is manifest. One additional dimension was the anti-planter or anti-capitalist one. Though in the available records there is no explicit reference to any specific grievances and aspirations of the tea garden workers, there is no doubt that the Oraons and other tribals involved in the Duars agitation *acted as workers*. In their 'defiance of garden management' and 'refusal to work', about which the planters and DPA showed great concern, there was evidence of class conflict of an incipient nature. In the particular movement under examination the latter dimension came to be subsumed under autonomous manifestation of anti-colonialism.

The anti-imperialist and anti-capitalist affinities in the Duars, however, did not exclude community and, in this case, tribal affinity. In fact, the response to foreign rule and planter domination came to be encapsulated in tribal religious consciousness, a dimension which made many aspects and expression of the Duars agitation largely incomprehensible to the planters and colonial officials. It was also this tribal cultural identity which inevitably gave rise to some ambiguities. But while one can hardly ignore the importance of this identity, it needs to be stressed that it did not lead to displacement of anti-imperialist and anti-planter consciousness.[52] Rather, the Oraon religious beliefs and practices contributed towards the strengthening of this consciousness.

The Duars agitation, as noted above, began as a continuation of Chhotanagpur Tana Bhagat movement and was ini-

[52] Cf. Guha, *op. cit.*, pp 169-70.

tially an example of *vertical* mobilization embracing Oraon plantation workers. But it represented much more than that. As mentioned earlier, the Duars agitation soon came to involve non-Oraon tribal, semi-tribal and even a few non-tribal workers, although the Oraons constituted the predominant element. The most clear evidence of participation of the non-Oraons is an incomplete list of convicted workers.[53] Besides the names of twenty three Oraons, it contained names of two Mundas, two Mahalis, one Goala (milkman, cowherd) and one Teli (oilpresser) all of whom had been sentenced to rigorours imprisonment for taking part in the movement. This testifies also the feature of *horizontal* mobilization. In fact, there is evidence of a convergence of both vertical and horizontal solidarities. And solidarity at the level of Oraon workers and also solidarity between Oraon and non-Oraon workers was more than just tribal and ethnic solidarity. These also signified self-consciousness of the workers about the exploitation and oppression experienced by them and entailed anti-imperialist and class solidarities. To restate, there was an *overlapping* of anti-British content of the movement, class solidarity and tribal or ethnic loyalty.

What were the actual mechanics for achieving, maintaining and consolidating these solidarities? The account of the genesis and unfolding of the tribal worker movement presented earlier shows that various mechanisms were combined in varying degrees. These were, among others, the pull of tribal ties and tradition, parleys and assemblies such as meetings held in the 'coolie' lines and also lonely places, the collective chanting of *mantras* or incantation, the use of community and tribal idioms and 'codes', the reforms in social and religious practices (e.g, eschewing of meat and strong drinks and prohibition of community dances and songs), the rumour about imminent British defeat and German victory, the vision of an independent Oraon Raj, the promise of land, and the power of religious, political and

[53] See *DPA Report* for 1917, pp 426-27.

community commitment to 'exterminate the sahibs' sanctified through 'the vow sworn by God, Germany and blood'. The experience of rise in prices of salt and food grains and information about fall in tea export were put to intelligent use to spread the rumour of British Raj in crisis. It appears that a roving band of young 'volunteers' or cadres' carried the message of the movement initially from Chhotanagpur to the Duars and later on from garden to garden and helped to forge and strengthen the soilidarities mentioned above.

The Duars tribal labour agitation, as in the case of any popular movement, had its share of fence-sitters, vacillators and collaborators. The flow of information to the managers illustrates the extent of collaboration. The authorities too encouraged dissidence and betrayal. In Gurjangjhora tea garden the manager tried to isolate two leaders from the rest of workers. In Duars as a whole the police authority rewarded the loyal workers with the position of special constables.

Under the circumstances, the solidarity of the workers involved in the movement found expression in the exercise of collective authority against the non-committed, vacillators and workers loyal to the authorities. The major instrument to get support from those who were undecided and also to deal with dissidence from the movement was social boycott or excommunication which was often accompanied by abuse and threat. This is what appears to have happened in the case of Charua and his wife.

There were several cases in which the workers saw through the management's game and foiled it. Faced with the dangers of dissidence and treachery, measures were taken to defend the movement and protect its leaders and 'cadres'. The practice of holding meetings and recitations in lonely places and under the cover of darkness was one such measure. The Gurjangjhora garden incident also prodives an illustration of protection given to leaders. Thus, when two leaders were summoned by the manager, a large body of workers went with them, and when the two were given an order to leave the garden, the workers accompanying them refused to part with them.

A distinctive feature of the movement that deserves to be mentioned was its democratic character. Most of the tribal movements in colonial India including the Tana Bhagat movement was centred around a supreme leader having prophetic power.[54] But the Duars movement, though an extension of the well-known Oraon movement, did not have any such leader. Available records highlight the role of garden *sardars* and also that of collective consultations through assemblies and gatherings.

Despite the presence of many significant dimensions, this particular variant of protest and struggle of tribal peasants turned into plantation workers soon ran its course. The impact of the movement on the subsequent socio-political life of the tribal and particularly Oraon workers remained ambivalent.

Before concluding this paper, one more observation needs to be made. That one is in relation to the nationalist attitude towards the Duars tribal labour agitation which had a distinct anti-British thrust — in fact, the earliest instance of popular anti-imperialist struggle not only in the Duars but in the district of Jalpaiguri as a whole. It is found that, may be because of patriotic consideration and/or some other reasons, the *Amrita Bazar Patrika*, a Calcutta-based nationalist daily, took a sympathetic view of this protest and struggle. But the nationalists of Jalpaiguri district itself, however, appear to have remained totally indifferent to it. That the Oraon agitation came to the notice of some of the nationalists of the district has been put on record.[55] But there was no awareness of its significance and the need for having any links with it. A major part of explanation lies in the wide socio-cultural gap that the *bhadralok* (upper-caste educated Bengali middle class) nationalists of Jalpaiguri had with the 'coolies'. Thus, tribal anti-imperialism and *bhadralok* nationalism remained distanced from each other.

---

[54] See Fuchs, op cit.

[55] Khagendra Nath Das Gupta, 'Swadhinata Sangrame Jalpaiguri Jela' in *Jalpaiguri Zilla School Shatabarshikee Smarak Patrika*, Jalpaiguri, 1976, p 4.

9

Bangladeshi Cultural Symbols and the Bangladesh State*

SHYAMALI GHOSH

In January 1983 General H.M. Ershad, the Chief Martial Law Administrator (CMLA) of Bangladesh, which was then under a Martial Law regime, made a statement favouring the establishment of an Islamic state in Bangladesh. He also publicly criticised the way in which Bangladesh had been observing *Shahid Dibash* (Martyrs' Day on February 21) because it lacked an Islamic content. He was reported to have indicated that henceforth the Day should be observed in the proper Islamic way. At the same time, moves were on to make Arabic a compulsory subject at the primary level of schooling. Resentment against these moves was expressed in statements by eminent citizens, banned political parties, a students' forum, and so on. Ershad's comment was seen as an attempt to disorient the 30-year-long awareness of *Shahid Dibash*. People were advised to observe the Day in the way it had always been observed in order to stall the spread of 'anti-culture' and the promotion of 'obscurantism.' Eventually the Day was observed in the usual manner. Meanwhile student unrest was quelled by police action; in the process some lives were lost.[1]

These events raise various general questions about the relationship between the state and society, the credibility of particular regimes, the issue of universal human rights, and so on. They also question the relevance and future of any

* An earlier version of this paper was presented at the 11th European Conference of Modern South Asian Studies, Amsterdam, July 1990.

[1] For some details see *Dainik Ittefaq* 15 and 20 January 1983, *New Nation* 20, 25 and 31 January 1983, 1 February 1983; *Holiday* 2 February 1983; *Far Eastern Economic Review* 10, 17, 24 January 1983 and 10 March 1983. Also see Enayetullah Khan, 'The bigots are back,' *Holiday* 22 January 1983.

religion or ideology which fails to take into account basic realities concerning social heritage, and cultural consciousness and development. Related to this is the following problem. Can a state or a state-supported religion dictate the course of national culture, in the process side-tracking that culture's other components? Can a single component of a culture represent the whole unless it is backed up by shared feelings and expressions? Is it possible for a state to effect culture change without clearly expressed popular approval? Such questions are particularly relevant in the case of Bangladesh.

The overwhelming majority of citizens of Bangladesh adhere to Islam. At the doctrinaire level this is an exclusivist religion, believed to have been divinely ordained to regulate every aspect of the life of its adherents. On the other hand, socio-cultural developments in Bangladesh suggest that this society on the periphery of the Islamic world has been evolving composite national cultural symbols. These symbols go beyond the arena of personal religious conviction and practices but do not undermine or question personal religiosity. This historical development is out of line with rigid injunctions flowing from the Islamic heartland which are popularly described as fundamentalist. Indigenous cultural development in the periphery, however, has been instrumental in creating an attitude towards religion as providing basic guidelines at the aggregate societal level, while leaving ritualism to individual discretion. This attitude leaves little room for religion as a subject to be either promoted or demoted by the state.

This paper discusses the language-related pattern of cultural development in Bangladesh. It does so not merely to present a particular case but also to evoke further discussions on cultural development and religious or ideological rigidity. This may be useful for understanding developments elsewhere in South Asia and beyond. This is particularly relevant in view of a growing awareness of religious revivalism as an autonomous factor in the evolution of bilateral and multilateral relations among countries in the Asia-Pacific region.

I

'Can I ever forget the Twenty-First of February — the day reddened with my brother's blood?'[2] Thus begins a song (known as *Ekusher Gan* or the song of the 21st), which in Bangladesh is a most emotionally stirring and sanctified one, next only to the national anthem (*My golden Bengal, I love thee*). The *Shahid Minar* in its present form was conceived as a mother extending her arms to protect her offsprings.[3] Both *Ekusher Gan*, which is self-explanatory, and the *Shahid Minar* commemorate the martyrdrom of Bengali-

[2] *Ekusher Gan* was written by the eminent Bangladeshi Journalist Abdul Gaffar Chowdhury, now residing in London. It was put to music by the popular Bangladeshi singer Altaf Mahmud who was killed in 1971. The song, divided into four stanzas, runs as follows:

'Can I ever forget the 21st of February
The day reddened with my brother's blood?
Can I ever forget February, a month filled with
teardrops of bereaved mothers, the February of
my blood-stained golden land?

Awake, like the destructive forces of nature
Let the earth be shaken by mounting rage against
the slaying of young lives.
At the crossroads of change those who suppress
popular demands by killing the golden boys—
will they be spared?
No, no. In the blood-smeared pages of history
The final verdict will be given by the 21st of February.

On that late winter night the moon kissed the
blue sky. The tuberoses bloomed in heavenly bliss.
Suddenly came a devastating storm.
We know the faces of these beasts of darkness.
There is only hatred in the hearts of mothers,
sisters and brothers for those who shoot straight
at the lifeline of the land to suppress demands.
Their hateful footsteps can be heard on the soil
of Bengal today. They do not belong to this land.
They are selling the future of this land.
They have snatched away our food, clothing and peace.

Awake, 21st of February. Even today brave men and
women perish in the oppressor's prison.
My slain brother's spirit is calling-
Awaken the latent strength of the people
We will again light the fire of anger in every
nook and corner of the land in February.
Awake 21st of February.'

Translated by the author of the article who is grateful to Ms. Urmi Rahman of London for the Bengali text of the song.

speaking youths at the peak of the Language Movement in 1952.

In the late forties and early fifties the Language Movement was an important phase in the cultural-political development of the people of Bangladesh, and hence a significant factor in the building of their identity.[4] The observance of February 21 has therefore always been an integral part of Bangladesh's cultural development and the *Shaheed Minar* has been a cultural property closely linked with the historical emergence of Bangladesh.

Customarily, the Day began with a *Prabhatpheri*,[5] followed by offerings of flowers at the base of the Minar, decoration of the premises with *Alpana* (floral-geometrical drawings on the floor), and the putting-up of posters around it. The Alpana designs was also drawn on the main route to the Minar through which year after year people would come in silent procession, barefooted and wearing black badges. Afterwards they would visit the Azimpur burial ground where the martyrs of 1952 are buried. Here too flowers were offered. Seminars, meetings and cultural functions were held right from the beginning of February; they highlighted the significance of martyrdom in the struggle to give the Bengali language its legitimate place in the language policy of the Government of Pakistan. Every year numerous publications were brought out on this occasion and till the time the Day was declared a holiday, a day-long *hartal* (strike) used to be

---

[3] From accounts of some participants. Originally it was a small brick-and-mortar columm built immediately in 1952 and rebuilt several times after demolition by government agencies.

[4] For some details of the Language Movement see Badruddin Umar, *Purba Banglar Bhasha Andolan O Tatkalin Rajniti* (Bengali) (East Bengali's Language Movement and Politics of the Time) Volume I Dhaka, 1970; Kamruddin Ahmad, *A Socio-political History of Bengal and the Birth of Bangladesh*, 4th edition, (Dhaka, 1975), pp. 110-11. Since 21 February 1952 the number 21 became so meaningful that the author of the United Front Manifesto for the Assembly elections in 1954 decided to accommodate 42 proposed points into 21. In the elections the United Front literaelly ousted the Muslim League, the party in power since 1947. See Abul Mansur Ahmad, *Amar Dekha Rajnitir Panchash Bachar* (Bengali) (Fifty years of Politics that I have seen) Third enlarged edition (Dhaka, 1975), p.323.

[5] *Prabhatpheri* is an early-morning procession during which suitable songs are sung - a popular form for expressing patriotic/nationalist sentiments during the anti-colonial struggles in the Indian subcontinent.

observed on *Ekushe*.[6]

After Bangladesh became a sovereign state, *Ekushe* was officially designated as a day of national mourning. Before that it had been observed as a day of resistance and repeated efforts by the Pakistani regime to disrupt its observance and undermine its significance had met with failure. On the contrary, it acquired further significance as a symbol of Bengali cultural autonomy in the context of the autonomy movement launched formally with the Six Point Charter of Demands in the mid-sixties.[7]

II

The Language Movement of 1948-52 was a resistance movement in immediate reaction to the language policy of the Pakistan Government. This policy undermined the legitimate claim of the Bengali language to be one of the state languages, if not the only state language because it was the majority's language in Pakistan. In 1948, M.A.Jinnah, the founding father of Pakistan and the then Governor-General, announced that Urdu would be the national language of Pakistan. This became a political issue but it also had clear

[6] The processionists included men and women from all walks of life, belonging to all age groups. The Day has been observed as a holiday since the massive anti-government movements of 1968-69. All the cultural and other functions held on the occassion and throughout the month of February highlighted various aspects of the Bengali language, its place in the minds of the people, its richness and the oppressive nture of the Pakistan Government as reflected in its maltreatment of Bengali. One of the very popular songs that used to be sung says: 'Ora Kathay Kathay Shikal Paray Amar Hate Paye, Ora amar Mukher Bhasha Kairha Nite Chay' (They put me in chains on any pretext, they want to forcibly take away from me my own language). There were frequent references to a bereaved mother, East Bengal, in the poems. In a very moving poem, Sikandar Abu Zafar said that the road strewn with bones, smeared with blood, and covered with wilted flowers would unmistakably lead to a mother's house. See Sikandar Abu Zafar, "Mayer Barir Path' (The Path to Mother's House), Kabir Chowdhury (ed.), *Ekusher Shankalan* (Bengali) Ekusher Collection (Dhaka, 1971), pp. 177-78.

[7] Hasanuzzaman, 'Purba Bangla Chitra' Unashattarer gana abhyutthan parabarti ashampradayik shanskriti rajniti dharmanirapekshatar darshan' (Bentali) (Portrait of East Bengal. The Philosophy of the non-communal culture, politics and secularism after the 1969 mass upsurge) *Prekshit* (Dhaka) February 1987, pp. 71-93. Hasanuzzaman establishes his point through a survey of a number of writings by eminent writers like Abul Fazal, Mofazzal Haidar Chowdhury, of Political Parties Students Organisation, etc. See also Umar's article in Kabir Chowdhury (ed.), no. 6, pp. 59-63.

religio-economic underpinnings in the proposed Islamic State of Pakistan ('proposed' because Pakistan's first constitution was then still in the making). During the course of the Pakistan movement Urdu had been made an important religio-cultural adjunct of the two-nation theory on the basis of which Pakistan was born. For the Bengalis the imposition of Urdu implied cultural hindrances but also had economic implications. It was seen as a tool for depriving Bengalis from participating in various economic activities including government jobs.

Orthodox Bengali Muslims had, during the colonial period, considered Bengali to be an un-Islamic language. The same attitude was also adopted by the Pakistani state. When in 1948, and finally in 1952, the state of Pakistan began its onslaught on the Bengali language, it was not just that the lingua franca of the majority of Pakistanis was being denied its due political status. The action was perceived as applying a deliberate brake on the progress of the Bengali language and Bengali literature, a denial of the people's right to self-expression. Language being the major vehicle of cultural development, the state policy was thought to be an encroachment on the indigenous culture itself.

Against this background, the observance of February 21 ought to be considered an institutionalised system of customs, a cultural symbol of Bangladesh. To interpret it as un-Islamic may be in line with the thoughts of those who believe that 'from an Islamic view point what is cultural is largely religious.'[8] But at an analytical level, culture and customs are seen as a 'surface refraction of what goes on in the human mind.'[9] And what goes on in the human mind is of course greatly influenced by the environment, the social heritage of language, habits, ideas and beliefs (which includes religion, but not religion alone), and the accustomed mode of communication. Can the outcome of such a com-

[8] Sardar Ziauddin, *The Future of Muslim Civilization* (London, 1979), p. 274.

[9] Refferred in Angele P. Cheater, *Social Anthropology - An Alternative Introduction* (London, 1989), p.37.

plex evolutionary process be set aside because of a dogmatic or limited understanding of what constitutes culture?

This misinterpretation of culture in the case of Bangladesh springs obviously from the belief in certain quarters that Islam is an all-pervading system which guides and controls all thoughts and actions of an adherent. This might have been true during the early days of Islam in its heartland or in some highly protected set-up with 'Islamic curtains' all around. But in the Islamic pockets away from the heartland, Islam was not the only cultural contact point and the human mind was conditioned in a different way. This was the case in Bangladesh.

If the State, represented by the Government, moves against popular feeling, it may find it difficult to operate without taking recourse to its coercive apparatus, as was evident in 1983.[10] Even though the state did not have its way on that particular occasion, such state intervention may impede cultural development and consequently the formation of a solid cultural identity. Alternatively, such state encroachment may also accelerate the process in the opposite direction, as was evident during the Pakistani regime. The attempted tampering with language-related cultural expressions in East Pakistan only strenghtened the cause for democratisation and autonomy as envisaged by the Six Point Charter of Demands — which were believed to have advanced Bengali cultural development.[11]

III

The conflict between religious orthodoxy and indigenous

[10] In 1972, the state had to give in to popular preference in a different way - by resuming religious recitals over the state-controlled electronic media which were initially banned by the Government of Bangladesh.

[11] A typical example was restrictions on broadcasting of songs by Rabindranth Tagore for their non-or anti-Islamic contents. Besides protestations by eminent people including Maulana Abdul Hamid Khan Bhashani, there was a spurt in the singing of Tagore songs. (See *Ganaprajatantri Bangladesh Sharkar Tathya Mantralaya,* Hasan Hafizur Rahman (ed.), *Bangladesher Swadhinata Juddher Dalilpatra Dwitiya Khanda* (Bengali) Dhaka, 1982, pp. 281-82).

cultural development in Bangladesh is not just a contemporary scenario. The majority of the people of what is now Bangladesh have been living through it almost always in the last 500 years. Bengal was first acquainted with Islam through visiting Arab traders but large-scale conversion took place much later, between the 14th and 15th centuries, mostly by *Sufis* of syncretistic traditions. Hence, although the number of Muslims went up considerably, initially orthodox Islamisation was at a low ebb. Added to Sufi tolerance was the shared life experience of the people irrespective of their religion. They continued the same socio-cultural practices, based on shared rural economic activities, the vagaries of nature, and the cycle of the seasons. In this way the deviant Islam of Bengal evolved, much like that of Indonesia. This has been interpreted by some as 'Bengali Muslim Subculture' at the popular level. The local *Ulema* tried to rectify this but were not successful. Later, however, the deviation, or the 'subculture,' was challenged more seriously by the 19th century Islamic revivalists.

In Bengal the Tariqah-i-Muhammadiya, the Taiyuni and Ahl-e-Hadis movements inspried by Shah Waliullah's teachings are cited as examples. The Faraizi movement is also cited as an Islamic revivalist one. There are different scholarly opinions, however, regarding its exclusively religious character, its communal overtones and its focus on agrarian relations. The Faraizi movment began as a purification of Islam of all local innovations, to bring it back to its unadulterated pristine form, which was believed to have guaranteed social justice. It lasted for about 25 years during which it was transformed into a peasant movement against the Zamindars and local administration. At the level of the urban elite, the emphasis on religious exclusivity of Muslims generated a sort of extraterritorial pull at the expense of the indigenous subculture. Some enthusiasts refused to accept Bengali as their lingua franca, some even published Bengali books paginated from the right to the left following the Urdu/Arabic model of writing.

The common Muslims appear to have been much impressed by tales about the heavenly heartland of Islam but Urdu and Urdu-based culture remained as alien as ever. Attempts at cultural Islamisation by the *ashrafs* (elite Puritans who claimed to be descended from Middle Eastern Muslims and their neo-ashraf associates such as a section of the urban intelligentsia and the rich landowners) were quite successfully resisted by the educated among the *ajlafs* (the indigenous masses) for the time being. However, the strength of the pro-British ashraf/neo-ashraf combine lay in the fact that they could capitalise on the politico-economic antagonism of Muslims against the Hindu community and had the resources to influence Muslim public opinion to a great extent.

Ultimately, in the 20th century, these forces were successful to the extent that people were motivated by perceived and actual socio-economic compulsions to support the creation of Pakistan, a promised homeland, that would end all their miseries. But this did not signify giving up their 'subculture' or the language-related development of their own culture.[12]

The Language Movement of the forties and fifties and its commemorative practices were therefore rooted in the controversies over the status and development of the indigenous culture. The events of the eighties are a continuation of the same cultural struggle, now with the Bangladesh state as a party to attempted Islamisation.

The Bangladesh state began as a secular entity. In the Constitution of Bangladesh, enacted in 1972, secularism was one of the four fundamental principles of state policy. These

[12] For further details see, Asim Roy, *The Islamic Syncretistic Tradition in Bengal,* New Jersey, 1983); 'The Bengal Muslim "Cultural Mediators" and the Bengal Muslim Identity in the Nineteenth and Early Twentieth Centuries' *South Asia*, New Series, vol. 10, nos. 1-2 June 1987, pp. 11-34; Rafiuddin Ahmed, *The Bengal Muslims 1871-1906 - A Quest for Identity,* (Delhi, Oxford, New York, 1981); (ed.),*Bangladesh: Society, Religion and Politics* (Dhaka, 1985); Mustafa Nurul Islam, *Bengali Muslim Public Opinion as Reflected in the Bengali Press, 1901-30* (Dhaka,1973), pp. 270-81; Ali Anwar, 'Muslim MInd and Society in Bangladesh: An Historical Retrspect', Asghar Ali Engineer (ed.), *Islam in South and South East Asia* (Delhi, 1985), pp. 185-229; Kamruddin, no.4, pp.1-43; A.K. Najmul Karim,the Dynamics of Bangladesh Society, (New Delhi, 1980) Narahari Kaviraj, *Wahabi and Faraizi Rebels of Bengal* (New Delhi, 1982). Shamasuddin, Abu Zafar, *Sociology of Bengal Politics* (Dhaka, 1973). Ahmad Sufia, *Muslim Community in Bengal 1884-1912* (Dhaka, 1974).

were not enforceable as such but Article 8 stated that these formed the foundation of the state. According to Article 12 the principle of secularism was to be realised by eliminating communalism, by not granting a political status to any particular religion, by avoiding the abuse of religion for political purposes, and by not discriminating against or persecuting anyone on the basis of his/her religion. These provisions, although criticised by some, were generally accepted as a true reflection of the spirit of the Liberation War and the preceding mainstream political developments. The fact that religion had become a political non-issue in erstwhile East Pakistan was amply demonstrated in the first-ever general elections of Pakistan in 1970, which heralded the break-up of Pakistan and the emergence of Bangladesh in 1971. Most of the candidates of the so-called *Islam Pasand* parties lost their deposits in East Pakistan. In the first general elections of Bangladesh, held in 1973, such parties could not contest because they were banned following the constitutional provisions cited earlier. Their members, who were accused of being anti-liberation because of their active help to the Pakistani occupation army in its genocidal atrocities had gone into hiding, some fleeing the country for fear of reprisals.[13]

But the secular status of Bangladesh changed when the civil-military bureaucratic elite representing the Pakistani legacy reasserted its dominance under the leadership of General Ziaur Rahman after the assassination of Sheikh Mujibur Rahman and some of his close associates between August and November 1975. Initally the slogan of '*Joi Bangla*' was replaced with '*Bangladesh Zindabad*.' In the Seratunnabi Conference in Dhaka in 1976 opinions were expressed which favoured an Islamic set-up. This was followed by protests from others. These protest were understandably low-key because the country was under a Martial Law regime. Tawab, the then Air Chief and one of three

[13] For some details see, Ahmed Moudud, *Bangladesh: Era of Sheikh Mujibur Rahman* (Dhaka, 1983); Rounaq Jahan, *Bangladesh Politics: Problems and Issues* (Dhaka, 1980).

Deputy Chief Martial Law Administrators, had participated in the Conference and he was eased out immediately. But a new lease of life was given to the Islamicists by the abrogation of the constitutional provision which prohibited the use of religion for political purposes. Through several other ordinances the constitution was so amended that Bangladesh officially ceased to be a secular state. A declaration of absolute faith in the Almighty Allah was inserted. The name of the state remained the Peoples' Republic of Bangladesh but an invocation to the Almighty Allah was introduced at the beginning of the Constitution. The amendements also envisaged the consolidation, preservation and strengthening of relations with Muslim countries based on Islamic solidarity.[14] In other words, the national objectives were changed so that Islamisation became a state subject by implication.

But such formal changes by successive governments with a narrow support base could not easily change the cultural moorings of the people. Even the enactment of the 8th amendment of the constitution, which states that Islam will be the state religion of Bangladesh, did not effect this. *Shahid Dibash* and other cultural activities continue in the usual manner because the Language Movement is inextricably linked with the existence of Bangladesh as a sovereign entity. Whether the present policy makers are genuinely orthodox Islamicists or motivated by political expediency or personal aggrandisement, they can overlook this basic fact only at the cost of societal chaos. Such chaos will in no way contribute towards either the promotion of the state-proclaimed definition of Islamic culture, or an indigenous cultural development.

The Islamic tilt of the present government has already added to social tensions in Bangladesh. The Bangladesh Nationalist Party (BNP), founded by General Ziaur Rahman and now led by his widow, the present Prime Minister Begum Khaleda Zia, came to power through a fair and free election with the help of the Jamat-e-Islam (JeI), which re-

---

[14] Jahan, no. 13 Shyamali Ghosh, 'Constitutional Changes in Bangladesh', *India Quarterly*, vol. XLII, no. 4, October-December 1976, pp. 390-404.

ceived a new lease of life under Ziaur Rahman's rule. He even allowed Golam Azam to return to Bangladesh clandestinely in 1977 and unofficially lead the JeI. Azam had led the party in erstwhile East Pakistan and had fled to Pakistan because of his anti-liberation role in 1971; subsequently he had been denied Bangladeshi citizenship. General Ershad was vocally anti-JeI and on several occasions acted against fatwas given by *ulema*, but he paid no heed to the popular demand to expel Azam from Bangladesh. Golam Azam has obviously been encouraged by the present regime's obligations to the JeI and its consequent Islamicist attitude, particularly projected by the Prime Minister. Azam was reportedly elected *Amir* (Chief) of the JeI in December 1991. The opposition parties demanded an explanation from the government as to how a Pakistani passport holder could actively participate in Bangladeshi politics. They also demanded in the *Jatiya Shanshad* (Parliament) that he be tried in court However, the Home Minister called this demand illegal and unconstitutional. Following this a 101 member 'people's court,' consisting of prominent intellectuals and freedom fighters, was formed. This people's court decided to try Azam for crimes against humanity unless he was expelled from the country. The people's trial was held and Azam received a guilty verdict. In response to this, the government arrested Azam pre-emptively to save him from any possible physical assault. The members of the people's court were chargesheeted for unlawful activities and they were arrested. A large number of socio-cultural organisations have, however, supported the trial. The BNP leadership was not united over the issue. And followers of the JeI and its student front, the *Islami Chhatra Shibir*, took to the streets and attacked the offices of pro-trial newspapers.[15]

Therefore the political rehabilitation of anti-liberation forces, started by Ziaur Rahman, and continued by Ershad and Begum Zia, is another facet of the Islamisation role of

[15] For details of the Golam Azam Controversy see *POT* Public Opinion Trends Analysis and News Service (Bangladesh Series) New Delhi, December 1991 - May 1992.

the Bangladesh state. But once again the spirit of the Liberation War which cherished secular ideals and Bengali culture has activated the people. The success of the recent *hartal* called by the opposition on the Azam issue is one pointer. Another is JeI's poor record in successive elections.

Besides the JeI and a number of similar Islamic political organisations, there is another strand of Islamic orthodoxy which has been more popular, particularly among decision makers. This strand is represented by esteemed '*pirs*' (holy men), perhaps the most eminent of which is presently Shah Sufi Hazrat Maulana Hashmatulla Naqshbandi Mujaddadi, founder of the *Bishwa Zaker Manzil* at Atroshi in Faridpur. He is popularly known as the Pir Saheb of Atroshi. It is well known that pirs and *dargas* (shrines) are not formally recognised by heartland Islamic orthodoxy. By their allegiance to pirs, the Islamicist rulers of Bangladesh have in fact given support to the heterodox, syncretistic Islamic tradition of Bangladesh. The popularity of tolerant Islam (as represented by the Sufis) combined with state encouragement to hard-line Islamicists (as represented by the JeI) shows that there is a lack of consensus regarding Islamisation within the state, and this explains partly why state intervention in cultural development has failed.

The inconsistence of Islamisation can also be linked directly to the question of the constitutional legitimacy of successive regimes between 1975 and 1991.[16] It appears to reflect a lack of conviction which would be natural because even those who wield power in Bangladesh are products of Bangladeshi culture and social heritage. They must also be aware of the danger of communalisation in the multi-religion

[16] Ershad, the same CMLA (later President of Bangladesh) who had criticised the 'un-Islamic' manner in which *Ekushe* was observed, did not mention anything about it in his address to the nation on 30 January 1983. the constitutional Amendment making Islam the State religion stops just there without any operative clause. Although reportedly he has not personally visited the Shahid Minar after 21 February 1983, he has written poems commemorating the Day. In these poems he uses words like Alpana which, according to his own assertion in January 1983, is un-Islamic. At the 1971 memorial the eternal flame also continues to burn despite objections by the Jamaat-e-Islam, which denounces it as an un-Islamic practice.

society that Bangladesh is. In the long run communalisation would be neither in the interest of the ruling group nor in that of society as a whole. Probably it would not be wide of the mark to surmise that the occasional invectives against un-Islamic practices and the half-hearted measures towards 'Islamisation' are meant only to make Bangladesh appear to be moving towards Islamisation. This provides Bangladesh with a better bargaining position in the Organisation of Islamic Countries, especially with regard to getting easy financial assistance, bilaterally or multilaterally, from the Islamic heartland as well as making it possible for many Bangladeshi citizens to be gainfully employed in this region. A major portion of Bangladesh's foreign exchange earnings comes from Bangladeshis working in the Petro-dollar countries of West Asia. However, if the process of Islamisation in Bangladesh would require the state to seriously challenge the existing indigenous cultural symbols, it would no doubt lead to endemic civil strife.

In the ultimate analysis, the inner strength of Bangladesh's cultural milieu decides the course of her cultural development and identity, irrespective of what the state desires or what narrowly based orthodox groups might wish. And if social heritage is a major factor in cultural development, we can probably predict the outcome if democratic forces are allowed free play. Only an institutionalised regimental state might attempt to raise an 'Islamic curtain' in Bangladesh. In order to achieve this, it would have to overcome formidable internal resistance as well as face a international criticism regarding human rights.

It is of course up to each individual Bangladeshi to decide how she or he wishes to indentify with the social and cultural heritage and the country's national identity.

My analysis would indicate, however, that so far the indigenous social heritage seems to have the edge over religious orthodoxy. The Bangladesh state cannot overlook the role which cultural symbols played in its making, even if it would prefer to do so: these symbols are the symbols of the very sovereignty of Bangladesh. Furthermore, these symbols signify the struggle of the oppressed against the oppressor, and those who distort or suppress them will be identified with oppression. Political demands become stronger when they include protests against the suppression of cultural symbols.[17]

[17] This has been amply demonstrated by the downfall of President Ershad, and the current anti-government agitations.

10

Honour and Resistance: Gender, Community and Class in Bengal, 1920-40*

SAMITA SEN

In Bengal, in the 1920s and 30s, women were repeatedly depicted as victims of male sexual violence in a variety of political discourses. This essay seeks to examine some issues that arise from such deployments of gender and the specific ways in which women were represented in communal and jute mill labour politics. The metaphor of rape and molestation of women was prominent in nationalist, communal and radical race and class rhetoric. In all these discourses, this metaphor served the dual purpose of symbolically expressing anxieties felt in the wake of rapid social change and portraying exploitation in vivid and personalised terms. As an evocative means of inspiring public rhetoric, it contained enormous potential for mobilising protest and resistance.

The political potential of the portrayal of women as victims of male sexual violation lay in the male violator symbolising the threat of an oppositional community. Thus in radical race discourse, the rapist was a European, in Hindu nationalist and communal discourses, he was a Muslim. In radical class discourse, such men were managers, police, or those perceived as agents of the management. The boundaries of the 'community' which suffered violation through the defilement of women was constantly redefined in shifting political contexts. At the centre

* This article has drawn on my Ph.D dissertation. Samita Sen, "Women Workers in the Bengal Jute Industry, 1890-1940: Migration, Motherhood and Militancy", Cambridge University, 1992. The dissertation is being revised for publication and this article reflects a preliminary stage in that process. I have benefitted greatly from discussions with Joya Chatterji, Indira Chowdhury-Sengupta, Subho Basu, Rama Goyal, Anil Sethi, Ajay Skaria, Arjan de Hann and Sanjay Reddy. Joya chatterji and Indira Chowdhury-Sengupta have been particularly kind in making their manuscripts available to me. I have drawn liberally from their work.

of this metaphoric deployment of the image of the despoiled woman lay a notion of 'honour' (*izzat*). This concept, typically embedded in the corporate family was associated primarily with the regulation of women's sexuality and her 'purity'. Honour in this sense was susceptible to violation from men outside the kin group, or within it. The notion that women are the repository or the conduit of kin or caste-based honour and status was not unique to Bengal, or even to South Asia, though the relation of kinship ideologies to cultural codes of status and honour had specific expressions in constraining rules of conduct like seclusion and in ideologies of female purity. The latter was especially important in the agrarian society of the Gangetic belt where under the predominant system of 'male' plough cultivation, women, especially from wealthy land-owning families, were not allowed to work in the field. Excluded from the primary productive activity of the household, women were evaluated primarily in terms of their reproductive capacities, that is, their fecundity and especially their ability to provide the family with male heirs. The need to safeguard the transfer of property to 'real' heirs also meant ensuring the correct paternity of women's children, ideologically buttressed by the notion of honour. An interrelationship between kinship, status, seclusion and the control of women's sexuality articulated the notion of women's sexual purity or 'honour' (*izzat*) with the honour and status of the corporate family. In this sense, the construction of 'honour' was not only not individual but transferable and was in fact, transmitted to succeeding generations. The corporate family thus shared in the women's honour.[2] This notion of 'honour'

[2] E. Boserup, *Women's Role in Economic Development*, London, 1970; Jack Goody, *Production and Reproduction*, Cambridge, 1976; P. Jeffery, *Frogs in a Well: Indian Women in Purdah*, London, 1979; Hanna Papanek, "Purdah: Separate Worlds and Symbolic Shelter", in H. Papanek, and G. Minault, (ed.): "*Separate Worlds: Studies of Purdah in South Asia*, Chanakya Publications, Delhi, 1982; Hilary Standing, *Dependence and Autonomy: Women's Employment and the Family in Calcutta*, London, 1991; N. Yalman, "On the purity of women in the castes of Ceylon and Malabar", Man: *Journal of the Royal Anthropological Institute*, 93, 1, pp. 25-58. The cultural uniqueness of Bengali kinship has been emphasised in some anthropoligical studies. R.B. Inden, *Marriage and Rank in Bengali Culture*, Vikas, 1976; R.B. Inden and R.W. Nicholas, *Kinship in Bengali Culture*, Chicago, 1977; L. Fruzetti and A. Oster, "Seed and earth: a cultural analysis of kinship in a Bengali Town", *Contributions to Indian Sociology*, 10, 1, pp. 97-132.

constructed in the context of the family was extended to a wider community. This essay is concerned with the symbolic articulation of the notion of honour in this extended sense. In nationalist, communal and radical class discourse, fiction and reportage projected the sexual abuse of women by men who were ascribed oppositional identities as a violation of a community's 'honour' to symbolise oppression and to mobilise resistance.

The woman as a victim of class, racial or communal violence then became a cipher in conflicts between men, divested of agency in political movements and a mere signifier of a community's political self-expression. Despite their power as political metaphors, such portrayals of the woman as a victim muted female experiences of social change, economic exploitation and political struggles. These myths about the sexual defilement of women sometimes signalled economic and racial exploitation and were used at times to mobilise political resistance. However, such uses displaced issues of sexual oppression into discourses of class, race and communalism. Communal rhetoric at the end of the 1920s, for example, sought to fuel opposition to legislative intervention into the age of marriage by drawing on the political challenge the Hindu elites faced in Muslim majority regions of eastern Bengal. This twin threat was symbolised in the myth of abduction of Hindu women by Muslim men.

Similarly, in the urban working class context, economic and sexual exploitation were sometimes encoded as violations of individual and community 'honour'. In the jult mill towns of Bengal, myths about violation of women's honour may have served to express the insecurities and instabilities of a heterogeneous migrant community operating in a labour surplus market. Such myths served to obscure exploitation of women within the working class. But their emotional potency gave them a special valence in moments of class and racial antagonism.

The prominence of notions of community 'honour' in

moments of class protest acquires special importance in the context of Bengal's labour historiography. In studying political movements among jute mill labour in Calcutta, historians have been bitterly divided regarding the relative primacy of class and community consciousness in mobilising and harnessing workers' grievances. The ties within and among communities based upon religion, caste and kin have been labelled 'pre-capitalist' and have been considered inimical to the development of a full-blown 'class' consciousness. The religious differences between Hindu and Muslim workers, moreover, translated into occasional physical confrontatioin. The 'communal' question has received special attention, presumably due to the larger political context of an increasing polarisation between Hindu and Muslim politics in Bengal in the thirties and forties. That the gradual growth of confrontational communal politics in the province was reflected in similar political alignments within the working class casts doubt on the understanding of religious and communal differences as a 'pre-capitalist' hangover which Indian labour had not thrown off effectively enough to allow class consciousness the requisite primacy. Chakrabarty's recent endeavour has been to free labour from the 'emancipatory narrative' of class by relocating working class politics within the specificity of a 'pre-capitalist culture'. This has intensified the debate about the contesting claims for primacy of class and community consciousness in working class politics.[3] Das Gupta has explained this lack, i.e., the inability of the working class to give primacy to the politics of confrontation with capitalists rather than to the communal politics of the period, in terms of the uneven economic development dictated by colonial imperatives. The 'enclaved' nature of Indian industrial growth is seen to inhibit the growth of a working class.[4]

Whatever be the relative merits of 'class' and 'community'

---

[3] D. Chakrabarty, *Rethinking Working Class History, Bengal 1890-1940*, Princeton, 1989.

[4] R. Das Gupta, "Material Conditions and Behavioural Aspects of the Calcutta Working Classe 1875-1899", 1979, *Occasional Paper No.* 22, Centre for Studies in Social Sciences, Calcutta, 1979.

as the primary interpretive framework for understanding labour politics, for the purposes of this essay it is useful to note that the metaphor of violation of 'honour' was played out in varying degrees and in different ways, not only in 'communal' (in the sense of Hindu-Muslim antagonism) discourses, but in other discourses of class and community identities. It has been recognised that ties of caste and kin, region and language, were equally divisive of working class solidarity, though these have not been seen to have the same prominence as religious affiliations in working class politics. The continuities of caste, kin, local village-based and language-based community loyalties, which cut across class solidarity, have been explained in terms of the economic compulsions of working class practices. These ties are said to have served as life-lines for workers operating in an uncertain and overstocked labour market where informal networks based on locality, caste and kin provided access to employment and sustenance and support in the urban environment.[5]

What these diverse stories have taken for granted is that they are being told about men — adult men who, by their participation in wage-labour in 'modern' industry qualify for this contested 'class' consciousness. The 'hierarchical and inegalitarian' culture of the working class as conceived by Chakrabarty is blind to the inequalities and hierarchies of gender. He explains, 'Most of the jute labourers were adult males, women on the average forming about 16 per cent of the labour force between 1921 and 1930.'[6] Thus, the lower numerical proportion of women actually working in the factories has justified their absence in histories of class. This presumes that class can be explained exclusively in terms of relations in the workplace and assumes an inextricable link between factory employment and the development of class consciousness. The critical question of the reproduction of the working class, outside the physical domain of wage

[5] A.K. Bagchi, "The Ambiguity of Progress: Indian Society in Transition", *Social Scientist*, Vol. XIII, No. 3, 1985.

[6] D . Chakrabarty, *Rethinking Working Class History*, p.9.

labour as well as within it, is ignored.[7]

The jute mill worker was typically a migrant from a village in Bihar, U.P. or Orissa. He came to the city alone, or with men of his family, caste or village, leaving his wife and children in the village. As a result, the proportion of women in jute mill towns was very low. Some of the men set up a second household in the town with local women or with other women who had migrated to the town alone. Jute mill workers also suffered severe economic exploitation, earning individual wages which did not meet subsistence requirements, and had only uncertain access to employment in towns and cities flooded with migrant labour. The household was destabilised, there was a flux in gender relations that raised anxieties about cultural and material reproduction. This social crisis was echoed in the prominence given to the notion of 'honour' in both community and radical class discourses at moments of intra-class and inter-class conflict. The notion of honour was, after all, embedded in the reproductive exigencies of kinship ideologies of the Gangetic belt from where the majority of the jute workers hailed. It thus provided a potent and emotive means to express the anguish of economic and familial trauma. In the case of Bengal's jute mill labour, the fear and anxiety, it can be argued, about cultural and material reproduction was an important element in the relationship between class and community identity.

This essay seeks first, to explore the imaging of the woman as a victim of male sexual violence and its construction as the violation of community 'honour' in communal discourse and in the discourses of racial and class resistance. It attempts next to place this symbolic use of the notion of honour in the context of social anxieties about gender relations, especially among the jute mill workers of Bengal. It

---

[7] Das Gupta has made an initial attempt to address this issue by arguing that it was the labour of wives and children left behind in the villages by migrant workers that supplemented the colonial industrial sector to maintain the working class family at a 'sub-subsistence' level. R. Das Gupta, "Migrant Workers, Rural Connexions and Capitalism: The Calcutta Jute Industrial Labour, 1890s to 1940s", *Indian Institute of Management (Calcutta) Working Paper Series*, April, 1987. Mimeograph.

argues that the figure of the woman as a victim of sexual abuse echoed deeply felt sentiments. Real or fictional villains from outside the working class or a community could be blamed for specific oppressions. The manager or the supervisor raping the working woman symbolised the disruption of the household, even as it masked the sexual oppression of the woman within the household by men of their own class or community.

Nationalism and Communalism: The Hindu Woman as Victim

In the late 1920s and 1030s, when communal polarisation in Bengal politics was gradually sharpening, a public furore was created around accusations of molestation of Hindu women by Muslim men in the predominantly Muslim majority districts of eastern Bengal. The stereotyping of Muslim men as sexually savage and the metaphor of Muslim violation of Hindu womanhood had already been established in nationalist rhetoric. Through history-writing and fiction, myths like that of the introduction of purdah following the Muslim invasion and the segregation of Hindu women as the reaction of a beleaguered Hindu community to the threat of rape and molestation by barbarous Muslim men, were enshrined in nationalist common sense.[8] The

[8] Even Katherine Mayo, whose virulent indictment of the position of Hindu women in India caused a furore in the thirties, ascribed Purdah to Muslim invasion. Katherine Mayo, *Mother India,* London, 1927. There is surprisingly little by way of a satisfactory explanation of the historical origins of purdah in India. What seems fairly certain is that seclusion and veiling were known before the tenth century A.D., the period of the Muslim invasion. Many historians argue, however, that the practice became, through imitation of the invaders and the need to protect women in politically unstable times, more diffused among wider segments of society only after the Muslim invasion. A.S. Altekar, *The Position of Women in Hindu Civilization,* Delhi, 1962; A. Appadorai, (ed.) *Status of Women in South Asia,* Bombay, 1954; K.M. Panikkar, "The Middle Period", in T.A. Baig (ed.) *Women of India,* Delhi, 1958. Some popular articles in contemporary journals even attributed the practice of child marriage to Muslim invasion. The explanation being that the threat of violation by Muslim men prompted fathers to marry off their daughters early. See, for example, "Strijatir Paradhinata" [The Dependent Status of Women], *Bharat Mahila,* Poush, 1320 B.S. (1913) p.277. This article also attributes *Abarodhpratha,* i.e. purdah to Muslim invasion. For a discussion of purdah in Bengal, see Dagmar A.E. Engels, *The changing role of women in Bengal, c1890-c1930. With special reference to British and Bengali discourse on gender,* Ph.D. Thesis, London University, 1987.

underlying Hindu paradigm in nationalist fiction and history-writing has been explored recently by many scholars.[9] While nationalism cannot be related to communalism in any straightforward way, it cannot be denied that nationalist rhetoric, especially in late nineteenth century Bengal, appropriated the colonial construction of Indian society as deeply divided by religion, and used predominantly Hindu religious imagery to define an Indian identity. As Chatterji points out, such manipulation of Hindu religious imagery does not amount to a 'communal' intent in the nationalist rhetoric, since the aim was to mobilise popular religious sentiments against colonial rule rather than against an oppositional religious community. Communal ideology, in contrast, defined identification with one religious community as the basis for political conflict with other religious communities - in this context, the Hindus and the Muslims were posed in a permanently conflictual relationship.[10] In this sense, the new communal rhetoric of the 1920s and 30s marked a crucial parting of the way from nationalist ideology. But, the Hindu imaging that had been written into nationalist fiction and history a scarce half century ago provided a continuum for anti-Muslim characterisa-tions in communal political rhetoric.

The image of the Muslim man as sexually threatening was depicted most frequently in historical novels. In one sense, these historical novels were the most powerful and

---

[9] L. Dumont, *Homo Hierarchicus. The Caste System and its Implications*, Chicago, 1980; Ravinder Kumar, 'Class, Community or Nation? Gandhi's Quest for a Popular Consensus in India', in the *Essays in the Social History of Modern India,* Calcutta, 1986; J.R. McLane, 'The Early Congress, Hindu Populism and Wider Society' in R. Sisson and Stanley Wolpert (eds.), *The Congress and Indian Nationalism: The Pre-Independence Phase,* New Delhi, 1988; Gyanendra Pandey, *The Construction* of *Communalism in North India,* New Delhi, 1990; Gyanendra Pandey, 'Hindus and Others: The Militant Hindu Construction', *Economic and Political Weekly,* 28 December, 1991, pp. 2997-9; Mushirul Hasan, *Nationalism and Communal Politics in India, 1885-1930,* New Delhi, 1991; Prakash Chandra Upadhyaya, "The Politics of Indian Secularism', *Modern Asian Studies,* Vol.26, No. 4, 1992, pp. 815-853; Indira Chowdhury-Sengupta, "Colonialism and Cultural Identity: The Making of a Hindu Discourse, Bengal 1867-1905", Ph.D Thesis, University of London, 1993; Joya Chatterji, *Bengal Divided: Hindu Communalism and Partition 1932-1947*, Cambridge University Press, forthcoming.

[10] Joya Chatterjee, *Bengal Divided.*

popular means of writing a nation into history. In peopling history with subjects who experienced history, historical novels not only provided an immediate and emotive genre, but in giving the concerns of the so-called private sphere the status of history, it enabled a powerful deployment of the myth of sexual violation of Hindu women by Muslim men as metaphors both of oppression by an alien ruler and for resistance to it. The literature is replete with characteristically lecherous and licentious Muslim rulers and nobles who abduct and molest the women of Hindu chieftains and *rajas* who resist Muslim invasion.[11] Though the intention may primarily have been the construction of a tradition of patriotism and resistance in the 'national' past, this was quintessentially a Hindu past where Hindus relentlessly battled alien Muslim oppression.[12] The *sati* entered this new cultural discourse as an icon of resistance. In the narrow sense *sati* referred both to the woman who immolated herself in the burning pyre at her husband's cremation, and to this practice of immolation.[13] The practice had been banned by a controversial law in 1829.

[11] Early examples of this area in Rangalal Bandopadhyay, *Sura Sundari* (1868), and Jyotirindranath Tagore's *Asrumati,* (1879). The latter depicts an attempt to abduct Rana Pratapsingh's daughter. Similar incidents are found in Bankim Chandra Chatterjee' Rajsinha, Mrinalini, Durgeshnandini, in *Bankim Rachanabali,* Vol I, Calcutta, 1969. Many of Dwijendralal's Ray's plays draw on similar imageries See, *Tarabai* (1903), *Durgadas* (1906), *Mebarpatan* (1908). Rathindranath Ray, *Dwijendralal: Kabi O Natyakar,* Calcutta, 1971.

[12] There are numerous examples of such rewriting of history in novels and verses. Some of the prominent of these were: Nabinchandra Sen, *Palasir Juddha,* (The Battle of Plassey), (1876), Calcutta, 1984; Bankimchandra Chattopadhyay, *Rajsinha,* (1893), *Bankim Rachanabali,* Vol I, Calcutta, 1969; R.C. Dutt's novels, *Maharashtra Jibanprabhat* (1878) and *Rajput Jibansandhya* (1879). See Dr. Bijit Kumar Dutta, *Bangla Shahitye Aitihashik Upanyas,* [The Historical Novel in Bengali Literature], Calcutta, 1980. But historical novels were not the only genre for rewritting a glorious Hindu past. See for example, Bankimchandra Chattopadhyay, "Bangalar Itihas", [History of Bengal], (1874), *Bankim Rachanabali,* Vol II, Calcutta, 1969; Kedarnath Datta, *Bharatbarsher Itihash,* [History of India], Calcutta, 1860; and Bhudeb Mukhopadhyay, *Puravritta-sar,* [Essence of Past], Calcutta, 1860. For more detailed discussions on history-writing in nineteenth century Bengal see, Indira Chowdhury-Sengupta, "Colonialism and Cultural Identity: The Making of a Hindu Discourse, Bengal 1867-1905"; S. Kaviraj, "The Myth and Praxis: The construction of the figure of Krishna in Krishnacarita", Occasional paper, Nehru Memorial Museum and Library, 1987, "Imaginary History", Occasional paper, Nehru Memorial Museum and Library, 1988; Partha Chattopadhyay, "Itihaser Uttaradhikar", [Inheritance of History], *Baromas,* April 1991. Also see, Romila Thapar, Harbans Mukhia and Bipan Chandra, *Communalism and the Writing of Indian History,* New Delhi, 1987.

[13] In a wider sense, the term *sati* is used for pure, chaste and devoted wives.

In its new incarnation as an icon of nationalist resistance, royal Hindu women were typically depicted as voluntarily embracing death by fire in preference to dishonour at the hands of the barbarous Muslim invader. The issue was shorn of much of the complexities that surrounded it in the early nineteenth century debates over its criminalisation. The fascination with the spectacle of *sati*, its conflation with *jauhar*, the mass immolation of women, drawn from Rajput legend, and its unproblematic incorporation into nationalist mythology, flowed from a reinterpretation of the practice in terms of heroic resistance of Hindu women to threats of sexual violation by the Muslim conqueror.[14] The story of Padmini was perhaps the most popular and was repeatedly reproduced in verses, plays and short stories. The first in these series of renditions of the glorious act of *jauhar* of Padmini, the exquisitely beautiful wife of Bhimsingh of Chitor, who died to defend her honour from Alauddin's lecherous intent, was by Rangalal Bandopadhyay in 1858. Abanindranath Tagore's short story "Padmini" in his *Rajkahini* written in 1904, is

[14] Many of the heroes and heroines of this prolific genre written up as plays, novels, short stories and long poems were drawn from Tod's work. J. Tod, *Annals and Antiquities of Rajasthan*, (1829), Reprint London, 1914. Perhaps the first of the better known examples of such rewritting of Rajput legends was in Madhusudan Dutt's play *Krishnakumari* (1861). In the introduction, Madhusudan wrote, "This plot is taken from Tod, Vol.1, p-461". See, Muhammad Manirujjaman (ed.). *Madhusudan Natya Granthabadli*, Dhaka, 1969. The heroine Krishnakumari does not commit *sati* in the strict sense of the term, i.e., she did not immolate herself in the burning pyre of her husband, but she commits suicide. The theme was picked up by Jyotirindranath Tagore in his *Sarojini ba Chitor Akraman*, (1875). See Dr. Sushil Ray, *Jyotirindranath*, 1963. This play made a great impression. Rabindranath Tagore's song, "*Jval Jval chita dvigun dvigun, paran shanpibe bidhaba bala*" [exhorting the fire of the funeral pyre to burn twice as fiercely for the widowed young girl to immolate her life in it] was sung at the scene of the *sati*. Binodini describes her experience as an actress playing the scene, "While playing [Sarojini] we used to become immersed in it. Not just we [the players], but the audience would also become completely involved...[In] one scene in "Sarojini', Rajput women are singing as they ascend the funeral pyre. This scene used to enrapture the audience. The pyres would be burning in three or four different places, the first would be raging two or three feet high.... One by one groups of Rajput women... sang as they walked around the fire and fell into it. Immediately a spray of kerosene would make the fire burn more fiercely, and that would kindle a woman's hair or clothes - but nobody paid it any attention - they still walked around the fire and jumped into it. I cannot quite express in words the kind of excitement that gripped us then." Binodini Dasi, "Amar Katha" [1912] in Soumitra Chattopadhyay and Nirmalya Acharya (ed.), *Amar Katha O Ananya Rachana*, Calcutta, 1969, Reprint 1987, p. 100-1.

perhaps the most well-known version.[15] In defining what constituted heroism of Hindu women, nationalist discourse thus recovered from *sati,* often condemned as barbarous in the social reform discourse, a heroic sub-text that was rewritten as a powerful and evocative icon of resistance.[16] This myth of nationalist resistance woven around heroic Hindu women resisting spoilation by fictional Muslim villains was particularly vulnerable to communal readings and with the sharpening of Hindu-Muslim conflict in provincial politics, became imbued with a different political content. The repeated imagery of Muslim kings looting and plundering the indigenous Hindu populace and raping Hindu women fed into the stereotype of the sexually savage Muslim male and was later deployed in more explicitly communal political rhetoric.[17] The ethnicised image of the sexually pure and chaste Hindu woman, the *sati-lakshmi,* became the symbol of the health of the community, the repository of the community's traditional values and of its 'honour'. The metaphor of rape and defilement of Hindu women by Muslim

[15] Rangalal Bandopadhyay, *Padmini Upakhyan* (1858). This was followed by an anonymous play *Padmini* (1894). Abanindranath Tagore published *Padmini,* a short story in his *Rajkahini* in 1904. In 1906, Khirodprasad Bidyabinod wrote the play *Padmini.* They were followed by Haripada Chattopadhyay in 1915 and Jogendranath Gupta in 1925. Many historians have searched in vain for the historical validation of the legend. The consensus appears to be that if there was a Padmini, she was the daughter of Hamir Shankar of the Chauhan dynasty and the wife of Ratnasingh, a chieftain in central India. Dr. Kalikaranjan Qanungo, *Rajasthan Kahini,* Calcutta, 1968. See, Barun Kumar Chakrabarty, *Toder Rajasthan O Bangala Sahitya* [Tod's Rajasthan and Bengali Literature], Calcutta, 1981.

[16] There are numerous other examples of such iconography of *sati.* Rangalal Bandopadhyay, *Karmadevi,* (1862); Rabindranath Tagore, "Bibaha", (1899), *Katha, Rabindra Rachanabali,* Vol. I, Calcutta, 1961; Rajanikanta Gupta, *Arya Kirti,* Calcutta, 1986. Rajendranarayan Mitra, editor of the periodical Nirmalya, wrote a collection of stories from Rajput legends in two parts entitled *Rajmangal.* (1912). The second part was called *Satikshetra* and contained stories about Padmini, Dhatri Panna, Sarojini, Krishnakumari and Jodhabai. See also Manomohan Ray *Satir Mulya* (1922). Indra Chowdhury-Sengupta explores in more detail the conflation of the two notions of *sati.* Legitimated by the mythical reconstruction of *sati,* the term *satitva* could now embrace feminine heroism and resistance as well as purity and devotion to accomodate the code of conjugality prescribed for the *bhadramahila.* Indira Chowdhury-Sengupta, "Colonialism and Cultural Identity: The Making of a Hindu Discourse, Bengal 1867-1905".

[17] Joya Chatterji points out that the characterisation of Muslim men as sexual savages was doubly derivative in the way it drew on European imperial discourse on Islam. Joya Chatterji, 'Class, Culture and Communal Conflict'. For the Orientalist construction of Arab male sexuality see E. Said, *Orientalism,* London, 1978. Also see, B. Turner, *Marx and the End of Orientalism,* London, 1973.

men could thus be represented as a threat to the whole community in Hindu communal discourse. Women not only functioned as symbols of identity or 'tradition' in these wars of communities, but their roles as repositories and conduts of the community's 'honour' often marked them out as victims of violence. And it provided a 'legitimate' basis for political action by the community on which the dishonour had been perpetrated.[18]

In the 1920s vernacular newspapers like the *Ananda Bazar Patrika* and other dailies like the *Amrita Bazar Patrika* began to carry horror stories of rape and abduction of Hindu women, especially Hindu widows, by Muslim men. The Women's Protection League was set up in 1925 and it 'rescued thousands of outraged and abducted women and conducted numerous cases against culprits...'.[19] In 1927, *Gharer Katha*, edited by Surendra Kumar Bandopadhyay, reported the 'torture of women' especially in northern and eastern Bengal.[20] In July 1928, the *Ananda Bazar Patrika* reported four cases of abduction in Kusthia alone. On 4 September 1929, there were six such cases reported in the *Ananda Bazar Patrika,* and in the next seven days eleven more cases were reported. The *Ananda Bazar Patrika* screamed headlines like *Nariharan O Mushalmaner Kartavya* [Abduction of Women and the Duty of Muslims],[21] and published statistics to prove that though more Muslim women were abducted than Hindu women, on the whole there were many more Muslim offenders.[22] By emphasising the commu-

---

[18] G. Pandey, 'Hindus and Others: the Militant Hindu Construction', *Economic and Political Weekly,* XXVI, 52, 1991 and Tanika Sarkar, 'Woman as Communal Subject: Rashtrasevika Samiti and Ram Janmabhoomi Movement', *Economic and Political Weekly,* XXVI, 25, 1991. Also see, S. Sen, "Motherhood and Mothercraft: Gender and Nationalism in Bengal", *Gender and History,* V, 2, 1993.

[19] *Welfare,* December 1925, p.797

[20] *Gharer Katha,* No. 1, Aswin-Agrahayan 1334 B.S.

[21] *Ananda Bazar Patrika,* 4 September, 1929.

[22] On 24 August, 1929, *Ananda Bazar* reported, "Terrible cruelty by Muslims in Matibhanga - Hindu women stolen, Hindu neighbourhoods ransacked, one woman murdered, many Hindus hurt". In one issue there were several items on this subject: *Sudhangshubala Haran* [Abduction of Sudhangshubala], *Lilabati Haran [*Abduction of Lilabati], *Maimansinghe Nariharaner Prabalya,* [The Exacerbation of Abduction of Women in Mymensingh] *Nariraksbmar Prastab* [The Proposal to Protect Women]. *Ananda Bazar Patrika,* 4 September, 1929. In 1929, the Allahabad Court reported the rising rates of crime against women all over the country and asked for punishment as well as prevention. *Ananda Bazar Patrika,* 16 August, 1929.

nity identity of the offenders and marginalising the significant evidence that 'more Muslim women' were victims of sexual assault in Bengal than Hindu women, *Ananda Bazar* deliberately sought to cast the issue in communal terms. The myth of the 'abduction of Hindu women by Muslim men' continued to excite the emotions of Hindu and Muslim politicians, but in the spate of accusations and counter-accusations, neither side gave any importance to the evidence, or even acknowledged that Muslim women were equally vulnerable.

Ananda Bazar's reporting of the rape and abduction of Hindu women led to a meeting convened at the Albert Hall in Calcutta on 22 August, 1929, by the editor of the newspaper, Satyendra Nath Mukherjee, who was active in communal politics in the thirties.[23] An intense debate was sparked off by provocative speeches about the rising number of Hindu women being sexually violated by Muslim men.[24] The point at issue was the violation of Hindu male honour.

> ...The chastity of Hindu women is held in high esteem amongst the Hindus and the violation or the attempted violation of chastity is the most outrageous offence to the Hindu mind...the Government is indifferent to a matter so sacred to the Hindu heart...[25]

The meeting at the Albert Hall resolved that,

> ...The Hindu community all over Bengal and Assam, specially where they were isolated [are] to form themselves into well-organised bands for the protection of the honour of the women and to arrange so that the girls are taught in the use of offensive and defensive force by means of weapons suited for the purpose to protect their honour.[26]

The theme of self-protection was stressed repeatedly in popular and political platforms. At the provincial Hindu

---

[23] He was described, in a note from a government official, K.B. Roy, as a Hindu politician, the self-appointed and 'stoutest champion of Hindu women, and an uncompromising critic of Moslem conduct...". Note dated 5 September 1929, West Bengal State Archives, [henceforth WBSA], Home Political Confidential [henceforth Home Poll. Cofdl.] 535 of 1929.

[24] *Ananda Bazar Patrika*, Editorial by Ramananda Chattopadhyay, 23 August, 1929.

[25] From the Secretary, Bengal Provincial Hindu Sabha, to A.N. Moberly, Member, Executive Council, Government of Bengal, West Bengal State Archives Home Political Confidential 535/29

[26] WBSA, Home Poll Cofdl 535/39

Sabha meeting, Narendranarayan Chakrabarty tabled a proposal to protect women from Muslim attack.[27] Ramananda Chattopadhyay reporting the meeting in an editorial in the *Ananda Bazar* Patrika, launched a virulent attack on Muslims alleging that 'respectable muslim families do not appear to mind housing stolen wives to help the louts and goondas' and when cases of abduction were taken to court, 'the muslim population of the village crowded at the courts as though it was a titillating event'. He pointed out that there was an 'epidemic of abductions' of Hindu women by Muslim men, especially in rural Bengal as in the Noapara and Nodail thana. Women's Protection Societies, therefore, ought to be formed in all villages.[28] The Albert Hall meeting also demanded that the government institute a committee of enquiry consisting of five members of the Hindu Mahasabha, three from the Women's Protection League, and five to be nominated by the government from the Legislative Council to enquire into the causes of abduction and suggest remedies.[29]

Muslim politicians reacted sharply to this meeting by calling another meeting at Albert Hall on 25 August. Ahmed Ali, who had been present at the earlier meeting of the 22nd, reported a speech made by Swami Satyananda, who allegedly

> asked the Hindu youths of Bengal why they were not using their bombs and revolvers against the Muslim untouchables who had

---

[27] *Ananda Bazar Patrika*, 4 September, 1929.

[28] *Ananda Bazar Patrika*, 23 August, 1929. The idea of Muslims lacking in 'culture' and being essentially sexually savage was earlier mentioned in the same context of abduction and molestation of Hindu women by Saratchandra Chattopadhyay. "If the significance of education is the broadening of the mind and the culture of the heart, then I have to say that there can be no comparison between the two [Hindu and Muslim] communities. In the matter of the abduction of Hindu women, I often see journalists ask why the Muslim leaders remain silent. Why do they not protest against the repeated perpetration of such a grave offence by the men of their community? What is the meaning of their silence? I think the meaning is very clear. It is only a sense of tact that prevent them from actually admitting that they do not make objections precisely because given the opportunity they would be happy to join the rank of the offender [in abducting Hindu women]" Saratchandra Chattopadhyay, "Bartaman Hindu-Mussalman Samasya" [The Current Hindu-Muslim Problem], *Sulabh Sarat Samagra*, Calcutta, 1989, reprint 1991, p. 2135.

[29] WBSA, Home Poll Confdl 535/29. A note from a Secretary, however, suggested that one or two 'reasonable' Hindus and Muhammmedans presided over by a European Judge would be more useful in getting at the facts and making them public. Ibid.

> been abducting their womenfolk instead of against the Government and advised them not to fight against Government until the untouchables had been disposed of first.[30]

Ahmed Ali also reported that Sarala Dasi mentioned in her speech that a verse in the *koran* enjoined that if 'Moslems could outrage non-Moslem women they would win religious merit...'. Muslim politicians at the meeting not only repudiated these Hindu accusations as false and exaggerated but retorted with counterclaims that,

> In all the cases of abduction reported...the women were offenders of the first degree, and that the facts were always distorted and misrepresented for the purpose of convicting muslim youths. Hindu women were more likely to be morally affected for the worse than Moslems because of the frequency with which they visited the theatres and because of the large quantity of obscene literature which they read.[31]

This characterisation of sexual deviancy became part of a mutual campaign between Hindu and Muslim politicians. This myth of abduction of Hindu women was not merely a metaphoric deployment of communal stereotypes, it was a myth in a more ordinary sense in that it falsified reality. Though there was a general "increase in the number of cases in kidnapping and abduction group of offences...,"[32] in the late 1920s, there was little statistical or any other evidence to show that the incidence of molestation of Hindu women by Muslim men was significantly higher than molestation of women within these communities. In fact, police reports show that the numbers merely reflected the larger Muslim concentration in the areas from which these cases were reported. Proportionate to the population, the number of offences of such nature by Muslim men were perhaps a little lower than by Hindus.[33]

The issue remained alive throughout the thirties. News-

---

[30] WBSA, Home Poll Confdl 535/29. The Government reporter notes, "[*P.S.* - It is a hopelessly exaggerated version of what was actually said.]"

[31] Speech by Akram Khan, 25 August, 1929, at the Albert Hall, Calcutta. Reported in WBSA, Home Poll Confdl 535/29.

[32] Home Poll Cofdl 535/29.

[33] WBSA, Home Poll Confdl, 535/29.

papers and journals quoted statistics as evidence of increasing vulnerability of the Hindu community honour in Muslim majority districts of eastern Bengal, perhaps expressing symbolically its heightened sense of political disenfranchisement in the wake of the Communal Award.[34] In 1932, *Jayasree*, under the headline, "Torture of Bengali Women", argued that in the past six years many women had been tortured and raped and that the offenders were mostly Muslims. They admitted that some Muslim women were also abducted, but argued that Hindu women raped by Muslim men were far in excess of Hindu women raped by Hindu men.[35] In 1939, the Modern Review noted that there was no decrease in crimes against women in Bengal.[36] In 1936, in an editorial in response to a speech by the Governor headed, 'Daring abduction of Women by gangs of ruffians', the *Ananda Bazar Patrika* once again took up the issue. The Governor, they reported, said in his speech that the incidence of abduction of women as 'serious offence' had declined from 1934 to 1935 by some 30 per cent while the offences in other classes had increased by about 7 per cent. The editorial points out that these police statistics were not a good indicator of the extent of the crime because a large majority of such crimes were not reported due to poverty and the fear of social stigma. Therefore, not much reliance, they averred, should be placed on the observed decline in the incidence of cases of abduction. The Governor was also reported to have said in his speech that the problem was not communal, because a large number of muslim women were abducted. The editorial while agreeing that this was true, argued,

> ...If the Governor investigated the matter a little further he would find that among the offenders, the larger majority are Muslims rather than Hindus. Therefore, even if it is not a communal problem, the

[34] Joya Chatterji, *Bengal Divided.*

[35] *Jayasree,* Aswin, 1339 B.S., p. 539.

[36] 1141 cases of offences against women were reported to the police during the year 1939, of these 98 were of kidnapping, 250 of abduction, 485 of outraging modesty, 249 of rape and 9 of buying and selling of minors for prostitution. *Modern Review,* July-December, 1940, p. 359.

Muslim community has a special responsibility and duty in the matter. We have no doubt that if the educated and respectable Muslim community was conscious of this vice of abduction of women and took responsibility for its mitigation, the problem in Bengal could have been dealt with more easily. After the Governor's speech, if the police on the one hand, and the Muslim community on the other, become more active in the performance of their duties, then we will be very happy. Needless to say, the Hindu community also has a great duty to control this vice of abduction of women and that no Hindu will deny this responsibility.[37]

The editor of *Ananda Bazar* had convened the meeting at the Albert Hall to protest against the abduction of Hindu women by Muslim men in August 1929, at a time when Hindu 'nationalist' agitation against the Age of Consent Bill intended to raise the age of marriage for women was gathering momentum. The interest of the Hindu middle class in the problem of child marriage and especially child widows had reawakened and issues about control of women's sexuality became inextricably bound with nationalist and communal discourses. Soon after the Albert Hall meeting, *Ananda Bazar* published a special supplement on women on 5 October 1929. Many of the articles, some written by women, focused on the problems of the Sarda Bill and its disastrous implications. At the centre of the debate was the concern over child widowhood and the 'problem' of widows losing caste and therefore being deprived of access to family resources and having to take recourse to prostitution. Some opponents of the bill in eastern Bengal foresaw higher incidence of abduction and rape of women as a direct consequence of raising the age of marriage. Gurusaday Dutt, asked to sound public reaction to the bill, reported from Mymensingh.

Cases of abduction of Hindu and Mahmmedan girls by Mahmmedan rowdies is extremely common and it is feared that compulsory postponement of marriage will offer a great temptation to such cases happening...[38]

---

[37] *Ananda Bazar Patrika*, 29 July 1936, p. 6.

[38] WBSA Letter from G.S. Dutt, District Officer, Mymensingh to The Commissioner of the Decca Division, 25 February, 1930, Home Poll Confdl 73 (1-8) of 1930.

Similar fears were expressed in Chittagong. The district officer reported that, "Offences against person are common in this district... and the poorer women and girls work in the fields, draw water..."[39] It was feared that raising the age of consent would endanger the women who had to go out of the house to work. In fact, the majority of cases reported were of attacks on low and intermediate caste women. Among the cases reported from June to September 1929, there were women from Kumbhakar, Tanti, Namasudra, Paramanik and Kapali castes.[40] There was only one mention of a Brahmin girl being abducted in a town. In eight other cases, the caste of the women was not mentioned. And the overwhelmingly large proportion of women reported to have been molested were widows.[41]

From the middle of the nineteenth century when the idealisation of womanhood sought to define and circumscribe women's identity within marriage and motherhood, widows, especially child widows, posed a special problem. Despite the influence of Victorian puritancial ideals of a pure and passionless womanhood, male fears of a powerful and devouring female sexuality seem to have lingered beneath the construction of the 'angel of the hearth'.[42] This had been illustrated in the debates over child marriage and widow remarriage in the nineteenth century.[43] In the 1920s when controversy over the Age of Consent Report raged, contradictory and ambiguous attitudes to widow remarriage revealed the tensions within constructions of woman-

---

[39] Letter from H.R. Wilkinson, District Officer, Chittagong to M.A. Momin, Commissioner of the Chittagong Division, 19 February, 1930. Home Poll Confdl 73 (1-8) of 1930

[40] *Ananda Bazar Patrika,* June - September, 1929.

[41] *Ananda Bazar Patrika,* July 1928; 4-11 September 1929.

[42] M. Borthwick, *The Changing Role of Women in Bengal,* 1894 - 1905, Princeton, 1984, p. 228.

[43] Iswar Chandra Vidyasagar, who compaigned for legalisation of widow remarriage, was at first concerned at the mounting evidence of illicit sexual liaisons involving widows and consequent abortions. Later, the advocates and the contestants of widow remarriage returned repeatedly to *shastric* injuctions. *Sambad Prabhakar,* 28.1.1262 B.S., 1855 AD, in K.S. Bhattacharjee, *The Bengal Renaissance: Social and Political thoughts,* New Delhi, 1986. Also in Shri Charan Basak, *Balabidhabar Bibaha,* Calcutta, 1922.

hood.[44] Widowhood, manual labour and prostitution were seen to go together.[45] Official documents did not question this characterisation. A.Mackenzie, Secretary to the Government of Bengal, pointed out, 'In Bengal the prostitute class seems to be chiefly recruited from the ranks of Hindu widows.'[46] The 1921 Census enumerated 78,957 child widows in Bengal, of whom 2845 were under 5 years. *Welfare* found these figures sufficient evidence to comment, 'the evil of this widowhood has resulted in the increase of the number of fallen sisters in cities and towns'.[47] Such tenuous evidence was used to suggest that widows, who had been outcast for failing to adhere to the norm of celibacy, *samajparitaktya*,

---

[44] This tension is very evident in Saratchandra's novels. Several of his novels feature women - widows or married women - who had been ostracised because of sexual transgressions, and had become 'prostitutes' or fallen women. His depiction of them as endowed with traditional womanly 'virtues' earned him some criticism. In reply, he writes to Lilabati Gangopadhyay, 'I had once in my youth collected the life-stories of 6-700 Bengali "fallen" (*Kulatyagini*) women. I wasted a great deal of time, effort and money on this endeavour. But I also learned a strange lesson. It is true that I earned a bad reputation, but I knew for certain, that 80 per cent of these women are married women. Widows are few. What if the husband is alive, what if he keeps strict guard, my dear sister; it is only through great sorrow that a woman destroys her true nature. It is not because of attraction to other men, or from a terrible lust. When they destroy such an integral part of themselves, it is not because they are tempted by something wonderful outside in the world, but they accept this great sorrow to escape an even worse existence.' Sarat Chandra Chattopadhyay, *Aprakashita Patrabali, Saradiya Basumati,* 1966.

[45] The word for widows - rarh - being used interchangeably with prostitutes indicated clearly the assumption that widows were sexually available. Such a use could not have been accidental. O'Hanlon mentions that the same was true in Marathi. R.O'Hanlon, *For the honour of my sister countrywomen: Tarabai Shinde and the critique of gender relations in colonial India,* Oxford University Press, forthcoming. Two examples from Bengali ditties popular in eighteenth century Calcutta clarify the point:

> '*Ghor podley chhagoley maray*
> *Rarh holey sabai eshey sanga korte chay*'
> ('When a hut collapses, even the goat tramples on it. When one becomes a widow, everyone comes to arrange a Sanga with her.')
> '*Ajob Sahar Kolketa*
> *Rarhi bari juri gari michhey kathar ki keta*'
> ('A strange city is this Calcutta. Whores and houses, carriages and cars abound. And how fashionable it is to lie!')
> Sumanto Banerjee, *The Parlour and the Streets: Elite and Popular Culture in Nineteenth Century Calcutta*, Calcutta, 1989, pp. 56 and 84.

[46] National Archives of India, Delhi, Home Judicial No. 5829, A. Mackenzie to H.L. Dampier, Official Secretary to the Government of India, Calcutta, 17 October, 1872. Later in 1926, another official noted, 'Among the Brahmins, marriages take place at the age of 12, and the widows may not remarry, so that if young, they frequently become prostitutes. Traffickers recruit young widows from the provinces and send them to the towns.', WBSA, Home Poll. Confdl., 129 (1-2) of 1926.

[47] *Welfare*, December 1925, p. 797.

women who were denied access to familial resources for a variety of reasons like marital infidelity, inchastity or barrennness and victims of rape and seduction, took to prostitution for lack of other alternative means of survival.[48] On the one hand, this provided an argument in favour of their remarriage,[49] on the other hand, the fear of rape and abduction of unmarried girls provided an argument against raising the age of marriage. Thus child marriage and widow remarriage were two important questions around which issues about the control and regulation of women's sexuality were being debated in the 1920s and 30s. Societal anxieties stirred at the threat of reformist and legislative intervention into gender relations — a domain the Bengali Hindu elite had sought to mark out as the primary domain of their control free from colonial domination.[50] These anxieties were ultimately deflected into a communal rhetoric, the threat of Muslim preeminence in provincial politics of Bengal constituting, especially in the post-Communal award era, the primary challenge to Hindu elites.[51] In thus eliding social and political anxieties, the myth of the abduction of Hindu women provided a compellingly emotive and vividly personalised symbol of the challenges and threats faced by the Bengali Hindu elites.

Race, Class and Community: The Working Class Woman as Victim

The division of colonial society on racial lines had partly been justified in nineteenth century colonial discourse through

---

[48] Balai Chand Adhya wrote to the *Amrita Bazar Patrika* from Chinsura, that Hindu girls abducted and 'outraged' lost their place in society and that the door to earning any honest livelihood being closed to them they are forced to become 'public prostitutes to keep body and soul together'. *Amrita Bazar Patrika,* 1 August 1937.

[49] One article by Saralabala Dassi is of particular interest. Writing with anger and irony, she talked of the progress of the Women's Movement and said that society must sanction widow remarriage, otherwise women would continue to leave their homes and families *(Kulatyagini). Ananda Bazar Patrika,* 25 October, 1929, p.11.

[50] The marking out of a 'private' domain of gender relations in the nationalist discourse has been discussed in greater detail in S. Sen, "Motherhood and Mothercraft".

[51] See Joya Chatterji, *Bengal Divided.*

the characterisation of a pure passionless white woman threatened by the unbridled lust of the lascivious native male. The representation of white men as the natural protectors of white women was contingent on the representation of the native male as bestial and without any sexual control. This patriarchal racism underlay the tremendous publicity given in Bengal to a few incidents of alleged assault on white women by native men. The reports usually seemed to have implicated men in menial services, though in the political construction of the reportage, very little attention was paid to the class of the native men alleged to have assaulted a white woman. 'Native men' were seen as a homogeneous class, and the act of assault interpreted as expressions of 'race hatred'.[52] In turn, from the closing years of the nineteenth century, nationalist discourse repeatedly highlighted the sexual threat to Indian women posed by white men. In this case, the women were usually from the working class, and depictions of rape and assault, violation of 'honour', was used as a vivid and personalised metaphor for racial and class exploitation. The profligate white man was a symbol of political and economic exploitation and betrayal. The erosion of loyalism among the Bengali middle class and the gradual sharpening of the nationalist rhetoric destroyed the paternalistic image of the coloniser, to be replaced by the image of the predatory and sexually threatening white male. The myth of violation of Indian women by white men was used in strongly emotive ways as idioms of resistance.[53] European planters,

[52] This theme has been explored in the context of the Anti-Ilbert Bill Agitation in 1993-4 in Mrinalini Sinha, "Chathams, Pitts and Gladstones in Pettycoats: The Politics of Gender and Race in the Ilbert Bill Controversy, 1883-4." in N. Chaudhuri and M. Strobel, *Western Women and Imperialism: Complicity and Resistance*, Indiana University Press, 1992.

[53] The Indigo Revolt, the refusal by peasant to cultivate indigo under duress from white planters, provided the context for one of the first examples of the use of the metaphor of sexual molestation of a woman to inspire public rhetoric against class and racial exploitation. *Neel Darpan* by Dinabandhu Mitra depicts a peasant woman, Kshetromoni, being assaulted and molested by a white planter. Dinabandhu Mitra, *Neel Darpan*, Dhaka, 1860. Accusations of sexual violation of peasant women figured prominently in petitions against planters and the committee appointed to enquire into the state of indigo cultivation felt it necessary to exonerate planters from these charges. "As to outrages on women, which, more than any oth er might offend the prejudice and arouse the vindictiveness of a people notoriously sensitive as to the honour of their families, we are happy to declare that our most rigid inquiries could bring to light only one case of the kind. And when we

managers, and supervisors were repeatedly characterised as sexually abusing working class women. In the context of the tea plantations of Assam and Northern Bengal such characterisations assumed legendary proportions.

The *Shishusahay O Matrimangal Samiti.* [The Society for aid to children and welfare of mothers] 'investigated many cases of women's oppression and have instituted legal proceedings. Apart from these they have done their utmost to aid the community of mothers *(Matrijati)* in many other ways'.[54] The Secretary of the Organisation was Santosh Kumari Gupta, well-known as a pioneering jute trade union organiser.[55] In September 1924, Santoshkumari Gupta wrote in an *Ananda Bazar* Editorial,

> Due to the ineffectiveness and cowardice of Indians, the number of cases of assault on women is steadily increasing. Our heads are bowed in shame when we recall this low bestiality of our own people. But this is not where our shame ends. With increasing frequency we hear of the bestial white men perpetrating terrible physical torture on our women. Of all the sorrows of our unfree and enslaved condition, this is the most degrading.[56]

She cites the high incidence of molestation of women workers by white planters and managers in the tea garden of Assam. One incident is described in detail.

> On 19 May, in one estate, at 2 a.m., the manager Mr. Johnson and his assistant manager went to the coolie lines in a car. There they went to a hut and called a woman by her name. They broke open the door and both the husband and wife came out. The husband was pushed out of the way and the woman, Gedama was dragged

came to examine into its foundation, as seriously affecting the character of one planter, and through him the body of the planters in a whole district, or as affording any clue to the excitement of the past season, we discovered that there were very reasonable grounds for supposing that no outrage on the person of the woman had ever taken place." Report of the Indigo Commission appointed under Act XI of 1860 with the Minutes of Evidence taken before them and Appendix, pp. xxi-xxix, excerpt from S.D. Punekar and R. Varickayil, (ed.) *Labour Movement in India, Documents: 1850-1890*, Bombay, 1989.

[54] *Ananda Bazar Patrika,* 15 August, 1924, p.4.

[55] At the peak of her power in December 1924, the AITUC asked her for an affiliation of unions. She was the President of the Sir Stuart Hogg Market Employees' Association, she was closely associated with the postal union and she also tried to organise a boatmen's union. Deputy Inspector General, Criminal Investigation Department, Intelligence Bureau, [henceforth DIG CID IB] Secret, 1923 and 1924.

[56] *Ananda Bazar Patrika,* 10 September, 1924, Editorial.

> into the car. They took her to the assistant manager's bungalow. Gedama was screaming at the top of her voice. The assistant manager pulled her into a bedroom and there raped her four times consecutively. In the morning, at about 5 a.m., she returned home in tears. In the meanwhile, the husband and awakened the neighbours and they all collected in front of the assistant manager's bungalow. Gedama came and told them the story of her rape. After this, all the Telegu workers, about 40 on that estate, left the estate and went to the nearest railway station.[57]

There is not the same pervasive legend about sexual abuse of jute mill women by white managers and supervisors as there is about plantation women. Accusations of sexual abuse against European managers and supervisors appear, however, to have been commonplace and could sometimes provoke working class protest in the form of strikes. Protests against sexual harassment by managers and clerks betrayed racial and class antagonism. Individual cases of assault and sexual harassment could become the basis for concerted protest by women - sometimes with the support of male workers. Women, in protesting, or even in participating in protest, against sexual abuse by European managers and supervisors, or against *durwans* and *jamadars,* the latter being perceived as agents of the management, often invoked the notion of honour. They were thus drawing on a metaphor that struck a chord of sympathy in their follow workers - men and women - conflating potential anger against sexual exploitation with class conflict. In this women workers were themselves acting in their capacity as workers to reinscribe their gender oppression. They were tapping an emotional reservoir articulated to an oppressive construction of gender when they invoked the notion of honour to win the support of men of their class and community. Women workers were drawing what gains they could from the contradictory position they occupied vis a vis the managers and working class men. The advantages, in the form of support of male workers against sexual abuse by managers and supervisors, that flowed from exploiting this contradictory social position, did

---

[57] ibid.

not, however, mean that they could surmount the contradiction within which they were caught. Their capacity to act against the management was drawn from precisely that discourse which emphasisted their incapacity to act, a discourse depicting them as the passive and powerless victims needing protection from aggressive male sexual threat.

One interesting oft-quoted example of collective protest by women against sexual harassment was the strike in the Hooghly Mill. On 16 September, 1920, some women workers walked out of the mill demanding the dismissal of the assistant-in-charge accusing him of 'improper' conduct and more specifically alleging that he had 'struck' one of the women. The mill had to be closed and the next day the assistant was actually dismissed.[58] This was a rare success story. In most cases such strikes could not be sustained and when the unions took them up they were sometimes diverted to other economic issues like wages. In 1923, the Union Jute Mill at Entally went on a complete strike (of 3000 workers) in protest against the assault on a woman worker by an European assistant. According to the manager this was merely a rise to avoid the stricter discipline enforced on women workers.[59] The 4500 workers of the Dalhousie Jute Mill at Champdany went on strike in July 1921 to protest against the harassment of a woman worker by a European assistant. The dispute was resolved amicably and work resumed two days later.[60] But matters were not always so easily settled. While in most cases these strikes were short-lived and quickly resolved, in cases involving women, there was a tendency towards outbreaks of violence. At the Fort Gloster Old Mill, for example, a charge was brought against Erfan Ali (a spinner) for throwing bobbins at Mr. Howrie, an assistant. The defence case was that he had merely pointed out that except Manik's (a weaver) 'kept' women everyone was cleaning the machinery.[61]

---

[58] WBSA, Commerce Commerce, July 1921, A 40-45, 2R-67-1.
[59] DIG CID IB, Secret, Weekly Reports, 1923.
[60] DIG CID IB, Weekly Reports, Secret, 8-14 July. 1921.
[61] *Amrita Bazar Patrika,* 14 August, 1928, p.10.

These strikes demonstrated the immediate mobilising potential of accusations of sexual harassment in organising resistnce against racial and class exploitation. Managers often took care to point out that these allegations were trumped up to win support for strikes. That may indeed have been the case on certain occasions. This is not to say that cases of sexual harassment did not occur. It is quite likely that European managers and supervisors did sexually abuse women workers in mills. In conditions of a labour surplus market and an informal recruitment system and the social reality of fragmentation and enforced mobility, women too might have been compelled to deal in sexual currency. The point I wish to emphasise here is that, such traumas, fictionalised, could enter political rhetoric as an explicit illustration of class exploitation which aroused an emotional recognition from working class men and women. In linking personal tragedies to political resistance, the theme of sexual abuse could become imbued with powerful mobilising potential.

In same cases, charges of sexual abuse against European managers and supervisors provided ammunition to ballast strikes and could be used as a means of mustering support for strikes which appear to have included a range of issues about wages and working conditions. The workers found it 'legitimate' to stage a strike on the issue of women's 'honour' and, therefore, used it to strengthen their case even when apparently other causes had precipitated their protest. On 28 April 1931 in the Bally Jute Mill, forty 'workers of the preparing department', some of who were women, went on strike. They were protesting against the dismissal of a new recruit. The strike failed because other workers refused to join the strike, and the forty strikers were easily replaced. On 2 May they were forced to vacate their quarters and two of the female strikers filed a petition charging the Manager with 'outraging their modesty'.[62] In many cases when the declared reason for a strike was protest against assault on women

[62] DIG CID Secret, 4-11 April, 1931.

workers, police reports, and management statements often pointed to other underlying issues as the 'real' cause of the dispute. Such diversions were meant to divest strikes of the 'legitimacy' workers sought to give them by charging managers with sexual assault, or to defuse the potential for violence. The management preferred not to deal with issues involving 'dishonour' to women. On 6 January 1923, when 9,500 workers of the Old and New Clive Mills struck work in protest against the 'objectionable procedure of searching the persons of the female workers while leaving the mill premises', the manager pointed out that the 'real' reason was the previous dismissal of some weavers. Similarly, when the preparing department of the Gourepur Mill No.2 went on strike in protest against the assualt on a woman worker by an European assistant 'by pulling her clothes', the issue was quickly diverted and the subsequent accounts of the strike refer to the dismissal and assualt of a *sardar*.[63] During the labour unrest of 1928, it was alleged that 'it was a popular story that the Ludlow strike started owing to the conduct of some of the 'young American mill assistants' and there were many 'hints of indiscreet actions by the young managers' in this mill. However, subsequent reports on the progress of the strike and its final settlement deal merely with the issue of union membership and victimisation of strikers.[64]

The image of the woman as a victim of violent abuse by managers and police was powerful precisely because it personalised political resistance. Its evocative power as a metaphor of oppression made it useful as an interpretive framework and it can be found in newspaper reportage, strike pamphlets and trade union statements. Middle class mediation and trade union rhetoric continually portrayed working class women as victims of abuse, providing, in moments of protest, ammunition for mobilisation against state or managerial violence. Condemnation of police or state

[63] DIG CID IB, Secret, 1923.

[64] Centre for South Asian Studies, Cambridge, *Benthall Papers, Box I, G.C. Godfrey to Edward Benthall*, 13 December, 1928.

violence against working class protests gained strength and credibility from references to atrocities on women and children. One leaflet distributed by Niharendu Dutt Mazumdar refers to police violence which had 'not even spared children of 10-12 years of age. They have insulted our mothers and sisters. They forcibly entered our *basti* homes...They even took all our women by force to the mill.'[65] But such portrayals also represented women workers as divested of agency in moments of protest and underlined the image of the passive and powerless woman, on whose body class oppression inscribed its violent message.

The Ludlow strike of 1928, in which women took an active initiative provides the best example of how emphasis on portrayals of women workers as victims of brutal violence overshadowed the recognition of their acts of protest. A popular daily, sympathetic to the cause of labour said,

> ... after this the other women workers were beaten up ruthlessly. They were pulled by their hair and dragged up. Many have been seriously injured. One 60 year old woman was beaten to unconsciousness and the union volunteers removed her to a hospital. It has been said that a one-year old baby was torn from his mothers' breast and flung to the ground...4 women and 2 men workers have been arrested...[66]

The 'Infant Torn from Mother's Arms'[67] caused most disquiet, and persuaded the District Magistrate, Gurusaday Dutt, to personally investigate the case. The matter became grist for inter-union rivalry, K.C. Roychoudhury protesting against 'the exploitation of women in labour disputes'.[68] Earlier, in the Ludlow Mill when there was an assault by the blacklegs on the strikers' families, a 7000 strong meeting condemned

---

[65] Issued 4 June 1937, WBSA, Home Poll. Confdl. 331 of 1937.

[66] *Ananda Bazar Patrika*, 11 June 1928, p. 6. Another description rang along the same lines, '...the Manager induced women leaders of the strike to come to his office... Thereafter the gate were locked up and ... police and jamadars continued to intimidate them all along... 7 leaders were severely assaulted... Rest of the women were indiscriminately assaulted and forcibly dispersed, dragged by their hair. . The outrage has been so barbarous as to form an unprecedented chapter in the history of labour throughout the civilized world...' *Amrita Bazar Patrika*, June 15, 1928.

[67] Appeared as a newspaper headline in *Ananda Bazar Patrika*, 13 June 1928, p.7.

[68] DIG CID IB, Weekly Reports, Secret, 1928.

'injury to women and children to break strikes.' One newspaper headline proclaimed *'Striloker lanchhana'* (Humiliation of Women).[69] A more direct reference to an attempt to use violence against women workers to capture public attention was in 1939.

> Labour Minister is bent on crushing the labour movement.... Instances of assault on even women workers by the police and European managers were cited by him [Sibnath Banerjee], but in all cases the Minister remained indifferent...[70]

The image of the woman as a victim spilled beyond the paradigms of racial and class resistance into a more comprehensive vulnerability to male violence in the context of communal conflict within the working class. Chakrabarty has shown how Hindu and Muslim workers traded insults in the highly coded and symbolic language of woman's honour.[71] Since women's honour involved the honour of the community, violation of *izzat* provided a 'legitimate' basis for political action. In the twenties, and more especially the thirties, mutual charges of violations of 'honour' of women between Hindus and Muslims tied in with the wider deployment of such metaphors in the communal discourse in Bengal already discussed above. In 1938, a report on Hindu-Muslim conflict in Kankinara mentioned attacks by Muslims on 'Hindu houses and women'.[72] In the National Jute Mill at Rajgunj in Howrah, a strike on 4 November 1938 was followed by notices that failure to rejoin work would lead to dismissal. When 400 Muslim workers from the mill quarters attended the mill the next day, 300 strikers were reported to have entered the quarters and 'started molesting the women and children in the [Muslim] coolie quarters throwing brickbats and damaging property. The workers rushed out and ...a riot started'.[73] 'Acute communal tension' was reported among workers of the Anglo-India Jute Mills in April 1937 when

[69] *Ananda Bazar Patrika,* 2 May, 1928.
[70] *Amrita Bazar Patrika* July 9, 1939 p. 7.
[71] Dipesh Chakrabarty, *Rethinking Working Class History, Bengal 1890-1940,* Princeton Unversity Press, 1989, p. 199.
[72] WBSA, Home Poll. Confdl. 260 of 1938, also cited in D. Chakrabarty, *Rethinking Working Class History,* p. 216.
[73] WBSA, Home Poll. Confdl. 403 of 1938.

the Hindu workers had gone on strike and the Muslim workers were 'unwilling' to join them.[74] Another report on Kankinara around the same time said, 'In the Kankinara Mill quarters, the Muhammedans have for some time...[been] in the habit of ...exhibiting their private parts to the Hindu women of the same line...This caused considerable ill-feeling which [had] been augmented by the strikers'.[75]

Community provided a basis for identity that often cut across class identity to divide working class solidarity. Whether or not community identities along religious lines were products of deliberate propaganda by the state, or by organisations like the Arya Samaj and Muslim League,[76] the construction of a community identity, and a notion of honour flowing from it, could be defined by language, habitat or religion.[77] The lines of community identity shifted continually across the interstices of these definitions, drawn and redrawn in moments of crisis and protest. At such moments, 'honour' of women could be subsumed within any of these varying definitions of community and it could be deployed in a variety of different contexts. As in the instances cited above, community identity could merge with the division of workers into strikers and blacklegs. In times of working class unrest, a conflict between 'loyal' workers or 'blacklegs' and strikers could have explosive potential for violence.[78] In the Rajgung riot mentioned earlier, the clash between 'Hindu strikers' and 'loyal Muslim workers' was supposed to have led to the

[74] WBSA, Home Poll. Confdl. 403 of 1938.

[75] WBSA, Home Poll. Confdl. 403 of 1938.

[76] D. Chakrabarty, 1989, *Rethinking Working Class History*, 1989, p. 199.

[77] Ibid., p.216.

[78] During the Ludlow Jute Mill strike of 1928, on 28 April, five days after the strike had commenced, the manager with 60 men hired from Calcutta began to evict workers from their quarters. These men were usually confined in the mill upto 7 pm, but on this particular day they were released at 5 pm and they came to the lines and started assaulting the strikers' family. The strikers who were holding a meeting received the information and rushed to the place with their leaders Kalidas Bhattacherjee (Bengal Jute Workers Association) and Hemanta Kumar Basu who were presiding over the meeting. They found that 2 women had already been severely injured, the locks were broken and belongings were scattered outside. The description of the clash reads, 'Gurkha durwans were preparing to evict bodily some women workers, which enangered workers into a clash with the police'. *Amrita Bazar Patrika*, July 15, 1937, p.6.

molestation of women and children in the muslim *coolie* quarters.[79] In the general strike of 1929, the threat of dishonouring the wives and daughters of non-striking men was used as an incentive to draw more men into the fold.[80] The lines of community division could as easily follow from linguistic or regional differences. A riot between Bengalis and 'upcountrymen' ensued (November 1928, Bauria) when the Bengalis received a piece of 'false information' that the upcountrymen 'had entered [their]...villages...and had been molesting their womenfolk.'[81]

In strikes and protests against managerial harassment, women workers could themselves initiate or participate in the invocation of honour as a paradigm of resistance. In order to wrest the ability to challenge authority they reinforced the metaphor of the victim woman, by calling upon its emotive strength to legitimise their actions. It was a male construction of women's honour, one which imprisoned women in their victim status, that was deployed most successfully in moments of communal conflict within the working class. Despite the power of such emotional imaging to underscore oppression and muster resistance, women were, primarily, the passive site on which such conflictual imageries were played out, and were often mere pawns in battles between men. The emphasis on women as signifiers of community honour bolstered the passive and powerless image of the working class woman. The role of the victim was extended from subjection to police and managerial brutality in moments of class conflict to a more comprehensive vulnerability to physical abuse within and outside continually shifting categories of community.

Women Workers in the Jute Industry

Women workers were, however, not only vulnerable to

[79] WBSA, Home Poll. Confdl. 403 of 1938.
[80] Royal Commission of Labour in India [henceforth RCLI], Vol.V, Pt. 1, p 411.
[81] *Amrita Bazar Patrika,* 27 November, 1928.

violence and sexual oppression by men outside the community or the working class. The ubiquity of community constructions of violation of honour in the discourse of class and racial resistance tends to conceal and deflect the reality of sexual relations between working men and women within the same community. While, the image of the working woman being sexually violated by men from outside the community gained powerful credibility, it also serv ed to distort perceptions of immediate and direct sexual exploiters of women. Working class women were continually vulnerable to sexual violence, in the *basti,* the street and the mill. The sexual abuse of women transcended class or community boundaries, and women who lived and worked in jute mill towns in severely adverse conditions were subject to physical, emotional and material exploitation within the household.

The low sex ratio, the high crime rate, the loss of household stability, the social and cultural alienation enforced by migration, and the unfamiliarity of urban life and factory work characterised the lot of the migrant jute worker. In the mills women worked as many as eight to ten hours in the day and returned home to housework and childcare in slums which offered to ameliorative facilities. In addition, they faced the reality of poverty and uncertainty of employment which undercut household stability. The economic and social assault on the household may have undermined traditional forms of common law marriages and altered customary modes of control over women's sexuality. The anxieties generated by the disruption of productive and reproductive control over the household may have accentuated preoccupations with women's and, therefore, the family's and the community's 'honour'.

It is difficult to say with any certainty how women themselves perceived their sexual vulnerability in the mill, the slum and the street. Some commonsense speculations may perhaps be permissible here. The overwhelmingly masculine environment with the inevitable accompaniment of violence against women reinforced their insecurities. This was sometimes expressed as a need for 'protection'. Women recognised the difficulties of living and working without male support. Given the uncertainties of employment and the informal nature of recruitment, *sardars,* clerks and managers often exacted payment for favours in sexual currency. Durgabala Dasi from the Fort Gloster Mill whose mother and father, father's sister and two husbands also worked in the same mill, said, "How can a woman stay alone? Is it good? People will say bad things about you and gossip. It is better to have a man". So she married a second husband of her choice when her first husband, to whom her parents had married her, died.[82]

Sexual harassment by *durwans* and *jamadars* led to outbursts of violence and short-term strikes. The ubiquitous *sardar,* however, often had a special role to play. Some *sardars* exercised control over the workers both in the workplace and in the slums. This gave them greater power to exact sexual favours from women workers. It is misleading to call the *sardars* a direct recruiting agent, in so far that the mills did not pay the *sardar* to assist migration from the village. Such recruitment may have played some role in the very early years of the industry but by the turn of the century, a situation of overwhelming labour surplus obviated such investments in recruitment. The *sardar* was typically a labour supervisor - and there were three or more *sardars* in every department. The line *sardars,* supervising a small group of workers were under a head *sardar.* As labour supervisors, they were a bridge between the management and the workers - their value to the management lay in their ability to control labour and regulate its supply to mills while their control and authority over labour in the workplace depended to some extent on networks of power outside the mills. In the absence of formal recruitment channels, the informal networks of caste, village and kin were

[82] Interview, 2 December, 1989.

important for access to jobs[83] as well as for providing a safety-net in an uncertain urban environment where migrants had few source of sustenance.[84] The system of *badli* or temporary workers, who were employed on a 'daily' basis or in the very short term, typified the informal system of recruitment. To the management, this was an easy means of ensuring a flexible labour supply - to be recruited when necessary, either as blacklegs or for expansion of production. For workers, it meant chronic insecurity of employment, and a higher premium on permanent jobs. It also meant that a group of workers were constantly dependent on patronage for access to employment.[85] The low level of wages, providing bare individual subsistence, entailed chronic indebtedness. Thus the worker was embedded in a complex network built up around working class *bastis*, for access to work, credit and housing. Some *sardars* straddled these and could regulate and control access to jobs, credit and housing, but apart from the *sardar*, the clerks, *darwans* and *jamadars* within the mill, and traders, shop-keepers, the local toughs *(goondas)* outside the mill, were involved in servicing the workers. The scope of a few clerks in the Bally Jute Mill has been described thus by A.D. Khan,

> ...The case of the workers is that they had to pay the various clerks of the Jute Department for securing employment. Homage in cash was also exacted from time to time as security for tenure of jobs, while religious festivals became occasions for special peace offerings. It is alleged that registers were so manipulated that the men received more wages than were due to them, the arrangement

[83] This is obvious from the oral evidence of workers recorded by the Royal Commission on Labour. Of the ten workers interviewed, two had been recruited by a *sardar*. The others had come through 'relatives' and 'friends'. In the case of Abdul Halim, the sardar was the friend who provided cash in times of need and ensured the security of his job. *RCLI* Vol. V, Pt. 2, pp.76-80.

[84] D. Chakrabarty, *Rethinking Working Class History,* 1989. The role of the jobber has been examined in considerable detail in the context of the cotton textile industry in R.S. Chandavarkar, 'Workers' Politics and the Mill Districts in Bombay between the Wars', *Modern Asian Studies,* Vol.XV, 1981.

[85] The workers of weaving and spinning departments of Gauri Shankar Jute Mill wrote to Niharendu Dutt Mazumdar on 22 May, 1937, they alleged that *Sardars* had to pay a deposit to the Mill clerk for their employment which they subsequently extorted from he workers. Ritlall *Sardar* was charged Rs. 100 for his appointment, Pearilall, line *sardar* was charged Rs. 40 for a transfer. Piro Shaftier was charged Rs. 75 for an appointment and Chhattu was charged Rs. 50. DIG CID IB, 168 of 1992.

> being that they would refund the excess amounts to the Babus... There was the further allegation that Tripura Babu forced many of the men to buy their provisions from his brother's shop at Uttarpara on pain of dismissal...Mr. Kitching wondered why the men should, all of a sudden, have experienced righteous indignation at the clerk's dishonesty.... There is little doubt that the wages of these bogus tickets had to be drawn through the workers, who must have exacted a price for their connivance, so that when there was a hitch among the partners the truth leaked out.[86]

Sardars, clerks, *durwans* and others who had a certain amount of control over important resources - like jobs, credit and housing — often bargained for sexual favours from women. Women found it difficult to enter and retain employment without some kind of patronage or protection.[87] The Chief Inspector of Factories mentions. '...women without "friends" are cruelly exploited by the *sardars* and time-keepers through whom they get employment...'.[88] This could, of course be interpreted in various ways. According to a sociological survey in 1950-51, 49 per cent of the 347 women interviewed in a jute mill at Howrah, said that they joined that particular mill because they had a male relative already working there. The author adds, 'it is indeed not usual for a husband or father...to allow his wife or daughter to be working outside for the whole day unless there is someone working with her whom he can trust to work with the women.'[89] The fracas in Fort Gloster mill mentioned earlier had its ori-

---

[86] *Report of the Court of Enquiry appointed under Section 3 of the Trade disputes Act, 1929 (Act VII of 1929), to investigate the Trade Dispute between Messrs. George Henderson & Co., Ltd., of 101/1, Clive Street, Calcutta, Managing Agents, Bally Jute Mill, Bally, District Howrah, and the workmen of the Weaving and Jute Departments of the said Mill,* Government of Bengal, Calcutta, 1941.

[87] Mr. Williamson of Kinnison Jute Mill told Curjel that he preferred not to employ young girls, because they were more likely to be attacked. Older women tended to work in batches together. He had tried 'sirdarinis' to avoid the exploitation of women workers by the sardars, but the experiment failed, it is said, because they were less satisfactory than the men, and took higher bribes. *Curjel Report,* Appendix B, Serial No, 1.

[88] Chief Inspector of Factories to Government of Bengal in Industrial Commission Report, 1908, WBSA, Comm. Comm. November 1919, A 11-25 Unlike the cotton mills of Bombay, Jute Mills never employed women supervisors. The Royal Commission on Labour had recommended it but the IJMA rejected the proposal. WBSA· Commerce Commerce, July 1932, B322.

[89] M.N. Rao and H.C. Ganguly, "Women Labour in Jute Industry of Bengal - A Medico-Social Study", *Indian Journal of Social Work,* Vol. II.1950-1951, p.184.

gin in the new manager failing to appreciate the rules - he drew attention of the *sardar* to the fact that Manik's 'kept' woman was not working while all the others were busy cleaning the machinery. This started the trouble that ended in a spinner throwing a bobbin at the new manager.[90] Curjel definitely states that it would be difficult for women in the mills if they were not under protection. This could mean a different kind of sexual exploitation of women workers. 'One of the most deplorable features in the immorality of the system,' Sherwood Eddy wrote, '[is that] the power of the foremen...enables them to make immoral overtures which if refused may lead to dismissal'.[91] Kashinath Shau whose mother worked in the Titagarh No. 2 Mill remembers a quite famous incident from the forties. For some time, a woman in the preparing department was being harassed by a *Sardar* who held out the hope of ensuring her permanent employment. Finally unable to fend him off, she made a rendezvous and 'hurt him very badly when he arrived'.[92]

The *sardar* traversed a grey area between the workers and the management, and while some of them were more powerful, many were not set apart from the community of the workers. *Durwans* and *jamadars* were, however, seen more as direct agents of the management, especially in times of trouble when they were used to break strikes. An accusation of sexual harassment against the *durwans* could provoke concerted protest from men and women. The Gourepur Jute Mill had gone on strike on 9 September 1923 over an alleged insult offered to a woman worker by a mill *durwan*. In 1928, the Meghna Jute Mill in Jagatdal was closed on 6 March because some *durwans* had used 'improper' language to the woman workers on the occasion of the *holi* festival. The millhands protested upon which the *durwans* assaulted some of the workers. As a consequence nobody came to work the next day.[93]

---

[90] *Amrita Bazar Patrika*, August 14, 1938, p. 10.
[91] George Sherwood Eddy, *the New World of Labour*, London, 1924.
[92] Kashinath Shau, Interview, Titagarh No. 2 Mill, 12 December 1989.
[93] DIG CID IB Weekly Report, Secret, 1923 and 1928.

The notion of 'honour' thus proved potent, when its violation could and did promote solidaristic class protest. In depicting working men's crimes as symptoms of capitalist exploitation, the metaphor of honour concealed the disturbing implications of exploitative sexual relationship between working men and women. The notion of honour had a political utility for women workers who could deploy it against managers, supervisors and working class men perceived as agents of the management, to win support of other working class men. But its radical implications were severely limited, since it could only remain a defensive weapon and its terms were inflated from the value given to chastity and 'purity' of women in kinship ideologies. Its power as a defensive weapon was even more limited in the context of the household because its ability to regulate relations between working class men and women eroded with the weakening of stable kinship patterns in the industrial towns. The deployment of the notion of honour as a paradigm of resistance in class, racial and community contexts evaded the reality of intense sexual exploitation of working women by working men.

To begin with, life in the *bastis,* much more than in the workplace, was particularly brutal to women. There was a high level of sexual violence both within and outside their marital relationships. The incidence of child molestation seemed to have been particularly high. *Amrita Bazar Patrika* in 1937 reports ten cases of rape of girls under 10 years in mill quarters and *bastis*, four cases of rape of women over 10 years, Amrita Bazar Patrika and Ananda Bazar Patrika together report 10 instances of rape in 1935, 9 in 1929. As early as the 1890s police inspectors were reported to have been unfairly harassing some women workers of a jute mill on the 'pretext' of some personal feud among the workers.[94] The descriptions of these incidents are brief, but they reveal that the main target of attack were women and girls who were caught alone and anawares. Despite this evidence, Shanti

[94] Kanailal Chattopadhyay, K., (ed.) *Bharat Shramajibi,* Calcutta, 1975.

Pasreecha, one of the first lady welfare officers engaged by Jardine Skinner and Company for the Kankinara and Reliance Mills, has argued that rape was a rare occurrence in mill areas because, with high congestion and overcrowding, it was not possible to catch women in helpless positions, or even alone.[95] The incidence of rape of very young girls may then have been because they were more helpless and were more likely to be caught alone since they did not work in the mills. Sunia (10 years) was kidnapped from her parents from the *coolie* quarters of Khidirpur.[96] Ansia Bibi (17 years) was abducted 'when her husband had gone to the Mill' and taken to Dumdum where she was raped several times before she escaped.[97] Dhania (8 years) was returning from the public privy when Ganga Chamar offered her a treat and took her home, gagged and raped her.[98] When her parents who were mill hands were 'away on duty', Kachi Dasi, (10 years) was raped by her neighbour.[99] Abdur Rahim (55 years) raped Bagum Bibi (7 years) having tempted her to come to his room by offering her sweets.[100] When her father and mother 'went to work in the mill', Mir Hussein, who also worked in the mill, returned in the afternon and raped Chhabian (10 years), having first tied her hand and feet.[101] These examples can be multiplied.[102]

[95] Interview, Shanti Pasreecha, Calcutta, March 1989.

[96] *Amrita Bazar Patrika,* 24 August, 1928, p.6.

[97] *Ananda Bazar Patrika,* 27 June, 1935, p.8.

[98] *Amrita Bazar Patrika,* 25 July, 1939, p.4.

[99] *Amrita Bazar Patrika,* 22 July, 1939, p.4.

[100] *Amrita Bazar Patrika,* 3 March, 1937, p.4.

[101] *Amrita Bazar Patrika,* 17 August, 1937, p.12.

[102] When Savitri was alone, she had not gone to the mill because she was ill, her husband and 'co-wife' had gone to the mill, two engine drivers of the mill finding her absent in the mill came to her house in the afternoon, and tried to abduct her. *Amrita Bazar Patrika,*July 8 1908, p. 7; Lakshmi was dragged out of her house and taken away and gang -raped, 'when her father was not at home'. *Amrita Bazar Patrika* June 25, 1937, P.7; Chandia (12 years) lived with her brother. While she was sleeping, he and his wife left for work in the mills. Their neighbour entered the house and invited her to his room. She refused, and he picked her up in his arms and carried her to his room, which was adjacent, gagged and raped her. Ibid. The very young age of the girls involved in these instances is suggestive. Dr. P. Sengupta who practices law in Patna, remarked that rape of very young girls was a frequent occurrence. She relates this to the superstitious belief current that intercourse with a pre-puberty girl is a cure of gonorrhoea. (Interview, Patna, March, 1991). It may also be mentioned here that rape and child molestation may have been a more

Other than rape and abduction, women were subjected to various kinds of harassment. Sarat Chandra De worked in Kamarhati jute mill and when his tenant Jatiram left his house and rented a room in Satyabala's house, he began by abusing and ended up assaulting Satyabala.[103] Bagit Kunjra stole a widow's baby to force her to marry *(nika)* him. He was also trying to force a widow, Kulsum of Kharda Bazar, to sell him her house at a cheap rate. He terrorised prospective customers so that she was ultimately forced to sell to him at his price and move into hired rooms herself. Dookhalia had asked for the money she had lent to Basiram, who promptly beat her up to avoid payment. Turahin, Parbati and Ramrath were beaten up by Kunjra in course of an argument. Turahin was beaten up again later because she had dared to lodge a complaint against him.[104]

Such instances can be further multiplied from newspaper reports alone, though one would suppose that only a small percentage of the cases would find their way to the police, let alone to the court and then to the newspapers. The vulnerability of very young girls who were special targets of crimes like rape and abduction, might have prompted mothers to take young daughters with them to the mills. Often, however, the dauthers had to be left at home for domestic purposes. One girl was raped, for instance, when she was collecting cow-dung,[105] another when she had gone to the tank to fetch water,[106] one was kidnapped when she had gone to the corner shop to buy provisions, a fourth when she had gone to the street hydrant to wash

---

common occurrence than the (lack of) evidence would seem to suggest. The reporting of such incidents was restricted to mill areas and city slums. Middle class families were far more chary of airing their grievances in public. For girls in middle class families, the loss of status and honour involved in loss of chastity might have been greater. We get only brief flashes of the possibility of such occurrence in middle class families from women novelists. See, for example, Maitreyee Debi, *Na Hanyate,* (It Does Not Die), Calcutta, 1974.

[103] WBSA, Home Poll. Confdl, 200 (1-7) or 1925.

[104] WBSA, Home Poll. Confdl, 376 (1-8) of 1925.

[105] *Ananda Bazar Patrika,* 22 February, 1928, p.5.

[106] *Amrita Bazar Patrika,* 3 May, 1939, p.4.

[107] *Amrita Bazar Patrika,* 21 September, 1939, p.5.

utensils.[107] Tasi, who was eleven years old, was stolen from the *coolie* quarters of Garden Reach when she had gone to collect firewood.[108]

The need for 'protection' against such sexual violence often prompted women to enter into relatively more stable relationships with men. These sexual relationships were characterised as 'temporary' in official and elite discourse because they fell outside the increasingly narrowly defined legal norms of sacramental or contractual marriage. While these 'temporary' marriages did not necessarily represent radical departures from traditional marital arrangements current among lower and intermediate castes, the economic uncertainties and the demographic imbalance, for instance, of the urban industrial environment did weaken sanctions against extra-marital sexual relationships and patterns of stable cohabitation. Women remained in a weaker position in the so-called 'temporary' marriages, though the characterisation of such marriages as extra-legal also conferred on women a limited freedom to terminate these arrangements.

The 'temporary' marriage tended to victimise women more than men because in many cases women, unlike men, did not have the option to return to the village. This was important because men had wives and families in the village to whom they were committed to send money regularly. Such men saw their alliance with women in the city as 'temporary' because they were themselves not permanently settled industrial workers and would go back to their village periodically. This made the 'temporary' wife more insecure and vulnerable in these 'temporary' marital relations. Such alliances also increased the vulnerability of the wives of migrants left behind in the village. In Bhojpuri folk songs sung by women, the absence of the husband and the possibility of a sowatin, usually translated as a co-wife, is poignantly por-

[108] *Ananda Bazar Patrika,* 4 May, 1935, p.12.

trayed.[109]

For the 'temporary' wife in the city, the problem arose when the man had saved some money and wanted to go home to his village. Women, who had migrated without their families, had to forego the 'rural' tie that most men retained. Women usually migrated when rural resources were exhausted or when they were marginalised in the family. For those women who migrated in these circumstances, migration itself often implied a loss of status. As a result, there was an irrevocable break with the rural past, as severance much rarer for single male migrants.[110] Since women's access to family resources was conditional on their behavioural and relational role fulfilment,[111] those women who migrated outside the family context, could not hope to return to the family home once they had lost 'honour' from migration. Many women thus did not have the option to return periodically, or ever, to the village. This is further borne out by the fact that among colonial emigrants a larger proportion of men than women returned to India.[112] In the 1920s and 30s, the majority of the women did not in fact return home for confinements and periodic visits. Dr. Dagmar Curjel, who undertook a survey of women workers in Bengal's mills, mines and

---

[109] '*...I will give thee O crow! a leaf platter of milk and rice, If thou will bring me news of my beloved in a foreign land, Sweetheart of thy beloved! Say not "beloved" or "loved one" Thy beloved is entangled with a young Bangalin, I ask thee, O crow! a strange matter. In what feature is the young Bangalin beaugiful?*
Slender of loin is she, and beauteous is her face, bees hum about her hair
I would draw her dagger and take away my life, for thou dost praise exceedingly that wanton one.'
G.A. Grierson, Seven Grammars of the Dialects and Sub-dialects of the Bihari Language, calcutta, 1883, p. 126. In a similar song, the woman sings, '*...thy beloved also hath fallen captive to a young tamorin.*
Alas! what is that country and that land like, and what the young tamorin...
Poison will I pound and venom will I eat, for he hath set that wanton before me. Das Bulaki sings this ghato at a fit season, singing it, singing it, and her friends consoled the deserted one.' Ibid.,p.125

[110] D.F. Curjel, Report of Dr. Dagmar Curjel on the Conditions of Employment of Women Before and After Childbirth, 1923. [henceforth *Curjel Report]* Main Report, p.2.

[111] Kalpana Bardhan, "Women's Work, Welfare and Status: Forces of Tradition and Change in India". *Economic and Political Weekly,* Vol.XX, No.50, December 14, 1985.

[112] Letter from F.E. Pargiter, Uncer-Secretary to the Government of Bengal, General Department, to the Secretary to the Government of India. Revenue and Agricultural Department, Bihar State Archives, General Emigration, May 1885, No. 6-8.

plantations in the 1920s, makes this pathetically clear.

> When up-country men workers have saved money they often return for a time to their family land, but neither on such occasion nor (when) they eventually return to settle in their own country, do these men often take back with them the women whom they brought down...in the large majority of cases women who once come to the mills do not return to their own country.[113]

In this sense most of the women who could not return to the village, had even less bargaining power than men and were truly proletarianised. When in Jagaddal, 115 women, made redundant by the introduction of new machinery, were offered passage home, none applied for it. The Manager said this was because 'the large majority of them are permanent residents in the mill areas'.[114] A survey in 1930 showed that the category of workers who could be regarded as 'settled' or permanent migrants were second generation immigrants who were born in the mill 'lines' or in the neighbourhood. They were usually employed in the jute mills and rarely returned to their native village. Gilchrist comments that in many cases they were the 'illegitimate children of jute men and women workers... and a large number of these women and the children, who are born of the (temporary) unions never leave the areas where they work'.[115]

It was not a notion of honour drawn from ideals of female purity and chastity that allowed working women an opportunity to negotiate the reality of brutal sexual exploitation with its concomitant violence within the household and the neighbourhood. The unfavourable sex ratio, and the extralegal character attributed to their 'temporary' marriage,

---

[113] *Curjel Report*, Main Report, p.2

[114] They had been retrenched by the Anglo-India (Middle) Jute Mill in Jagaddal and were offered by the Managing Agents, under pressure from Niharendu Dutt Mazumdar, an opportunity to apply for tickets to return home to their country home. There were not a single such application. The Agents had made it clear that they would not give cash and would make sure that the ticket they gave would have to be used for returning home and could not be sold. WBSA Commerce Commerce, March 1941, B181-184.

[115] The survey included 79553 workers. Apart from this 3.5 per cent of 'permanent' migrants, the rest returned to the village periodically, and the largest sample, almost 85 per cent returned at least annually. *RCLI*, Vol. V, Pt. 1, Memorandum from the Government of Bengal, and R.N. Gilchrist, *Labour and Land*, Calcutta, 1932, p.10.

which, on the one hand, made them vulnerable to male desertion and violence, gave women, on the other hand, one advantage. The 'temporary' alliances could be broken by either the man or the woman. Within the given structure of alliances and social organisation this gave her a very limited freedom of choice. That is obvious in the many tussles that centred round them. In this sense, and because women could take the initiative to break the alliances, which being 'informal' and therefore, without the force of law (as in case of middle class marriages) to enforce exclusive rights to her sexuality, the alliances were 'negotiated bargains'. An implied 'loss of honour' may not have stopped them from invoking the lack of legal marriage ties when it worked to their advantage. There are several instances when women deserted their husbands. When Moniruddin complained that his wife had been enticed away and concealed in 'a House of ill-fame', the defence came up with the argument that the girl was in fact not legally married to him.[116] Rambalak charged Dehri Routh with kidnapping his wife from Kanchrapara and bringing her to Bhadreswar. Ramratia refused to return, saying she was not married to Dehri Routh.[117] Saifulla of Naihati could not persuade his 'wife' to return with him from Kankinara where she had gone to protect herself from his assaults.[118] The next story is full of interesting features.

> On the complaint of Abdul Sovan of Manicktolla, Sheikh Hussani was charged...(and) prosecuted before Mr. M.M.Bose, Honorary Magistrate, Sealdah on a charge of enticing away Shamsul Bibi, wife of Sovan for immoral purposes when the latter was not at home. Azizur Rahman deposed that he was the son of the complainant. His mother Shamsul Bibi lived with his father. She at present was living with the accused...like his wife in the same room. Abdul Sovan stated that about 5 months ago...he could not find his wife...traced her.... at the house of the accused... the accused was not related to the complainant.[119]

[116] *Amrita Bazar Patrika,* 13 January, 1935, p.4.
[117] *Amrita Bazar Patrika,* 26 November, 1932, p.17.
[118] *Amrita Bazar Patrika,* 14 July, 1928, p.6.
[119] *Amrita Bazar Patrika,* 17 January, 1940, p.5.

Sovan claims his 'wife' was 'enticed' away, though she refused to return, and there was, in fact, no proof that they were over married. The son never said his father and mother were married. His mother 'lived with his father', and now she was then 'living with the accused'. The use of the term 'live with' for both cases signifies no great difference in the perception of the son between the two arrangements. the 'wife' *refused* to return to the 'husband'. In another case, the lack of evidence of a legal marriage proved conclusive, despite the complainant's claim of marriage.

> The prosecution case is that the complainant's married wife, Kalidassi had been enticed away by the accused... [and] concealed in the house of Hafiz Mea of Halisahar...Kalidassi in her evidence said that she was quite willing to go back to her former (first) husband [Dasu Bauri]...but her step-mother had been compelling her to live with the complainant as his mistress... The magistrate said... the girl [left] of her own accord.[120]

These examples should not, however, be read without caution. Despite the fact that some women could and did disregard 'loss of honour' to take advantage of the high rates of desertion and divorce to gain some advantages, the working class neighbourhood could brutally victimise women who sought to assert their sexual freedom. In these circumstances, the notion of honour could be inverted and used to sanction violence against women. Pasreecha mentions that it was usual for neighbours and friends to arrange a marriage for a young widow to protect her honour, ensure her security and to 'avoid complications'.[121] Some widows may not have been willing. In case of one widow, her unwillingness cost her dear.

> Mungri Passi alleged that one Wednesday morning the accused Sundar Passi and six others forcibly took her away from her house and confined her in a room for the night in a house at Cossipore. The next day they forcibly cut her locks, blackened her face and put a garland of small snails, shoes and earthenpots round her neck and made her sit on a donkey which paraded the streets and bustis of

[120] *Amrita Bazar Patrika,* 22 June, 1936, p.4.
[121] Interview, Shanti Pasreecha, Calcutta, March 1989.

> Narkeldanga. The woman said that Sundar Passi wanted to marry her but she refused and preferred to lead a life of liberty as she is a widow. The enraged Passi... with the assistance of his fellows tortured her severely.[122]

Such examples of sexual harassment and physical abuse of women warn against placing too much emphasis on the choices working women could exercise over the initiation or termination of sexual liaisons. In any event, a tenuous economic position and responsibility to maintain children, not to speak of sexual violence, may have prevented many working class women from exercising their choices. While divorce, second marriages and widow remarriage may not have been uncommon in the social practice of castes and communities who made up the large majority of the jute working class, economic disruption in the urban environment may have made these practices more fluid. Not only did extra-legal sexual relationships become more unstable, unemployment made it more likely that men would desert pregnant women who would then have to rear and maintain the children on their own. In times of unemployment and for women in very low paid jobs, a household unit based on marriage, or even relatively stable cohabitation, may have been desirable, or even necessary for survival.

This is not to suggest that upper caste and middle class norms of female chastity and the sacramental marriage were necessarily relevant to the realities of working class women's lives. Despite their greater vulnerability in these sexual arrangements, 'temporary' marriages may have helped to ameliorate the social reality of fragmentation and enforced mobility that undercut experienced household stability. This consideration might have in a sense also compensated for any 'loss of honour' since they had in fact already lost 'honour' to the extent that they could no longer return to their family home. It is unlikely that many women had any real choice. Men's wages barely suficed for individual subsistence and

[122] *Amrita Bazar Patrika,* 17 May, 1936, p.8.

women's wages were lower. Women and children, therefore, rarely earned enough to live on. Thus even 'tempporary' families, apart from being a source of affection and human warmth, were also necessary for survival. Only by pooling their wages together could working 'families' feed and house themselves and their children. Given the intense economic and sexual exploitation faced by working class women, the experience of family for women might have been less an oppressive structure than a bulwark against the atomising effects of poverty and legal and political restraints.[123]

'Temporary' marriages thus increased working women's security even as it added to their vulnerability. The deployment of notions of 'honour' in moments of class, racial or community conflict by working class men, and in some cases by working women, concealed complex negotiations of ideals of chastity and purity within which such a notion of honour was embedded. Such negotiations modified, and in some cases intensified, sexual exploitation of women within the household and the working class neighbourhood. In the elite and official discourses such negotiations were depicted as sexual deviancy. The retention and imposition of dominant standards of sexual behaviour involved the characterisation of violence and sexual laxity as being endemic to the working class.

Conclusion

The deployment of a notion of 'honour' inflated from kinship ideology to include an extended community in-

[123] Jane Humphries points out that in particulr cases, the working class family may also have been the locus of resistance. And in that sense, rather than an area of male exploitation, in working class women's experience, the family may have provided the basis of class consciousness and resistance. "Class Struggle and Resistance of the Working Class Family", *Cambridge Journal of Economics,* 1, September, 1977. In other migrant situations, it has been argued, that the family provided important means of socialisation of children in both 'cultural' and survival skills. In that sense, family could be a locus of racial and class resistance. Evelyn Nakano Glenn, "Racial Ethnic Women's Labour: The Intersection of Race, Gender and Class Oppression", in C.E. Bose, R. Feldberg and N. Sokoloff, (ed.) *Hidden Aspects of Women's Work,* Women and Work Research Group, New York, 1987.

volved the portrayal of women as the passive victims of profligate men ascribed oppositional identities. This emotive imagery was used as a paradigm of resistance in moments of class and racial protests to mobilise and harness anger. It was, however, also a means of conflating femal experience of class and racial exploitation with sexual abuse. The image of the sexually violated women afforded a potent and personalised emblem of exploitation but it also served to obscure sexual exploitation of women within the household and the working class neighbourhood. In the context of jute mill labour, the marking out of men in authority like managers, supervisors and men of oppositional communities as sexually predatory, masked the real and direct secual violence working men perpetrated on working women of their own communities. While it was true that it was evasion of the realities of working class sexual violence that allowed the effective political use of the metaphor of honour in some situations of class and communal conflict, the middle class and official characterisation of sexual laxity among the poor was equally an evasion of the realities of severe economic and social exploitation faced by the jute working class. The working class woman thus alternated between the image of the victim, and the image of the morally flawed poor.

This essay has attempted to explore these images and to outline some of the concerns about familial and household disruption that lay under them. The patterns of sexual relationships between working men and women in the mill towns reveal that while women, subjected to economic constraints and enforced mobility entered 'temporary' marriages that ameliorated some of their economic and physical insecurities, they were also at the unequal end of these relationships.

The Jute Industry and Its Workers: Changes in Stratification in Eastern India

Arjan de Haan

If there is a city in the world which has become the prototype of underdevelopment and pauperisation, it is Calcutta. After the golden age of the nineteenth century, the city fell into decay when Delhi became the capital of British India and Partition caused serious problems. Similarly, one of old Calcutta's most flourishing industries, jute manufacturing, declined progressively after it received severe jolts during the economic crisis of the thirties, when Calcutta was cut off from its supplying districts after 1947, and when synthetic yarn began to replace jute in the world market.

There is a tendency in studies of the jute industry to see it as bound to decline from its inception because it was a capitalist-colonial enterprise *par excellence.* Dipesh Chakrabarty (1989), in particular, has stressed the industry's 'mercantile' character, which he supposes to have been a more fundamental problem than even the crisis of 1929. Also, the effects of the development of the industry are generally assumed to have been negative. The population is supposed to have hardly benefited, if it did not actually suffer because of it.[1] In the avail-

[1] For the negative impact of the growth of industry under colonialism, many references can be cited. For example, Sen and Banerjee ([1983], p.32) write: 'Many of Calcutta's problems are carry-overs from the past when the city had grown for nearly two centuries in the typical colonial pattern...The sectors of factory industries...were dominated by British capital and had very little positive linkage with the province's own economy...' Of course, Marxists like Ranajit Das Gupta (1979) and trade-union leader Indrajit Gupta (1953) emphasise the bad conditions in which the workers have to live and work. See also Goswami (1985). Nirmala Banerjee (1989) describes the negative consequences of modernisation for women. Studies on the villages from which the migrants came, although mentioning the positive effect of the income, stress the negative effects of the 'money-order economy' (Das [1986], p.220), particularly on family life (see also Yang [1989], p.198-199; and Banerjee [1989]).

able studies on jute labour, the labourers themselves and their point of view have been overlooked. My field data[2] show clearly that the workers have a quite different, and often much more positive view of the industry (and also the *sardar*, for example) than the historians.[3]

In this paper I will challenge the thesis that the industry had mainly negative effects and I will show that the decline of the industry is the result of a set of factors which were partly of human making and not inevitably linked up with this type of industry; under more appropriate policies the jute industry could have developed better. I will also argue that its consequences for the labour force were not negative, that many people benefited and that those people who did not benefit, did so of their own choice, presumably because they had better alternatives. In other words, I will show that the industry clearly produced trickle-down effects.

In the first part of the paper I describe the development of the industry, focusing on the period since the twenties. I show that the decline of the industry was not inevitable. The second part describes conditions in the industry and refers to the role of the state in improving these conditions after Independence. The two final parts are concerned with the groups of people who joined the industry, why they did so, and who benefited. The third part addresses the question of why relatively few Bengalis joined the industry, and the final part describes the people who came to the industrial areas.

1. *The Jute Industry: from 'Trading Mentality' to 'Sick Industry'*

The jute industry has never given rise to clear feelings of

---

[2] In 1991 I conducted fieldwork among jute labourers and other migrants in Titagarh, north of Calcutta, the second major concentration of jute mills. I have collected histories of about 70 families, focusing on their patterns of employment, and I intend to describe the development of a group of labourers over a period of 60 years, from 1930 to 1990. This paper contains a first preliminary analysis of the research data.

[3] The research in India has been made possible by a grant from WOTRO, The Netherlands Foundation for the Advancement of Tropical Research. Carrying out field work would not have been possible without the assistance of Gautam Sanyal.

pride among Bengali people. Historians have not written about the industry in a positive vein. Chakrabarty called the industry, as it existed in the thirties, 'anachronistic,' and he wrote that its economic policies and technological choices were determined by a 'trading mentality' (Chakrabarty [1989], p.64). A major analysis of the industry, especially for the period since Independence, is lacking for 'unfathomable reasons' (Goswami [1991], p.237). I think, however, that the reasons for this neglect are not far to seek. From the beginning the industry has been dominated by Europeans and, later, by Marwaris. During most of the history of the jute industry, three-quarters of the labourers were non-Bengalis. Bengalis have generally occupied only intermediate positions in the industry. The industry excited little interest among Bengali historians and social scientists, and they never produced an analysis of the political economy of the industry, its changes after Independence, or its present state of health. Consequently, the following can be no more than a sketch of what happened since the beginning of the century.

1.1 *The Industry in Colonial Times: a 'Mercantilist Spirit'?*

The early history of the jute industry has been well explored: the flourishing of mills on both sides of the river Hooghly, the dominant role of British Managing Agents and managers described as 'Coolies from Dundee,'[4] and so on. In the meantime the romanticism of the early writers has also been sufficiently counterbalanced by Nationalist and Marxist perspectives. Up to the middle of the twenties, the story was one of almost uninterrupted growth and high profits, and in Dundee it is nowadays still said that a part of the city had the largest concentration of millionnaires in the world; they became rich by making sand bags during the First World War.

[4] As the subdivisional Officer of Barrackpore called them just after Independence. 'Notes to successor' of the Subdivisional Officer, Barrackpore (hereafter 'Notes of SDO'), a collection of notes from October 1934 to 1950, placed at my disposal by the present S.D.O. of Barrackpore, Mr. K.P. Sinha.

With the advent of the thirties, however, the story changed completely.

According to Chakrabarty ([1989], pp.36 ff.), it was not so much the Great Depression as the industry's incapacity or unwillingness to respond to increasing competition which led to its crisis. The industry refused to develop on scientific grounds, it continued to focus on low-quality and cheap products, and it was able to do so since the mills formed an oligopoly, formalised in the Indian Jute Mills Association (IJMA). In response to the crisis, the industry resorted to limiting its production - a policy which it was to follow till well after Independence. Chakrabarty seems to argue that this pursuance of the monopoly was bound to fail.

Goswami ([1991], pp. 237-39) has attacked some dominant ideas about the jute industry in colonial times. He denies that it was an exclusive monopoly of the British, and that there were effective barriers for Indians to enter the industry. He also argues that the industry did not posses oligopolistic power in the market for jute goods because the United States bought 40 percent of the gunny export. Finally, Goswami argues that the IJMA could hardly be described as an efficient cartel because it was characterised by a huge amount of free-riding, cheating and quarrelling. In Goswami's opinion, it was 'a primitive, inherently unstable, export oriented, capitalist industry...' With regard to the effects of the depression on the industry, however, Goswami has little to say.

I am not surprised that no significant restructuring of the industry occurred after the crisis of 1929. The crisis was external to the industry, and must have come as a surprise for everyone. From the industry's point of view, there must have been few or no immediate alternatives but to restrict production. A few years after the crisis a committee was appointed to investigate into the competition faced by the jute mills. In the late thirties, a research bureau was set up which tried to improve the quality of jute. But by the time the industry had recovered from the crisis - trading conditions returned to pre-depression levels in 1937, prices a few years later - the Second World War had started and this affected the organisation of the industry for years.

1.2 *The Jute Industry after Independence*

After Independence, the industry's advantageous situation disappeared. Partition separated the jute mills from their supply areas, now in East Pakistan. The industry in West Bengal suffered from increasing competition when jute mills were built in East Pakistan to take advantage of the cheap and high-quality jute being grown there. Till the late sixties, this competition was one of the main factors accounting for the West Bengal industry losing its share in the world market. Later this share was further threatened by competition from synthetics. East Pakistan's industry had the advantage of better and cheaper raw material, which accounted for more than half the value of manufactured goods. It also received export subsidies from Pakistan's government, whereas the industry in India had to pay an export duty during a few years in the fifties and late sixties. The cost of labour increased; although it accounted for only around 25 percent of the production costs, this made competing even harder. The attitude of the Government also changed radically. The unity among the British in Calcutta should not be exaggerated but the colonial government certainly did not put much in the way of the jute industry.[5] The atmosphere in which the Scottish Managers operated changed radically after Independence, as can be gathered from a note by one of the first Bengali Subdivisional Officers in 1949. Speaking about the 'Scotch-Marwari junta,' he said, 'Mill managers are Coolies from Dundee. Make them feel that you are superior and they would behave.'[6]

---

[5] See Charles Allan's ([1988], p.95-105) description of the sharp differences in status between the Indian Civil Servants, the 'box-wallahs' and the 'jute-wallahs', the traders in jute.

[6] Notes of SDO. The new Government did not have a negative attitude towards the industry as such, but it was not very active in stimulating the industry either. As one senior manager put it in a personal communication, the Government took the industry for granted.

After Independence, the industry adjusted to the new circumstances. There were attempts by the Government to increase the quantity and quality of jute produced and India did attain a high degree of self-sufficiency in jute, but - as the IJMA noted repeatedly - the quality remained low. The industry also began to modernise its production process. It tried to reduce labour cost by retrenching workers, particularly women. During the fifties, employment decreased very rapidly, although only one stage of the production process, jute spinning, was rationalised. There is little information about labour productivity; however, a study by Chatterjee (1962) shows that there was a considerable rise in labour productivity during the fifties. Nevertheless, investments in modernisation remained low. According to Sarkar ([1989], p.79), the industry spent no more than Rs. 50 million on mill modernisation in any year.[7] The industry continued its main strategy, producing at the lowest possible cost rather than improving its product or entering new markets. The main exception was carpet backing in which the industry made considerable progress during the sixties; later, however, this market was lost to synthetics.

Between 1950 and 1965, production showed an upward trend, although a somewhat erratic one. Exports also remained high, and in 1964 reached the highest level since Independence, according to the IJMA. It was therefore not surprising that in 1961 a spokesman for the industry told the Central Wage Board that he was quite optimistic about future prospects, or that the Board concluded that the industry would be able to bear the extra burden of a wage increase.[8]

---

[7] Contemporaries often argued that the jute industry did not sufficiently modernise and diversify its production. There is undoubtedly some truth in this argument. Even the IJMA admitted that they spent only 0.2 percent of their sales on Research and Development, whereas their competitors in the USA spent 4 to 5 percent (Annual Report 1969, p.13).

[8] Report of the Central Wage Board for Jute Industry 1963, report reproduced in IJMA (1985). The report shows that the average gross profit of the industry was 9.1 percent between 1951 and 1955, and 5.6 percent between 1955 and 1959. The profit rates in all industries were 9.2 and 9.0 percent in these two periods.

1.3 *Crisis of the Jute Industry*

In the early sixties the situation still looked bright: there was a growing demand for carpet backing, and the Soviet Union had begun to buy large amounts of jute goods in the late fifties. But after 1965 the condition of the industry deteriorated rapidly. At least four factors were important in this decline. Perhaps the main factor was the shrinking of the export market. In 1965 over 900,000 tons jute goods were exported; in the seventies the annual export varied between 317,000 and 707,000 tons. A dramatic fall occurred during the second half of the sixties, but the export market for sacking had already been lost by then: the export of hessian declined from 448,000 tons in 1965 to 270,000 tons in 1972, and the export of carpet backing, once seen as a saviour of the industry, did not grow nearly as much as was hoped for.

Second, after the devaluation of the rupee in 1966, an export duty was imposed on jute goods. This was the second time a duty was imposed. The first time was during the Korean War, and the duty had provided an umbrella for the setting up of mills in East Pakistan, which subsidised its export, and other countries. The duty on jute goods in 1966 annulled the effects of the devaluation, which was intended to improve the competetiveness of Indian exports. The effects of this duty did not go unnoticed and a high IJMA official told that representatives of the industry did plead for the abolishment of the duty. The view of the (Central) Government on the industry remains to be investigated - the same IJMA official argued that the government perceived the industry as possessing a monopoly - but the export duty shows the large change in the role of the state compared to the colonial period.

The third factor which contributed to the decline of the jute industry was the withdrawal of British capital. This had been happening since Independence. The foreign owners were not interested in investing new capital. Ownership was slowly taken over by Indian entrepreneurs but at the moment when they actually took over managing power, it was too late to influence the direction of the industry. By the mid-seventies the financial position of the industry had seriously eroded.[9] Only a few companies were successful over a long period and those often had other reserves from which they could support jute production.

The fourth factor was labour. Not too many labour problems occurred after Independence. All negotiations were conducted in a constitutional manner, there were not very many strikes, and the wage costs did not rise very much. Around 1970, however, the situation changed fundamentally. A top manager informed me about the serious mistake made by the jute mills, and especially the IJMA, after the first United Front ministry came to power in West Bengal. In 1969 the unions formulated a charter of demands. The IJMA thought that it would never come to a general strike, and it did not accept the Government offer. It may be argued that from then on the IJMA lost control over labour, its strategies to play off the unions against each other failed, and within five years it was confronted with four general strikes, the first since 1937. In 1970 the IJMA wrote that over a period of one-and-a-half years, the share of wage costs in total manufacturing costs increased from 22 percent to 27 percent, which was only the beginning. According to Sarkar ([1989], p.41) it increased from 16 percent to 28 percent between 1960 and 1980, and labour unrest did not diminish. Although increasing labour unrest and increasing wage costs by themselves posed enormous problems to the industry, one factor was perhaps at least as important. Since Independence, the workers had become more secure in their jobs because it had become more difficult to dismiss workers, and *badli* (substitute) labour had also obtained more rights. It was agreed that 90 percent of the working complement of a factory had to be made permanent, and 15 percent *special badli.* For the in-

[9] A study by the Central Statistical Organisation (CSO 1981) shows that the financial capability of the jute industy, while having improved till 1965, eroded quickly after that year.

dustry this meant that labour became highly inflexible, which perhaps contributed to the frequent closures of the mills as we know them now. The wage structure also changed in a remarkable way; at present production and wage are hardly linked, and unions have strongly resisted linking them, although nowadays many union leaders would agree that a culture of productivity is lacking.[10]

It is clear that the mid-sixties formed a turning point of the industry. In retrospect it is amazing how its problems accumulated. Because of its dependence on raw jute, the development of the industry remained variable, as it had always been. The years between 1966 and 1968 were years of bad crops. From 1965 onwards export markets began to decline rapidly, and one wonders whether the Government could not have done more to resuscitate the export trade. When the export duty was finally removed, most of the harm had already been done. Insufficient capital was available because of the gradual withdrawal of British money, and from 1970 Indian capital shifted from Bengal towards other places in India. There were additional problems, like the deteriorating condition of Calcutta's port and a worsening electricity supply. On top of this came the labour problems.

1.4 *Underdevelopment?*

I have argued that what happened to the industry was not inevitable. The type of colonial enterprise which the jute industry represented was not predestined to the long and deep crisis which overcame it after the mid-sixties. From the crisis of 1929 till the mid-sixties adaptions were possible and they were attempted with some success. The more recent

[10] In the jute industry the wage is composed of various parts, the main being the basic wage and the Dearness Allowance (DA). While the DA is connected to the increase in prices of consumer goods, the basic wage is related to production, and differs from one department to the next. In 1963, when the minimum wage was Rs.80 per month, half of this was composed of the basic wage. Since then, the basic wage has not changed, unlike the DA. In 1991, while the wage in the mills is over Rs.1600 per month, only Rs.40 is related to production.

decline can be blamed only partly on the colonial heritage. There were specific reasons why the situation deteriorated. First, one has to take account of the fact that the jute industry has always shown erratic trends, mainly because of its dependence on raw jute, and thus on the vagaries of nature. Even a monopoly like the IJMA in the twenties could not influence this factor. The crisis of the thirties had a most adverse effect on the industry because it depended almost completely on the world market. After the worst years of the crisis were over, the Second World War broke out, followed rapidly by the upheaval of Partition and Independence. During the fifties the industry adjusted fairly well to its new circumstances but things went seriously wrong during the sixties. The impact of competition from synthetics is well known. We know less about the withdrawal of British capital which occurred just when large investments were needed. It is also difficult to determine the effect of the change in labour relations. It is well known that wages increased but both the inflexibility of labour and labour unrest played an important role from the late sixties onwards.

Increased external competition meant that the jute industry could never be as profitable as it had been in the past. By the same token, and justly so, labour could never become as cheap as it used to be. It may be argued that there was therefore something inevitable to the decline of the industry. But I maintain that the situation which developed from the late sixties was not inevitable. A more cautious policy could have given the jute industry a new, more dynamic lease of life.

2. *Conditions of Labour*

There is a fundamental difficulty in discussing conditions in the industry from an outsider's point of view. For a middle-class observer, jute mills are noisy and dusty places where only poor wages are earned. The surrounding *bastis* where the workers live are crowded; open drains give these quarters a terrible smell, and the houses are tiny and unventilated. But how do the workers see these places?[11] No doubt, living conditions are considered to be poor, especially the lack of space which makes it difficult to accommodate one's family. Working conditions are viewed critically, and the work load is now considered as high. Wages also are said to be insufficient to cover family expenses. But if we compare these conditions to those at the places of origin of the workers, or even the surrounding countryside, the picture changes radically. A working day which lasted from sunrise till sunset will not have been uncommon for peasants or agricultural labourers. Jute work, even weaving, is not necessarily harder work than harvesting. Employers have never done much to improve housing conditions but still they supplied filtered water - a novelty as the employers proudly pointed out. Electricity was also available long before it became available in the villages.

2.1 *Wages*

From the perspective of the migrant workers, the wage is the most important consideration. There is little doubt that wages in the jute industry have always been comparatively high. Nowadays an unskilled agricultural labourer in Bihar earns a wage somewhere in between Rs.10 and Rs.20. A jute labourer earns around Rs.50 to Rs.60 in factories which pay the official wages, and around Rs.30 in factories which do not stick to central agreements. The difference between wages in agriculture and industry also existed in the past. In 1911 a coolie in Saran, the major labour-supply district, would earn between two annas and three annas three paisa; in the jute mills the daily wage for an unskilled labourer was over five annas.[12]

[11] Historians have paid surprisingly little attention to this question. They cite (colonial) reports about the bad conditions, but when it comes to the question of organised protest, they never consider the possibility that conditions in the jute mills might have been reasonably satisfactory from the perspective of workers. During my fieldwork, I came across an almost unanimous opinion among jute workers that conditions had been better in the past, especially during British rule.

[12] Yang (1989), p.197. According to Foley (1906), citing IJMA figures, weekly wages varied from Rs.1-0 for a child worker to Rs.6-8 for a trained male weaver.

It was possible for the workers to save from their wages. The IJMA often cited figures on remittances from post offices in the jute-mill towns. During my field research I came to the conclusion that it was possible for a general worker to save a considerable portion of his wage. Of course, the amount which could be saved differed with personal circumstances, but workers generally said that they could save at least half of their wage, and often three-quarters. In 1991 a single worker would spend about Rs.300 on food, and about Rs.25 and Rs.50 on house rent, out of an average monthly wage of about Rs.1600. Workers also get substantial retirement benefits, although nowadays many of the funds are empty. From their savings they have to maintain the family in the village. But even if only Rs.800 is sent home, this is still more than a labourer could earn in Bihar.

What happened to the wage since the beginning of this century? From the turn of the century till the crisis of the thirties, nominal wages increased steadily, and real wages remained more or less stationary despite considerable fluctuations.[13] A reduction in working hours significantly decreased nominal wages during the Depression but they recovered towards the Second World War. During that war real wages decreased precipitously because of huge price rises; employers softened the blow somewhat by supplying food rations.

After the experience in the Second World War, industrial wages were linked to the increase in consumer prices. While during the colonial period the wages were set almost unilateral by the industry, after Independence the state and unions became very important in determining wages. In 1948 the minimum monthly wage in the jute industry was raised from Rs.46 to Rs.58.50, although Gupta (1953) remarks that even so they did not regain their pre-war levels.[14] In 1951 and 1955

[13] This is based on the trend described by Mukerji (1960). However the earlier figures in particular are quite unreliable (see Bagchi [1972], p.123)

[14] According to Sanyal (1960), the 1951 real wage level was still below the 1939 level; in 1954 it was almost three percent higher.

wages were raised again. In the fifties real wages did not show much change: the real wage in 1958 was hardly higher than in 1951.[15] In 1958-59, the Occupational Wage Survey concluded that the jute industry was among the low-wage industries. Till 1968 this trend continued: nominal wages increased but real wages remained more or less the same. After 1968, however, real wages began to increase rapidly. In 1970 they were one-third higher than in 1960. Further increases are shown in the following table.

REAL WAGES IN THE JUTE INDUSTRY, 1960-1976
(Index: 1960=100)

1960	100
1965	107
1970	125
1975	143
1976	149

Source: *Central Statistical Organisation (1981)*

By the end of the eighties, real wages were about twice as high as in 1960. Clearly, then, real wages showed a moderate increase until 1968 but then came a real rise, just when the crisis of the jute industry came about.

2.2 *Wages and the Sardar*

In 1973 the Labour Secretary of the Government of West Bengal added a special comment to the annual publication *Labour in West Bengal.* He discussed the labour unrest which occurred during the late sixties and defended it. According to him, it had been caused by the low wages in the 'imperial industries':

> 'Historically depressed level of wage among a highly conscious working class having rising expectation of standard of living inher-

[15] These calculations are based on the figures provided in annual Government publications, '*Labour in West Bengal and the West Bengal Labour Year Book*'.

> ently creates a situation of potential strife and confrontation, but fortunately due to the maturity and reasonableness of labour leadership, things have remained much more peaceful than what the situation warrants.' (Labour in West Bengal 1973, appendix, p.vi)

The Labour Secretary also gave an explanation for these low wages:

> 'in jute and coal mines, through Sardar system and contractor system, workers were recruited from perennially poverty-striken districts of U.P. and Bihar. This system of recruitment and quasi-feudal management of the industries ensured an abominably low level of wages.' (Labour in West Bengal 1973, appendix, p.i)

His idea was that the working class became conscious of its depressed conditions at the end of the sixties. I agree that the workers had not benefited significantly in real terms till the sixties, but I do not agree with the explanation given by the Labour Secretary. First, I think that he held a stereotypied view of the role of the recruiters, or sardars. Like many scholars, officials and reports on industrial labour, he projected the image of the powerful *sardar*, a headman from the village who not only recruited labour, but also controlled the workers in mill and town.[16] Chakrabarty has given a fairly long analysis of the functioning of the sardar. It would lead too far to go into the details here but I wish to stress that I find his analysis hardly convincing.[17] In my field research I have found a picture of the sardar which is quite different from the generally accepted one. There was, and is, extraction of bribes by *sardars*, clerical staff ('*babus*') and management. Also, the sardar commanded respect, and sardars may

[16] See for example the 1951 Census, Vol. VI, part 1A, p.319: 'A *sirdar*, whose home is in one of these districts brings down to a factory a gang recruited from among the poorer of his co-villagers, maintains some sort of control over them while they are employed and generally looks after them till he takes or sends them home again.'

[17] Two aspects are especially important here. First, the personal evidence given by the jute workers in the report of the Royal Commission on Labour in India (1931) fails to reveal the omnipresence of the sardar. Second, Chakrabarty ([1989], p.109 ff.) emphasises that a large part of the sardar's authority was based on fear and the use of naked physical force. He then describes the practices of the goondas in the bustees, and this creates the image that both had the same functions and means of operation. Although he emphasises that the sardar cannot be equated with the goonda, and suggests that the sardar also needed a kind of legitimacy, the image of violence and fear remains.

also have been money lenders. But the power of the sardar was much more restricted than is generally supposed. The sardar was a common worker, a person with a little more experience, and he was in charge of 15 to 50 workers. Recruiting was mainly through personal relations, and the sardar was part of these personal relations.[18] Since there was never a serious shortage of labour, there was little active recruiting in the villages. Old workers told us that much of the recruiting happened at the railway station where sardars, but also babus, asked the incoming migrants from where they came and exhorted them to come to work in his mill. Many of these migrants had relatives there and did not need to pass through this channel. In order to get a job, it was sufficient to pay some money or donate some food. But the workers told us that force had never been used to this end; to give some tea, *pan* (betel) or money to a senior person was socially accepted. Social relations in the mill towns were predominantly personalistic, often based on inequalities in existence in the villages of origin. Power relations no doubt played a role in this but workers denied that their lives had been controlled by the *sardar*. There were various channels to get a job; the presence of a sardar in one's network of relations simply provided an extra opportunity.

Second, I do not agree with the Labour Secretary that from the late sixties, when leftist parties came into power in West Bengal, the workers were liberated from these recruitment practices and the quasi-feudal management, or that they now became conscious of their rights. I do believe that workers had rising expectations. Also, the workers have always protested against unjust practices, and often demanded higher wages. But what happened in the late sixties was something different. Trade unions had always been formed along political lines, but political power relations had changed fundamentally. The countervailing power of the

[18] 'Personal relations' has a wide meaning here. Belonging to the same area creates an a-priori affiliation.

IJMA disappeared. The Communist Government now chose the side of the unions to a much larger extent than the Congress Government had ever done. But despite the new Government calling itself Communist, relations of production in jute manufacturing did not change. Power relations in the mills and towns did not change fundamentally either: the power of the union or political leader increased, the power of the sardar decreased, but the relations remained personalistic and paternalistic.

2.3 *Wages: More for Fewer People*

It has been argued that the workers in the organised sector did not form a labour elite because they did not get a higher wage than workers in the rest of the economy.[19] Information about the development of wages in the so-called informal sector is hard to come by. Nevertheless, the stories of people who have worked outside the jute industry indicate clearly diverging income trends. For example, many said that until the sixties it was possible to earn significantly higher incomes in rickshaw-pulling. For this reason, many of those who worked in the informal sector preferred not to work in the jute industry. From around 1970, however, their incomes tended to lag behind wages in the jute industry; the latter were adjusted at least to price increases and often more than that, and various benefits were introduced or improved. At the same time incomes in the informal sector eroded, partly because of an increasing surplus of labour.

These diverging trends clearly show the development of a labour elite within the urban labour market, and the importance of state intervention in this. This conclusion is not new in the Indian context but I wish to stress that the existence of a 'labour surplus' juxtaposed to secure workers in the organised sector is not a natural phenomenon, and that it is

[19] Tulpule and Datta (1988) showed that after Independence the increase in real wages in Indian industries did not grow much faster than the National Income, i.e. the average income of all workers.

not related just to population growth. We may remember Marx' criticism of the Malthusian assumption that unemployment was caused by the natural growth of population; Marx argued that it was related to economic (capitalist) development. In the case of the West Bengal jute industry, unemployment is to some extent of a human making, the result of the form of development which was 'chosen' in India and which resulted in giving a larger part of the product to a smaller part of the population. Wage increases and job security in the fifties resulted in saving labour. State intervention fuelled the process, by putting emphasis on capital-intensive modernisation simultaneously with rising the wages of the working class. Since the late sixties, the Communist Government emphasised the rights of the workers, but secured these benefits for an increasingly smaller portion of the population.

3. *Those Who Did Not Join*

The period till the twenties was characterised by a relative shortage of labour - especially for the more skilled jobs - and this continued for a considerable time. Local labour became short with the explosive growth of the industry around 1900. Ranajit Das Gupta has shown that local labour was replaced by immigrant labour, mainly from the north-western part of Bihar and the eastern part of the United Provinces (now Uttar Pradesh, UP). From then on jute labour and other unskilled industrial labour has been performed mainly by non-Bengalis.[20] Why is it that so few Bengalis joined the industry? A number of explanations have been offered but I

[20] There are no reliable figures about the trend in the proportion of migrant labour. The yearly figures of 'Labour in West Bengal' are unrealiable, because they are based on figures supplied by the factories, which are known not to take this serious. Probably the most reliable recent survey is the one by Bhattacharjee and Chatterjee (1973), who showed that, around 1970, 87 per cent of the jute workers came from outside Bengal, although they have settled more permanently than before. Since then, there is a trend towards more Bengali labour, but the influence of this is not large. In the sample of Indrani Mukherjee (1985), 90% of the workers of Kinnison Jute Mills belonged to migrated non-Bengali communities, and 78% maintained links with the land by visiting this at least once in every two year. My field study confirms that the labour force is still predominantly non-Bengali.

find none of them satisfactory. I will briefly refer to these explanations under four headings: the affluence of Bengal; the character of the Bengali; alternative opportunities; and employers' strategies.

3.1. *The Affluence of Bengal*

Probably the oldest explanation was the relative prosperity of the Bengali peasants, which made it unnecessary for them to join the industry. The Indian Industrial Commission of 1916-18 noted that the density of population was relatively high but that this did not force many people to find employment outside agriculture.

> 'Not only do the inhabitants multiple and thrive, but large numbers of people have to be imported from other provinces to assist in the cultivation and marketing of the crops. In many of the districts of Bengal, according to the 1911 Census Report "the people are so prosperous that they can afford to look down upon menial work and leave most of it to immigrants from Bihar and the United Provinces who serve as earth-diggers, palki-bearers, domestic servants, boatmen and general labourers."'[21]

This idea was held widely and firmly till the end of the colonial period. In the Census of 1951 it was discarded as a myth (see below) but also for the earlier period it is now maintained that while Bengal as a whole may have been relatively prosperous, this was not true for the entire agricultural population. The 'Dufferin Report' of 1888 shows that even then there was a considerable portion of the population which had to rely on labour only. Throughout Bengal, 26 percent of the households depended solely on labour, and it

---

[21] Indian Industrial Commission 1916-18. Further, the District Magistrate of Howrah wrote: 'People of this district do not go out to other places in quest of labour; they have their own lands to till and it appears from the reports of the mill managers that they cannot have these people during the tilling and reaping season when up-country and Orissa people take their places, but this is only for short time.' (West Bengal State Archive, Commerce Department, Commerce Branch 1W-15. A 1-15, May 1919). Foley (1906) noted that it was unnatural to recurit in the districts of Raniganj, East Bengal, Darjeeling, Murshidabad, Jessore and Khulna, because the people were too prosperous. Paul Greenough (1982) describes the 'prosperity of Bengal' as a cultural construct, an ideal formulated by Bengalis, and contrasts this with the material situation under colonialism.

was considerably higher in the western districts of Midnapur, Malda and Murshidabad. An even higher percentage of households had labour as an additional source of income (quoted in Van Schendel and Faraizi [1984], p.9-10). Since the late nineteenth century, the agricultural economy of Bengal has been declining. For a large proportion of the Bengalis taking up industrial work may not have been necessary but this was not the general picture. A substantial group of people, especially in West Bengal, did need other sources of income, a need which has increased since then. There were certainly districts in Bengal from which migrants might have been expected to come.[22]

3.2. *The 'Bengali Character'*

Apart from the 'affluence-of-Bengal' argument, but often related to it, racial or cultural explanations have often been put forward, and not only by the colonial authorities. These explanations attribute particular characteristics to Bengalis. First, they were thought to be immobile by nature. The Census of 1921 observed:

> 'Economic pressure, when it is not very great, has little effect on migration, for it requires an effort to uproot the Bengali from the soil on which he was born.' (Census 1921, Vol. V, p.139, see also the Census 1881)

The Census of 1921 also called Bengalis 'originally stay-at-home people.' Mitra, the Superintendent of the Census of 1951, criticised this idea.

> '... traders, businessmen, artisans, craftsmen, and even agriculturalists in Bengal, as migration figures since 1881 have proved, have always travelled far and wide in search of a living, and ... used to migrate a great deal more before than they do now.' (Census 1951, Vol. VI, 1a, p. 295)

Other sources also show that the idea of immobility is

[22] Still, an agricultural labourer in Bengal (for example in Burdwan, as was told to us by a jute worker who came from Burdwan) would earn a higher wage than a labourer in Bihar, or, more relavant: the difference in income between agricultural labour and jute labour existed also in Bengal, but was not so large.

untenable. There is considerable evidence of extensive migration between districts in Bengal which was probably larger at the beginning of this century than around 1950. This migration was generally from west to east, and seasonal.[23] There is no reason to believe that the population of Bengal was immobile but it remains to be explained why their migration generally remained limited to agricultural occupations.

A second characteristic attributed to Bengalis is that they were not willing to give up agricultural work because they preferred to work in the open field rather than in a factory. This refers especially to low castes such as Namasudras, Bauris and Bagdis.[24] Labour from 'tribal areas' was seen as unsuitable for jute mills.[25] This 'unsuitability' was clearly a myth but at the same time it was a myth that worked: once certain patterns of migration and employment were established, these did not change easily.

A third explanation under this heading refers to Bengalis as unwilling to do manual labour. Bengalis, it is argued, joined the jute mills only in skilled mechanical jobs or administrative jobs. This point of view was held by British employers but it also held true for parts of the local population, the sons of zamindars, and for artisans. Mitra, the Census Superintendent of 1951, discarded the 'myth' of the affluence of Bengal and criticised the idea of the immobility of the Bengalis. He replaced these myths by another:

> 'It was been argued that the reason why the Bengali does not go into

[23] Van Schendel and Faraizi ([1984], pp.50 ff.). According to the Census of 1951 (Vol.VI, 1a, p.298), interdistrict migration in Bengal declined already between 1911 and 1921, and it declined even further till 1951. This was caused, according to the Census, by the growth of population density: the districts were not able to absorb more migrants.

[24] This is probably an image of lower castes held by higher castes. I found this even among jute workers: a Bengali higher-caste jute worker from Burdwan district told me that he had taken four or five people from his village who joined the industry but left after a few days. The reason for this was, in his opinion, that they came from the open field ('math') and could not adjust to working in a factory.

[25] See Foley (1906) who notes that people from the following districts were not suitable for jute work: Santal Parganas (who went to coal and tea), Hazaribagh (Assam), Manbhum, Bankura (partly 'too jungly'), Midnapore (Santals refuse to go) and Sambalpur (also too jungly).

industry as mill-worker as much as a man from other states of India is his opulence in agriculture which makes him disdain work at the mill...this story of agricultural opulence is largely a myth and as even a brief account of industries in decayed towns teaches us he is not loth to work with his hands at boiler and furnace. The reason is probably to be found elsewhere and it seems that what is held as virtue for some is held as a shortcoming against the Bengali workman. The latter is more precision worker, an artisan, a craftsman with a sense and gift of individual design, a sense of freedom of fabrication, than a mass producer.' (Census 1951, Vol.VI, la, p.433)

It would not be difficult to point out the interests behind these 'myths' created first by the colonial authorities and later by Bengali rulers. I would argue that if we free these myths from their racial connotations, they do have something to say about the existing division of labour and the segmentation of the labour market. If we turn the descriptions of the 'character' of Bengalis into sociological categories, they do give us indications as to why certain groups joined the industries and others did not. To explain how this segmentation came about, we have to look at economic conditions; to these I turn now.

3.3. *Alternative Ppportunities*

It is important to realise that Calcutta's economy has been booming till the sixties, and that employment remained available till then. On an aggregated level one might say that the shortage of labour disappeared from 1920 onwards: the population grew faster after 1920, the crisis of the thirties decreased employment opportunities, Partition caused a break in the stream of migrant labour to the east and an influx of people into West Bengal, and the Second World War put an end to employment opportunities in Burma. One might expect that it had become difficult to find work since the Second World War. In my field research I found that this was not the case. The general experience of the workers, jute workers, rickshaw pullers and small vendors alike, was that up to the late sixties it was not difficult to get a job. People remember that even around 1962 loudspeakers were used to attract labourers. From the late sixties onwards, however, it has become increasingly difficult to get a job.

It is my assumption that it was possible for Bengalis to shun industrial work in these circumstances. Clerical employment was expanding in Bengal at the same time as industrial employment. Industrial workers may even have been able to start small production units themselves.[26] This may be illustrated by the case of the refugees from East Bengal. Few of these have joined the industry. Before I began my fieldwork I assumed that it was not possible for them to enter the industry because employment opportunities had already been cornered by Bihari workers. But this was not the case. At that time there was a shortage of workers because of the war and Hindu-Muslim riots. The government also took measures to stimulate industrial employment among the refugees. Nevertheless, they did not join in large numbers, and the employers wrote (again) that Bengalis were not interested in, or adaptable to, industrial work.[27] Close to Titagarh there is a large colony of refugees from East Bengal, settled on land granted to them by the government. In line with the general pattern hardly any of them joined the industry. Most were engaged in artisanal production, especially the production of bangles from conch shells; this had been their caste occupation in East Bengal. We interviewed only one member of this group who worked in a jute mill, but as a mechanical worker. It is not likely that entry into the industry was impossible for the refugees. Recruitment in the mills follows networks of kinship and friendship, which would give the kin and friends of early migrants an advantage. But till the late sixties getting a job was not difficult, and Bengali entrants would not be without contacts because most of the clerks are Bengalis.

---

[26] This probably happened more often in the more skilled industries as in the case of the Mahisyas who were an agricultral caste, then took up work in engineering factories, and later started small engineering units (Owens and Nandy [1977]). See also Morriss ([1982], p.657) for a similar argument.

[27] See 'Managers Reports to Directors' for the years around 1950, in the company archives of Thomas Duff and Company.

3.4. *Employers' Strategies*

Migration studies have shown that the so-called unwillingness of local labour to work in factories was no more than a myth created by employers when local labour demanded higher wages or started getting organised. Employers often tried actively to replace local labour by migrant labour.[28] For the jute industry, however, there is little or no evidence from which one can deduce such a policy. In the most extensive report on recruitment of labour during the expanding phase of the industry, Foley noted that Hindustanis were generally more regular, stronger, steadier and more satisfactory workers, but he concluded:

> 'One naturally asks what recruiting agency is used to supply this constantly increasing enormous demand, and it is somewhat astonishing to find that no recruiting on any systematic method is done at all.' (Foley [1906], p.9)

Prentice, the Magistrate of 24-Parganas, wrote in 1919:

> 'Local labour is insufficient for mill requirements. All offering is accepted and none is displaced by imported labour. Indeed the mills can usually employ more labour than is available, whether local and imported, and ordinarily there is no surplus though this year labour is comparatively easy to obtain owing to high prices and general scarcity.' (WBSA, Commerce, Commerce, 1W-15, A 1-15, May 1919)

There are no references to mill owners complaining that local labour was too expensive, not willing to work or leaving regularly.[29] The evidence collected by the Indian Factory Labour Commission (1908, 'IFLC') shows that opinions varied as to which labour was better. Bengali labourers left more frequently because their villages were close to the mills. Up-

---

[28] See e.g. Breman ([1990], p.18) and Chakravarty ([1978], pp.277 ff.) for migration in the colonial period, and Teerink ([1989], p.34 ff.) for migrant labour in the sugarcane harvest in Gujarat. Note that their use of terms like 'recruitment', 'catchment areas' and 'sourcing' suggests an active policy on the part of the employers or the state.

[29] An exception is the following reference in Basu ([1988], p.12): the IJMA preferred migrants because Bengalis would not respond to the cash stimulus, and migrant labour was more steady and regular in attendance.

country labourers, on the other hand, left en-masse during the 'hot season,' causing a temporary scarcity of labourers.

Although there are insufficient data to substantiate this point fully, the introduction of electric light and the subsequent lengthening of the working day during the first decade of this century must have played a role. The IFLC wrote:

> 'many of the upcountry hands prefer the long hours from 5 AM to 8 PM...the local (Bengali) weavers seemed on the whole to prefer the shorter hours...as many of them lived at some distance from their work.'[30]

But even in this case the employers did not show any preference: the Bengalis simply left the mills which had extended the working days and their place was taken by migrant labour. They were not pushed out.

3.5. *Why Did Bengalis Not Join?*

The question of why Bengalis did not join the jute mills deserves much more attention than I can give it here. We need to explore migration streams in Bengal as a whole, and specifically how and why patterns of migration developed. These lie outside the scope of my research and therefore the existence of a non-Bengali enclave and the fact that neither the poor from the western districts of Bengal, who fell victim to the 1943-1944 Famine, nor the refugees from East Bengal flooded the mill towns remains puzzling. Up to the late sixties the labour market was not closed, and there is no evidence of employers trying to oust local labour.

The role of the state is hardly relevant in this respect. There was no policy to oust local labour and to recruit mi-

---

[30] IFLC, (1908), 'Inspection Notes' p.126. See also the oral evidence of T.W. Clarck, manager of Kanknarrah and Kamarhatty jute mills (no.170, p.254): 'With a ten hours' day he felt convinced they would get a great deal more local labour. The Bengali would not come at 5 A.M....' The weavers in Budge Budge Mill, one of the mills south of Calcutta where relatively many Bengalis worked, said that they would be more satisfied with a lower wage and shorter working hours (evidence no.192). The working day stretched over 15 hours, and this affected mainly the weavers. They did not work the full 15 hours but in various informally organised shifts they worked about 12 hours.

grants. After Partition, there were some attempts by the Government of West Bengal to help the refugees from East Bengal to find employment in the industry, but these attempts were of a limited scope, and had little succes. A 'sons of the soil' movement has remained absent in West Bengal.

Different groups had various reasons for not being interested in the industry. The local elite could hardly bear the sight of up-country labour and the sound of the factory whistle. The sons of local landholders certainly did not need to, or want to, join the industry, except in clerical positions. They formed only a small portion of the population, but I would suggest that the aspiration to become a clerk did influence larger parts of the population. During the expanding phase of the jute industry and the economy as a whole, the idea developed of jute work as *'choto kaj'* or low-status work. This idea spread to a large section of the population. Even today it is said that Bengalis do not want to join the jute industry because of status reasons, and specifically because the dowries in their families may become lower. One may add to this that perhaps similar considerations played a part among some migrants but that it is easier to do low-status work far away from home. The idea of jute labour as low-status employment was very probably prevalent among the artisans as well. Because of the expanding economy most artisans did not need to join the mills. There was sufficient demand for labour and for the products of small-scale industries, so the lower classes were not forced to join the industry.

What remains to be explained is why the many small peasants and landless labourers in Bengal did not join the jute industry. Conditions in Bengal were certainly more favourable than in Bihar: the income of an agricultural labourer was higher. Nevertheless, there was a rural 'proletariat' in Bengal, particularly in the western districts, which one might have expected to be attracted to the industry. They did actually migrate, but not to the industry. The stereotyped explanation was that they were 'too jungly' or preferred agricultural work. As an individualistic explanation this makes little sense but it can still be assumed that once a certain pattern of migration has come into existence, and once it has become customary for certain migrants to take up certain jobs, this pattern will not easily change. One might say that stereotypes may become self-fulfilling prophesies, and thereby reinforce themselves. For historical reasons, Bihari migrants started out in kinds of work that differed from those of Bengali migrants. In the next section I shall show that for the former jute labour was an extra opportunity which presented itself. They replaced Bengali labourers but did not push them out; the Bengalis left of their own accord.

4. *Those Who Joined*

I have analysed why relatively few people from areas near the jute mills joined the industry. In this section I describe who joined the industry and why. First, I discuss the areas from which they came and I indicate why its was from these areas that migrants came. Second, I discuss the migrants' background and present a hypothesis, based on the scarce material which is available, concerning which people migrated and benefited from the industry. Finally, I describe the pattern of differentiation among migrants in the jute-mill town of Titagarh.

4.1. *The Recruiting Districts*

The areas from which jute labourers have migrated are quite clearly circumscribed and they have remained largely the same during this century. The western part of Bihar and the eastern part of UP form the most important area. The northern coastal area of Orissa comes next; from this area fewer migrants seem to have joined the jute industry after the beginning of the century. A third area is the coastal area on the border of Orissa and Andhra Pradesh, which is partly

Oriya-speaking and partly Telugu-speaking.[31] Another group of workers comes from the area around Raipur in Madhya Pradesh, but this stream has also declined.[32] The only detailed information on the districts from which workers came was supplied to Foley by Thomas Duff and Company in 1906. These figures showed that Saran was the district which supplied by far the largest group of migrants, followed by Ghazipur and Arrah, as the Table reveals.[33]

MAIN RECRUITING DISTRICTS FOR JUTE-MILL LABOURERS, 1906

	% of jute-mill workers	% of population which migrated
Saran	20	7.91
Ghazipur	8	7.61
Arrah/Shahabad	8	6.96
Ballia	6	8.57
Patna	6	4.79
Monghyr	6	4.09
Muzaffarpur	3	2.64
Cuttack	3	?

Source: Foley (1906) first column computed from information supplied by Mr. Nicoll to Foley, appendix pp. ix ff.

The concentration of workers from Saran is most remarkable and has been widely discussed. Saran is generally depicted as a very poor area with a high population density. No detailed study of the development of this district is available, yet is likely that the condition of the poorer population has stagnated during the last 100 years. In the 1880s, the Collec-

[31] Foley (1906) noted that many people from this last area went to Burma, and that it might therefore be good recruiting ground for the jute mills. This advice was not followed, as far as I know, but when the Second World War made it impossible to go to Burma, many migrants came to the jute mills from this area.

[32] It might be relevant to note that all these areas were on one of the three main railway lines from Calcutta: to Delhi, to Madras, or to Bombay. The areas were therefore very well connected with Calcutta.

[33] Arrah town was the headquarters of the former district of Shahabad, which was known as the district of Bhojpur, the main recruiting district for overseas migration. Saran was less prominent is the supply of overseas migrants. (Tinker [1974], pp.40 ff.)

tor of Patna wrote:

> 'The condition of those who support themselves entirely by labour is rather worse than that of the better class of petty cultivators. They are almost always paid in kind, the usual allowance of a grown man being 2 to 2,5 seers of the coarsest and cheapest grain, value about 1,25 annas.'

They also found employment for only eight months a year (Nolan [1888], p. 4). According to the Dufferin report, agricultural labourers in the western districts of Bengal earned 2 shers of clean coarse rice (Van Schendel and Faraizi (1984, p. 15; one sher is 0.9 kg.).[34] During our visit to Saran in April 1991 we were told that a day labourer could earn 2 kg. of wheat, or any other grain except rice, with a money value of about Rs. 8. Although this provides only a very rough indication, we may conclude that the condition of the poorest has not changed very much.

It is not possible to determine when migration from Saran started but it existed before the colonial period. The large scale of migration has been ascribed to various reasons: high population density, high rates of rent, the absence of local industries or industrial decline during the 19th century, and the 'industriousness' of people from Saran. Space does not permit to discuss all these factors but I am convinced that none of them was singularly determining. Saran is a district which has been dependent upon remittances from outside for a very long period. Migrants have long been going to East Bengal to do agricultural work from November till March. The work was seasonal and the migrants returned to their villages at the beginning of the hot season. This pattern of migration existed before the first jute mills were built and it was only to be expected that so many joined the mills and that employers perceived them as 'industrious' people. For the migrants the jute industry was simply an extra option

[34] Around 1900 it was estimated that of a total population in Saran of about 2.5 million, a quarter of a million had little or no land, and the same number lived below subsistence level (Kerr, cited in Foley [1906], p.38-40). According to the 1951 Census, there were 427,264 landless labourers, and 42 percent of the families of agricultural labourers were indebted (Roy Chaudhury [1960]).

which opened up in Bengal. And in their view it was not the worst option: the income was relatively high, and employment was stable and not seasonal. Moreover, although the work is officially classified as unskilled manual labour, many workers called it *naukri* (service), and it increased their status at home.

4.2. *Who Migrated?*

Was it the poorest people who migrated? Contemporary writings pictured the labour force as consisting of the poorest people who came to the jute industry as their last resort. In the words of the Census and the Royal Commission on Labour, they were 'pushed, not pulled'; and this idea was repeated in the writings of historians. A first reading of the available historical material gave me some cause to doubt this (De Haan [1993]). My field research has convinced me that the image of migrants as victims of economic development needs to be corrected.

Data on land ownership are scarce, and in my research I found the information which people supplied on the land they owned to be unreliable.[35] Most migrants said that they had come because of a shortage of land. They usually have a small plot of land, not enough to maintain their families. A survey held in the late forties found that 59 percent of the workers were landless, 21 percent owned less than two bighas (two-thirds of an acre) and 20 percent owned more than 2 bighas (Chattopadhyay [1952], p.29 ff.). The most recent large survey among jute workers was held around 1970; it showed 42 percent of the families of workers not to own any land and 29 percent to own less than 1 acre (Bhattacharya and Chatterjee [1973], p.303). A survey held in Bihar in

[35] I found that migrants generally overstated the amount of land they owned in the village, probably because land ownership is an important indicator of status. On the other hand, one may also expect migrants to tell that they possess less land than they really own, if they expect measures to improve their condition. I think the first possibility is more likely. Having conducted my fieldwork only in an urban area, it was of course not possible for me to check these data, or to compare the characteristics of migrants with those who stayed behind.

the eighties revealed that 39 percent of all migrants (not just jute workers) were landless and that 38 percent had less than 2.5 acres (Oberai et al. [1989], p. 36). Interestingly, however, this distribution did not differ very much from the distribution of the total population in the sample. This leads me to the conclusion that people with land migrate almost as often as landless people.

In my field study this diversity in the pattern of land ownership was confirmed. To some extent, the pattern coincided with the regional distribution of the migrants. The people from Bihar and UP very often possessed some land. The Telugu-speaking people from the Orissa-Andhra border area did not own land, but the Oriya-speaking people from the same area did. However, people with and without land had often migrated from the same area. The amount of land which landed migrants owned clearly was not sufficient to maintain their families, but this insufficiency in itself is not an explanation for their decision to leave home. There were many other people who might migrate for the same reason, e.g. those to whom the migrants gave their land in sharecropping.

Almost all people whom I interviewed replied that they had migrated and started work in the jute mills because of some crisis in their home village, the insufficiency of their land, or the unprofitability of their business. But shortage of land or family need do not fully explain migration. Even people with considerable amounts of land said that they needed a higher income. In all cases, people felt that it was necessary to leave home but why they felt so was ultimately a personal matter.

The idea of people being pushed rather than pulled towards the city becomes even less tenable when we consider the pattern of migration. Migrants to the jute mills have shown a peculiar pattern for a very long time. They have largely retained their migratory character, i.e., they still maintain strong links with their 'native villages,' sometimes even after a period of a hundred years. Very often their wives, children and other close relatives still live in the village, they define the village as their home and they go back there every year for one or two months.[36]

We should not see the migrant labour force as the bottom layer of rural society, as those who were pushed out. Rather, the immigrants form a replica of rural society - or an extension of it since links with the villages have been mostly retained. My thesis is that people from all strata of rural society have migrated to Calcutta. It is true that migrants need contacts but good information about working conditions in Calcutta was available in the villages of Saran. Migrants were coming and going on a regular basis and because labour was scarce a contact was easily established. All groups of people arrived in Calcutta, thereby reproducing the rural stratification in the city. Caste became less important in the urban surroundings but did not disappear altogether: traders often took up trading in the city, and Rajputs often became *darwans* (watchmen) at the mills or joined the higher ranks in the local unions.[37]

4.3 *Differentiation among the migrants*

Studies have shown that all groups and castes joined the industry. Although this is true, one should not imagine the population of the industrial town as a complete melting pot, in which all rural differences disappeared. Regional differences remained very strong: there was a clear separation between 'Oriya lines,' 'Madrassi lines,' and the more diffuse areas in which Biharis lived. People from different areas continued to use their own language, although many knew one or two other languages. Although all castes are repre-

[36] The study of Bhattacharya and Chatterjee (1973) suggests that the workers have become more permanent, that their floating character has slowly disappeared. My study contradicts this partially. The work has become more permanent, labour turnover has decreased and length of service has increased. But at the same time, they have retained their links with the village, they still take long leaves, with the paid holiday of 14 days plus an unpaid leave, for which they often produce a medical certificate which they can buy from a doctor.

[37] The idea of a replica does not mean to suggest that the stratification was fixed, or even stable. As I shall describe below, there has been a large amount of mobility, both upwards and downwards.

sented in the industry, caste differences did not disappear. Caste remained a strong factor in terms of identities as well as of the jobs people took. Finally, religion continued to be important. Titagarh was an industrial town in which Hindus and Muslims mixed with surprising ease.[38] The differences did not disappear, however, and neither did stereotyped opinions about the other community. In economic terms too it would be wrong to draw one picture of all migrants. It is more realistic to stress the diversity within the group and the unequal development which has taken place among the migrants. It is not possible to isolate one specific factor which would explain why some people fared better than others. In fact, these divergent developments are still very poorly understood and need to be researched carefully.

What was once perhaps a homogeneous labour neighbourhood has developed into a highly diversified town. The percentage of people working in the industry has declined but this has not led to pauperisation. The sons and grandsons of the jute workers of old show a remarkable diversity in employment patterns, downwards from jute work into day labour and rickshaw pulling as well as upwards into more skilled jobs or self-employment in business. The urban labour market presents us with the paradox of strong segmentation combined with mobility. I shall first discuss segmentation and then consider how mobility is still possible.

The kind of job which a person took up was determined mainly by that person's contacts. When asked why they had taken the work they were doing at present, most people replied that they had been taken there by their father, a relative, or a friend. The network of relations, determined by family, caste, religion and/or region, was mainly responsible

[38] This is not to say that there have not been communal problems in the mill towns. Chakrabarty (1981) showed that communal problems started with the coming of migrants from North India. I found that Titagarh has been relatively quiet in this respect, not only according to the stories of people, but also (in the forties and fifties) according to the Managers' Reports of Thomas Duff and Company. I cannot really explain this fact, but one important factor may be that both groups were very large, that there was not really a minority group, and victimisation may be more difficult.

for the segmentation of the labour market. As a result, people from Ganjam district in southern Orissa worked mostly in the batching and beaming departments of the jute factories and up-country Muslims often worked as weavers. In this last case one might expect that these Muslims had also been weavers back home but this was the exception rather than the rule. Many weavers had not known the art of weaving when they came to Calcutta; their relatives took them into the mills and taught them the job. Conversely, many weavers, particularly from Andhra Pradesh, did not take up weaving in the jute industry. Some explained that people from UP and Bihar had taken the weaving jobs, others pointed to the fact that mill weaving was different from handloom weaving.

There is a strong segmentation in the labour market, but it is not 'organised' by anybody. It has little to do with employers' strategies or the economic background of the workers. It also does not seem to be related to some jobs being better than others. For example, the income from weaving generally was better than from work in other departments but the work was also much harder. Weavers were not considered a labour elite, as seems to have been the case among female jute weavers in Dundee. To some extent, the segmentation is merely a matter of coincidence. For some reason a group of workers started working in one department and once this pattern was established it reinforced itself through the personal way in which recruitment operated. As in the segmentation in migration streams, stereotypes are important here, e.g. Muslims are seen as weavers, Oriyas as coolies and Bengalis as unable to do hard work. In the case of segmentation within the mills, the stereotypes are highly arbitrary but no less effective. I would argue that the strong identities of the different groups, particularly regarding regional and religious background, reinforce the segmentation of the labour market.

There were few incentives for workers to move between the different segments. The pattern of migration did not stimulate mobility within the city: most workers came here with the idea to save money to improve their position back home and eventually to return to the village. The main employment changes, intra-generational as well as inter-generational, which we encountered were becoming a sardar, obtaining skilled work, or starting business or some other activity in the informal sector. I shall briefly discuss these changes and indicate why these happened.

During the last 20 years, many sons of jute workers were forced to take up day labour, rickshaw pulling, and the like. They may have been registered as badli workers in the jute mill but getting work in the organised sector is now practically impossible and requires a long waiting period at the very least. Many families are now downwardly mobile and therefore many have left. In the past, occupations like rickshaw pulling were also taken up willingly because it was then possible to earn an income which often exceeded the mill income. Now incomes in the mills have increased but incomes in informal activities have decreased. Many workers managed to become a sardar but this was not a big change in terms of income or even respectability. A sardar supervised only about 20 workers. For ordinary sardars opportunities to receive bribes have now become restricted; mainly head sardar and babus benefit from this.

There are many different businesses in Titagarh, even if we do not take into account the local Marwaris. Significantly, many of the better businesses are in the hands of people who came from districts slightly farther away from Titagarh than those which are the home of the common workers. Not surprisingly, members of business castes dominate local business but many jute workers also started business in the course of time. In these cases, personal motives were often crucial in explaining this change. Surprising (and parallel to the Muslim jute weavers) people often referred to their caste as their reason for going into business, even when none of their ancestors had ever been involved in it. Economic opportunities and personal savings were important in realising a switch to business but these formed certainly not the most important reason; many people with considerable savings never started business.

Finally, workers or their sons have found skilled work in or outside the jute mills. The level of education has risen very fast, although nowadays education by no means ensures a good job. Up-country labourers were able to get a better job in the skilled and clerical departments of the mills. In the past, these jobs were held almost exclusively by Bengalis; nowadays a significant number of non-Bengalis have found their way into them. As in the case of better-off businessmen, people with some initial advantages could benefit from these opportunities. But nevertheless it is important to realise that the road to upward mobility was not closed, certainly not till the mid-sixties.

Space does not permit me to go further into the question of social mobility. By way of conclusion I wish to say that different roads have been available to the 'proletariat.' The standard pattern has been for migrants to arrive in the city, to earn money and to remit it to the home village. This did not stimulate urban diversification. A second factor was that the labour market has been strongly segmented on regional, linguistic and religious lines. Because of these two factors, immobility has long been buttressed. The last 20 years, however, have seen a clear downward trend as a result of decreasing employment opportunities. Only a few families managed to be upwardly mobile by means of business or skilled employment. Their initial position is crucial here, and it is crucially determined by caste, contacts, schooling, economic opportunities and family composition.

4.4. *Migrants as Beneficiaries of the Jute Industry*

I have described which people benefited from the jute industry in Titagarh. Again, I cannot give a full overview because I have not studied those who did not migrate nor those who left Titagarh, but a few things are clear. Regarding the question of why Saran people migrated in such large numbers, I suggest that the answer is not simply that Saran was the poorest district. If Saran had been that poor, how could it have supported such a dense population? High population density, in combination with high land rents, landlord oppression and absent or declining industries, was a factor in migration but migration also made a high population density possible. Perhaps more importantly, Saran was a district which had built up perhaps the best migration links before the jute industry developed. It was only to be expected that migrants from Saran would dominate the labour force of this industry which made little effort to organise its own recruitment.

I have rejected the idea that only the poorest, or only the better-off, migrated to the city. Instead, I have suggested that the migrant town should be seen as a replica of rural society, as people from all strata of rural society can be found here. This leads me to the conclusion that a substantial proportion of the agricultural population benefited from the development of capitalist industry. Migrants were beneficiaries of the jute industry rather than its victims. They came to the industry to earn a relatively good income with which they were able to stabilise their position at home; they migrated to fend off proletarianisation in their home villages. Of course, the benefits were not equally distributed; some people benefited more than others and sometimes old patterns of stratification and inequality were replicated and reinforced. But in many cases old patterns of stratification did change: people moved up and down the social and economic ladder. It goes without saying that the growth and decline of the industry determined the fate of the group as a whole but divergent developments within the group cannot be explained in this way.

5. *Conclusion*

What was the contribution of the jute industry to Bengal society? In the literature this contribution is presented as quite negative because the jute industry is seen as a merely exploitative colonial enterprise. My argument comes close to a refutation of this argument. I do not deny that the industrialists were out to make profits and were usually successful. In this sense, they did exploit both workers and peasants. My argument is, however, that as far as the labourers are concerned the effect of the jute industry has been largely positive. It has provided an income to many poor people, albeit perhaps not to the very poorest. The rise of capitalism may well have had negative effects on rural society but this discussion is beyond the scope of this paper. The 'same' capitalism in the shape of the jute industry helped, however, to mitigate these negative consequences.

I have argued that most people might have benefited from the industry by joining it. Those who did not join were not faced by economic constraints but had other alternatives, or were constrained by cultural conventions. I have indicated why people from Saran joined, and why Bengalis stayed away. Many Bengalis did not need employment in the jute industry and many chose not to join for reasons of status. It remains to be explained why poor landless labourers from rural Bengal did not join the industry. The labour market was not closed and they could have got entry if they had tried. I have suggested that stereotypes like 'too jungly' indicate existing social and cultural patterns and patterns of migration and work with historical origins that proved difficult to change once they had come into existence.

Migration was, and still is, highly segmented and benefits from economic development do not trickle down in a equitable way. Migrants from different sections of Saran society went for the jute mills in a big way. But tribal groups did not make this 'transformation,' for reasons which are still poorly known. I suggest that these reasons are not to be found in the jute industry itself. From the available evidence, there is little to conclude that the character of the industry caused segmentation or indeed the new stratification that sprang up among the migrant workers. Neither has the state been instrumental in causing this segmentation. When the industry started, migration streams were already well developed, and state intervention was unnecessary. The post-colonial Governments have done almost nothing in altering this segmentation.

Clearly, not everybody benefited equally from the jute industry but there was a significant trickle-down effect. I have shown that the workers benefited from industrial employment even under colonial conditions. Also, I have tried to show that, despite external factors such as population growth and a colonial industrial heritage, the development and ultimate decline of the jute industry was not beyond the control of post-Independence Governments. After Independence, successive Governments claimed to represent the interest of the workers but actually only represented a section of the workers which decreased in size as a result of Government policies.

References

UNPUBLISHED

Indian Jute Mills Association. Report of the Committee, Annual Reports, unpublished, selected years since 1940.

Indian Jute Mills Association. Compilers (1985). Industrywise Tripartite Settlements, Report of the Central Wage Board and Summary of Omnibus Tribunal Awards in Jute Industry along with Clarifications.

Subdivisional Officer, Barrackpore. 'Notes to successor', a collection of notes, mainly handwritten, from October 1934 to 1950, placed at my disposal by the present S.D.O. of Barrackpore, Mr. K.P. Sinha.

Thomas Duff and Company, 'Managers Reports to Directors', 1930-56, University of Dundee, Archive Department, MS 86/V.

West Bengal State Archive, Commerce Department, Commerce Branch, since 1919.

PUBLISHED GOVERNMENT REPORTS

Foley, B. (1906). *Report on Labour in Bengal,* Bengal Secretariat Book Depot, Calcutta.

Government of India, *Census Reports,* (Several volumes).

Government of India, Labour Bureau, *Occupational Wage Survey (1958-59),* Vol. VI.

Government of West Bengal, Labour Directorate, *West Bengal Labour Year Book,* 1958 and 1959.

Government of West Bengal, Labour Directorate, *Labour in West Bengal,* Annual Reports since 1962.

Indian Factory Labour Commission (1908). *Report of the Indian Factory Labour Commission,* Government Press, Simla.

Indian Industrial Commission 1916-18 (Holland Commision), *Report,* Superintendent Government Printing, Calcutta 1918.

Nolan, Philip (1888). *Report on Emigration from Bengal to Burma and How to Promote it,* Bengal Secretariat Press, Calcutta.

Report of the Royal Commission on Labour in India, vol.1, vol.5. parts 1 and 2, vol 11, parts 1 and 2, London, 1931.

Roy Chaudhury, P.C. (1960). *Bihar District Gazetteers. Saran,* Secretariat Press, Patna.

ARTICLES, BOOKS, PAPERS

Allen, Charles, ed. (1988). *Plain Tales from the Raj. Images of British India in the Twentieth Century,* Futura Publications, London.

Banerjee, Nirmala (1989). 'Working Women in Colonial Bengal: Modernization and Marginalization', in: Sangari, Kum Kum and Sudesh Vaid (eds.), *Recasting Women: Essays in Colonial History,* Kali for Women, New Delhi.

Bagchi, Amiya Kumar, (1989). *Private Investment in India 1900-1939,* Orient Longman, New Delhi.

Basu, Subho (1988). 'Labour Movement in Bengal. From Community Consciousness to Class Consciousness: A case study of the jute mill worker (1881-1909)', Dissertation Master of Philosophy, Jawaharlal Nehru University, Delhi.

Bhattacharya, N., A.K. Chatterjee (1973). Some Characteristics of Jute Industry Workers in Greater Calcutta, *Economic and Political Weekly,* February 1973, pp.297-308.

Breman, Jan, (1990). *Labour Migration and Rural Transformation in Colonial Asia,* Free University Press, Amsterdam.

Central Statistical Organisation, Industrial Statistics Division, Ministry of Planning (1981). *Trends in Indian Jute Industry 1960 to 1976,* Bulletin No. ISD/7, New Delhi.

Chakrabarty, Dipesh (1981). 'Communal Riots and Labour: Bengal's

Jute Mill Hands in the 1890s', *Past and Present,* No.91, May 1981, pp.140-169.

Chakrabarty, Dipesh (1989). *Rethinking Working-Class History. Bengal 1890-1940,* Oxford University Press, Delhi etc.

Chakravarty, Lalita (1978). 'Emergence of an Industrial Labour Force in a Dual Economy-British India, 1880-1920, *The Indian Economic and Social History Review,* Vol.XV, No.3 July-Sept 1978, p.249-327.

Chatterjee, A.K. (1962). Trends in Labour Productivity in Jute Industry, *West Bengal Labour Gazette,* January 1962.

Chattopadyay, K.P. (1952). *A Socio-Economic Survey of Jute Labour,* Department of Social Work, Calcutta University.

Das, Arvind N. (1986). 'Agrarian Change from Above and Below: Bihar 1947-78', Ranajit Guha (ed.), *Subaltern Studies. Writings on South Asian History and Society,* Oxford University Press, Delhi etc., pp.180-227.

Das Gupta, Ranajit (1979). Factory Labour in Eastern India: Sources of Supply, 1855-1946. Some Preliminary Findings, *The Indian Economic and Social History Review,* Vol XIII, no.3.

De Haan, A. (1993). Migrant Labour in Calcutta Jute Mills: Class, Instability and Control, in: Peter Robb (ed.) *Dalit Movements, and the Meanings of Labour in India,* Oxford University Press, Delhi, 1993, pp.186-224.

Goswami, Omkar (1985). 'Multiple Images: Jute Mill Strikes of 1929 and 1937 Seen Through Other's Eyes', *Modern Asian Studies,* 21, 3, pp.547-583.

Goswami, Omkar (1991). *Industry, Trade and Peasant Society. The Jute Economy of Eastern India, 1900-47,* Oxford University Press, Delhi etc.

Greenough, Paul R. (1982). *Prosperity and Misery in Modern Bengal. The Famine of 1943-1944,* Oxford University Press, New York, Oxford.

Gupta, Indrajit (1953). *Capital and Labour in the Jute Industry,* All-India Trade Union Congress, Bombay.

Morris, Morris D. (1982). The Growth of Large-Scale Industry to 1947, *The Cambridge Economic History of India,* Vol.2, pp. 553-676.

Mukerji, K. (1960). Trend in Real Wages in the Jute Textile Industry from 1900 to 1951, *Artha Vijnana,* 2 (1), March 1960.

Mukherjee, Indrani (1985). *Industrial Workers in a Developing Society. A Sociological Study,* Mittal Publications, Delhi.

Oberai, A.S., P.H. Prasad, M.G. Sardana (1989). *Determinants and Consequences of Internal Migration in India. Studies in Bihar, Kerala and Uttar Pradesh*, Oxford University Press, Delhi etc.

Owens, Raymond Lee and Ashis Nandy (1977). *The New Vaisyas*, Allied Publishers, Bombay.

Sanyal, Arun with Shyamal Sen (1960). Labour Productivity and Shares of Wages to Production in Five Selected Industries for the First Five-Year Plan Period in India, *Bulletin of the Socio-Economic Research Institute*, Jan-March 1960, no.1, pp.46-52.

Sen, Asok and Alak Banerjee (1983). *Calcutta Metropolitan District in the Urban Context of West Bengal 1951-81*, Occasional Paper No.60, Centre for Studies in Social Sciences, Calcutta.

Teerink, R. (1989). *Women and Seasonal Labour Migration in India. Part II*, Research Report IDPAD, October/November 1989.

Tinker, H. (1974). *A New System of Slavery: The Export of Indian Labour Overseas, 1830-1920*, Oxford University Press, London.

Tulpule, Bagaram and Ramesh C. Datta (1988). Real Wages in Indian Industry, *Economic and Political Weekly*, October 29, 1988, pp. 2275-77.

Van Schendel, Willem and Aminul Haque Faraizi (1984). *Rural Labourers in Bengal, 1880 to 1980*, CASP, Rotterdam.

Yang, Ananad A. (1989). *The Limited Raj. Agrarian Relations in Colonial India, Saran District, 1793-1920*, Oxford University Press, Delhi.

12

Alternatives in Development and Underdevelopment: The Case of Bengal Agriculture

Abhijit Dasgupta

The search for an alternative paradigm to explain the problems of development and underdevelopment has assumed special significance in recent times. Both 'modernisation' and 'marxist' theories have failed to grasp many complexities in the development of the Third World. This paper deals with some alternative strategies in development and examines their effects regarding the agricultural sectors in West Bengal and Bangladesh in the seventies and eighties. The introduction of new technologies has stimulated agricultural growth in Bengal but the fruits of development have not reached the poor in Bangladesh as they have in West Bengal. This then raises the important question: *how did West Bengal achieve growth with equity?*

In order to examine the problem in some detail I have presented district-level data from Nadia in West Bengal and Kushtia in Bangladesh as both these districts experienced significant technological changes and agricultural growth in the seventies and eighties and both had a sizeable proportion of poor peasants including sharecroppers and agricultural labourers in the rural population. In West Bengal, the districts which made significant progress in agriculture are Burdwan, Hoogli, 24-Parganas and Nadia. In Bangladesh, these districts are Comilla, Chittagong, Dinajpur and Kushtia. These areas are also known as the 'green revolution' belts of Bengal. It may be pointed out that one of the reasons behind selecting Kushtia and Nadia for a detailed study is that before independence in 1947 these two districts were one. After

1947, the eastern part became a district of East Pakistan known as Kushtia and the western part remained as Nadia district within the state of West Bengal, India. This kind of selection naturally gives an opportunity to make a comparative study of the differential impact of development policies in an area which had the same kind of agrarian structure during the colonial period and same agro-climatic conditions.

Various official surveys carried out in Nadia district during the nineteenth century and the first half of the twentieth century (Hunter 1875, Kemm and Pringle 1928, Mitra 1953) present a picture of dismal agricultural conditions. The district had an extremely hierarchical land holding structure. Till 1790 the land was owned entirely by the Nadia Raj. From the later part of the 1790s the district land was split into 261 separate estates, held by 205 registered proprietors[1] The Nadia Raj had to meet heavy land revenue dues, thus land sales became inevitable. Anxious to raise money, the Nadia Raj offered portions of its estates to others on nominal rent. These portions were called *taluk* and the owners came to be known as *talukdars*. For some time the *talukdars* paid land revenue dues on their *taluks* through the Nadia Raj but subsequently it was decided to treat these *taluks* as separate estates and land revenue due upon them was paid directly to the government and not through the Raj. By 1809, the Nadia Raj had only one-fifth of its original estate.[2] This marked the transition in the landholding structure in Nadia. The intermediaries came into prominence. The erosion of the power of the Nadia Raj became imminent when *patni taluk* was introduced in the district. The assessment of some estates under the Permanent Settlement was very high and in order to ensure easy and timely realisation of rent, a number of leases were given to middlemen in perpetuity. These tenures were called *patni taluk*; in effect, they were leases which bound the holder (*patnidar*) by terms and conditions similar to those in which a superior landlord was bound to the state.

[1] Kemm and Pringle ([1928], pp. 51-53).
[2] Kemm and Pringle ([1928], p.58).

Undertenure holders of *patnidars* were called *darpatnidars* and those created by *darpatnidars* were called *sepatnidars.* This process of sub-infeudation led to a complicated tenancy arrangement in the district during the colonial period.

One such complicated tenancy arrangement was known as the *utbandi* system. Under this arrangement rent was determined by an appraisal of the crop on the ground. The tenancy right passed on from year to year and sometimes from season to season.[3] One could get a better idea about the most widespread tenancy arrangement e.g. sharecropping in the district during the later part of colonial rule from a report prepared by the government of Bengal in 1940. An attempt was made to find out what share of the produce was paid by the sharecropper or *bargadar* for the use of land, and whether it was customary for landlords to provide bargadars with seeds, implements, manure, threshing ground, and so on. The survey also looked into the following questions. Did the crop share generally paid by the *bargadar* include the cost of inputs? If not, which additional share was to be paid on this account? Was the advance paid to the *bargadars* repaid in cash or kind and with or without interest? The survey found that in Nadia the *bargadars* used to pay 50 percent crops to the landlords. However, in the case of sugarcane cultivation the sharecroppers were allowed to retain only one-third. The landlords paid 50 percent seeds for paddy cultivation and no other inputs for production. For consumption loans, the *bargadars* paid 50 percent interest to the landowners.[4]

In the forties and fifties the sharecropping system grew steadily all over rural Bengal. Nadia was no exception. The percentage of land under sharecropping increased in Nadia from 24.1 in 1940 to 31.4 in 1950. The growth was phenomenal also in districts like Dinajpur where it increased from 14.5 percent in 1940 to 37.2 percent in 1950. In Jalpaiguri it increased from 25.9 percent to 50.9 percent during the same period. Sharecropping arrangements had spread particularly

[3] Kemm and Pringle ([1928], pp.62-66).
[4] Government of Bengal ([1940], pp.3-20).

in areas inhabited by backward castes and tribes.[5]

One of the reasons for selecting sharecropping arrangements for a study of the differential impact of new technologies was that the percentage of land under sharecropping system was high in some parts of Nadia district even in the seventies and eighties. The sharecropping arrangement was particularly popular in the village Bira in Nadia district where a survey was carried out. In 1988, out of a total of 132 households in the village, 13 were entirely dependent on sharecropping, 61 were landowners-cum-sharecroppers and 10 were relying on sharecropping as well as wage labour. Therefore, as many as 84 households, or 63.6 percent were directly or indirectly dependent upon sharecropping. Moreover, a study of the sharecropping system under new technologies assumes significance as agriculture under sharecropping is often described as inefficient and unproductive.[6] Is this the case with sharecropping arrangements in the green revolution belts of West Bengal or Bangladesh? Before going into this question, I would like to point out some of the factors which led to a high percentage of sharecroppers in the village Bira. Firstly, absentee landownership emerged during the later part of colonial rule and continued in the post-independence period. Landowners who were residing in neighbouring villages and towns had to rely on sharecropping. In 1988, 56 percent of village land was owned by people residing in neighbouring villages or in towns. A more important factor in influencing the high percentage of sharecroppers in the village was the increase in the number of migrants since partition in 1947 and subsequently their cultiving land as sharecroppers. In Bira, most sharecroppers were Namasudra refugees from East Bengal who had arrived after 1947. In the case of Bangladesh, the Land Occupancy

---

[5] Sen [1972].

[6] Many economists have agreed with the Marshallian position that sharecropping results in an under-allocation of variable inputs. Marshall observed, "when the cultivator has to give to his landlord half of the returns to each dose of capital and labour that he applies to the land, it will not be in his interest to apply any dose the total return to which is less than twice enough to reward him" ([1920]p.644).

Survey (LOS) of 1978 recorded 20.9 percent of land under tenancy, which according to many is an underestimation.[7] Anyhow, LOS data showed that 90.7 percent of the leased-in area was under sharecropping arrangements in the early seventies.

Therefore, on both sides of the border sharecropping is the dominant form of tenancy. In 1989, in the village Naopara in Bangladesh, 32 households out of a total of 209 combined wage labour and landownership with sharecropping and 10 households were entirely dependent on sharecropping. Therefore in both West Bengal and Bangladesh villages the percentage of land under sharecropping and number of households dependent on sharecropping were significant. This accounts for the importance of this group in the agrarian structure.

The growth in the number of agricultural labourers in both West Bengal and Bangladesh since the fifties is a well-known phenomenon. In many areas the introduction of new technologies and improvement in agricultural productivity led to a dependence on wage labour. In West Bengal, a steady rise in the number of agricultural labourers as percentage of agricultural workers could be seen in the census data. In 1951 agricultural labourers as a percentage of agricultural workers was 25.91, which increased to 28.24 in 1961 and to 44.28 in 1971.[8] Growth was especially noticeable in Nadia district. In 1961 the percentage of agricultural labourers to total agricultural workers in Nadia was 27.93, which increased to 42.20 in 1971 and to 46.9 in 1981.[9] In 1989, 34 Bira households (26 percent) were either landless labourers or labourer-cum-sharecroppers or labourer-cum-landowners of small plots.

In Bangladesh too the percentage of rural households which may be described as functionally landless (owning 0.5 acres or less of land other than homestead sites) went up to 50.2 in 1977. In Kushtia district it was 46.6 percent. However,

---

[7] Jannuzi and Peach ([1979], pp.102-3).

[8] *Census Reports*, from 1951 to 1971.

[9] *Nadia District Census Handbook*, 1961, 1971 and 1981. Definitional changes between the censuses have slightly inflated the percentage.

if one takes rural households owning no cultivable land (no land other than homestead sites), then it was 28.8 percent in Bangladesh as a whole, and 24.8 in Kushtia.[10] Khan (1977) offered another yardstick to measure rural poverty in Bangladesh, by comparing the rise and fall in the number of 'poor' and 'extremely poor' people. Poor people are those with income less than adequate for meeting 90 percent of recommended calorie intake, and extremely poor are those with less than adequate income to meet 80 percent of calorie intake. He observed that the number of 'extremely poor' had increased from 25.1 to 42.1 percent between 1968-69 and 1973-74, while the number of 'poor' people increased only from 76.0 percent to 78.5 percent.[11] The sharp increase in the proportion of 'extremely poor' indicates the process of pauperisation in rural Bangladesh. In Naopara, as many as 101 households (48 percent) were functionally landless in 1989.

New Technologies in Agriculture in Nadia

An extensive network of underground irrigation developed in Nadia district during the seventies and eighties. In 1970, River Lift Pumps (RLP) irrigated 4,500 acres which increased to 22,400 acres in 1974-75. Similarly in 1970-71, 45,700 acres came under Deep Tube Well (DTW) irrigation, which increased to 51,000 in 1974-75. The increase in the acreage under Shallow Tube Well (STW) was particularly striking: it increased from 35,000 acres in 1970-71 to about 80,000 acres in 1974-75. As a result of all these efforts, the percentage of gross cropped area under irrigation in Nadia district increased from 10.8 in 1971-72 to 23.4 in 1980-81.[12] The development of the irrigation network increased the cropping intensity in the area. In the seventies a phenomenal increase in the acreage under wheat could be noticed in the district. An increase in the acreage under boro rice and jute

[10] Boyce ([1987], p.222).
[11] Khan ([1977], p.39).
[12] *Nadia District Rural Development Agency Report*, ([1989], pp.5-9).

also took place during this time.

The district-level data also show an increase in the use of HYV seeds, fertilisers and pesticides in Nadia in the seventies and eighties. The HYV intensity or percentage area under HYVs in 1978-79 for aman rice was 37.7 and for aus rice 38.3. The fertiliser intensity (or nutrient kg per hectare per crop) went up from 11.9 in 1970-72 to 49.3 in 1978-80.[13] An intensive use of irrigation and other inputs led to an increase in food production. For example, the production of boro rice increased to 1,264,000 tonnes. The production of wheat increased from 71,000 tonnes in 1967 to 527,000 tonnes in 1976. An upward trend was also noticed with regard to the production of other cereals and pulses.[14]

Agricultural growth has not been uniform in all the blocks of Nadia district. Irrigation intensity and input use were high in Karimpur, Tehatta, Nakasipara and Ranaghat blocks, areas where an effort was made to build an irrigation infrastructure with DTWs and STWs. The Comprehensive Area Development Corporation (CADC) played a catalytic role in spreading new technologies in Ranaghat by installing DTWs and STWs, and by providing inputs, credit, storage and marketing facilities. Bira village is within the administrative jurisdiction of Ranaghat block and benefitted from the CADC programme.

A Case Study

We may now consider the nature of technological growth in Bira, and its impact on sharecroppers and agricultural labourers. Bira is located in southern Nadia district. In 1988, it had 132 households and a total population of 808, spread over three residential areas, namely Hindupara, Musalmanpara and Mathpara. The residents of Hindupara and Mathpara arrived in the village as refugees from the border-

[13] Boyce ([1987], pp.176-80).
[14] Boyce ([1987], pp.58-59).

ing districts of Bangladesh (e.g. Jessore, Kushtia and Khulna). Musalmanpara, on the other hand, had only Muslim households who were the original inhabitants of the village. The technological infrastructure improved right from the mid-sixties when the CADC installed a DTW in the north-eastern part of the village. The DTW, which had an average command area of about 100 acres, ensured the supply of water to the high lands during the cultivation of summer crops. Within a short time, the DTW became indispensable for all other crops. Privately-owned STWs supplemented water supply to the low-lying areas.

The spread of irrigation has facilitated the use of HYV seeds in the village for crops like *aus*, *aman*, *boro*, jute and vegetables. The use of HYV *aman* and *aus* seeds (e.g.IR-50) increased the yield rate of *aman* by 12-15 maunds and that of *boro* by 20 *maunds* per *bigha* of land. In 1987-88, the CADC fulfilled 30 to 40 percent of the demand for HYVs in the village. On average the Bira cultivators used fertilisers worth Rs.250 per *bigha* of HYV paddy land.[15] Along with fertilisers, pesticides became an integral part of HYV paddy cultivation. The yield rates of almost all the major crops showed an upward trend after the introduction of irrigation, HYVs and fertilisers. For instance, the yield rate of aman paddy, which was between 10 and 12 maunds per *bigha*, increased to about 20 *maunds* a *bigha* where HYVs were used. The use of DTW on high land helped the farmer to grow a second crop. The increase in the gross cropped area (net sown area × cropping intensity) led to an overall increase in the crop acreage. The rise in aggregate output in the village was a result of both an increase in the yield rate and an expansion in the gross cropped area.

At this point let us consider who played the key role in spreading the new technologies in the village and who were the beneficiaries. As we have seen before, a sizeable portion

---

[15] This includes 40 kilogrammes of phosphate, 30 kilogrammes of urea, and 12 kilogrammes of potash.

of village land is sharecropped and the spread of new technologies was spearheaded by the sharecroppers. The efficiency of the sharecroppers was closely linked with the tenurial security. This tenurial security was offered through a government programme which came to be known as *Operation Barga (OB)*. For the purpose of registering the names of sharecroppers the state government formed squads comprising of state government officials, District Land Reforms Officers, Block Development Officers (BDOs) and members of the local unit of the West Bengal Provincial Kisan Sabha (WBPKS). These squads opened up camps in the village, recorded the names of sharecroppers, and distributed deeds. In 1979, Operation Barga covered 1,009 mouzas in Nadia district and had recorded tenurial rights of as many as 26,402 sharecroppers.[16]

In 1979, Operation Barga helped in recording tenurial rights of 82 *bargadars* who cultivated 124.29 acres of land in Bira. Some *bargadars* who lived outside the village but

---

[16] The decision to introduce Operation Barga was taken in June 1978 at a state-level workshop of government officials; the programme was launched on July 5, 1978. By April 1979, the programme had succeeded in registering the names of 666, 682 bargadars or sharecroppers in 29,033 mouzas spread over 14 districts. (Govt. of West Bengal ([1979], p.57).

In April 1979 and April 1980, Operation Barga had succeeded in recording the names of bargadars in various West Bengal districts in the following way:

Districts	No. of Monzas	No. of *bargadars* recorded in April 1979	No. of *bargadars* recorded in April 1980
Midnapur	8,950	1,12,721	1,69,419
24 Parganas	2,794	84,138	1,17,239
W Dinajpur	2,016	64,130	76,026
Bankura	2,537	49,702	67,206
Malda	1,539	49,657	54,314
Burdwan	2,155	49,905	55,347
Hoogli	1,843	46,905	55,347
Cooch Behar	696	40,699	49,796
Birbhum	2,120	38,595	50,409
Murshidabad	1,949	35,870	40,972
Jalpaiguri	408	35,902	41,013
Nadia	1,009	26,402	32,547
Howrah	643	24,835	26,647
Darjeeling	374	8,149	8,582
Total	29,033	666,682	8,540,740

Source: Government of West Bengal (1979) and Bandyopadhyay ([1980],p.7).

According to another official report, 1,296,136 sharecroppers had been registered by 30 June 1984.

leased in land in Bira too succeeded in having their names recorded. As far as the use of new technologies by newly-registered sharecroppers and landowner-cum-sharecroppers was concerned, most households (between 60 and 70 percent) used irrigation water from the CADC-controlled DTWs and STWs, as well as HYV seeds and fertilisers.

For example, Din Mohammad, a 70-year-old landowner-cum-sharecropper, leased in 1.75 acres and owned about 4 acres of land. Din recorded his name at the time of Operation Barga and used irrigation, HYVs and fertilisers on his own as well as on leased-in land. He was encouraged to use new technologies after his name had been registered under Operation Barga. Clearly, security of tenancy gave confidence to sharecroppers to use new technologies more intensively.

An examination of the size of holdings of sharecroppers registered under Operation Barga in Bira shows that 51 percent owned 1.50 acres or less (see *Table I*). Some critics of Operation Barga argued that the programme had strengthened the position of small and medium farmers in West Bengal. For example, Chattopadhyay ([1984], pp. 86-88), who surveyed two villages in Nadia to study the impact of Operation Barga, observed that small and medium farmers were the beneficiaries of the programme. However, in Bira more than half of the beneficiaries owned 1.50 acres or less, as indicated by *Table 1*.

TABLE I
SIZE OF HOLDING OF SHARECROPPERS REGISTERED UNDER OPERATION BARGA IN BIRA VILLAGE (NADIA DISTRICT, WEST BENGAL).

Size (acres)	Amount of land (acres)	Percentage
0.00-0.50	20.00	17
0.51-100	26.96	21
1.01-1.50	16.23	13
1.51 and above	61.10	49
Total	124.29	100

Perhaps at this point some of the other criticisms against Operation Barga may be considered. Rudra ([1981] p.43) observed that Operation Barga was a party-based struggle, tenants belonging to the opposition parties were evicted to give room to tenants belonging to the ruling party. Similarly, Chattopadhyay ([1984], p.89-92) pointed out that in one of the villages bargadars owing allegiance to other or no political or peasant organisations were unable to contact the administration and claim their due. As a result, Operation Barga was viewed in that village as an exercise by CPI(M) activists for their local camp followers. All the 12 bargadars who recorded their names belonged to the peasant wing of the CPI(M). In Bira, however, the magnitude of barga recording showed that the programme rose above party lines. Beneficiaries of Operation Barga in fact had different political leanings or were a-political.

Operation Barga has also been criticised on the ground that it meant very little to the poor sharecroppers who lacked financial resources to cultivate land with better inputs and agricultural implements. Very little was done to offer financial support to the sharecroppers. With regard to the availability of credit, Chattopadhyay ([1984] p.85-86) found that the bargadars lacked financial resources. The panchayats failed to disburse loans. However, in Bira during 1987-88, 56 percent of the sharecroppers received bank loans amounting to Rs.66,231,55.[17] Besides cash loans, the registered sharecroppers also received assistance in the form of seeds and fertilisers from the CADC. Bandyopadhyay ([1985] p.31) also found that commercial and cooperative banks offered the much-needed financial support to bargadars. In his survey of 13 villages in West Bengal he noticed that loans from institutional sources which were offered to the recorded sharecroppers, accounted for about 56 percent of total loans.[18]

---

[17] The programme for the disbursement of loans was undertaken at the instance of the District Rural Development Agency. These loans are popularly known among the villagers as 'DRDA loans.'

[18] According to West Bengal Government (1979), at the state level, out of the target number of 79,837 bargadars and assignees of vested land, 59,114 were provided with bank loans in 1979, of which bargadars accounted for 50 percent.

Bandyopadhyay even showed how other infrastructural facilities besides agricultural loans were developed to break age-old dependency relationships between landowners and sharecroppers. The small farmers-cum-sharecroppers who benefitted from Operation Barga later played an important role in spreading new technologies in West Bengal agriculture. A tendency to accumulate capital, to reinvest it in agriculture and to maximise profit was noticeable among these farmers. Both irrigation and cropping intensity were higher on their land. Hiring of labourers by these new enterprising small farmers-cum-sharecroppers is also a common phenomenon in recent times.[19]

In Bira the number of agricultural labourers' households increased after Partition (1947). Hindu refugees from East Bengal arrived in the late forties, mid-sixties (the largest group, after the Indo-Pak War) and early seventies (with the Bangladesh war of liberation). Most refugees arrived empty-handed and eventually adopted wage labour as their occupation. The number of agricultural labourers also swelled in the sixties due to the eviction of sharecroppers. In this period, tenancy-reform legislation created fear in the minds of the landowners regarding their control over leased-out land. As a result, evictions took place on a large scale in many parts of West Bengal. The evicted sharecroppers were left with very little option but to rely on wage labour. A natural population growth of three to four percent per annum also stimulated the rise of wage labourers in Nadia as well as in Bira village.

A number of changes are noticeable in the living conditions of agricultural labourers in Bira in recent times. The land-reform package of the early seventies had a provision for an increase of the minimum daily wage to Rs.8 for a standard eight-hour working day. The wage rate was subject to revision with increases in the cost of living. In 1988, the minimum wage for a labourer in the village went up to Rs.12 a day. Perceptible changes could be noticed with regard to

[19] These issues have been discussed in detail in Dasgupta ([1990], 109-20).

the creation of additional man-days for the workers. The development of irrigation infrastructure, the increase in cropping intensity, and more specifically the launching of the 'food for work' programme helped to create additional employment opportunities for agricultural labourers. Besides this, under the surplus-land redistribution programme, wage labourers (especially those who belonged to the 'scheduled caste' and 'scheduled tribe' categories) were given preference over others. As a result, some Bira labourers who belonged to the Namasudra caste benefitted from this programme in the seventies. Agricultural labourers also enjoyed rights over homestead land as a result of changes in land legislation.

Bangladesh

In 1987 Bangladesh had a population of 104 million who lived on a territory of 55,600 square miles or 144,000 square kilometres. Bangladesh was the ninth most populous country in the world. Some basic indicators of development give an idea about the economy of Bangladesh. In 1985-86 per capita income in Bangladesh was Tk.4,400 (equivalent to US $147). However, the poorest 40 percent of the population had a substantially lower per capita income (approximately Tk.2,450, or $82). In recent times, the per capita daily consumption of food has fluctuated around 2,000 calories. In 1983-84 about 37 percent of the population of Bangladesh consumed less than 1,800 calories per capita per day. Therefore, one-third of Bangladesh's population had an extremely low food consumption over a long period of time.

Agriculture was the largest economic sector in Bangladesh, contributing 57 percent of the GDP and absorbing three-quarters of the labour force. Agricultural products accounted for two-fifths of the income from merchandise exports.[20] As in West Bengal, in Bangladesh too a series of

[20] Hossain and Khan ([1989],p.5).

programmes were undertaken for agricultural growth. These programmes helped the spread of new technologies in agriculture. Some aspects of technological growth in the seventies and eighties may be considered.

The Bangladesh government tried to build up an infrastructure for irrigation from the mid-seventies. A number of projects were undertaken for the development of surface and ground-water irrigation. RLPs, DTWs and STWs were imported and sold to farmers at subsidised rates. Funds were allocated for the development of canal irrigation. The first major ground-water irrigation project, the Ganges-Kobadak Project (GKP), received substantial financial assistance for its expansion.[21] As a result of all these efforts, the total irrigated area increased from 10 percent in 1969 to 25.7 percent in 1984-85. The fertiliser intake in agriculture showed an upward trend from the mid-seventies. The total consumption of fertiliser grew from less than 2,000 metric tonnes of nutrients in 1950-54 to about 11,000 metric tonnes in 1959-60. Fertiliser consumption went up to 356,000 metric tonnes in 1977-78. In the early eighties, virtually all HYV boro, HYV transplanted aus and tobacco received fertiliser.[22]

Expansion of the area under HYV seeds showed a marked improvement from the late sixties, as a result of large-scale imports of HYV seeds from the International Rice Research Institute (IRRI) and the Indian Council of Agricultural Research (ICAR). After its inception in 1970, the Bangladesh Rice Research Institute (BRRI) brought out 16 different HYV seeds. As a result, by 1985 nearly one-third of the cereal area and 97 percent of wheat had come under HYVs.[23] All these data indicate how Bangladesh, like West Bengal, made progress in the use of new technologies in agriculture.

---

[21] the total cost of the Ganges-Kobadak Project was estimated at US $49.3 million, of which $37 million came as an asian Development Bank loan and 10.9 million was provided from the government of Pakistan/Bangladesh. The UNDP offered assistance to cover the cost of staff training, consultancy services and technical assistance.

[22] Boyce ([1987],p.179).

[23] Boyce ([1987], p.179-80).

Like neighbouring Nadia district in West Bengal in Kushtia too there was a rise in the use of irrigation, HYVs and fertilisers in the seventies and eighties. An irrigation infrastructure had developed in Kushtia with the inception of GKP in the mid-fifties. The introduction of irrigation in Kushtia through GKP has increased cropping intensity by ensuring cultivation of at least two crops per year. In most cases, farmers in the GKP command area were producing either HYV *aus*, *aman* and pulses or HYV *aus*, tobacco and pulses.

Before the seventies, the use of chemical fertiliser was quite restricted, only 4.6 kg of nutrient per hectare of gross cropped area in Bangladesh, which increased to 28.6 in 1978-80. The increase in fertiliser intensity was particularly high. It went up from 22.1 commodity kg per hectare per crop in 1969-70 to 107.0 in 1978-80. In 1976-77, 19.8 percent gross cropped area was fertilised in Bangladesh.[24] Although the national figures on HYV intensity or percentage area under HYVs in 1976-77 was low (only 6.4 for aman and 8.0 for aus paddy), the district-wise data show the popularity of the new technology in Kushtia. HYV intensity for aman in 1976-77 in Kushtia was 16.4 and for aus 10.5.[25] All these data indicate that the development of irrigation infrastructure helped the spread of HYVs and fertilisers in agriculture. Thus, like West Bengal, some parts of Bangladesh too experienced the 'green revolution' in the seventies and eighties.

A Case Study

Naopara village is located in northern Kushtia district. In 1988-89, Naopara had 209 households, of which 204 were Muslim and 5 Hindu. The village land was used extensively for agricultural purposes. Out of a total of 385.45 acres, 256.08 acres (66 percent) was under cultivation. GKP ensured a good supply of water to about 90 percent of the

[24] Boyce ([1987], p.179-80).
[25] Boyce ([1987], p.180).

cultivable land in the village. In most areas, villagers grew two crops, either *aman* and jute or *aus* and a *rabi* crop during the winter. The users of GKP irrigation water had switched over from traditional to HYV crop cultivation. The cultivation of HYV crops on irrigated land necessitated a greater use of fertilisers and pesticides.

In contrast to the developments in Bira, the introduction of new technologies had an adverse effect on the sharecroppers and agricultural labourers of Naopara. In 1989, 39 households (18.6 percent) were dependent on sharecropping. In Bangladesh, sharecroppers generally make an oral contract for a year or more with the landowner. But sharecropping contracts for only one crop are also common as landowners often use hired labour on a plot of land for one crop and lease out the same plot for the second crop. Sharecroppers bear all production costs except land revenue and irrigation charges. They pay half the produce to the landowners. The factors influencing a Naopara landowner's decision to lease out land differed greatly from those in Bira. For example, if land was far from the owner's residence, the landowner was often compelled to lease out. Landowners residing in Kushtia and Mirpur towns preferred leasing arrangements. Those who held white-collar jobs, and households without able-bodied adult males also depended on sharecroppers. In other words, contracts were made more out of compulsion than out of choice.

Sharecroppers in Naopara did not enjoy any tenurial rights although land reforms ordinance, 1984 was passed to protect their interest. As a result, the eviction rate was high. The landowner's dissatisfaction with the yield rate was a common point of dispute. Sharecroppers who were unable to use HYVs or fertilisers were likely to face the threat of eviction. In 1989, five evictions were reported and in all cases the landowner complained of negligence on the part of sharecropper, especially their inability to raise the yield by using new technologies. In Naopara termination of contract and eviction had become a regular phenomenon after the arrival of the canal-water irrigation. Landowners now prefer wage labour to sharecropping because it gives them higher returns. Evicted sharecroppers in Naopara eventually join the ranks of the rural proletariat.

The second vulnerable category in the agrarian structure consisted of the agricultural labourers. Among various types of agricultural labourers in Kushtia, the '*jon majours*' were those who worked on the basis of daily wages paid in cash. They were employed for almost all essential agricultural work (e.g. land preparation, sowing, weeding, transplanting and harvesting). In 1989, a jon majour received Tk.20 as daily wage. The largest group in the village were, however, the '*khola*' labourers who worked under a landowner as a group for one crop or for a year. *Khola* labour was similar to the '*thika*' labour prevalent in many parts of India. *Khola* labourers divided wages equally among the members of their group. In Naopara as many as 101 households were dependent on wage labour, especially on *khola* labour. The spread of new technologies had improved employment opportunities for the labourers but corresponding changes in the wage rate or working hours had not come about in the village.[26] During the early seventies a labourer received about Tk.10 in daily wages, which increased to Tk.20 only in the late eighties. Thus the rise in the real wage rate was insignificant compared to the rise in the cost of living in Bangladesh. In fact, the real wage has been declining over the last two decades,

[26] Even at the national level in Bangladesh, real wages rose hardly at all, and in some periods the real wage rate had actually declined. This happened in the early fifties in the wake of declining terms of trade for agriculture, and also in the mid-sixties and mid-seventies.

AGRICULTURAL WAGES IN BANGLADESH SINCE 1973-74

Year	Money Wage (Tk/person/per day)	Real Wage (Tk/person/day at 1973-74 cost of living	Wage rate in Kg. of coarse rice
1973-74	6.69	6,69	2,36
1974-75	9.05	5.33	1.57
1975-76	8.82	7.09	2.61
1976-77	8.93	7.32	2.96
1977-78	9.44	6.41	2.43
1978-79	10.88	7.28	2.53
1979-80	12.46	6.79	2.16

Source: Khan ([1984], p.86).

resulting in deepening impoverishment among the rural poor.

Indebtedness among agricultural workers was common in Naopara. Khola labourers borrowed both in cash and in kind. These were short-term loans, borrowed during the lean periods and repaid after the harvest. A high rate of interest was extracted on both cash and kind loans. For example, a labourer who borrowed Tk.100 during the lean period paid Tk.150 after a gap of three months. For borrowing one maund (40 seers, or 36 kg) of paddy during the lean period, a labourer would have to repay one maund and 20 seers of paddy after the harvest. Some labourers had become involved in usufructuary mortgage, especially to meet contingent expenditures e.g. medical treatment, death, and social functions such as weddings. A failure to repay resulted in complete alienation of the pawned articles.

The vulnerable position of agricultural labourers in Naopara might be explained by referring to some disputes. In June 1989 agricultural labourers in the village received Tk.25 as daily wage. However, one of the landowners arranged to hire a labourer from outside at the rate of Tk.20. This sparked off reactions among the local labourers who objected to the idea of hiring labourers from outside the village. The local labourers refused to work. The matter was referred to some of the older members of the village for a settlement. They upheld the right of the landowner to hire labourers from outside. Disputes over working hours were also common in the village. In general, a labourer worked either from 6 a.m. to 2 p.m., or from 8 a.m. to 4 p.m , with two breaks for sundries and lunch. However, landowners were reluctant to allow two breaks. The dispute over the working hours once again was referred to a committee of elders who approved of only one interval of half an hour for the labourers.

Mobilisation and the State

The two crucial factors which have influenced the process of development and underdevelopment in West Bengal and Bangladesh may now be considered. In the case of West Bengal, the process of mobilisation of the rural poor by the West Bengal Provincial Kisan Sabha (WBPKS) played an important role in protecting the interests of the sharecroppers and agricultural labourers. The process of unionisation helped to raise consciousness among these groups. The WBPKS mobilised the sharecroppers around demands for protection of tenurial rights by registering the names of bargadars and by fixing their share. Since the early sixties the WBPKS has been raising the demand to confiscate surplus land and to redistribute it among poor sharecroppers. For the labourers, the WBPKS has demanded fixed working hours, higher wages and more employment opportunities.[27]

The peasant organisations adopted various methods to realise their demands. The district and local committees of the WBPKS organised processions, demonstrations, *gheraos*, forcible occupation of land, and collective ploughing and harvesting of disputed lands. The organised protests did not remain within the boundary of the village. Whenever a government official e.g. the Block Development Officer, the Agricultural Extension Officer, the Junior Land Reforms Officer or the Director of the CADC ignored the demands of the peasants, the local unit of the WBPKS arranged demonstrations, gheraos, or picketing at the offices of these officials. For example, in 1986-87 when the CADC-run DTW broke down and the Director of CADC refused to take immediate action, the farmers and labourers of Bira organised a 'dharna' at the CADC office. Some more examples can be cited to show how poor peasants of Bira put pressure on the landowners. When some of the landowners of Musalmanpara refused to pay the stipulated wage rate of Rs.12 and a midday meal to the labourers, village members of the WBPKS called a strike and the landowners had to concede to the demand for the stipulated wage. In most disputes involving

[27] The CPI(M)-led WBPKS in West Bengal had no separate organisation for landless labourers, although the CPI did have one called 'Khetmajdur Union'.

a landowner and a sharecropper, or a landowner and a labourer, the local unit of the WBPKS became an important arbitrator. The peasant organisations checked some of the negative effects of technological growth e.g. eviction of sharecroppers, displacement of small cultivators, payment of an insufficient wage to the agricultural labourers.

The absence of peasant organisations in Bangladesh and hence lack of mobilisation of the peasantry have left poor farmers in Bangladesh at the receiving end. An attempt to organise the peasantry under *Krishak Samitis* was made in the late fifties under the leadership of Moulana Bhasani. However, the imposition of Martial Law led to an end to all activities to mobilise the peasantry. The *Krishak Samitis* were revived in 1963 after the lifting of Martial Law. But attempts to mobilise the peasantry once again were undermined when Moulana Bhasani, the peasant leader, severed his links with the East Pakistan Communist Party (EPCP). Very little was done to mobilise the peasantry in the sixties and seventies. In 1982, another attempt was made to form the *Sammilita Krishak Sangram Samiti* (United Peasant Action Committee). This time too the idea to form a broad-based United Front for the peasantry failed when the partners of the front divided over the question of participation in the general elections of 1986. Thus in Bangladesh the peasantry never achieved the sense of cohesion which their counterparts in West Bengal developed. This made their position in the agrarian structure vulnerable. Eviction of sharecroppers is widespread in Bangladesh. Agricultural labourers too are at a disadvantage and there is no perceptible improvement in the wage rate or the working hours. Following the terminology proposed by Marx, it can be argued that the peasantry in Bangladesh is a class-in-itself rather than a class-for-itself.[28]

The process of development and underdevelopment in West Bengal and Bangladesh cannot be explained without referring to the role of the state. In West Bengal, the state

[28] Marx [1969], p.102.

gradually took on a more supporting role in protecting the rights of sharecroppers and labourers. A review of the land-reforms programme shows this. 'Operation Barga', the programme to register the names of sharecroppers, is a case in point, as are the enforcement of provisions regarding land-ceilings, the redistribution of surplus land, the exemption of revenues for small farmers. In Bangladesh, the state under military rule, and even after liberation, protected the interests of the landowning class.[29] In various spheres e.g. distribution of agricultural inputs, agricultural taxation policy, public works programme one could notice a deliberate attempt by the state to protect the interests of the rural rich. In the mid-seventies land-ceilings were raised from 100 to 300 bighas to appease the landed gentry. Empirical studies have shown how the use of modern inputs e.g. irrigation, seeds, fertilisers and institutional credits benefitted the rural rich in Bangladesh.[30] The introduction of new technologies in West Bengal and Bangladesh agriculture has stimulated agricultural growth and improved food production. But the benefits of technological growth have not reached to the poor in Bangladesh as they did in West Bengal.

References

Bandyopadhyay, D. (1980). *Land Reforms in West Bengal,* Govt. of West Bengal, Calcutta.

Bandyopadhyay, N. (1985). *Evolution of Land Reforms Measures in West Bengal: a Report.* ILO Asian Employment Programme Working Paper Bangkok.

[29] Van Schendel (1982) and Rahman (1986) dealt with this problem in some detail. Van Schendel pointed out: "The State, in colonial times almost obscured by layer upon layer of zamindari landlords came much closer to the peasantry in pakistan times, and again after the breaking away of Bangladesh. Thus, while the state became a semaller and weaker unit, a process of *compression* could be observed: the distance between peasantry and state decreased and the power of dominant groups vis-a-vis the state increased. this process contributed to the strengthening of these groups within the peasantry" ([1982], pp.277-78). Cf. Rahman [1986], pp.12-14.

[30] Rahman ([1986], pp.12-14).

Bandyopadhyay, N. (1986). Operation Barga and Land Reforms Perspectives in West Bengal, *Economic and Political Weekly*, Vol. XVI, Nos. 25-26, pp. A 38-42.

Boyce, J. (1987). *Agrarian Impasse in Bengal : Institutional Constraints to Technological Change*, Oxford University Press, Oxford.

Chattopadhyay, B. (1984). *Tenancy Reform. The Power Structure and the Role of Administration : an Evaluation of Operation Barga*, Cressida, Calcutta.

Dasgupta, A. (1990). *Rural Proletarianisation in Eastern India and Bangladesh*, IDPAD - ICSSR Project Report, New Delhi

Government of Bengal (1940). *Proceedings (Official) on the Adhiar Movements in Some Bengal Districts*, Land Revenue Branch, Calcutta.

Government of West Bengal, (1979). *Tebhaga Theke Operation Barga* (in Bengali), Govt. Press, Calcutta.

Hossain, M. (1989). *Green Revolution in Bangladesh*, University Press Ltd., Dhaka.

Hunter, H.H., (1875). *Statistical Account of Bengal*, vol. 2, Trubner, London.

Jannuzi, F.T. and Peach, J.T. (1979). *Bangladesh: a Profile of the Countryside*, USAID, Dhaka.

Khan, A.R., (1984). Real Wages of Agricultural Workers in Bangladesh. in Khan, A.R. (ed.) *Poverty in Rural Asia*, ILO ARTEP Geneva.

Khan, A.R. & Hussain, M. (1989). *The Strategy of Development in Bangladesh*, The MacMillan Press, Hound Mills.

Marshall, A. (1920). *Principles of Economics*, MacMillan, London.

Marx, K. (1969). The Eighteenth Brumaire of Louis Bonaparte, in Marx and Engels (ed.,), *Selected Works*, vol.1, Foreign Language Publishing House, Moscow.

Mitra, A. (1953). *An Account of Land Management in West Bengal : 1870-1950*, Government of West Bengal, Calcutta.

Nandy, S.C., (1986). *History of the Cossimbazar Raj in the Nineteenth Century*, Dev Al Pvt. Ltd., Calcutta.

Pringle, J.M., and Kemm, A.M., (1928). *Final Report on the Survey and Settlement Operations in the District of Nadia 1919-25*, BSBD, Calcutta.

Rahman, A. (1986). *Peasants and Classes: a Study in Differentiation in Bangladesh*, Oxford University Press, Delhi.

Rudra, Ashok, (1981). One Step Forward and Two Steps Backward, *Economic and Political Weekly*, vol. XVI, Nos. 25-26, pp. A61-68.

Sen, S., (1972), *Agrarian Struggles in Bengal, 1946-47*. People's Publishing House, New Delhi.

Van Schendel, Willem, (1982). *Peasant Mobility: the Odds of Life in Rural Bangladesh*. Manohar, New Delhi.

Enactment of "Tebhaga" and Conditions of Sharecroppers: Some Findings from Two Deltaic Villages of Bangladesh

ANJAN KUMAR DATTA

1. *Introduction*

During the past decades there has been considerable debate on the relevance of production organisation in determining the pace of growth in agricultural productivity. It is now widely acknowledged that the existing hierarchy of interests in land, and the institutional arrangements within which land (as a vital means of production) is used can impede innovation and development in agriculture.

In Bangladesh there is noticeable inequality in the ownership of land. According to the latest agricultural census of 1983-84, five per cent of the farm households (those who own above 7.5 acres of land) own 26 per cent land. By contrast, 70 per cent of the farm households (owning less than 2.5 acres of land) own 29 per cent (BBS 1986:32). As a result of this inequality, the rich landowning households largely dictate the conditions under which poorer landowning households get access to land either as tenants or labourers. This provides them with ample opportunities to ensure accumulation of capital more through maintenance of intensive exploitation of low-productivity labour than through attempts to increase labour productivity. Furthermore, rich landowning households also use their position to manipulate the situation of landpoor households by intervening in land and non-land markets, often through various interlinked transactions.

At various points in time, landpoor peasant households, articulated their demands to change the institutional arrangements of agricultural production. Such articulations were confronted with either violence (as in the case of the *Tebhaga* movement of the 1940s, for details see Sen 1972, 1979) or by enacting some *ad hoc* reform laws without proper administrative and political commitment at the level of implementation.[1] In 1984 the Government of Bangladesh intervened (for reasons of growth and equity) in the agrarian structure and its organisation of production by enacting an ordinance called the Land Reform Ordinance of 1984. The Ordinance has three distinct features. These are:

1. Imposition of a ceiling on the acquisition of new land and provision for the distribution of *khas* land among landless households.
2. Introduction of *Tebhaga* and other rules assuring the rights of sharecroppers.
3. Introduction of a minimum wage law for agricultural labourers.

Against the backdrop of this Ordinance (particularly the tenancy reform), the present paper analyses the tenancy (more specifically share-cropping) relations as practiced in rural Bangladesh and the extent to which the Ordinance of 1984 influenced these at the micro level. The study draws on data collected from two deltaic villages in the south-west region of Bangladesh. However, before getting into a detailed analysis of data we present the main features of the tenancy reform of 1984.

2. *Tenancy Reform of 1984*

During the famous *Tebhaga* movement in the forties, one of the main demands of the peasantry was to establish their

---

[1] For discussions on Land reform Laws during 1950s and in post-independent Bangladesh see Siddiqui 1981A, 1981b, 1981C, Alamgir (ed.) 1981.

right on land as share-croppers and to increase the share of the produce going to the share-croppers. This movement was violently suppressed by the government. Later, in the Act of 1950, the right of share-croppers was not only ignored, but their position was equated with wage labour. Therefore, the system continued to be based on an inherently insecure and exploitative practice of crop sharing. Since then no changes had been made in land laws to regulate the share-croppers' position until the Land Reform Ordinance of 1984. In this Ordinance provisions were made to provide legal recognition of the rights of share-croppers and to safeguard their interests. Chapter V of the Ordinance deals exclusively with share-croppers and their rights. Various types of legal protection for the share-croppers and procedures for implementation are discussed and elaborated in different sections and sub-sections of this chapter. The main features of this Ordinance are the following:

- No person shall allow another to cultivate his land and no person shall cultivate the land of another person on condition of sharing the produce of such land between them without a contract in accordance with the provision of the law.
- The period of such contract shall be valid for five years.
- Persons cultivating land of others as *bargadar* (share-cropper) immediate before the commencement of this ordinance are recognised as *bargadar* and their rights as *bargadar* are guaranteed.
- No owner shall be entitled to terminate a *barga* (share) contract except in execution of an order, made by the prescribed authority, on the ground as specified under the law.
- The produce of any *barga* land shall be divided in the following manner, namely:
  a. one-third shall be received by the owner for the land.
  b. one-third shall be received by the *bargadar* for the labour.

c. one-third shall be received by the owner or the *bargadar* or by both in proportion to the cost of cultivation, other than the cost of labour, borne by them.

- The harvested crop of any *barga* land shall be stored for threshing and division either at any place belonging to the *bargadar* or at any place belonging to the owner, whichever is nearer to the *barga* land, or at any other place agreed upon between the parties.

This legislative intervention in the sphere of tenancy relations is undoubtedly a breakthrough. The Ordinance clearly recognises the rights of the *bargadar* and guarantees security in terms of tenure. But to what extent has this law been implemented? The data which we collected from two villages of south-western Bangladesh during 1987-88 show that the law is not implemented (at least in the area of research).

3. *The Area*[2]

3.1 *Location and Ecology*

The study villages, Sagardi and Nabagram, are situated in the south-west deltaic region of Bangladesh, and form part of Rajanagar *union parishad* under Paikgacha *upazila* of Khulna district. The district town is 40 kilometers to the north. Paikgacha *upazila*, the local administrative unit, is 20 kilometers to the south-west. The study villages are part of the physiographic region known as the 'immature delta', a broad belt of land that contains the *Sundarban* forests and the *Sundarban* reclaimed estate i.e., cultivable land (cf. Rashid 1977:40). The villages, being part of the delta, are intersected by numerous rivers. The rivers are subject to tidal fluctuation and the tidal range varies between +7.5 to -2.5 feet. Therefore, during the early phase of settlement, people had to invest much labour in clearing away bushes

[2] In this study pseudonyms are used for union, village and individual names.

and constructing embankments around their land to protect their houses from flooding and to ensure crop production. Originally these jobs used to be done by hired labourers. In the 1960s the state initiated a scheme, the Coastal Embankment Project, to construct embankments and sluices along the coastal belt of the country to protect and ensure lives of people and livestock and to protect crops from being damaged by flooding and saline intrusion. Such embankments and sluices were constructed in the research area in 1967-69.

3.2 *Crop Production*

The ecological constraints described above have had a profound influence on the cropping pattern. The land is basically mono-cropped, with paddy the principal crop on land protected by embankments. The paddy which dominates the crop production in these villages is transplanted *aman* paddy. Occasionally, a second crop such as sesame, jute, chillies and winter vegetables is grown, depending on the availability of rain water and draught power. The two villages together have a cropping intensity of 111. This performance is lower than the national average of 153 achieved during the period 1983-84 (BBS 1985:455). This low cropping intensity is due to the salinity of the water and the prevailing system of production. Before going into the details of land use and production organisation, however, we shall discuss some basic characteristics of the population.

3.3 *Population and Households*

According to the census of 1987, the study villages have a population of 1,309 spread over 209 households, with an average of 6.3 persons per household. The number of household members is the lowest for the landless category and shows a steady rise with the increase in landowning status. Among the landless, average household size is 4.94, for the highest landowning category (households owning land above 7.51 acre) it is 9.

Nearly all households in both villages are engaged in agriculture, either as operators or as labourers. Cultivation is reported to be the main occupation for the majority (60 per cent) of households. Two-thirds of the total village income comes from land. Among the non-land sources of income, wage labour constitutes a quarter of total village income. Ninety households (43 per cent) were found to be selling labour to varying degrees.[3] Apart from the above, trading, fishing and catching of shrimps (postlarve) are other sources of income available to these village households. However, access to non-land sources of income is greatly determined by the position of households in terms of ownership of land. In the subsequent section we deal with the distribution of land and the way access to land and employment on land is regulated.

3.4 *Ownership and Distribution of Land*

Compared to the national average of 0.25 acres per capita (BBS 1986:xii), people of the study area have an average of 0.43 acres cultivable land per capita. However, in spite of such a favourable land:person situation, many do not have access to any land at all while many have access to far more than the average household. Therefore, distribution of land or access to land remains of crucial importance to the majority of households. In the area land is distributed between people and households as follows:

[3] District figure for labour households is reported to be 44.5 per cent by 1983-84 census (cf. BBS 1986:100).

TABLE 1
PERCENTAGE DISTRIBUTION OF POPULATION AND LAND ACCORDING TO DIFFERENT CATEGORIES OF HOUSEHOLDS IN 1987[4]

Land Category (acres)	Distribution (%) Pop	HH	Average HH size	Land Owned Acre	%	Land per Capita	Land per owner HH
00	19	23	5.0	-	-	-	-
0.01-1.00	25	27	5.8	31.6	6	0.1	0.6
1.01-2.50	23	23	6.3	82.8	15	0.3	1.7
2.51-5.00	13	12	6.7	106.4	19	0.6	4.1
5.01-7.50	8	6	8.7	74.6	13	0.7	6.1
>7.51	12	9	9.0	264.9	47	1.7	14.7
Total	100	100	6.3	560.4	100	0.4	2.7

Note: Pop = Population, HH = Household.

Data on landownership show a skewed distribution pattern.[5] About a quarter (23 per cent) of all households do not own any land at all. Many of them also do not possess any other significant means of production. Consequently, the majority live mainly from selling labour power against wages and by doing all kinds of petty odd jobs in the agricultural and non-agricultural sectors of the economy. They form the poorest group. If a peasant household with land up to an acre is considered marginal then 27 per cent of households fall into this category and they own only 6 per cent of cultivable land. Households owning more than five acres comprise only 15 per cent but they own 60 per cent of the total agricultural land.

The inequality is also reflected in the landownership figure per household and land:person ratio over different landowning categories.[6] The average land per owner household is 2.7 acres. The figures vary from 0.6 to 14.7 acres as we move upwards through the landowning categories (i.e.,

[4] All figures for land are in acres.

[5] As the Table shows, the land distribution in the area is more skewed than at the national level (see remarks in page 319). On the other hand, the percentage of landless households is lower than the national average.

[6] Gini-concentration ratio is estimated to be 0.528 (based on the number of households). This implies a significant concentration of landownership.

from category II to VI). Similarly, whereas the average land:person ratio is 0.4, its variation ranges from 0.1 to 1.7 acres. The second observation becomes more meaningful and interesting when we take into account the demographic characteristics of households. Our data show that higher landowning categories have larger households than lower landowning categories. In spite of their household size, the higher land categories have much higher land per capita than the lower ones who also have smaller household size. This distribution per capita shows the extent to which households and people differ in terms of ownership of the most vital means of production i.e., land. The question arises, who gets the income from the land, and under what conditions is this arranged. In the following sections, we shall deal with tenancy relations as a mechanism of production organisation and shall try to shed lights on the influence of the tenancy reform of 1984 on the position of the share-croppers.

4. *Land Tenancy Relations*

4.1 *Extent and Forms*

In our study villages, a significant amount of land is cultivated by non-owners who have obtained access to the land by establishing tenancy relations with its owners. Of the total land owned by village households, 28 per cent is cultivated under various tenancy arrangements. The proportion of tenant households is even higher. Sixty-four per cent (133 households) are involved in tenancy relations in one form or another, each of which has a well defined content and specific conditions. This is determined not only by economic considerations (in the narrow sense), but also by a host of socio-political factors. In our villages, identified tenancy relations include mortgage, lease and share-cropping. The distribution of households and land under different forms of tenancy relations is shown in Table 2.

The Table shows that among the different forms, share-cropping is the most important both in terms of involvement of number of households and of frequency of land transactions. We will therefore make a detailed analysis of share-cropping relations and see to what extent the enacted laws are being implemented.

4.2 *Share-cropping: The Dominant Form of Tenancy*

Under this system the landowner rents out the land to a tenant for cultivation. The cost of cultivation is normally borne by the tenant. Occasionally costs of inputs are shared. In the study villages, only harvest labour cost is shared. The rest is paid by the tenants. The product is shared between the landowner and the tenant in certain stipulated proportions. The general conception about share-cropping in Bangladesh is that the product is shared on a 50:50 basis between the landowner and the tenant.[7] But in our study villages share-cropping on a 50:50 basis is more the exception than the rule.

4.3 *Extent of Share-cropping*

The number of households involved in share-cropping is quite large: 110 households (53 per cent of the total). Of these, 71 households rent in land, while 31 rent out and a total of 8 households are involved in both renting in and renting out of land under share-cropping contract. A significant amount of land is transacted under share-cropping arrangement via the participating households: 254.4 acres is share-cropped in by village households, equalling 36 per cent of the total land cultivated by the village households. This gives an average of 3.2 acres of land per share-cropper household. On the other hand, the village households also rent out 141.8 acres (25 per cent) of land to sharecroppers, implying an average 3.6 acres rented out by each household. Table 3 shows the number of households and the total amount of land operated under share-cropping contract in the study villages.

[7] See the following studies: BBS 1977a, 1978; Hashemi 1988; Hossain 1981; Jannuzi and Peach 1980.

TABLE 2

DISTRIBUTION OF HOUSEHOLDS AND LAND PER LAND-SIZE CATEGORY UNDER DIFFERENT TENURIAL RELATIONS

# of HHs	Land owned in Acre	Share-crop in # of HHs	Share-crop in Land	Share-crop out # of HHs	Share-crop out Land	Mortgage in # of HHs	Mortgage in Land	Mortgage out # of HHs	Mortgage out Land	Lease in # of HHs	Lease in Land	Lease out # of HHs	Lease out Land	Land Operated in Acre	# of Operating HHs
49	—	13	29.3	—	—	1	0.3	—	—	14	9.6	—	—	39.2	24
56	31.6	29	75.0	6	3.9	—	—	3	1.9	17	15.4	1	0.7	115.5	49
48	82.8	19	62.6	10	16.3	1	1.2	9	3.8	6	13.3	1	0.6	139.2	41
26	106.4	7	44.6	6	19.3	2	0.5	1	0.2	1	0.7	—	—	132.7	22
12	74.7	4	15.6	3	2.2	—	—	1	0.5	—	—	—	—	87.6	12
18	264.9	7	27.3	14	100.1	1	1.3	3	5.7	—	—	—	—	187.7	15
209	560.4	79	254.4	39	141.8	5	3.3	17	12.1	38	39.0	2	1.3	701.9	163

TABLE 3
NUMBER OF HOUSEHOLDS AND AMOUNT OF LAND TRANSACTED UNDER SHARE CROP CONTRACT

Variable	No. of Hhs[8]	Amount of Land	Average land per Hh
Sharecrop In:	79	254.4	3.2
Sharecrop Out:	39	141.8	3.6

The high incidence of share-cropping, both in terms of number of households and amount of land, clearly shows the importance of share-cropping as a relation of production. It is therefore important to identify the participants in this relationship and the terms and conditions under which they enter into it. An analysis of the influence of such relationships on determining a household's position in the production process and thereby in the social framework, is important for our understanding of agrarian class relations in the rural economy. We shall start with the participants in share-cropping relationships: the share-croppers who rent in land and the landowners who rent it out.

4.4 *The Share-cropper and Share-cropped Land*

In the study villages, 79 households (38 per cent of the total) are found to be share-croppers. These households do not, however, form a homogeneous category. They come from different landowning categories and their command over share-cropped land varies. Table 4 indicates the landownership category of share-cropper households and the extent of their command over share-cropped land.

[8] Eight households have been counted twice as they rent in as well as rent out land.

TABLE 4
NUMBER OF SHARE-CROPPER HOUSEHOLDS AND THE AMOUNT OF SHARE-CROPPED LAND PER LAND-SIZE CATEGORY

	Land Category	No. of share-cropper HHs.	Land Shared (in Acres)	Average Land per Share-cropper HH
I.	00	13	29.3	2.5
II.	0.01-1.00	29	75.0	2.6
III.	1.01-2.50	19	62.6	3.3
IV.	2.51-5.00	7	44.6	6.4
V.	5.01-7.50	4	15.6	3.9
VI.	>7.51	7	27.3	3.9
	Total	79	254.3	3.2

Many share-croppers come from the lower landowning categories: 53 per cent are from categories I and II. Forty per cent of total households in these two categories are share-croppers. Together, they cultivate 104.2 acres of land on a share-cropping basis, which is around 41 per cent of the total share-cropped land cultivated by village households. In the middle landowning category IV, seven households (27 per cent of the total) share-crop land and have the highest command over share-cropped land. Households of this category form nine per cent of total share-croppers and control 18 per cent of total share-cropped land. On average, each share-cropper in this category rents in 6.4 acres of land, almost double the total average figure of 3.6 acres. Among the higher landowning categories of V and VI, 37 per cent (11 households) share-crop land. They form 14 per cent of share-cropper households and together cultivate 17 per cent of total share-cropped land.

The spread of tenancy in essence reveals the very different functions of tenancy. Indeed, 41 per cent of total share-cropped land goes to the landless and marginal peasants of categories I and II, but at the same time category IV rents in 18 per cent of share-cropped land. In the first case, the average rented-in land is 2.5 acres, while in the latter case it is 6.4 acres. For the first category tenancy could be seen as 'a survival strategy', in the second case this is clearly not so. It is even less so for the larger landowners of category VI, of whom seven rent in land at an average of 3.9 acres.

4.5 *Sources of Share-cropped Land*

Land rented in by share-croppers comes from village landowners as well as from landowners belonging to other villages. Some share-croppers rent land only from village landowners while others rent it only from outsiders. A number of households maintain relations with both village landowners and outsiders. An analysis of data on share-croppers and their relations with landowners from their own villages and outside shows that 28 households (35.5 per cent) are totally dependent on village landowners for all of their share-cropped land. Another 19 households (24 per cent) have share-cropping relations with village landowners as well as with outsiders, while 32 households (40.5 per cent) have share-crop relations only with outside landowners.

When sharecropping contracts are analysed in relation to the residence of landowners, we find that 42 per cent of the contracts are made with village landowners while 58 per cent are with outsiders. The importance of outside sources for share-cropped land is also reflected in the amount of land which the share-croppers cultivate. In these villages, of the total share-cropped land 53 per cent comes from outside sources. The data on the village households' high degree of involvement with outside landowners via share-cropping relations therefore indicate that as far as the process of agricultural production is concerned, the villages do not operate in isolation. The data show that the villages are integrated into a wider economy and society.

4.6 *The Landowners: Share-croppers' Counterparts*

As we have seen, land share-cropped by the village households comes from landowners of the study villages and from outside. We now turn our attention to these landowners.

Out of 160 landowning households in the study villages, 39 households (24 per cent) share-crop out either all or part of their land, totalling 141.8 acres, or 50 per cent of all land owned by them. Among these 39 households, 17 share-crop out all their land to others. These 17 households belong to different landownership categories by size. Table 5 shows the number of households which share-crop out their land and the amount.

TABLE 5
AMOUNT OF LAND SHARED OUT BY DIFFERENT CATEGORIES OF HOUSEHOLDS

Land Category	No. of HHs	Land owned Acre	HH # of HHs	Share-out Land Owned	Land Land Sh.out	Sh.out as % of tot. land of Cat.	tot. land owned	No. of HH Sh. out all land
0.01-1.00	56	31.6	6	3.9	3.9	12	100	6
1.01-2.50	48	82.8	10	17.6	16.3	20	92	6
2.51-5.00	26	106.4	6	28.5	19.3	19	68	3
5.01-7.50	12	74.7	3	21.4	2.2	3	10	-
>7.51	18	264.9	14	211.8	100.1	38	47	2
Total	160	560.4	39	283.2	141.8	25	50	17

Note: HHs =Households, Sc =Share-crop, Sh.out =Share-out, tot. =total

The large variation among landowning households in terms of the proportion of land share-cropped out is due to very distinct conditions and considerations. Landowners in category II share out their land due to lack of inputs necessary to undertake production. In this category six households share-crop out their total holdings. Only one of these has a cow, the others do not have any cattle. Consequently, they share-crop out their land. Four of them work as labourers. The other two are one-person households: both men are widowers and have no children. Both also work as private tutors for children. Several of these households often fail to meet their subsistence needs (from their own income), and have to borrow money from the rich landowners against an exorbitant rate of interest. When such loans go beyond their financial capacities and they cannot repay, the debtors give their land to their creditors under a share-cropping contract. This acts as collateral and the creditor keeps on cultivating the land under share-cropping until the total loan is repaid. In our villages three poor households rented out their land to others as a collateral for a loan. Households that share-cropped out their total land for these reasons are exemplified by UB.

> UB is aged 35 and heads an extended household of seven members: his wife, aged 26, a son of five, a daughter of three, a widowed sister of 30, a niece of eight and his mother of 70. He owns only 0.5 acres of land located within the village boundary. His other material possession is a cow. In the past UB used to cultivate his land and sell his labour, but the returns were not sufficient to maintain his household. To meet his deficit he took an advance of *Taka* 500 from a landowner against an interest of 25 per cent per year. UB could not earn sufficient money to pay back his debt. After two years he gave his 0.5 acre land to his creditor. The terms of the contract were fixed at 50:50 share and the share-cropper (in this case the creditor) enjoys the right to share-crop this plot of land until UB has repaid the principal loan of *Taka* 500 plus two years' interest which equals *Taka* 281.[9] However, during the period in which the creditor enjoys the right of share-cropping, no interest was charged on this loan.

Among the other 33 households that share-crop out land, two from category III do not have any agricultural implements. Only one household has a cow. The two households share-crop out their land and work as agricultural labourers. Another two households in this category share out all their land because of a shortage of labour power. One is a widow who has only two minor children. The other is an old man of 77 whose only son, who used to look after cultivation, was sent to jail in 1986 on charg of murder. Since then this household has shared out all its land. From the same category, three households share-crop out all their land to meet the

[9] Interest rate is compound. If the borrower cannot repay the principal and the interest accrues on such an amount within a year, the accumulated amount of the first year becomes the principal for the second year, and so forth.

collateral for loans taken out under terms similar to those of UB. These three debtor households took out loans under different circumstances. One is a school teacher, who has been accused of involvement in the killing of the local *union parishad* chairman. He was sought by the police and to avoid arrest he had to hide; later, to get his name off the police record, he had to bribe the police. For this purpose, he borrowed *Taka* 1500 against the right to share-crop his 1.33 acres of land. The other two households were brothers who took out credit to pay for their mother's cancer treatment; she died after long suffering.

The rest of the households share-crop out their land for a combination of socio-political and economic reasons. There are some who find it difficult to combine cultivation with their usual occupation such as employment in school or in a commercial firm. For others, the traditional perception of 'status', defined in terms of non-involvement in cultivation, is an additional consideration.

In the largest landowning category, some households find their landholding too big to cultivate themselves. The amount of household labour available and the problems of proper management and supervision very often restrict the use of hired labour above a certain level. The problem of supervision also relates to the dispersal of the plots over a large area (holdings are often spread over different villages of the region). These factors cause large landowners to rent out their land. With the change in terms and conditions of tenancy, particularly share-cropping (these will be considered in more detail below), landowners also find it profitable to rent out land on this basis. Apart from these economic and management considerations, political factors also stimulate large landowners to rent out small parcels of land to small and marginal peasants. Many do so to a number of peasants (even to the landless) in order to cultivate a political clientele, and frequently do so on the pretext of kinship or 'community' feelings.

Landowners will also rent out land to the person from

whom it was bought. There are also specific economic and political reasons for large landowners to rent out land to the lower landholding categories. On the enactment of the Land Reform Laws,[10] many large landowners concealed their surplus land either through fictitious transfer or by transferring it in the name of a 'loyal client', i.e., *benama.* As part of such a deal they rent out a sizeable amount of land to their clients and followers.

4.7 *Socio-Economic Background of Landowners*

If we examine the backgrounds of various landowners who are involved in share-cropping arrangements, the data confirm our earlier observation. Data were collected on the socio-economic background of landowners. Two methods were used: one consisted of interviewing 79 share-cropper households of the study villages; the other combined interviewing the landowners concerned with observing their involvement. The second method was, however, restricted to landowners from the study villages.

Share-croppers were asked about their landowners and their place of residence, and the amount of land they received from each landowner. Later, they were asked to indicate the three most important landowners,[11] for each of whom a set of data was collected. These included landownership status of the landowner, management of farm, nature of involvement in the agricultural production process, and involvement in socio-political activities of the village or region. Through this method we were able to collect information on 133 landowners.[12] While comparing the two sets of data (and also having cross-checked the informa-

[10] According to the 1972 Land Reform Law the ceiling on land ownership was put at 33.3 acres. In 1984 a new Ordinance fixed the ownership ceiling at 20 acres per household. For details see GOB 1972a, 1972b, 1984a.

[11] Criteria to judge that importance were based on the amount of land received from a landowner.

[12] The actual number of landowners is lower. A landowner who rented out land to a number of share-croppers was counted more than once. Therefore, the number of landowners actually refers to the number of contracts.

tion with our case-study materials and field observations), we found that there was no remarkable variation between the responses of the share-croppers and those of the landowners. We therefore present only one set of data in Table 6: the response of the share-croppers.

TABLE 6
NUMBER OF HOUSEHOLDS WHO RENTED OUT LAND AND THEIR SOCIO-ECONOMIC BACKGROUND PER LANDSIZE CATEGORY

	Land category	# of Hhs.	Do they operate Land Yes	No	NK	Managt. of Cultivation only Self	Self& Lab	Only Lab	NK	Participate in SP Activities Yes	No	NK
I.	0.00											
II.	0.01-1.00	6	-	6	-	-	-	-	-	-	6	-
III.	1.01-2.50	11	1	10	-	-	1	-	-	3	8	-
IV.	2.51-5.00	12	7	5	-	3	3	1	-	4	8	-
V.	5.01-7.50	7	1	6	-	-	1	-	-	2	5	-
VI.	>7.51	55	40	15	-	-	15	25	-	39	15	1
	NK[13]	42	28	11	3	-	12	15	1	20	21	1
	Total	133	77	53	3	3	32	41	1	68	63	2

Note: HHs = Households, Lab. = Labour, SP = Socio-Political, NK= Not Known.

The Table shows a large group (40 per cent) of landowners who rent out land but do not cultivate any land themselves. Even those who cultivate a part of it, use hired labour. In fact, only around 4 per cent of households that operate a farm do so with family labour only. This applies to all size classes with the exception of category II.

However, the nature of involvement in cultivating the land varies from category to category. Households from all land categories participate in agricultural production along with hired labourers, but the degree of that participation varies considerably. For example, in categories III, IV and V (between 1.00 and 7.50 acres), all with the exception of one household participate in cultivation with family labour; in

[13] Households whose position was not known mostly belong to the upper land categories of V and VI (owning five acres and more). This observation is based on discussions with our informants.

category VI (>7.51 acres), however, only 15 households (37 per cent) participate in cultivation, while the remaining 25 (63 per cent) are totally dependent on hired labour. Among households whose land position was not known, 12 (43 per cent) participate in cultivation, while 15 households (54 per cent) depend fully on hired labour. Thirty-five households (45 per cent) out of 77 who operate some land, use family labour or a combination of family and hired labour. Of the remaining landowners, 41 (53 per cent) are totally dependent on hired labour for cultivating their farm. This group of landowners is very similar to the 'traditional landowners' who use their land resources for political and economic gain. An analysis of landowners' participation in village or regional socio-political activities illustrates the situation further.[14]

In our villages, 68 landowners (51 per cent) are involved in socio-political activities. This applies to all land categories except category II. The highest proportion of landowners involved in socio-political activities is found in category VI, followed by those whose land position is not known. Seventy-one and 48 per cent of landowners from these two categories, respectively are involved in socio-political activities of the village and region.

4.8 *Terms and Conditions of Share-crop Contracts*

Share-cropping contracts are all oral contracts. Out of 140, no written contract was found in either village. However, we found a variety of terms and conditions attached to share-cropping contracts, which have changed over the years. Based on our own observations since 1981 and on discussions with the villagers, it was clear that the changes were all in favour of the landowners (e.g., providing *begar* (free labour services) to the landowners, payment in advance

[14] Socio-political activities included membership in the village *shalish* (village court), having decision-making power in the *shamaj* (congregation), standing and/ or nominating candidates for local (*union parishad*) elections, representation in different committees involved in development work, e.g. food-for-work committee, school committee, etc.

at varying rates). The terms and conditions under which households participate in share-cropping of land can be divided broadly into nine different arrangements, as follows.

1. All input costs paid by the share-cropper, output is shared between share-cropper and landowner at a ratio of 50:50.
2. All input costs paid by the share-cropper, output is shared at a ratio of 37:63.
3. All input costs paid by the share-cropper, output is shared at a ratio of 33:67.
4. A share system of 50:50, all costs paid by the share-cropper. Landowners claim certain free services (called *begar*) which may be specified or remain unspecified at the time of negotiation. The range of such *begar* varies from six to more labour days per acre, depending on the relationship.
5. All input costs paid by the share-cropper, output shared on the basis of 50:50, but after harvest the share-cropper pays a *selami* to the landowner. The rate of such *selami* varies from 1.5 *maunds* to three *maunds* of paddy per acre of land tilled, which is about 5-10 per cent of the total harvest (1 *maund* =40 *seers* =36Kg.).
6. A share system of 50:50, all costs paid by the share-cropper. After harvest the share-cropper pays a *selami* to the landowner, at a rate varying from 30 *seers* to 1.5 *maunds* per acre of land cultivated. The share-cropper also provides *begar* at the rate of 3-6 labour days per acre of land cultivated.
7. A share system of 50:50, all costs paid by the share-cropper. In addition, the share-cropper pays a cash advance to the landowner, ranging from *Taka* 600 to 1,500 per acre. The landowner repays the amount after the harvest without any interest if he wants to retake his land.
8. A share system of 50:50, all costs paid by the share-cropper. The share-cropper pays an advance to the landowner, the rate of which varies from *Taka* 300 to

1,200 per acre. The share-cropper also provides *begar* of three labour days per acre of land cultivated.

9. All input costs paid by the share-cropper. Output shared on a 50:50 basis. The landowner advances an obligatory credit of 3 *maunds* paddy per acre which is realized at harvest at an interest of 50 per cent. The landowner also rents out a pair of cattle (under *bota*[15]) for every 3.33 acres of land cultivated against a rent of 10 *maunds* of paddy per pair of cattle. This condition is found only in one case where a landowner shares an amount of 13.33 acres among four share-croppers, two from the village and two from outside.

These arrangements include certain general conditions that are applicable to all sub-sets, as follows.

a. All by-products, mainly paddy straw, go to the landowner.
b. The cost of harvesting labour is shared by share-cropper and landowner. Harvesting labourers are paid in kind from the gross product. The costs are thus shared between share-cropper and landowner according to the ratio of the crop share arrangement.
c. After harvest, all crops go to the landowner's threshing place. The share-cropper provides all necessary labour for threshing (with the exception of fields that are harvested under *malabhaga*) and after threshing gets his share. However, some exceptions are found to this practice when share-croppers are from higher landowning categories. They often thresh at home and deliver clean paddy to their landowners. If the threshing is done at the share-cropper's place (which is mostly the case with absentee landowners living in towns, such as Khulna), the share-cropper brings the crop to the landowner at his own expense. In such a case, however, a meal is often served to the share-

[15] Renting of cattle against paddy for a certain period of time (especially for a work season).

cropper when he brings the produce. Occasionally the cost of hiring a boat (transportation is by country boat) is borne by the landowner, depending on the arrangement between share-cropper and landowner.

d. The choice of crops to be grown and decisions regarding the hiring of harvest labour (selection of harvest labour has great economic and political significance[16]) are mostly made by the landowners.

The amount of land transacted and the number of households involved under different terms of the share-cropping contract varies from one land category to another. The following Table shows the significance of different terms and conditions of share-cropping contracts.

TABLE 7
PERCENTAGE DISTRIBUTION OF SHARE-CROPPED LAND UNDER VARIOUS TERMS AND CONDITIONS OF THE CONTRACT BY LAND CATEGORY

Land category	50:50	63:37	67:33	50:50 Begar	50:50 Selami	50:50 +B&S	50:50 +adv.	50:50 Adv&B	50:50 S,B&BO	Total
00	50	-	5	23	17	-	-	5	-	100
0.01-1.00	6	3	6	17	15	19	8	6	10	100
1.01-2.50	28	7	14	14	21	4	12	-	-	100
2.51-5.00	32	-	-	-	40	-	28	-	-	100
5.01-7.50	11	-	-	-	42	-	47	-	-	100
>7.51	62	5	-	-	12	-	21	-	-	100
Total	30	3	6	11	22	7	15	3	3	100

Note: B&S= *Begar* and *Selami*, Adv.= Advance, Adv.&B = Advance and *Begar*, S,B&BO = Selami, Begar and *Bota*.

[16] Harvest labourers are often asked to pay an advance to the landowners as security deposit which is refunded after harvest. For this amount the landowners do not pay any interest, but they invest this advance in money lending. In case labourers do not pay an advance they are asked to provide *begar* services for a number of labour days. The number of days to be provided as *begar*, however, depends on the mutual relationships between the landowner and labourers, and the acreage of land to be harvested.

The political significance relates to the selection of harvest labour. Since 'harvesting' is 'better remunerated', labourers often approach the landowners for such job. Thus the landowners select some labourers rather than others, thereby giving the former sense of privilege and keeping them loyal and content.

Only 30 per cent of land (76.8 acres) is cultivated on a 50:50 crop share basis, by 46 per cent of the share-cropper households (36 share-croppers). This is much lower than the figure usually given in Bangladesh for 50:50 crop share.[17] For the rest of share-cropped land, either the terms are such that over 50 per cent of the crops go to the landowners, or in addition to the 50 per cent share, extra appropriation is made by the landowners through economic (advance/*bota*) or non-economic means (*begar*). The additional extraction of *selami* and advances are imposed on a substantial amount of share-cropped land. Of the total share-cropped land, 22 and 15 per cent are cultivated under these two conditions, respectively.

Analysis of land share-cropped under different conditions and the landowning position of share-croppers reveals a number of interesting aspects. Share-croppers from all landowning categories pay some additional economic and non-economic benefits over the 50 per cent share of crop. Following Cheung, these could be termed 'compensatory payments' (1969: 89-91). However, there is a clear distinction in the payment of such extra benefits by share-croppers of different categories. Share-croppers belonging to higher land categories, i.e. IV and above, make such additional payments only in economic terms (such as *selami* or advance). The lower-category share-cropping households make their payments both in economic and non-economic form. Non-economic payments include *begar* (free labour service), political support, etc.

In total, 39 acres of land (15 per cent) are taken for share-cropping by paying an advance to the landowners. This advance payment (an additional condition imposed above the normal terms of share-cropping) gives the share-cropper more security in the sense of tenure for a longer period of

[17] Jannuzi and Peach, based on the 1977 land occupancy survey, write '...share-cropping terms are most commonly 50 percent of the crop at harvest time (according to the 1977 survey, 93.3 per cent of all tenant and owner-cum-tenant households report this share percentage)' (Jannuzi & Peach 1980: 24, emphasis added). For similar evidence see BBS 1977a, 1978; Hossain 1981.

time. In most instances, we have observed that share-croppers from higher landowning categories who rent in land through advance payment, exercise their rights over their rented land more like a 'part owner' (cf. Mukherjee 1957: 19). Households which rent in land against advance payments often share out the same land or part of their own land to households of lower landowning categories under different terms for economic and socio-political gain.

Share-croppers from lower landowning categories rent in land by paying additional amounts of the crop to the landowners in the form of *selami* or services in the form of *begar*. These payments are mostly made after the harvest. Only for a small percentage of their total share-cropped land (i.e., 12 per cent) are advance economic payments offered, and then for specific reasons. For example, we found three households from category III who share-crop 7.7 acres of land against an advance payment. All three households are in petty trading. Lacking sufficient capital to buy land, these households invest money in advance payments in order to get land under a longer-term share-crop contract.

The nature and degree of control exercised by share-croppers in deciding the pace of work (e.g., transplanting), employment of harvesting labour, threshing, etc., also varies significantly from one category of share-cropper to another. We have observed that among lower categories of share-croppers (I-III) the schedule of planting the fields was mostly dictated by their landowners. Consequently, many of these poorer tenants had to hire in labour to complete the work within the stipulated period, although they had sufficient family labour to do the job if it could be stretched over a rather longer period. For these share-croppers of categories I-III, the landowners decided in almost all cases on the employment of harvesting labour. Furthermore, these share-croppers had to carry the crop to the threshing floor of the landowner. Threshing was done by the tenants with their own labour and draught animals. If the share-cropper used the landowner's cattle, threshing costs were deducted from his share. Among these lower categories of share-croppers, there were only two cases in which employment of harvesting labour and threshing were done by the share-croppers. After threshing, the share-croppers carried the crop to the landowner's place, and the by-product of paddy straw was kept by the share-croppers against a small payment.

As opposed to this situation most of the share-croppers in the 'larger' categories (IV-VI) decided on the recruitment and employment of harvesting labour themselves. We found only three share-crop contracts involving 10 acres of land (11 per cent of the total share-crop land) where harvesting labour was employed by the landowners. However, crops were usually threshed at the landowner's place. Ten share-croppers out of 18 (55 per cent) threshed the product at their own place and then transported it to the landowner.

Thus, evidence shows that two distinct trends are evolving within share-cropping relations. Firstly, the larger landowner dealing with a poor tenant (given the unequal power relations) is increasingly assuming responsibilities and taking control over the production process. In this situation the landowner intervenes in the process of production and thus divorces the tenant from his responsibilities and control over the production. Secondly, there are better-off share-croppers who not only decide on the production process but also control the labour process. In most cases (as reported above) they also exercise their rights over the share-cropped land for a longer period of time.

4.9 *Share-Cropping and Socio-Political Support*

Apart from the terms and conditions that are explicitly stipulated during the time of negotiation, other conditions remain implicit, the most important being political support. Since half the landowners (51 per cent) are involved in village or regional socio-political activities, they often use tenancy relations as a means to achieve or strengthen their socio-political power base. We have observed that on many occasions landowners dictated to the share-croppers for whom they should vote or what stand they should take in the village *shalish*, and so forth. If share-croppers show unwillingness or reluctance to do this, the landowners can use their power (i.e., ownership of share-cropped land) to keep control or to buy the support of a new clientele. Table 8 below shows to what extent landowners used political control in relation to their share-croppers.

TABLE 8
PERCENTAGE DISTRIBUTION OF SHARE-CROPPERS PROVIDING SOCIO-POLITICAL SUPPORT TO THEIR LANDOWNERS ACCORDING TO LAND CATEGORY

Land Category of Share-cropper	No. of Share-croppers in the Category	Share-croppers Number	Provide SP Support Percentage
00	13	7	54
0.01-1.00	29	18	62
1.01-2.50	19	9	47
2.51-5.00	7	1	14
5.01-7.50	4	-	-
>7.51	7	-	-
Total	79	35	44

The Table reveals that 44 per cent of the share-croppers cannot freely exercise their socio-political rights. They are dictated by their landowners in the socio-political activities of the village or region. Among share-croppers of the landless category, 54 per cent follow their landowners' decision and/ or support them in socio-political matters. For share-croppers of category II the percentage is even higher, rising to 62, followed by 47 per cent for share-croppers of landowning category III. It is noticeable that among the higher landowning categories (IV-VI), only one share-cropper of category IV provides political support to his landowner, while for categories V and VI it is totally absent. It should be remembered that landowners who ask for political support are mostly from upper landowning categories (owning land over 2.51 acres). According to our information, of all landowners involved in socio-political activities, 96 per cent belong to these categories. Thus, when we analyse the position of share-croppers extending political support to their landowners and the position of landowners involved in socio-political activity, then the above data clearly demonstrate a dividing line and show the hierarchy of relations in terms of different interests.

4.10 *Share-cropping and Labour*

The crop-shareing relationship between a landowner and a share-cropper is often linked with a labour contract. We found two types in our villages: one is a normal labour contract under which the share-cropper is paid according to the prevailing market wage for the period during which he works for the landowner; the other is a free labour contract locally known as *begar* contract, which is included in the terms of a share-crop contract. Based on such a *begar* contract, landowners reserve the right to appropriate labour time from the share-croppers without payment, although occasionally a meal may be provided. The linkage between a share-crop contract and a labour contract (whether paid, *begar,* or a combination of both), however, depends on the relative economic position and bargaining strength of the participating households.

Share-cropper households of categories I and II are mostly bound to their landowners through a labour contract. Among landless share-croppers, 46 per cent of households are bound to their landowners in this way. Among them, 57 per cent provide *begar* to their landowners. In category II, 59 per cent of the households are linked to their landowners through a labour contract and 88 per cent provide *begar.* This is followed by category III where 21 per cent are linked through a labour contract and 75 per cent provide *begar.* In category IV and above, linkages between share-crop and labour contracts cease to exist. Twenty-two of the total of 27 share-croppers (i.e., 81 per cent) who are linked to their landowners through a labour contract provide *begar*.[18] This is a very high figure. The scale and importance of *begar* as a method of surplus extraction embodied in a share-crop contract can be understood from the following case study.

> RA is a landless peasant of Sagardi. He share-crops in 2.33 acres of land from one of his kin brothers. The terms are fixed at 50:50 share of the product plus provision of *begar*. The number of labour days to be provided as *begar* was not fixed during the time of negotiation, only the nature of jobs was broadly mentioned. As part of the *begar* contract, RA had to work for his kin brother/landowner for a substantial number of days. His work included tilling and preparation of 2.66 acres land cultivated by his landowner. This took about 70 labour days. During transplantation of the landowner's fields, RA had to assist him in hiring and managing labourers. RA had to go to different *hats* (weekly village market) to hire labourers. Normally one trip to the *hat* would cost one working day. He had to make three such trips to hire labourers for transplantation of his landowner's field. During dinner time he would serve food to the labourers. Often during such services he had his meal at the landowner's place. Before harvest RA had to prepare the threshing floor. After threshing, in addition to his own share of straw (i.e., straw from his share-cropped land of 2.33 acres) he had to dry and store all the straw coming from his landowner's own farm. During such workdays only two meals were served to him. Moreover, throughout the year he did all the shopping for his landowner, or if the landowner did the shopping, he carried the load from *hat* to home. The *hats* are located 6-9 kilometers away from the villages.

The extent of such surplus appropriation through *begar* is very high in the village. While talking to share-croppers and landowners, we got the impression that many of the large landowners hardly hire labourers except for peak agricultural operations. RB is one such example.

> RB owns 13.33 acres of land. Of this he shares out 11 acres to three share-croppers and 2.33 acres he cultivates under his own management. The share-crop contracts are all 50:50 plus provision of *begar*.

---

[18] Rendering of *begar* (compulsory free services) to the landowners is also found in other districts, including Comilla which is considered the agriculturally most developed region. According to the response of tenants in Comilla, 52 per cent provide free labour to their landowners, compared to 9 per cent in Mymensingh and 5 per cent in Rajshahi. Based on the responses of landowners, the study notes that 42 per cent of landowners in Comilla, 13 per cent in Mymensingh and 17 per cent in Rajshahi received compulsory free services (cf. Taslim 1988:661).

> The number of labour days he gets through share-crop relations is very high. He told us during one social evening[19] that, except for transplanting and harvesting of fields, he does not employ any labour for his 2.33 acre farm. All the labour necessary comes from his share-croppers. Moreover, he has four big houses which need regular thatching (maintenance, re-thatching, etc.). The labour input necessary for cutting straw comes partly from the share-croppers (the other part comes through harvest labour contracts). The roofing of the houses is also done by the share-croppers. One of his share-croppers, who gets a larger share of land than the others, takes responsibility for tapping RB's date palm trees. He also prepares RB's kitchen garden. RB hardly goes to the market for shopping, most of which is done by his share-croppers. When visitors come to his place, share-croppers are asked to be around for all kinds of services. The day we were invited, two of his share-croppers worked the whole day in exchange for a meal. One of them travelled a distance of two kilometers four times to get and/or deliver certain food.

In the study area we have also found a 'reverse' labour contract between landowners and share-croppers. Poorer households which share-cropped out their land to richer households, often work as labourers for their share-croppers. We found three households that did so. One worked during harvesting, while two others worked during a large part of the year. In all these cases share-croppers are from landowning category IV and above, while the landowners are all from category II.

4.11 *Share-cropping and Credit*

Credit relations within share-cropping arrangements can be divided into two types: credit received by share-croppers from their landowners, and credit received by landowners from their share-croppers. The share-cropper very often goes to the landowner for credit in the case of a share-cropping relationship between a poor share-cropper and a well-to-do landowner. We have also found landowners belonging to

[19] During our fieldwork we were sometimes invited by the villagers to have a meal, tea or a coconut at their homes. RB once offered us a meal in this way.

categories II and III who in times of crisis approach their better-off share-croppers for short term credit. The credit is in cash, in kind,[20] or a combination of the two.

According to our data, many share-croppers (44 per cent) of landowning categories I-III are indebted to their landowners. The highest number of indebted share-croppers are in category II, in which 55 per cent are indebted to their landowners. This is followed by share-croppers of category III (37 per cent) and category I (31 per cent).

In such a credit operation, no extra collateral is asked for, but the total product of the share-cropper acts as collateral. The credit is realized immediately after threshing the paddy. Such instantaneous repayment is made to ensure security of tenure and future support. In the absence of the availabibity of institutional credit, a good record of 'informal' loan repayment is the 'best insurance' for share-cropper households to get an advance in periods of unforeseen financial crisis. However, if the credit amount exceeds the expected share of the tenant, the landowner normally asks for additional collateral, which may be mortgage of the tenant's land (if he has any) or signing a deed or contract on a non-judicial stamp or cartridge paper, stating details of the repayment procedure. Tenants who have no land, sign to work as a labourer at the creditor's call during any time of the year, either at a pre-stipulated wage or at the prevailing market wage during the time of work. We found only one case in category II where the share-cropper had signed a deed promising transfer of his land in case of failure of repayment. But these contract conditions also state that even after transfer of the ownership title, the tenant will retain the right to cultivate the land as a share-cropper. We found four other share-croppers whose land had been either sold or mortgaged to the landowners under such terms during the last five years.

A certain rate of interest is also charged on such credit, depending on the mode of credit advance and on the rela-

[20] Kind credit is in paddy.

tionship between share-cropper and landowner. When credit is advanced in kind, 50 per cent interest is normally charged per six months. In some cases it is more. We found three different interest rates charged when credit was advanced in cash: 25 per cent, 30 per cent, and a total of 30 *seers* of paddy for *Taka* 100 (which comes to 125 per cent) for a period of six months. For credit advanced in kind, interest rates were again different. The prevailing rates were 50 per cent, 75 per cent and *Taka* 400 for one *maund* of paddy (100 per cent).

However, independently of the mode of credit advance or rate of interest, realization is always in kind. The cash amount is converted into kind (paddy) based on the market price of paddy prevailing at the time of payment. Therefore, we have 'two different interest rates': one for lenders of credit and one for borrowers. For example, if a lender converts kind into cash at the time of advancing the loan, or converts cash into kind at the time of realization, he earns a substantial interest due to price differences of paddy at two particular moments of time. For the borrower conversion has a different logic, because he has no option but to deal through his product, i.e. paddy. Therefore, for poorer households that take credit (in cash or in kind) the rate of interest is much higher than the stipulated one. Thus, when we convert the cash component into kind and then calculate the interest rate based on the repaid amount (kind) and its market price, we arrive at the following rates of interest.

TABLE 9
MODE OF CREDIT ADVANCEMENT AND RATE OF INTEREST

Mode of Credit Advancement	Rate of Interest in Percentage Stated	After Conversion
Credit in Cash:	25	87.5
	30	95.0
	30 *seers* paddy/Taka 100	125.0
Credit in kind:	50	50.0
	75	75.0
	400 *Taka*/ one *maund* paddy	100.0

Clearly, within the framework of credit relations, a large percentage of the produce gets transferred from share-croppers to their landowners. Taken together, such credit and production relations leave a very small proportion of the production in the hands of the share-croppers. As a consequence, the two villages show no visible inter-linkages between input market and product market. Control over the product market is hidden under the repayment system of credit. Therefore, the product market operates rather freely. Out of 79 share-cropper households, not one reported that there is a commitment between share-croppers and landowners for the product to be sold to the latter. Operation of the credit market has two distinct implications. Firstly, it gives the resource-rich landowning households power to manipulate the situation of debtor households through extraction of their product. Secondly, owing to this procedure of repayment in kind, the creditor restricts the entry of outside traders in grain. This in turn gives richer households the opportunity to dictate the conditions under which one can have access to various markets (i.e., land, labour, credit or cattle).

5. *Some Concluding Observations*

Our data provide ample evidence that in spite of the enactment of a *tebhaga* system, the real terms and conditions of sharecropping contracts remain very different, and can even be described as "reverse *tebhaga*". More importantly these terms are continual deteriorating and a majority of the sharecroppers explicitly told us that the terms of sharecropping contracts are becoming harder.[21] Over and above the 50:50 crop share, landowners are imposing many additional economic and non-economic conditions when negotiating a share-crop contract. If the share-croppers fail to comply with

[21] Similar evidence on the deteriorating terms of the sharecrop contract in the post-tenancy reform period has also been documented in other studies. See Rahman 1986, Jansen 1986, Hashemi 1988.

the demand of the landowners, they often get evicted from the land. However, the application of these conditions to the share-croppers does not follow a uniform pattern. Certain categories are more affected than others. We have observed that among the 69 share-croppers who had had tenancy relations for more than two years, 67 per cent were evicted from their share-cropped land due to their unwillingness and/or inability to comply with the landowners' demand. Households that were evicted came mostly from lower landowning categories. Moreover, an analysis of political relations between share-croppers and landowners shows that share-croppers were asked to extend political support to their landowners or their nominees. It is important to note that all share-croppers of these two lower categories showed their awareness of the negative consequences (in the sense of loss of share-crop land, change of terms, or other social harassment) if they should violate the landowner's instruction. Such forms of coercion, together with economic control either through the share ratio, *selami* or credit, put a large number of share-croppers at the discretion of the landowners. The extra-economic and non-economic conditions under which share-croppers operate clearly demonstrate a dividing line among the different categories. Those of the lower categories, specifically the landless and those owing only a small amount of land, are far more vulnerable than the others. An analysis of the production and labour process shows that share-croppers of these lower landowning categories have hardly any control over the production process. Moreover, apart from careful control and supervision of harvest operations, landowners frequently intervene in the decision-making process at different stages of production. We have observed in several cases that landowners determined the schedule for the preparation of land as well as transplanting, on the grounds of efficiency or identification of the ideal period of cultivation. In many situations, this intervention forces share-croppers to buy additional labour and animal power at those specific periods, although in the long run some of their own resources remain unutilized.

Furthermore, many share-croppers of categories I and II have to provide labour to their landowners as part of the tenancy contract. As we have seen the number of labour days provided by share-croppers is very high (see case studies in section 4.10). However, the wages they earn through these labour days are very low. Our interviews and discussions made this quite clear. A normal labour day would be paid at a rate of *Taka* 34, but the 'attached' labour day in a share-cropping contract would yield only *Taka* 26, or 23 per cent less than average earnings, which is a very big difference. The picture emerging from this analysis thus shows that share-croppers of categories I and II are exploited by their landowners through a complex interlinked transaction of land, labour and credit. More importantly, this process of exploitation is frequently reinforced further by the sanctions of socio-political institutions.

The production and distribution which take place in these villages ensure and create opportunities for certain classes to appropriate directly the surplus produced by other classes. This is more so in a situation of 'over supply' of labour and lack of sufficient employment opportunities, as the poorer households tend to cling to agriculture at the cost of self-exploitation. On the other hand, the existing institutional framework of property relations gives power to landowners to dictate and regulate the terms under which one has access to land. The existing property relations and the organisation of production act as a mechanism to maintain very unequal relations of production.

Furthermore, since 84 per cent of the total share-cropped land is owned by households who belong to categories V and above, their economic and social position is an important factor to be taken into account. The economic position of the landowners, which also puts them in a better socio-political position (as economic and socio-political power are convertible), acts as an effective obstacle towards the implementation of legal changes in the existing system. Since most of the landowners are involved in village or regional socio-political activities, poorer households have very little opportunity to represent their interests in any forum or place their demands on the agenda for discussion or implementation. Rich landowners exert their influence not only over village affairs, they also frequently make their presence felt at higher levels as well. This is facilitated by the constellation of class forces who are in command of the state apparatus.[22]

However, given the nature and character of the state in Bangladesh and its structural position vis-à-vis the donors,[23] at times it is forced to formulate certain policies (sometimes as part of a process of legitimization) which are apparently in contradiction to the interests of the dominant classes. But in the long run the state either does not pursue the effective implementation of these policies, or in case they are implemented, this is done in such a manner that the rural rich can take advantage of them and use them to strengthen and consolidate their power. For example, after the enactment of the 1984 Land Reform Ordinance, the state started initially with the distribution of *khas* land among the landless. But when the process of *khas* land distribution was seriously questioned and some political parties and peasant organisations took an active interest in it, the state shifted its emphasis from distribution of *khas* land to the implementation of *Operation Thikana*, which is politically a softer option and does not require acquisition of much land to settle the landless households. Furthermore, during recent years the state has not, apart from the passing of the *tebhaga* law, taken any initia-

[22] In Bangladesh the state apparatus is controlled by an alliance of dominant classes and fractions which, following Poulantzas, could be designated as a "power bloc" (Poulantzas 1979:24). The 'power bloc' which dominates the state apparatus of Bangladesh is represented by the civil and military oligarchy, the commercial and industrial bourgeoisie and the landed aristocracy. This is a fairly stable alliance. The background of the members of Parliament, ministers, and the various economic policies of the government clearly attest to our observation.

[23] The 'power bloc' maintains its domination over the state apparatus, but at the same time the state is heavily dependent on international forces. This is evident from the sources of finance as reflected in its development budget. While presenting the annual budget of 1989-90, the Finance Minister informed the nation that "87 per cent of annual development programme will be financed by aid" (Haque 1989:26).

tive to implement it or to register the existing share-croppers as a step towards eventual recognition of their rights. Thus the government, as a result of its lack of political commitment, failed to pursue the implementation of *tebhaga* through its administrative set-up.[24] The tenancy reform has got very little or no operational significance at all. It failed to influence the lives and working conditions of the tenants, at least in these two villages. Consequently, the Ordinance could not stimulate productive efficiency or ensure distributive justice. To sum up, we conclude that in these villages, where economic and political power follows, or is determined by, the production process, a mere passing of a law without sufficient legal and institutional back-up is of little relevance for changing the structure of production. This calls for administrative support from the state machinery, and more importantly concerted actions from the tenants and poor labourers themselves. In any case, it is the latter group from whom surplus is being extracted by the non-producing class, either through tenancy or labour arrangements, or a combination of both.

References

Alamgir, Muhiuddin Khan (ed.) 1981. *Land Reform in Bangladesh*. Dacca: Center for Social Studies.

Bangladesh Bureau of Statistics 1977. *Summary Report of the 1977 Land Occupancy Survey of Rural Bangladesh*. Dhaka: July.

Bangladesh Bureau of Statistics 1978. *Summary Report of the 1978 Land Occupancy Survey of Rural Bangladesh*. Dhaka: December.

Bangladesh Bureau of Statistics 1985. *1984-85 Yearbook of Agricultural Statistics of Bangladesh*. Dhaka: Ministry of Planning.

Bangladesh Bureau of Statistics 1986. *The Bangladesh Census of Agriculture and Livestock 1983-84*. vol.1. Structure of Agricul-

[24] Some may differ on this point and may argue that the government had the political will but was constrained by the bureaucratic machinery and other institutions of class society. Subscribers to this viewpoint may be requested to study the 'Operation Barga' system of West Bengal, India, for a different experience.

tural Holdings and Livestock Population. Dhaka: Ministry of Planning, May.

Government of Bangladesh 1984. *The Land Reform Ordinance, 1984*. Ordinance # 4, Dhaka: January 26.

Haque, Wahidul 1989. *Annual Budget 1989-90, Budget Speech, Part I,* Dhaka: Ministry of Finance, June.

Hashemi, Sayed, M 1988. Land Ownership and Tenure Reform in Bangladesh. *Study Prepared for Bangladesh Agriculture Sector Review,* Dhaka: UNDP, October.

Hossain, Mahabub 1980. Desirability and Feasibility of Land Reform in Bangladesh. *The Journal of Social Studies*. Vol. 8, April.

Jannuzi, F.T. and Peach, J.T. 1980. *The Agrarian Structure of Bangladesh: An Impediment to Development*. Colorado: Westview Press.

Jansen, Erik. G 1983. Rural Bangladesh- Competition for Scarce Resources. *DERAP Publication, No.162,* Bergen: The Chr. Michelsen Institute.

Mukherjee, Ramkrishna 1957. *The Dynamics of a Rural Society*. Berlin, Akademie Verlag.

Poulantzas, Nicos 1979. *Classes in Contemporary Capitalism*, London: Verso.

Rahman, Atiur 1986. *Peasant and Classes: A Study in Differentiation in Bangladesh,* Dhaka: The University Press Ltd.

Rashid, Harun-Er 1977. *Geography of Bangladesh,* Dhaka: University Press Ltd.

Sen, Sunil 1972. *Agrarian Struggle in Bengal 1946-47*. New Delhi: People's Publishing House.

Sen, Sunil 1979. "Tebhaga Chai", in Desai, A.R. (ed.) *Peasant Struggles in India.* New Delhi: Oxford University Press.

Siddiqui, Kamal 1979. Political Economy of Land Reform in Bangladesh. *The Journal of Social Studies,* No. 6.

Siddiqui, Kamal 1981A. *Bangladeshe Bhumi Sanskarer Rajnaitik Arthaniti*. Dhaka: Bangladesh Institute of Development Studies.

Siddiqui, Kamal 1981B. Land Reform Legislation in the 50's and 60's. in Alamgir, M. K. (ed.) 1981. *Land Reform in Bangladesh,* Dhaka: Centre for Social Studies.

Siddiqui, Kamal 1981C. Land Reform Measures in the 70s in Alamgir, M.K (ed.) *Land Reform in Bangladesh*. Dhaka: Centre for Social Studies.

Contributors

SEKHAR BANDYOPADHYAY: Department of History, Victoria University of Wellington

SWARAJ BASU: Department of History, Indira Gandhi National Open University, New Delhi

RATAN LAL CHAKRABORTY: Department of History, Dhaka University

ABHIJIT DASGUPTA: Department of Sociology, Delhi School of Economics, University of Delhi

RANAJIT DAS GUPTA: Indian Council of Historical Research, New Delhi; formerly of Indian Institute of Management, Calcutta

ANJAN KUMAR DATTA: The Institute of Social Studies, The Hague

SHYAMALI GHOSH: School of International Studies, Jawaharlal Nehru University, New Delhi

ARJAN DE HAAN: Department of History, Erasmus University, Rotterdam

DESPINA ILIOPOULOU: Department of Sociology, York University, Toronto

SMRITI KUMAR SARKAR: Department of History, Kalyani University, Kalyani, West Bengal

SAMITA SEN: Trinity College, University of Cambridge

WILLEM VAN SCHENDEL: Department of History, Erasmus University, Rotterdam

Glossary

ahir	agricultural caste
aag	fire
ajlaf	the indigenous masses
alpana	geometrical drawings on the floor
aman	late summer rice, autumn season
amir	chief
antebasi	dwellers on the periphery
antyaja	low-born mixed caste
aranya	forest
ashraf	elite puritans who claimed to have descended from middle eastern Muslims
aus	early summer rice, early summer season
babu	gentleman
badli	substitute
bargadar	sharecropper
basti	slum
batwara	partition
bazar	market
begar	free labour service
benama	fictitious transfer of land
bhadrolok	gentry
bigha	unit of land measurement=0.33 acres
beradari	Hindu community
baishnab	followers of vaishnavism
bota	renting of cattle against paddy
chandal	untouchables
chotolok	low-class people
chowkidar	watchman
coolie	porter
dasi	maid
daroga	local head of police
davottar	rent-free land given to shrine or temple
dewan	revenue collector

durwans	peon
ekusher gan	song of the twenty first
futwa	religious opinion given by *ulema*
gandha banik	spice dealer, a caste
ghat	a path of descent to a river
guru	teacher
hari	sweeper caste
hartal	strike
ikrarnama	agreement
izzat	honour
jamadar	sweeper
jatra	a form of folk theatre
jhum	swidden cultivation
jotedar	intermediary landowner
jumma	swidden cultivator
khola	daily wage labourer
krishak samiti	farmers' association
lohar	metal working caste
mahajan	merchant, moneylender
mangal karya	auspicios work
mudi	grocer
napit	barber
patni	ferrymen
patnidar	intermediate tenure holder
pir	holyman
rabi	winter crop
raja	king, ruler
ryot	tenant
sampraday	community
sardar	a village leader, a labour contractor
seer	a measure of weight = 0.9 kg
selami	advance
shahid dibas	martyr's day
boro	winter rice
sufi	a Muslim mystic
talukdar	an intermediate holder
tanti	weaver

taka	monetary unit of Bangladesh
teli	oilpresser caste
ulema	scholars in Islamic jurisprudence
upazilla	sub-division
utbandi	temporary tenancy
zamindar	superior landlord/revenue collector
zamindari	estate of a zamindar

Index